A HISTORY OF
CHRISTIAN THOUGHT

VOLUME II

THE WEST
FROM TERTULLIAN TO ERASMUS

A HISTORY OF CHRISTIAN THOUGHT

BY

ARTHUR CUSHMAN McGIFFERT

VOLUME II

The West
From Tertullian to Erasmus

CHARLES SCRIBNER'S SONS

NEW YORK · LONDON

TO
MY COLLEAGUES
IN UNION THEOLOGICAL SEMINARY

PREFACE

Volumes One and Two of this History were originally meant to form a single volume covering the course of Christian thought from the beginning until the eve of the Protestant Reformation. When the manuscript reached the publisher, however, it was found unduly long for one volume and it was therefore thought advisable to divide it into two. Accordingly the first volume which appeared last spring included only the primitive period in east and west and the development in the east until the time of John of Damascus, while this one traces the development in the west from Tertullian, the first Latin Father, to Erasmus the Humanist. The circumstance that I had planned to devote but a single volume to the history down to the Reformation accounts for the scale of the work and also to some extent for the selection of material. Had I envisaged two volumes I might have allowed myself more space and greater breadth of treatment. Repeating what I said in my previous preface I may add that I hope later, if health permit, to continue the history down to our own day.

In the present volume, as in its predecessor, the method has been followed of dealing in considerable detail with a few important figures, and quoting freely from their writings, instead of passing many in brief review. It is my conviction that the fuller acquaintance with a limited number of thinkers thus made possible (particularly if they be representative and widely influential) contributes to a clearer understanding of the development of Christian

PREFACE

thought than a more superficial and merely hearsay acquaintance with a much larger number.

It is a pleasure to acknowledge my indebtedness to my colleague, Dr. William Walker Rockwell, Librarian of Union Theological Seminary, who has very kindly read certain chapters in proof and has given the Bibliography the benefit of his scrutiny; also to Mr. D. H. Schroeder, Assistant Librarian of Union, and Professor A. C. McGiffert, Jr., of the Chicago Theological Seminary, both of whom have helped me with this volume as they did with the first.

A. C. McGiffert.

Dobbs Ferry, New York
November, 1932.

CONTENTS

BOOK III

CHRISTIAN THOUGHT IN THE WEST FROM TERTULLIAN TO GREGORY THE GREAT

BOOK IV

CHRISTIAN THOUGHT IN THE WESTERN CHURCH OF THE MIDDLE AGES

CONTENTS

BOOK THREE

CHRISTIAN THOUGHT IN THE WEST FROM TERTULLIAN TO GREGORY THE GREAT

CHAPTER I

TERTULLIAN

ALTHOUGH the Greek and Roman churches did not finally separate until the eleventh century, from the second century on markedly diverse tendencies were making themselves felt respectively in east and west. At first Christianity in the west spread chiefly among Greek-speaking immigrants from the east. It is no accident, therefore, that for some time Greek not Latin was the language of occidental as well as of oriental Christianity. Gradually however the new religion became indigenous in the west. Its sacred books were translated into Latin and a Latin Christian literature began to appear. Inevitably, as time passed, Christianity was more and more affected by the spirit and temper of the Latin world. The difference between the two parts of the Empire was not so much a matter of race as of history and environment. The relation was not unlike that between America and Europe. Culturally the west was largely dependent upon the east. Its art, its literature, its philosophy were derivative not original. Its own prevailing interests were of another sort: utilitarian rather than aesthetic, practical rather than speculative, ethical rather than metaphysical. Matters of law and government received particular attention; the sovereignty of the State was made much of; and institutionalism with its inevitable emphasis on precedent and tradition enjoyed a large development. The influence of this changed attitude was naturally felt by Christianity. Theologians became interested in questions that had hitherto

3

attracted little notice and the doctrinal development took a new direction. The church as an institution acquired increased importance and much thought was given to its functions and authority. Man and his duties and responsibilities, together with the related subjects of sin and grace, came to the front and tended to crowd into the background the theistic and cosmological problems which largely absorbed the Christian thinkers of the east.

The difference between oriental and occidental Christianity would have been far greater but for the fact that the west got its Christianity from the east and for some centuries looked thither for theological leadership. Western theologians had little part in the theological controversies that filled so large a place in the life of the Greek church, but they accepted the results of the doctrinal development almost without question. As a consequence there was a large body of doctrine which the west shared permanently with the east. This common faith was binding on the whole church. All doctrinal development in Roman Catholicism presupposed it and was obliged to conform to it.

The divergence of interest and emphasis between east and west was first clearly apparent in North Africa where Greek influence was less felt than in Italy and Gaul. By North Africa is meant the strip of country lying along the Mediterranean coast from the Gulf of Sidra to the Atlantic and embracing, in imperial times, the three Roman provinces of Africa, Numidia and Mauretania. Cut off from the rest of the continent by mountain and desert it belonged rather to Europe than to Africa, as Egypt belonged to Asia. Coming under Roman rule in the second century B.C. the eastern part of the country, before many generations had passed, was thoroughly Romanized. Particularly in the province of Africa Italian colonists were living in large numbers and the relations between Rome and Carthage, the capital of the province and the administrative centre for the whole of North Africa, were close and intimate.

The population of the country was of mixed blood, old Libyan stock, Phœnician, and Italian predominating. Under the Romans Latin was the official and ultimately the dominant language, but Punic, generally prevalent before the period of Roman rule, continued to be spoken among the common people, and Greek remained for some time the language of polite society as well as of the literati.

When Christianity first found its way to North Africa we do not know, but before 200 A.D. there was a strong and flourishing church at Carthage, after Rome the most important city of the western world. There were also multitudes of Christians throughout the provinces of Africa and Numidia, though as yet comparatively few in the less populous and less Romanized province of Mauretania farther to the west.

For some generations North Africa was the theological centre of western Christendom as Alexandria was of eastern. In North Africa, indeed, was the real cradle of Latin Christianity, and there, as already said, the difference of interest and emphasis between the Christianity of the west and that of the east was first clearly apparent. Tertullian of Carthage, the first of the Latin Fathers, whose career fell in the late second and early third centuries, illustrates the difference in striking fashion.

In the entire history of Christianity there are few more interesting figures than Tertullian. He was born in Carthage of heathen parents about the middle of the second century. His father held high military rank and he was given the education usual for a youth of good family. He apparently studied law and perhaps practised for a time in Rome, but the greater part of his life was spent in his native city. His habits before his conversion to Christianity seem to have been neither better nor worse than those of his contemporaries. There are hints in his writings that he indulged in the pleasures and vices of the age, but he was largely free from the morbid self-consciousness that later characterized his compatriot Augustine. He became a Christian in middle life and was for some time a presbyter in the church of Carthage. Of the circumstances of his conversion we have no knowledge. His wife was a Christian but whether her Christianity antedated his and whether she had anything to do with his conversion we do not know; he says nothing about the matter in a work addressed to her. Not long after the opening of the third century he became a Montanist and remained a member of the sect until his death at an advanced age sometime after 220.

He was a prolific writer. His extant works, all of them written after he became a Christian and many of them in his Montanistic period, cover both apologetics and polemics and comprise a long list of practical tracts dealing with a variety of moral and religious questions. He wrote at first in Greek, the common language of Christianity in the west as well as the east until his time, but he soon abandoned it for Latin and all his writings, so far as they have been preserved, are in the latter tongue. Though he was not actually the first Christian to write in Latin he was the first important theologian to do so.

He created a Latin Christian vocabulary on a large scale, coining words freely and giving a technical Christian meaning to many terms in common use. He was the founder not only of the language of the western church but also of its theology so far as it was independent of the east. Ever since his day it has felt his influence and has shown the stamp of his genius and that in spite of his defection to Montanism, which destroyed his standing as a Catholic Father.

6

His character and temper are abundantly revealed in his writings. He was passionate, enthusiastic, restive and impatient, always at odds with himself and others, extreme in his views and in his expression of them, fanatical and intolerant, ascetic in his tendencies, a puritan of the puritans, rigorous in his moral principles and uncompromising in his moral judgments, violent and vituperative in his denunciations of those that disagreed with him, in his polemics sophistical and unfair and not above personal slander and flagrant misrepresentation. To score a point over an adversary he hesitated at nothing. In this respect to be sure he was at one with most of the polemic writers of the ancient church, but in the vigor of his language he surpassed them all. His literary style reflected his character: nervous, forceful, picturesque, full of paradox, antithesis and epigram, elliptical and compressed and often exceedingly difficult to translate.

He looked at everything with the eyes of a lawyer.[1] Religion and morals, the gospel itself, bore a legal aspect to him, and he gave the language and the theology of western Catholicism a legal cast which they have never lost. His interests were intensely practical; though a good deal of a theologian he seldom indulged in theological speculation and when he did he was usually moved by a polemic motive — to refute and overthrow the false teaching of one or another heretic. Practical duties and responsibilities were uppermost in his mind and the relationship between man and God which underlay them. He was not a systematic theologian, but his writings are full of ideas, often original and creative (he was in fact one of the most original of thinkers), and

[1] S. Schlossmann, in two articles entitled "Tertullian im Lichte der Jurisprudenz," in the *Zeitschrift für Kirchengeschichte*, vol. 27 (1906), undertakes to show that, despite the traditional opinion, Tertullian was not a lawyer and had had no legal training. His argument however is not convincing. Even if it were it could not be denied that Tertullian had the legal mind and looked at things in the legal way.

many of the doctrines of the Roman Catholic church took their rise with him or first received formulation at his hands.

Among his writings in defense of Christianity — a matter always much upon his heart — is his striking little tract on the testimony of the soul,[1] in which the common instincts of men are called upon to bear witness to God and divine judgment, and also his famous Apology which in content resembles the Greek apologies of the second century described in the previous volume, but is characteristically legal both in spirit and in form and is marked in many passages by a devastating sarcasm.

Stress is laid in the Apology on the Christians' loyalty to the Empire and the Emperor. They recognize the Emperor's appointment by God, they honour him and pray for him and support his throne by their pure and righteous living. Anticipating Arnobius and Augustine, Tertullian maintains, in reply to those who were blaming Christianity for all the ills from which the world was suffering, that those ills long antedated the coming of Christ, and as a matter of fact were far worse before his time than since. The work contains a long and interesting section (chapters 22 ff.) on demons and demoniacal possession, which reveals Tertullian's belief in their reality and evil doings and serves to supplement the references to the subject in Justin Martyr and Tatian.[2]

Among the most important of Tertullian's writings is an elaborate treatise on the soul, the first Christian work on psychology. It is unlike most of his writings and throws welcome light on certain characteristics of his thinking and certain aspects of his thought not so clearly revealed elsewhere. The soul, he maintains in agreement with the Stoics, is corporeal, as all that exists is. "Nothing is," he says, "if it be not a body"[3]; and elsewhere, "Everything that

---

[1] *De testimonio animæ.*   [2] See the previous volume, pp. 125 f.
[3] *De anima,* 7.

exists is a body after its own kind. Nothing is incorporeal except what does not exist." [1] Realist as he was Tertullian evidently found it impossible to conceive of existence in any other than corporeal terms. To deny the corporeality of the soul seemed to him, therefore, tantamount to denying its reality.

In support of its corporeality he adduced the usual arguments employed by the Stoics, including the inheritance of mental qualities, the interaction of body and soul, and the like. Not content therewith he appealed not only to the authority of the Scriptures but also to the testimony of a woman belonging to the Montanists, who had been vouchsafed the vision of a soul. According to Tertullian she declared that there had been shown her a soul in bodily shape, and that a spirit had been seen by her, not empty and void, but of a sort that might be grasped, soft and luminous and of an airy color and wholly human in form.[2] Tertullian could never rest content with mere rational arguments but must always clinch matters by appealing to an authority of some kind even if no better than an old woman's tales.

Being corporeal the soul has a form of its own — length and breadth and thickness. It is not identical with the body but permeates all parts of it, having its centre and directing power in the heart. It is not a function or a quality of the body, but rather the body is its instrument which it controls and uses for such ends as it will.[3]

Though corporeal the soul is spiritual, not material.

---

[1] *De carne Christi*, 11. Tertullian even went so far as to assert the corporeality of God. "Who will deny that God is a body although God is spirit? For a spirit is a body of its own kind in its own form." (*Adv. Praxean*, 7.) He maintained that God is corporeal not only because he would otherwise not be real, but also because if incorporeal he could not have created corporeal things (see my *God of the Early Christians*, p. 125). The contrast between Tertullian's view and that of Origen of Alexandria is very striking.

[2] *De anima*, 9.

[3] For this and what follows see *De anima*, 10–20; 40.

Breaking with the monism of the Stoics who recognized only one substance underlying all reality, Tertullian insisted that there are two substances, spirit and matter, both alike real and hence corporeal, but otherwise unlike and possessing each its own peculiar qualities. Spirit is simple and indivisible and hence indestructible; matter is compounded and can therefore be broken up and dissolved. It is interesting to notice, in this connection, that Tertullian, in agreement with Plato and with Christian tradition, took for granted the immortality of the soul and made its immortality an argument for its simplicity,[1] evidently feeling that the latter was not self-evident — another sign of his inability to conceive reality in other than corporeal terms.

The various faculties are functions of the soul, not parts of it, for it is indivisible and acts as a whole in all it does. It perceives material objects by the senses, spiritual objects by the mind. The senses are trustworthy and are never deceived, but our judgments about the objects cognized whether through the senses or the mind, are often erroneous. Like the body, the mind is not identical with the soul but is its agent and instrument, and hence the soul, which is free, is responsible for all the acts both of mind and body. The soul is not introduced into the body after birth, nor is it preëxistent, as Plato thought, but is propagated with the body [2] — a theory that came later to be known as traducianism. At death the two are separated, to be reunited at the resurrection.

This interesting and original work on the soul is very revealing, and while it may not do much to elucidate the subject in hand it throws a flood of light upon Tertullian's character and ways of thinking. Particularly instructive is

---

[1] Cf. *De anima*, 9, 51.
[2] *Ibid.* 4, 23 ff. Tertullian rejected not only Plato's theory of preëxistence but also the Pythagorean theory of transmigration. Cf. *ibid.* 28 ff.

the confusion into which he fell in his effort to maintain the corporeality of the soul while denying its materiality. As already remarked he spoke of it as extended (possessing length and breadth and thickness) and yet he insisted on its simplicity and indivisibility without apparently realizing the contradiction involved. Despite his insistence on the corporeality of all substance, he was not a materialist. He was simply a man of the street — a vulgar realist he might be called — unable because of his temperament and lack of philosophical training to think in abstract terms, and hence to conceive reality in other than physical forms, but convinced that man was an immortal spirit and that materialism meant the destruction not only of Christianity but of all religion and morality.

It is significant that he was not a philosopher before he was converted to Christianity, as Justin Martyr and Clement of Alexandria were, but was led by his Christian faith, partly perhaps for his own satisfaction, but chiefly for polemical reasons, to investigate certain psychological and philosophical questions that had not hitherto engaged his attention, or for that matter the attention of any of his co-religionists. He showed his native curiosity and his intellectual alertness in dealing with them, but at the same time he betrayed his want of philosophical training, and that despite the fact that in the work on the soul he mentions dozens of philosophers and shows an acquaintance with their opinions on the matters under consideration. Philosophy was not his forte, nor as a rule did he engage in philosophical inquiry or discussion. His real talents and his controlling interests lay elsewhere. As already said his dominant temper was legalistic and he looked at everything with the eyes of a lawyer. His legal spirit, indeed, appears in nearly all his writings. For that matter it is not altogether lacking even in the one that has just been described.

His idea of God well illustrates his general attitude. In his tract against Praxeas, the most theological of his writings, he formulated over against Praxeas' monarchianism a doctrine of the Trinity essentially legal in character. That God is triune means primarily that he is three persons in the legal sense, that is, three persons who share or own in common one substance or property. Tertullian's language at this point, though not the legal interpretation that attached to it, later had influence in east as well as west.[1]

Even more characteristic was his idea of God as a personal sovereign. It was as a sovereign, indeed, that he principally thought of him, and upon his majesty and authority he laid chief stress. He did not think of God as absolute being, as the metaphysical infinite or the all-inclusive whole, as the Greek theologians commonly did, but as a personal ruler to whom all men are subject. He accepted the common ideas of God as creator and providential governor of the world, the one who made and controls the physical universe as well as all living creatures. But with this aspect of God's work he was not primarily concerned, though he had a good deal to say about it in certain of his polemic writings, as for instance in his work against Marcion, who separated the creating from the redeeming God, and in his treatise against a Christian contemporary, the artist Hermogenes, in which the question under discussion was whether God created the world out of nothing or out of preëxistent matter. Hermogenes maintained the latter, Tertullian the former. Hermogenes, whose work on the subject is lost, was evidently moved chiefly by the desire to relieve God from responsibility for the evil in the world. This he did by attributing evil to the stuff of which the world was made as Plato had done. In other

---

[1] The Latin word for the Trinity (*trinitas*), occurs for the first time in Tertullian's *Adv. Praxean*, 2 and his phrases *tres personæ* and *una substantia* anticipated the orthodox trinitarian formula.

words he looked upon God as limited and bound by the intractable nature of his materials.

Tertullian on the other hand was moved by the desire to conserve the divine independence and omnipotence. "Liberty," he declares, "not necessity, comports with God. I prefer that he should have willed to create evil things freely rather than that he should have been unable to refrain from creating." [1] "Which then is worthier," he says in another passage, "that God created evil things of necessity or voluntarily? For he created them of necessity if he created them out of matter; he created them voluntarily if out of nothing. For now it is in vain that you are laboring to show that God is not the author of evil things, because even if he made them from matter they will have to be imputed to him who made them, however he may have made them. . . . But it is more seemly for him to have created voluntarily than under necessity, that is, out of nothing than out of matter. It is more worthy to believe that God is the free author even of evil things than to believe that he is a slave. Power of whatever sort better becomes him than pusillanimity." [2] In this last sentence we find the real secret of Tertullian's insistence on creation out of nothing. To create out of nothing argues much greater power than to create out of something and hence alone befits an omnipotent God.[3]

This consideration undoubtedly had much to do with the ultimate prevalence of the doctrine of creation out of nothing. So far as religious and ethical values are concerned they would seem to be conserved by Hermogenes' theory as well as by Tertullian's, with the advantage that the former

---

[1] *Adv. Hermogenem*, 16.

[2] *Ibid.* 14. For a fuller account of Tertullian's controversy with Hermogenes and of the doctrine of creation ex nihilo in the early church see my *God of the Early Christians*, pp. 157 ff.

[3] Theophilus of Antioch in his apology addressed to Autolycus (II. 4) has much the same to say. Theophilus also wrote against Hermogenes, but his work is no longer extant.

relieves God of the odium of creating evil. But to the theologians to limit the power of God in any way seemed impious, and when it came to be generally realized that the use of existing materials in the work of creation put limitations on him the vogue of the doctrine of creation out of nothing was inevitable. And that not simply among the theologians. Even the common believer wanted a god great enough to insure him all he needed both for this life and the next, and to suggest that God was less than almighty in any respect might well appear to threaten his adequacy.

Tertullian's chief concern, as I have said, was not with God's relation to the world of nature — the physical universe — but to the world of men and particularly to men as individuals. God is a sovereign; all men are his subjects. While Tertullian often used the common word Father in speaking of God it was authority rather than affection that was uppermost in his thought. The proper attitude toward God is humility and fear. "The fear of man is the honour of God," he says.[1] "Where there is no fear there is no amendment."[2] "How are you going to love unless you are afraid not to love?"[3] "Come then, you who do not fear God because he is good, why do you not boil over in every kind of lust? For this is the highest fruit of life, as I know, to all that do not fear God."[4]

Thus, according to Tertullian, virtue springs from fear. It is neither the product of love for God nor the spontaneous expression of the character of a child of God. Virtue is not harmony or beauty or self-realization; virtue is obedience to the divine law and the motive is fear of the penalty that will follow if the law be broken. At this point as at many others

[1] *De pœnitentia*, 7. It is interesting to compare the attitude of Tertullian with that of Epicurus who thought the fear of the gods the root of all evils and the only true worship of them the adoration of their virtues.
[2] *Ibid.* Cf. *Apologeticum*, 49.
[3] *Adv. Marcionem*, I. 27.
[4] *Ibid.*

Tertullian was a representative man and simply formulated in striking terms a common attitude of his day and of many a day to come.

The law demands obedience not because it is good and approves itself to man's conscience, but because it is law. "I hold it audacity," Tertullian says, "to dispute concerning the good of a divine precept. For it is not because it is good that we are bound to obey but because God commands it. To secure obedience the majesty of divine power has the prior right; the authority of him who rules is prior to the utility of him who serves. Is it good to repent or not? Why do you ask? God commands." [1] The law thus requires unquestioning obedience. If a man asks whether the precept be good, or if he obeys it because it is good, his obedience is not true obedience; he is following his own reason rather than God's will. All through Tertullian was interested to emphasize the absolute authority of God and the humility of man which expresses itself in blind obedience.

The principle of unquestioning obedience he carried over also into the intellectual realm. The divine law demands right thinking as well as right doing. The Christian must obey the rule of faith and neither deviate from it nor go beyond it. In his striking little work on The Prescription of Heretics, a capital example of his legal way of looking at things, Tertullian remarks, "At the outset I lay down this proposition, that there is some one definite thing taught by Christ which the nations are by all means bound to believe and for that purpose to seek in order that they may be able when they have found it to believe. Moreover there can be no endless seeking after the one sure thing that has been taught. You must seek until you find and must believe when you have found; nor have you anything farther to do than to keep what you have believed, provided you believe this

[1] *De pœnitentia*, 4.

15

besides, that nothing else is to be believed and therefore
nothing else is to be sought, when you have once found and
believed what has been taught by him who commands you
to seek nothing else than what he has taught." [1] And again :
"To know nothing contrary to the rule (*i.e.* the rule of faith)
is to know everything." [2]

Here, too, humility is the important thing. We are to
believe the rule of faith not because it is true and not because
it appeals to us as expressing the mind of Christ, but because
it is commanded. The more unreasonable it appears to us,
so Tertullian seems to think, the greater the merit of our
faith. [3] In his tract On the Flesh of Christ he declares, "The
Son of God died : it is absolutely worthy of belief because it
is absurd. [4] And having been buried he rose again : it is
certain because it is impossible." [5]

The contrast at this point between Tertullian and his
contemporary Clement of Alexandria is very striking.
Clement the philosopher, Tertullian the lawyer ; [6] Clement
broad-minded and hospitable to all truth, Tertullian as a
rule contemptuous of everything not given on authority.
And yet the latter also emphasized the reasonableness of
Christianity, particularly when addressing outsiders, and
made considerable use of rational arguments in its defense.

Tertullian was one of the group of old Catholic Fathers
who would exclude all heretics from the church. His tract
on The Prescription of Heretics, written before he became a

[1] *De præscriptione hæreticorum*, 9.

[2] *Ibid.* 14. Tertullian's rule of faith was substantially identical with the
Old Roman Symbol of which I spoke in the previous volume, chap. VIII. See
my *Apostles' Creed*, p. 47.

[3] Cf. *Adv. Marcionem*, II. 2 ; V. 5.

[4] Prorsus credibile est, quia ineptum est.

[5] Certum est, quia impossibile est (*De carne Christi*, 5). The particular
words Credo quia absurdum often attributed to Tertullian are not his.

[6] "What have Athens and Jerusalem to do with one another ? Or the
Academy and the Church ?" Tertullian asks in *De præscriptione hæreticorum*,
7.

Montanist, is perhaps the extremest and most sweeping statement of the principle that we have from the early church. In this tract he insists that heretics ought not to be argued with, though as a matter of fact he argued with them over and over again at great length, at least after he became a Montanist; nor should they be allowed to appeal to the Bible in support of their beliefs, for the Bible belongs to the church and heretics have no part or lot in it. "Accordingly we prefer to confront them with this principle, that we will decline to admit them to any discussion on the basis of the Scriptures. Before they are permitted to appeal to them it should be clearly seen to whom the Scriptures belong that no one may be allowed to use them who has no right to them." [1] Both the audacity and the sophistry of this are genuinely characteristic.

As a Montanist Tertullian receded from his extreme position and appealed to the Scriptures as well as to the revelations of the Montanistic prophets against the Catholic authorities. But even so he remained an authoritarian to the end. Truth is not to be discovered by investigation or speculation; it is given by divine revelation. There is a place for human reason in drawing conclusions from revealed premises, but the premises themselves are handed down from above. They are found and recorded in the Bible or the creed, or it may be in the inspired utterances of the new prophets. Beyond these no one may go. "By whom has truth been discovered without God? By whom has God been known without Christ? By whom has Christ been understood without the Holy Spirit?" [2]

In the west from Tertullian's day on dogma was a law; in the east it became in course of time, as we have seen,

[1] *De præscriptione hæreticorum*, 15.
[2] *De anima*, 1. And yet in this very work Tertullian used rational arguments on a large scale. The truth is his practice did not always agree with his theory.

a holy symbol. There was mysticism in the west as well as in the east, but in legalism not in mysticism the distinctive spirit of the west revealed itself, the spirit that found earliest and most complete expression in Tertullian.

It is significant and of a piece with his general attitude that Tertullian had a very definite doctrine of sin, a doctrine of a genuinely legal character. Sin has its seat in the will, not in the flesh, and its essence is disobedience to the divine law.[1] All sin therefore is guilt and as such punishable. Eternal death is not the natural fruit of corruption but the penalty for guilt. With this personal and legal notion of sin he combined a doctrine of original sin. In agreement with the Stoics, whom he refers to repeatedly and with whom he had much more in common than with the Platonists, he held, as already seen, that the soul is corporeal and is propagated with the body, not introduced into it from without. The soul shares in Adam's guilt and every man therefore is under condemnation and is punishable for his inherited guilt quite apart from any actual sins he may commit. In the beginning, Tertullian says, Adam was trapped by Satan into breaking the commandment of God, and "being consequently given over to death the entire human race, tainted by its descent from him, became a channel for transmitting also his condemnation."[2] And yet in opposing infant baptism Tertullian asked, "Why does the age of innocence hasten to the remission of sins?"[3] showing that he had not yet drawn the consequences of his doctrine as the church later did.

Original sin, according to Tertullian, has not completely destroyed freedom and the power to do right. The better nature of the soul, he says, "may be obscured because it is not God; it cannot be extinguished because it is from God."[4]

---

[1] Cf. De anima, 40.
[2] De testimonio animæ, 3.
[3] De baptismo, 18.
[4] De anima, 41.

The soul still possesses rationality and freedom and hence every man is responsible for his own actions. "The reward neither of good nor evil could justly be paid to him who should be found to have been either good or evil by necessity and not by choice." [1] Irenæus too, as we have seen, had a doctrine of original sin. Indeed his conception of man's need and of the salvation brought by Christ was based upon it. But he interpreted original sin in physical rather than legal terms, as corruption rather than guilt. The advance made by Tertullian, and it had wide influence in later times, was in bringing original sin under legal categories and thus holding all men punishable even before they had committed sins of their own. At this point we come upon one of the permanent differences between east and west.

In his doctrine of salvation Tertullian showed the same legal way of thinking. Salvation is wholly future and consists in escape not from death but from punishment. God is an avenging God and allows no sin to go unpunished. The whole human race, indeed, lies under condemnation for its guilt. Salvation and the way of salvation are both conceived in legal not mystical terms. Of Irenæus' idea of deification, the idea that characterized the mysteries, Tertullian shows no trace. There are mystical phrases to be sure in his tract on baptism, but they are merely traditional, and as a rule his language as well as his thinking is wholly devoid of mysticism.

Those who repent and are baptized are released from guilt and hence from punishment. Baptism is not to be received lightly and not too early in life. Rather it is to be deferred as long as practicable that there may be less danger of forfeiting its benefits by further sinning. "If any understand the weighty import of baptism they will fear its reception

[1] *Adv. Marcionem*, II. 86.

rather than its delay." [1] For centuries the postponement of baptism, thus advised by Tertullian, was a standing practice in the west.

The forgiveness attached to baptism is not given freely; it is bought by repentance which must be genuine and thoroughgoing. "It is at this price that the Lord has determined to award pardon. He proposes that immunity shall be purchased by the payment of repentance. If then those who sell first test the coin with which they are paid to see that it has not been cut or scraped or adulterated we believe that the Lord also when about to grant us so valuable a reward as eternal life first enters upon an examination of our repentance." [2]

Baptism and repentance must be followed by obedience or the Christian will fall again under divine condemnation. Continued obedience is as necessary as the initial repentance and baptism. In his work on penitence, written before he became a Montanist, Tertullian proclaimed in agreement with Hermas the possibility of a second repentance but no more for those who had sinned after baptism.[3] But if repentance after baptism is to be effective it must be accompanied by public confession and by works of satisfaction, that is by acts of humiliation and self-torture, including particularly severe fasting.[4] By temporary torments Tertullian says eternal punishment may be expunged; and in so far as a man has not spared himself in so far God will spare him.[5]

---

[1] De baptismo, 18. "We are not baptized that we may cease sinning but because we have ceased " Tertullian says in De pœnitentia, 6.

[2] De pœnitentia, 6.

[3] De pœnitentia, 7, 9. Later, as a Montanist, Tertullian was more rigorous, denying altogether the possibility of forgiveness for mortal sins committed after baptism. It was in his Montanistic days that he bitterly denounced Bishop Callixtus of Rome for declaring that he would forgive after suitable penance all sins of impurity including adultery (see Tertullian's De pudicitia, 1).

[4] Tertullian was a strong advocate of fasting. In his De jejunio, 17 he remarks in characteristic fashion: "Perhaps a well-fed Christian will be needed more by bears and lions than by God."

[5] De pœnitentia, 9–11.

Tertullian had an elaborate doctrine of post-baptismal sins, the sins of baptized Christians. Some of them are mortal, others only venial. In his work against Marcion he speaks of seven deadly sins : idolatry, blasphemy, murder, adultery, fornication, false witness, fraud.[1] In his tract on modesty, written like the work against Marcion in his Montanistic days, he says there are "some sins which we commit daily to which we are all liable. For to whom will it not happen to be angry unjustly and to retain his anger beyond sunset, or even commit violence, or carelessly to speak evil, or to swear rashly, or to break his plighted word, or to lie from timidity or necessity? In business, in official duties, in trade, in food, in sight, in hearing, how greatly we are tempted ! So that if there were no pardon for such sins no one would be saved. For these therefore there will be pardon through Christ, the successful suppliant of the Father. But there are also the opposites of these, the graver and deadly sins which will not be pardoned : murder, idolatry, fraud, denial of the faith, blasphemy, and particularly adultery and fornication, and if there be any other violations of the temple of God. For these Christ will no more be the successful suppliant ; these he who has been born of God will by no means commit, and he will not be a son of God if he commits them."[2] Here too the mortal sins are given as seven in number though the list is slightly different from that in the work against Marcion. In fixing upon the number seven Tertullian set the fashion for western theologians after his day though their lists were not always identical with each other or with either of his.

Keeping the divine law and making up by penitence and penance for minor defects in our obedience we earn the reward of eternal bliss in another world beyond the grave. Our bliss there will be proportioned to our deserts. "Why,"

---

[1] *Adv. Marcionem*, IV. 9.
[2] *De pudicitia*, 19.

Tertullian asks, "are there to be many mansions with the Father if not because of the variety in men's merits?"[1]

Tertullian was much interested in eschatology and had a great deal to say upon the subject. As a Montanist he was a premillenarian and believed in the nearness of the consummation. He pictured the future, particularly the future of the lost, in very realistic terms. One of the delights of the saved in heaven will be to watch the torments of the damned and realize their own good fortune in contrast with them.[2] The torments will be physical as well as mental. The existence of a literal hell where the fire is real is shown by volcanic eruptions, phenomena which confirm the words of divine revelation.[3] The contrast between Tertullian's materialistic rendering of the future life and the spiritual interpretation of the Alexandrian Fathers is very marked. In this matter, as in many others, he represented a wholly different point of view. As a rule the vivid sense of the future and the interpretation of it in sensuous terms have been commoner in the west than in the east. Premillenarianism to be sure was generally discredited in both parts of Christendom after the Montanistic controversy, but the minds especially of western Christians have always been largely preoccupied with thoughts of the future life, with its glorious rewards and its dreadful punishments.

Already by Tertullian, and more and more as time passed by the church at large, the present life was thought of as a mere probation for the life to come, without value in itself and possessing meaning only because in it rewards are laid up for the life beyond the grave. Other-worldliness was all-controlling in Tertullian's own life and in this too as in so many other matters he was typical of those that came after

---

[1] *Scorpiace*, 6.
[2] *De spectaculis*, 30. This was a commonplace in the Middle Ages.
[3] *De pœnitentia*, 12.

him. The supreme Christian virtues are humility and the spirit of other-worldliness. Possessed of these the Christian may pass safely through all the perils of the present life sure of enjoying the reward prepared for the saints in heaven.

Tertullian's influence in the west was enormous. He was a genuine westerner and he spoke a language the west could understand. To be sure his Montanism brought him into disrepute and prevented his being reckoned as a Catholic Father. But the great Cyprian was devoted to him and helped to keep his fame alive. His writings were preserved and continued to be widely read — a remarkable circumstance in view of the common treatment accorded the works of heretics and schismatics. And though theologians were chary of expressing agreement with him, many of his views and in particular his legal way of looking at things were permanently influential. Always God's sovereignty and majesty and avenging wrath have been more emphasized and the legal interpretation of Christianity and the Christian life has been more prominent and controlling in the west than in the east.

CHAPTER II

CYPRIAN

After Tertullian the greatest figure in the western church until the time of Augustine was Cyprian, bishop of Carthage from 248 or 249 until his death as a martyr in 258. Born in Carthage of heathen parents of wealth and social standing he became a Christian in mature life. Of the motives that led him to embrace Christianity and of the circumstances of his conversion we have no knowledge. He has something to say on the subject, it is true, in the third and fourth chapters of his Epistle to Donatus. He speaks there of his worldliness and of the darkness in which he was living until his sins were washed away in baptism and he was born again, when darkness gave way to light and weakness to strength. His language however is too general and too conventional to be of much help. But it is clear that, account for it as we may, his conversion was radical and thorough, for it resulted in a complete change in his way of living. Though he had inherited a considerable fortune, upon becoming a Christian he gave away the greater part of it in charity. He also abandoned his profession as a teacher of rhetoric in which he had gained a high place, and devoted himself wholly to the service of the church, being appointed a priest almost immediately and bishop very soon afterward.

In breaking with his past he not only gave up his accustomed occupations and pleasures and adopted a life of the strictest continence, he even turned his back on the writers whose works had constituted the staple of his education and confined his reading thenceforth to the Bible and Christian authors, particularly Tertullian. Nowhere in his works is there a reference to classical writers or a quotation from them. In this he was almost unique among the early Fathers, at any rate the better educated of them.

Though not personally acquainted with Tertullian, who died while he was still a youth, he conceived a great admiration for him, called him Master and studied his works assiduously. He nowhere quotes him by name but his writings show Tertullian's influence on almost every page. Though a less original thinker than the latter he was much saner and better balanced, and it was largely due to him that so much of Tertullian's thought found general acceptance in the west. He was a man of high ideals, of uncommon ability and of great force of character. He was also a preacher of considerable power. Not so much of a theologian and not so brilliant a writer as Tertullian he had rare administrative gifts which were revealed in his conduct of the affairs of the North African churches during a very difficult period. He became in fact and was generally recognized as the greatest and most influential prelate of his age. With a profound sense of responsibility he combined a keen appreciation of his own authority and dignity. He was accustomed to have his own way and for all his protestations of humility he often carried things with a high hand.

He was a less voluminous writer than Tertullian but we have several brief treatises from his pen, some of them of great importance, and in addition a large number of letters which reveal his character and principles with great clearness and at the same time constitute one of our principal sources for a knowledge of the history of the western church in the third century. His reputation and authority were so great that many works by other writers were ascribed to him or were issued under his name. There are still extant indeed several pseudo-Cyprianic writings, a few of them earlier, most of them later than his day.

Like Tertullian, and even more exclusively than he, Cyprian was controlled by practical interests. His general conception of Christianity was similar to Tertullian's. Whether he had had a legal education as some think, at any rate the legal way of looking at things was characteristic of him as it was of the older man. The sovereignty of God, the duty of obedience, the interpretation of the Christian life as a means of earning eternal bliss, the necessity of penance, all these Cyprian emphasized as Tertullian had done. His chief significance for us, however, lies in his theory of the church which he worked out under the pressure of practical emergencies. He nowhere formulates it in detail but it is reflected clearly enough in many of his epistles and particularly in his famous treatise on the unity of the Catholic church.

Cyprian's episcopate fell in a period of storm and stress. The Decian persecution, the most severe up to that time, broke out within a year after his accession and plunged the church in North Africa as well as elsewhere into serious trouble. He himself found it expedient to leave Carthage and go into retirement where he remained until the persecution was over. He did this apparently out of consideration for the good of the church, but naturally he was widely blamed for his flight and had much ado to maintain his standing and authority. The persecution moreover resulted in apostasy from the church on a large scale. While some stood firm and were exiled or thrown into prison the great majority denied the faith or secured from the authorities certificates that they had done so even when they had not.[1]

[1] Cf. *De lapsis*, 7; Ep. 14 : 1; 20 : 2. In referring to Cyprian's letters I have followed the numbering in Hartel's edition. In *The Ante-Nicene Fathers* the letters are arranged as in Migne's *Patrologia Latina*, but the numbering of the Oxford edition, which agrees with that of Hartel, is indicated in the footnotes.

Curiously enough some of these certificates on the original pieces of papyrus are still in existence. Whether entitled to them or not the holders of the certificates (libellatici as they were called) were generally regarded as apostates and were condemned for denying the Christian faith.[1] After the persecution was over many of them repented and wished to return to the communion of the church, and whether to pardon and readmit them became a burning question.

For some time it had been the custom in Rome and North Africa to readmit after suitable penance Christians who had been excluded from the church on account of fleshly sins. Callixtus, bishop of Rome from 217 to 222, had given official sanction to the custom and had claimed it as his right as successor of the Apostles to forgive all such offenders. He thus aroused the wrath of Hippolytus, the head of a rigorous sect at Rome. and of Tertullian as well. But the practice continued to prevail and was followed by Cyprian though not by all the African bishops. On the other hand that apostates could be forgiven and reinstated was not generally believed. Callixtus had said nothing about them in his edict. The church was not suffering persecution at the time and the question of their treatment was not under discussion. Like impurity and murder apostasy was regarded by Tertullian as an unforgivable sin, though he regarded it as less flagrant than sins of the flesh, because the latter were committed deliberately and were the fruit of lust, while denial of the faith was usually due to the pressure of persecution.[2] But in spite of Tertullian's opinion in this matter fleshly sins were generally regarded as forgivable while apostasy was not.

With the persecution of Decius, however, the situation changed. To insist on the permanent exclusion of the lapsed

[1] Cf. *De lapsis*, 27; Ep. 55 : 13 ff.
[2] *De pudicitia*, 22; so also Cyprian, Ep. 55 : 26.

meant to decimate the church. In spite of this Cyprian at first stood for the traditional custom and declined to readmit them, identifying apostasy, or the denial of the faith, with the sin against the Holy Ghost.[1] On the other hand the martyrs, as those were called who had been exiled or imprisoned for their faith, took a more lenient attitude and urged that the lapsed be readmitted. Some of them even went so far as to issue letters of pardon on their own authority without asking episcopal sanction.[2] They actually succeeded in winning the support of several presbyters of the Carthaginian church so that Cyprian found himself faced with a rebellion among his clergy.[3] Finally when it became evident that general sentiment was against him and that his authority, already weakened by absence from his post during the persecution, was not sufficient to compel submission, he yielded, insisting only that adequate penance should be required before pardon was granted and that readmission should be in the hands of the bishop alone.

Apparently he was led to yield not only by the exigencies of the situation but also by the conviction to which he finally came that to readmit the lapsed after suitable penance would be for their good as well as the good of the church.[4] It was in this connection that he insisted on his right as successor of the Apostles to forgive sins and readmit whomsoever he pleased, a right which he denied to the presbyters and also to the martyrs in spite of his high estimate of martyrdom. As said above, Callixtus had already claimed that the bishop as successor of the Apostles could forgive sins and readmit penitents to the church. Cyprian followed him but went further in basing the bishop's authority in the matter upon his possession of priestly functions which had been transmitted to him in regular succession from the Apostles.

[1] Cf. Ep. 16 : 2. [2] Cf. Eps. 18, 19, 22, 27.
[3] Cf. Eps. 43, 59. [4] Cf. Eps. 55 : 3 ff; 19 ff; also Eps. 15 and 16.

The bishop is not only the ruler of the church, he is also a priest and the only priest. He may delegate his priestly function to others and they may act for him but they have no independent priestly gifts. The presbyters, for instance, are priests not in their own right but only as the bishop's delegates and representatives.[1]

The bishop owes his appointment to God not man. He is wholly independent both of clergy and laity and his sovereignty is absolute.[2] To be sure Cyprian consulted freely with his clergy and strove as far as possible to meet the wishes of his people; but in the last analysis he was supreme and insisted that all should recognize his supremacy.[3] In the controversy with certain of his clergy concerning the treatment of the lapsed it was their defiance of his authority that chiefly incensed him.[4] In his emphasis upon episcopal authority he went so far as to insist that the church is founded on the bishops and that apart from them there is no church. Thus he says: "Thence through the vicissitudes of time and succession the ordination of bishops and the business of the church move on, so that the church is founded on the bishops and every act of the church is governed by these same rulers." [5] And again: "Whence you ought to know that the bishop is in the church and the church in the bishop, and that if anyone is not with the bishop he is not in the church." [6]

In the struggle with his opponents Cyprian was led also to lay emphasis upon the unity of the church, in the first instance of the local church under the control of its bishop, and then of all the churches under the control of the collective episcopate. It was in the interest of the principle of unity in the local church that he sided with Cornelius,

[1] Cf. Eps. 17 : 2; 43 : 3; 59 : 5; 63 : 14; 66 : 5.
[2] Cf. Eps. 3 : 3; 59 : 2, 5; 66 : 1, 4.
[3] Cf. Eps. 38–40.   [4] Cf. Eps. 16, 17, 43.
[5] Ep. 33 : 1.   [6] Ep. 66 : 8.

bishop of Rome, in the latter's controversy with Novatian. Cornelius, a member of the laxer party in the Roman church, which advocated leniency in the treatment of the lapsed, was chosen bishop immediately after the close of the Decian persecution. Thereupon the stricter party seceded and elected the presbyter Novatian, a man of the highest character and a theologian of considerable importance.[1] According to custom Novatian announced his accession to the bishops of the principal sees including Cyprian. But though the latter was more in sympathy with Novatian's attitude toward the lapsed than with the laxer attitude of Cornelius he declined to recognize him, insisting that Cornelius was the rightful bishop of the Roman church and that Novatian who had been elected later was in schism.[2]

Similarly he found occasion to insist on the unity of the church at large under the control of the united episcopate, in opposition not only to Novatian but also to Felicissimus and other schismatics who were opposing him in Carthage and in other parts of the province. "There is one church throughout the world," he says, "divided by Christ into many members, likewise one episcopate diffused in a harmonious multitude of many bishops."[3] Again: "God is one and there is one church and one chair founded upon Peter by the word of the Lord. Another altar cannot be set up nor a new priesthood created besides the one altar and the one priesthood."[4]

The unity of the church, already insisted on by Irenæus, was so important to Cyprian that he published a treatise on the subject, the most famous of all his writings, entitled On the Unity of the Catholic Church. This one Catholic church

---

[1] Novatian's treatise *De trinitate*, one of the most notable works of the third century, is especially important as an admirable summary of the western theology of his day. It shows throughout the overmastering influence of Tertullian's thought.

[2] See Eps. 44, 45, 55 : 8. [3] Ep. 55 : 24; cf. 68 : 3. [4] Ep. 43 : 5.

is not a mere community of Christians, it is the sole ark of salvation outside of which no one can be saved. "If anyone could escape," Cyprian says, "who was outside the ark of Noah he also may escape who is outside the church." [1] "Outside the church there is no salvation." [2] "He cannot have God as father who has not the church as mother." [3]

The difference at this point between Cyprian and earlier Christians was not that he asserted that no one could be saved apart from the church, for upon this there was general agreement from primitive days, but that he identified the church with a particular institution, the Catholic church, which was founded upon and had its existence in those bishops who held their office in regular succession from the Apostles. This church alone, he claimed, was in possession of saving grace and apart from it there was no salvation. Apart from it indeed there was no church and there were no Christians. [4] It was to be sharply distinguished from all heretical and schismatic bodies, from all other so-called churches which claimed to be Christian but were not. Irenæus had declared that the bishops as successors of the Apostles are the guarantors and interpreters of apostolic truth and that those who do not accept the truth taught by them are heretics and beyond the pale of salvation. Cyprian went further and asserted that even though they may be orthodox they cannot be saved unless they are within the one Catholic church. In other words schismatics cannot be saved any more than heretics. Indeed schismatics are heretics, for they do not accept the true church, belief in which is itself an essential part of the Christian faith. [5]

[1] *De catholicæ ecclesiæ unitate*, 6. The figure of Noah's ark had been already used by Callixtus.

[2] Salus extra ecclesiam non est (Ep. 73 : 21).

[3] Habere non potest Deum patrem qui ecclesiam non habet matrem (*De unitate*, 6).

[4] Eps. 55 : 24 ; 66 : 8.

[5] Cf. Eps. 51 : 1 ; 69 : 7 ; 70 : 2.

The schismatic like the heretic is worse than the apostate who has denied the faith in persecution. "There is a worse crime," Cyprian says, "than that which the lapsed seem to have committed who nevertheless as penitents offer God full satisfaction for their crime. Here the church is sought after and entreated, there it is opposed ; here there may have been necessity, there the wickedness is voluntary ; here he who has fallen has injured only himself ; there he who has attempted to cause heresy or schism has deceived and drawn away many ; here only one soul is damned, there a multitude are endangered. The one knows he has sinned and laments and mourns ; the other puffed up in his sin and rejoicing in his very transgressions separates sons from their mother, seduces sheep from their shepherd, disturbs the sacraments of God ; and while the lapsed has sinned but once, he sins daily. Finally the lapsed who afterwards suffers martyrdom is able to obtain the promise of the kingdom ; while he who is put to death outside the church cannot share the rewards of the church." [1]

Outside the Catholic church there is not only no salvation, there is nothing truly Christian : no forgiveness of sins, no Christian baptism, no Christian faith and charity, no real martyrdom.[2] Schismatics, however holy and righteous they may be, are devoid of all the Christian virtues and graces and are children of Satan and without God in the world.

In 255 or thereabouts a sharp controversy broke out between Cyprian and Stephen, at that time bishop of Rome, concerning heretical baptism.[3] It had long been the custom in Rome to receive into the communion of the church without rebaptism those who had been baptized by heretics or schismatics. Hands were laid upon them by the bishop to seal their repentance and admission to communion, but

---

[1] *De unitate*, 19.   [2] Cf. Eps. 55 : 2 ; 66 : 8 ; 70 : 2 ; *De unitate*, 14.
[3] See Eusebius, *H. E.* VII. 2-5.

they were not baptized again. This custom was continued by Stephen. Cyprian, on the other hand, following the practice of the African and Oriental churches, insisted on rebaptizing such persons on the ground that there was no true baptism outside the Catholic church.[1] Though he regarded the Roman practice as unsound and denounced it in unsparing terms he was willing that the Roman church should go its own way in the affair,[2] but Stephen was less complaisant. Emulating the example of one of his predecessors (Bishop Victor of the late second century), who had excommunicated the churches of the Orient for celebrating Easter on the wrong date, he broke off communion with the churches of the east, and of North Africa as well, for declining to follow the practice of Rome in admitting heretics without rebaptism. Like Victor he was evidently moved chiefly by the desire to assert his authority over other churches, and in this case particularly over Cyprian, whose power he was jealous of and wished to curtail. The result was that although in certain of his epistles Cyprian had spoken of the church as founded upon Peter and had seemed to imply that whoever is not in communion with the bishop of Rome is outside the church [3] he now proceeded on the assumption that he and his fellow-bishops in Africa and elsewhere were quite independent of the bishop of Rome and that their authority was fully equal to that of the latter. The church in fact has its unity, so he maintained, not in any single bishop but in the collective episcopate.[4]

The unity of the church finds its legitimate expression in ecclesiastical synods in which the collective episcopate declares its will. Episcopal synods had been common both in east and west for some generations. In them the bishops of

---

[1] Cf. Eps. 70, 73, 74.
[2] Cf. Eps. 72 : 3; 73 : 26.
[3] Cf. Eps. 43 : 5; 55 : 1; 59 : 17; 66 : 8; 70 : 3; 71 : 3; 73 : 7.
[4] *De unitate*, 5; Ep. 55 : 24.

a particular province or of a particular region were in the habit of considering all sorts of matters of common interest and deciding what action should be taken. It was in such gatherings, attended by neighboring bishops, that Cyprian found support in dealing with the question of the lapsed and in bringing recalcitrant clergymen to submission.[1] These were only local synods, but after Cyprian's time the unity of the entire Catholic church both east and west came to expression in general or œcumenical councils representing all parts of Christendom. Of these the Council of Nicæa of 325, of which I spoke in the previous volume, was the first. They were a natural and logical consequence of the principle of unity of which Cyprian made so much.

In a very true sense Cyprian was the founder of the Catholic church. That there was only one church of Christ and that all the local churches belonged to it had been widely believed from an early day, but so far as we know Cyprian was the first clearly to segregate the Catholic church — a world-wide institution all of whose parts were united in one indivisible whole — from all other Christian or would-be Christian bodies and to insist that this church alone was founded by the Apostles and that its bishops alone are in possession of the grace without which no one can be saved.

Cyprian's principles, whether under his influence or independently of him, were ultimately accepted everywhere. A contemporary, Bishop Firmilian of Cæsarea in Cappadocia, endorsed them in a letter to Cyprian which is still extant,[2] and they were not generally questioned after the middle of the third century either in east or west. They were the natural result of the controversies with Gnostics and other heretics, and of the schisms caused by disputes over ecclesi-

[1] Cf. *e.g.* Eps. 20 : 3; 31; 34 : 3; 55 : 6; 59 : 9.
[2] Ep. 75 in the collection of Cyprian's Epistles.

astical discipline, and it was inevitable that they should finally prevail in all parts of Christendom.

I have been speaking of Cyprian's theory of the Catholic church. He is important to us not only for this but also for his contributions to the doctrine of the sacraments. For one thing he brought them into closer connection with the church, denying that they are efficacious apart from it and putting an end to the notion that they have significance or value as private acts of religion. Baptism is valid, he insisted, only when administered within the Catholic church and by the bishop himself or his representative. If administered by the latter it has efficacy only when the bishop has laid hands upon the baptized person and thus imparted the Holy Spirit.[1] This practice did not originate with Cyprian. Even where heretics were not rebaptized it was the custom for the bishops to lay hands upon them before they were admitted to communion. There was as yet no separate sacrament of confirmation such as later came to be recognized, but the essence of it was already present in the division of baptism into two parts, the washing with water and the laying on of hands. This division corresponded to the twofold idea of baptism which had existed from an early day, baptism for the remission of sins and for regeneration. Sometimes the former had been emphasized, as for instance by those who interpreted Christianity chiefly in ethical or legal terms, sometimes the latter, as by those who interpreted it primarily in mystical terms. Often the two were confused and the difference between them overlooked, as by Justin Martyr.[2] Irenæus who combined the two interpretations of Christianity stressed both aspects of baptism[3] and after his time they were generally recognized as equally sound. Where the former was chiefly in mind the temptation was to post-

[1] Ep. 73 : 7, 9. [2] *Apol.* I. 61.
[3] Cf. *e.g.* his *Demonstration of Apostolic Preaching*, § 3.

pone baptism as long as possible. This tendency however was weakened by the growing recognition of the efficacy of penance which provided for sins committed after baptism, and finally gave way to the opposite tendency to baptize early that regeneration might not be delayed. This found justification in Cyprian's theory that even an infant who has committed no actual sins needs forgiveness for the original sin inherited from Adam.[1] The idea of original sin Cyprian took from Tertullian, but while Tertullian opposed infant baptism Cyprian favored it.

As Cyprian emphasized the ecclesiastical character of baptism and made it an exclusively Catholic rite he did the same for the eucharist. If performed outside the Catholic church it has no value.[2] Still more important was his interpretation of it as a sacrifice in which the priest repeats in a bloodless manner the sacrifice of Christ upon the cross.[3] It is true that it is not altogether clear whether Cyprian thought of the eucharist as a repetition of Christ's sacrifice, as it was later represented, or only as a commemoration of it.[4] But in either event the prominence which he gave to the sacrificial idea was of great significance. Commonly the eucharist was looked upon as the spiritual food on which the Christian's regenerate nature is nourished. As such it was connected with baptism viewed as the sacrament of regeneration. Cyprian emphasized the notion of it as a sacrifice for sin, either a repetition or a commemoration of Christ's sacrifice. He thus brought it into line with baptism viewed as the sacrament of forgiveness and if he did not actually suggest at any rate made possible the ultimate association of it with penance as a means of atoning for post-baptismal transgressions. Of this it will be necessary to speak again later.

---

[1] Cf. Ep. 64 : 5.
[2] *De unitate*, 8 ; Ep. 70 : 2. Cf. Ignatius of Antioch, Eph. 5.
[3] Cf. Ep. 63 : 4, 9, 14.
[4] Cf. Ep. 63 : 17.

As Cyprian brought baptism and the eucharist into closer and more exclusive connection with the Catholic church he did the same for penance. As already seen he insisted that the Catholic bishop alone has the right to forgive mortal sins and to readmit the offender to the communion of the church. This he may do because as successor of the Apostles and a priest of God he can impart divine grace. This meant that penance too, like baptism and the eucharist, is an ecclesiastical not a mere private affair, in other words that it is a sacrament in the full sense. This found expression in the words "remission of sins through the holy church," which formed a part of Cyprian's version of the Old Roman Symbol, the original of our Apostles' Creed.[1]

According to Cyprian the sacraments are valid only when performed by priests of good character and sound faith. Callixtus, followed by Stephen, bishop of Rome, had held that bishops should not be deposed whatever their character or conduct. They are accountable only to God and men have no right to pass judgment upon them.[2] Cyprian, on the other hand, like Cornelius, Stephen's predecessor, maintained the opposite. Bishops that were unsound in the faith or had committed mortal sins were to be judged by a council of fellow-bishops and if found guilty were to be deposed and excommunicated. They might afterwards, if repentant, be restored to the communion of the church but only as laymen.[3] But Cyprian went still further than this and insisted

[1] See the previous volume, pp. 157 ff. The article on the remission of sins apparently did not belong to the original text of the Old Roman Symbol and was probably added in the early third century. See my *Apostles' Creed*, pp. 46, 94, 155 ff. To the examples referred to there of early baptismal creeds in which the remission of sins is wanting may be added those given by H. Lietzmann on pp. 226–227 of a paper on "Die Anfänge des Glaubensbekenntnisses" in the volume entitled *Festgabe von Fachgenossen und Freunden A. von Harnack zum siebzigsten Geburtstag dargebracht* (1921). See also his "Die Urform des apostolischen Glaubensbekenntnisses" in the *Sitzungsberichte der preussischen Akademie der Wissenschaften*, Jahrgang 1919, pp. 269 ff.

[2] See Hippolytus, *Philosophumena*, IX. 12; Cyprian, Eps. 67, 68.

[3] See Eusebius, *H. E.* VI. 43, 10; Cyprian, Eps. 64 : 1; 65; 67 : 3, 6.

that unworthy clergymen, even if they had not been detected in their wickedness and deprived of their office, were incompetent to perform clerical functions.[1]

As a consequence the sacraments administered by such persons were invalid. Christians might thus be left in uncertainty as to whether they were actually receiving a sacrament. From the Catholic point of view this was a serious defect in Cyprian's theory. It was remedied as a result of the Donatist schism of which there will be occasion to speak in the chapter on Augustine.

[1] Eps. 65; 67 : 2.

CHAPTER III

FROM ARNOBIUS TO JEROME

In the century succeeding the death of Cyprian there were
no theologians of great importance in the western church
and no significant developments in Christian thought.
Soon after the beginning of the fourth century Arnobius, a
teacher of rhetoric in North Africa who was converted to
Christianity late in life, published an extended work in defense of his new faith, entitled Adversus nationes. He had
been a bitter opponent of Christianity for many years and
when the genuineness of his conversion was doubted he wrote
his Apology as a guarantee of good faith, a circumstance that
may explain the obvious haste in which it was written. The
work is in seven books. Of these only the first two are of
interest. The last five are devoted to a scathing arraign-
ment of heathenism, perhaps all the more severe because the
author's honesty had been questioned. In the main they
simply reproduce the current arguments and calumnies and
have little independent value or significance.

The first two books on the contrary are very fresh and
original. Arnobius took his start from the current accusation that the many ills from which the world was suffering
were due to Christianity. He denied that these ills were
any worse than in earlier days. Indeed he claimed that in
some respects they were not so bad, for at any rate there
had been less war in the world since Christ appeared. But
even granted that they were worse Arnobius retorts that the
ills men suffer, like the blessings they enjoy, are not sent by
the gods but are due wholly to natural causes. In this

connection he has many highly enlightened things to say that bear the flavor of what was for that day a somewhat extreme scepticism.

In pursuance of the same aim of cutting the ground from under the opponents of Christianity he attacks human reason and intelligence. Men are sadly ignorant and know very little about the universe in which they live. Indeed they are poor creatures generally and the lofty opinion they have of themselves is quite unwarranted. They are of no patrician race, Arnobius says. They are not the offspring of God and whoever maintains they are is guilty of blasphemy. They do not owe their origin to him any more than flies, beetles, moths and other insects. God made only what is good and useful.[1] Whence man and these other creatures came, whence evil in general comes, Arnobius confesses he does not know nor does he think it important. He is content, he says, to maintain only this, that nothing bad or harmful comes from God. "This we believe, this we know, in this one truth of knowledge and science we rest, that nothing has been made by him except that which is for the well being of all, is pleasant, is full of love and joy and gladness, and is attended with unbounded and incorruptible pleasures."[2]

Arnobius pours contempt upon the notion, generally prevalent among Christians, that the world was created for the sake of man.[3] Men are no better than brutes and to imagine that God had so high a regard for them as to make the world on their account is absurd. Instead of being the end of creation, men were made that evil might have an opportunity to spread, and "that there might always be miserable persons whose torments should entertain I know not what unseen and cruel power, hostile to humanity "[4] — a cynical statement that sounds strange enough on the lips of

[1] *Adv. nationes*, II. 46 ff.
[2] *Ibid*. II. 55.
[3] *Ibid*. I. 12; II. 38; cf. VII. 9
[4] *Ibid*. II. 46.

an early Christian. It is interesting to compare Arnobius at this point with Celsus, the second-century opponent of Christianity, who took much the same position. In becoming a Christian Arnobius evidently did not abandon all his old beliefs.

In his endeavor to show how mean and worthless man is Arnobius turned his attack upon the human soul. The long discussion of the soul in the second book was due to his desire to humble men and show the vanity of their pretensions. The soul did not come from God and is not naturally immortal. It is a poor thing and will enjoy immortality only if God wills to bestow it, only indeed if saved by Christ. In all that Arnobius said in disparagement of man he was moved by the desire to reduce the pretensions of human reason and thus make room for faith which alone has place in religion. Where salvation is at stake something must be done even if there be no sure grounds to act upon. In such a situation one must rely wholly on faith.

As a matter of fact, this is true, as Arnobius points out, in many other affairs as well. Because there is mystery everywhere, and our knowledge is so narrowly limited, faith must often be our chief if not our only dependence. In husbandry, in travel, in marriage, in all sorts of occupations and relationships, we cannot get along without it any more than in religion. To mock at Christians therefore for their faith is the height of absurdity.[1] Both they and their opponents believe many things they cannot prove, many things that are altogether incapable of proof. Both put their trust in teachers whom they follow, and if a comparison is to be made certainly the virtues and the wonderful works of Christ justify faith in him above any other teacher.[2] In his character and his miracles indeed Arnobius finds the chief ground for belief in Christianity.

[1] *Ibid.* II. 8 ff. [2] *Ibid.* II. 11.

As there are many gods, each with a different function, so Christ has his own peculiar function, namely, to give men salvation. This is so exclusively his work that no one can be saved, however upright and holy he may be, except through Christ. "Unless then I become a Christian I cannot hope for salvation? It is just as you say . . . For as with you certain gods have certain responsibilities, rights and powers, and you do not ask from anyone of them that which he is not able or free to grant, so it is the office of Christ alone to give souls salvation and bestow upon them everlasting life. For if you believe that Father Bacchus is able to give a vintage but not medicine, that Ceres can give crops, Æsculapius health, Neptune one thing, Juno another, and that Fortuna and Mercury and Vulcan are the donors each of certain particular things, this also you must accept from us that souls can receive life and safety from no one except from him to whom the supreme king has assigned this function and office. . . Therefore even if you are pure and have been purged from all stains of vice, and have conciliated the powers and moved them not to close the way to heaven or prevent your return thither, you will by no striving be able to attain the prize of immortality, unless by Christ's gift you perceive what immortality really is and are admitted to true life." [1]

Arnobius carried his hostility to the use of reason in religion so far as to declare that it was as culpable to attempt to prove the existence of God as to deny it. The knowledge that God exists is inborn; every man has an instinctive assurance of it, and to endeavor to confirm this assurance by the use of arguments is only to create doubt and undermine faith.[2] In the absence of any knowledge as to what the future has in store for us, and in default of proof in support of one or another alternative, it is wiser, Arnobius

[1] *Adv. nationes*, II. 65–66.   [2] *Ibid.* I. 32 ff.

says, to believe the more advantageous than the less.   Applying this to Christianity he maintains that it is wiser to accept
it than to reject it even though the issue be uncertain, for
if it shall prove true the one who has accepted it will enjoy a
blessed immortality, while if it prove false he will be no
worse off.[1]

Salvation is so important a matter that no one should
allow his attention to be distracted from it.   The world is
full of things we do not understand, of things whose source
or cause is hidden from us.   Who made man?   What is
the origin of the soul?   Whence did evil come?   Is the sun
larger than the earth or only a foot in diameter?   Does the
moon shine of herself or only with borrowed light?   "Leave
these matters to God," Arnobius says.   "Your affairs are in
a parlous state, I mean the salvation of your souls.   And
unless you apply yourselves to a knowledge of the Supreme
God there awaits you, when loosed from your bodily fetters,
a cruel death which will mean not sudden extinction, but
the long drawn out bitterness of excruciating torment."[2]

Many passages in Arnobius' work are marked by delicious
irony;   much of his scepticism and agnosticism is of a re-
freshing sort;   his attacks upon the assurance and self-confidence of the enemies of Christ are very effective;   but his
defense of Christianity leaves much to be desired.   For the
most part it is wholly negative.   Except for his references to
Christ's virtues and miracles there is indeed nothing positive
about it.

Arnobius was a layman, and whether because of ignorance
or indifference he gave expression to many beliefs quite out
of line with the orthodox theology of the day.   His ideas of
creation have been already referred to;   his view of Jesus'
earthly life was markedly docetic;[3]   in his interpretation of
Christ's relation to God he vacillated between ditheism and

[1] *Ibid.* II. 4.   [2] *Ibid.* II. 61.   [3] Cf. *ibid.* I. 62.

modalism.[1] Because of his docetism, and particularly because of his ideas about creation, he has been accused of Gnosticism, but his general position was as far as possible from that of the Gnostics. The accusation betrays the inveterate habit of mistaking superficial resemblances for real relationships, a habit which has wrought untold confusion in history.

Arnobius' deviations from orthodoxy in the matters just referred to need not detain us. They are of far less interest than his scepticism and anti-rationalism, for the latter were far from common in the early church. It is not surprising, in view of his general attitude as well as of his aberrations from the traditional faith in matters of detail, that his work should have failed to secure wide approval and should have been put upon the index by Pope Gelasius in the fifth century.

A point of view quite other than that of Arnobius was represented by his fellow-countryman and pupil Lactantius, whom the Emperor Diocletian some time before the end of the third century called to Nicomedia as a teacher of rhetoric. While there Lactantius made the acquaintance of Constantine and some years later, when already an old man, he betook himself to Gaul to tutor Constantine's son Crispus. Of his subsequent career and of the date of his death we have no knowledge.

If not already a Christian when he went to Nicomedia he was at any rate before he left, for it was there he wrote his essay on The Workmanship of God, and at least a part of his Divine Institutes. In addition to these works there are still extant brief treatises on The Anger of God and on The Death of the Persecutors, and an epitome of the Institutes, an admirable summary of the larger work written a number of years later. We need concern ourselves here

[1] Cf. *Adv. nationes*, I. 42 ff ; 53.

only with the Institutes, the most important of his writings and the one to which he owes his fame. It was written early in the fourth century at about the same time as Arnobius' Adversus nationes. Though also apologetic in its purpose, it is a work of a very different character, more comprehensive, more carefully wrought out, and written in a far better style. It is at once a defense of Christianity, an attack upon heathenism, and a systematic presentation of the author's religious and ethical principles. If not the most important it was at any rate the most ambitious work published by a Latin Christian before the time of Augustine.

It was the author's aim so to present Christianity as to appeal especially to the educated classes. He wrote an excellent style which won for him the name of the Christian Cicero; he quoted more or less extensively from the best known Latin writers, not only Cicero but also Seneca, Virgil, Horace, Lucretius and others; he appealed continually to recognized principles of human reason; he was neither eccentric nor fanatical; on the contrary his treatment was dignified and his thought moved for the most part on a high plane. Moreover he took a large view of the existing situation and attempted to meet it in a comprehensive and thorough-going way.

The trouble with the Roman world, so he believed, was that its philosophy was too little religious and its religion too little philosophical.[1] Christianity, he maintained, was fitted to mend both these defects, for it was at once a philosophical religion and a religious philosophy.[2] As such he strove to present it in his Institutes, and if the result was less satisfactory than might have been wished the failure was due to no lack of effort on his part. It was due rather to the unphilosophical character of the traditional Latin Christianity of the day and to the meagreness of his own philosophical

[1] *Institutes*, IV. 3.   [2] *Ibid.* I. 2; *Epitome*, 41.

gifts. The truth is he was no great thinker. He had none of the originality and speculative power of a Clement or an Origen, and though he was a better writer and probably more learned than either Tertullian or Augustine, he lacked their genius and made no important contributions, as they did, to the thinking of the western church. At the same time he had many interesting and instructive things to say, and he had a very definite idea of Christianity which comes out with uncommon clearness and fulness in his principal work and is well worth dwelling upon for a little.

Christianity, as he understood it, was a monotheistic religion whose principal tenet was divine providence. By this he meant not merely God's care and preservation of the world, but also and chiefly his moral government which consisted in rewarding the good and punishing the wicked everlastingly. This is a fundamental thesis of the Institutes. There is much else in the work but this forms the backbone of the whole. All true religion must include the belief that God will reward the good and punish the wicked in a world beyond the grave, that is all true religion must include the belief in divine providence. Only where there is true religion in this sense is there an adequate basis for morality.[1] "Neither can any honour be due to God," Lactantius says, "if he bestows nothing on him who worships, nor any fear, if he is not angry with him who does not worship."[2]

There is a long and interesting discussion in the third book of the chief good of man which Lactantius finds in immortality.[3] All else counts for naught as compared with this. By immortality he meant, as all Christians did, not mere endless existence but everlasting felicity. Its opposite is not death but everlasting misery. Virtue, he maintained, is not the chief end of life, as Cicero and other philosophers

---

[1] *Institutes*, III. 26 ff.   [2] *On the Anger of God*, 6.
[3] *Institutes*, III. 8 ff; cf. III. 27; VI. 9; VII. 5 ff; *Epitome*, 52 (57).

thought, for virtue is a means only not an end, a means to immortality which is the real and ultimate good. To make virtue the chief end of life and to pursue it for itself alone is mere folly.[1] The only sound reason for virtue is the eternal reward that is attached to it. Were it not for this we might as well indulge in all sorts of vice.[2]

In the fifth book of the Institutes (chapters 15–18) there is an illuminating discussion of the Greek sceptical philosopher Carneades' contention that justice and wisdom are incompatible, for justice requires consideration for the good of others even at the expense of our own advantage, while wisdom justifies consideration for our own good alone. Lactantius admits that this would be so were it not for the future reward that attaches to justice and makes it wise as well as right for us to treat others honestly and kindly even though we suffer in consequence. The way he thus rationalized, by appealing to a future life, conduct which by common consent was right and commendable then as it is now is very instructive.

In spite of his appeal to future rewards and punishments as the only adequate basis for right doing Lactantius insisted on the disinterested character of virtue. A good deed done for the sake of reward lacks the quality of true goodness; charity given in the expectation of a return is not genuine charity.[3] But when he spoke thus he was thinking of a reward from men not from God. No one should do good deeds to gain the applause of men, or to secure benefits from them in return. But to do good for the sake of a divine reward is an altogether different matter. The former is selfishness, the latter religion. It is extraordinary to see the naïveté and evident good faith with which Lactantius drew the distinction between the two. Good done for the

---

[1] *Institutes*, III. 27.   [2] *Ibid*. III. 17.
[3] *Ibid*. VI. 11–12.

sake of a return is not good, unless the return be from God when it is the highest goodness.

Lactantius was profoundly interested in ethics. He was not a speculative thinker and metaphysical questions did not attract him. He was not at all concerned, for instance, as so many Christian theologians were, with the origin and nature of the Logos, with the relationship between the Father and the Son, and with other similar ontological mysteries. Nor was he interested in natural philosophy or science. In moral philosophy, he says, there is utility, in natural philosophy there is only pleasure, and the former alone is worthy the attention of men of wisdom.[1] In natural philosophy moreover we are dependent largely on conjecture while in moral philosophy we may attain exact and adequate knowledge [2] — an interesting contrast with modern opinion.

The sixth book of the Institutes is really a treatise on ethics and presents the subject in an admirable way. The author does not content himself with discussing particular virtues and vices; he deals also with the nature of virtue. "Before I begin to expound the separate virtues," he says at the beginning of the fifth chapter, "it must be determined what virtue is." In dealing with the subject he quoted largely, and frequently with approval, from Cicero, Seneca and other non-Christian writers, but he differed with them in making morality religious and in giving it a divine instead of a merely human basis. Virtue, he says, has been wrongly defined by the philosophers, and he defines it himself as the worship of God.[3] He begins the sixth book, indeed, with a chapter on what he calls the chief and greatest part of his work, namely, the worship of the true God, which he declares is nothing else than right living.[4]

---

[1] *Institutes*, III. 7.   [2] *Ibid*. III. 3.

[3] *Ibid*. VI. 5. According to the *Epitome*, 53 (58), justice is the only true worship of God.   [4] Cf. also *Institutes*, V. 9.

It is interesting to notice in this connection that Lac=
tantius took over from the Stoic Chrysippus the interpretation of virtue as the overcoming of evil and as therefore
dependent on evil for its existence.[1]   Where there is no evil,
he says, there is no virtue, and hence there will be no virtue
in heaven.[2]   Evil is thus explained as a means to good.   It
exists that men may have wherewith to exercise their moral
powers.

Though, as already seen, Lactantius put the motive for
virtue in self-interest, even if of a sublimated kind, his moral
standards were of the highest.   He had, indeed, a splendid
conception of the good life and many of the things he says
about it are unsurpassed in ancient literature.   There was
something of the ascetic in him, as in most serious-minded
men of the age, but asceticism had a minor place in his ideal.
As compared with the majority of early Christians he was
extraordinarily free from it.   He believed in active rather
than passive goodness and he was too public-spirited and
too socially minded to be in sympathy with monasticism
which was beginning to make its appearance among
Christians.[3]

His ethical ideal may be summed up in two words :   peace
and brotherliness.[4]   His recognition of the superiority of
monotheism to polytheism was due in large part to its
moral effects.   Where one God is worshipped and served
instead of many all men are related to each other as his sons,
and peace and brotherhood are the natural result.[5]   Upon
both of these he laid the greatest stress.   More important
than anything else it was to have men the wide world over

[1] Cf. *ibid.* III. 29 ; V. 7 ; VI. 15 ; VII. 1 ff. and *Epitome,* 24 (29).
[2] *Institutes,* VII. 10.
[3] In *Institutes,* III. 23 he speaks disapprovingly of abandoning one's property.
[4] Cf. *ibid.* I. 18 ; V. 10, 23 ; VI. 10 ff.   In VI. 10 he calls humanity the
supreme virtue.
[5] *Ibid.* V. 8.

live together in amity. Anger he denounced again and again in the most emphatic terms. To conquer the mind and restrain anger, he says, is the part of the bravest man, of him who is most like God.[1] He also condemned, as Jesus had done, retaliation for injuries. Moreover he did not content himself with repeating Jesus' words, as many of the Fathers did, he showed what retaliation meant and what were the demoralizing effects of taking vengeance on others. After quoting from Cicero's De officiis that he is a good man who benefits whom he can and harms no one unless provoked by injury, he continues, "Oh how he spoiled a simple and true sentiment by the addition of two words! For what need was there of adding 'unless provoked by injury,' that he might hang vice on a good man like a most disgraceful tail and might represent him as devoid of patience, the greatest of all virtues? He said a good man would inflict injury if he were provoked. But from the very circumstance that he inflicts injury he must necessarily lose the name of a good man. For it is no less the part of a bad man to return an injury than to inflict it. For whence arise combats and wars and quarrels if it be not that impatience opposed to injustice often excites great tempests? But if you meet injustice with patience, than which virtue there is none more genuine or more worthy of man, it will forthwith be extinguished as if you poured water on a fire."[1]

Lactantius was particularly emphatic in his denunciation of war as of all shedding of blood, including capital punishment. Thus he says: "When God forbids us to kill he not only prohibits murder which is not permitted even by civil law, but he warns us also against things esteemed legitimate among men. Hence it will not be lawful for a just man whose armor is righteousness to engage in war, nor to accuse anyone of a capital crime, for it makes no difference whether you

[1] *Institutes*, I. 9.   [2] *Ibid*. VI. 18.

slay by the sword or by a word, because killing itself is forbidden. Therefore in this precept of God no exception whatever ought to be made, but it is always wrong to kill a man whom God willed to be a sacrosanct animal." [1]

Nowhere else in early Christian literature do we find more ringing declarations of the illegitimacy of war and of everything like it than are to be found in Lactantius' writings. It is not legitimate, he insisted, even to fight for one's own country, or to attempt to promote its advantage in any way at the expense of other lands.[2] Christianity he was sure was above everything else a religion of peace and brotherhood. This he regarded as its great glory, the feature which must commend it most strongly to the best and wisest men.

It is not surprising, in view of Lactantius' emphasis on ethics and on the justice of God in rewarding the good and punishing the wicked, that he should lay great stress on moral ability and the freedom of the will.[3] Though he mentioned Adam's fall he did not draw the conclusion so frequently drawn that man has lost the power to do right without divine help. He had, indeed, no doctrine of original sin as his countrymen, Tertullian and Cyprian, had. It is therefore not to be wondered at that he had no doctrine of regeneration and that he pictured Christ as a teacher and exemplar rather than a redeemer. Christ came not to transform the nature of man by uniting it with the nature of God, but to teach virtue and to teach it both by word and deed.[4] Every teacher, Lactantius says, ought to practise what he teaches, and hence God came in the flesh in order to practise what he taught.[5] Thus in Christ men have the example they need to enable them to live as God would have them live.

[1] *Institutes*, VI. 20; cf. I. 18; V. 17.
[2] *Ibid*. VI. 6.
[3] Cf. *ibid*. IV. 24–28.
[4] Cf. *ibid*. IV. 11, 14, 16, 23.
[5] *Ibid*, IV. 23–24.

Though he made so much of the moral aspect of Christianity Lactantius had little to say about forgiveness and nothing at all about penance. At this point as at many others he was very unlike his countrymen, Tertullian and Cyprian. His spirit was more akin to that of Justin Martyr and other second-century Apologists, including the North African Minucius Felix. That this spirit, so alien to that of Tertullian and Cyprian, also existed in the western church of the period is a fact of no little historical importance, as will appear later.

Lactantius' notion of true religion — the worship of one God and obedience to him in expectation of a future reward — differs not at all in essence from what is commonly known as natural religion. But he identified true religion with Christianity, and what is more, he declared that no one could be saved apart from Christ,[1] or outside the Catholic church.[2] His controlling interest and his general principles being what they were this seems strange. The reason for it he did not make clear. He maintained that God had revealed himself through the prophets and Christ, and that the revelation recorded in the Bible is the only true one. He maintained also that such a revelation was necessary;[3] but why he did not attempt to show as Justin Martyr had done when faced with the same problem.

In the fourth book of his Institutes Lactantius spoke at considerable length about Christ the divine Logos or Son of God : his birth from a virgin, his miracles, his death on the cross, his resurrection, ascension, and final return for judgment. But the connection of it all with his general conception of religion and ethics he failed to indicate. Indeed he made no attempt to show that human salvation necessarily depends either on what Christ was or on what he did. The

[1] *Institutes*, IV. 19; *Epitome*, 68 (73).
[2] *Institutes*, IV. 3. The Catholic church is referred to by Lactantius only in this chapter.
[3] *E.g. ibid.* I. pref.; II. 3; III. 3.

chapters on Christ seem to have been due rather to the apologetic desire to remove the existing prejudice against Christianity, whose Lord was a crucified man, and to show that even so it was monotheistic not polytheistic. Both here and in the seventh book, where in dealing with the subject of immortality Lactantius reproduces in detail the Judæo-Christian eschatology, he is on different ground from that which he traverses elsewhere in his work. In the fourth and seventh books he is speaking as a devout Christian who accepts unquestioningly the traditional faith of the church without troubling himself particularly about its significance. Elsewhere he speaks as a moral and religious philosopher profoundly convinced of the truth and immense practical importance of the doctrine of divine providence and of the conclusions to be drawn from it. The latter, as already said, was the real theme of his Institutes. Everything else was of minor interest to him.

In Christianity Lactantius found the highest moral principles and in Jesus Christ himself the most perfect example of virtue. In Christianity he found also the doctrine of future rewards and punishments, in his opinion the only sure basis for virtue. Very likely, indeed, it was on this account that he became a Christian, if he was not born of Christian parents as he may have been. But this was not the same as to believe that there is no salvation apart from Christ, still less that there is none apart from the Catholic church. He believed it apparently only under the influence of Christian tradition and without the support upon which he relied for his interpretation of the nature of true religion. At any rate he gave no reason for his belief and seems not to have realized that any was needed, or perhaps he did not consider the belief of sufficient importance to demand justification. The contrast at this point between the layman Lactantius and the ecclesiastic Cyprian is exceedingly interesting and significant.

During the half century after Lactantius there was little theological activity in the western church. In the east the Arian controversy was engrossing the attention of theologians ; in the west, though Hilary of Poitiers and some others took part in the controversy, there was no independent thinking on that or any other subject. The latter part of the fourth century, however, marked the beginning of a new period of great interest to the historian of Christian thought. The most imposing figure of the period was Ambrose, bishop of Milan. Born of a noble family prominent in public life he was made governor of the provinces of Liguria and Aemilia in northern Italy while still a young man. His headquarters were at Milan and he acquired such a reputation for wisdom and justice that when the bishopric of Milan fell vacant, though he was not even a baptized Christian, he was elected to the post and finally accepted much against his will. He held office for more than twenty years until his death in 397 and proved himself one of the greatest of bishops, the Cyprian of the fourth century.

He was a notable preacher and did much to commend Christianity, now the official religion of the Empire, to those, particularly of the educated class, that had stood aloof and had looked upon it with disfavor. In the controversy between the orthodox and the Arians he took the orthodox side and helped to undermine the influence of Arianism and establish the Nicene doctrine in the west. He was a conservative in theology and though not so bitter a heresy hunter as his contemporary Jerome he had no thought of showing quarter to Christians of heretical views. He took strong measures, too, against Jews and heathen, doing what he could to induce the civil government to proscribe every form of religion except orthodox Christianity. Though he was a man of the highest character, and had a deserved reputation for honesty and justice, his intolerance carried him so far that on one

occasion when the Emperor Theodosius ordered the restoration of a Jewish synagogue destroyed by a Christian mob,
he induced him to rescind his order.

Educated as a lawyer Ambrose knew nothing about theology until he was made bishop. He then devoted himself
diligently to the study of the subject and though he never
became an important theologian he wrote many exegetical,
dogmatic and practical works which were widely read and
had considerable influence. He was not an original thinker.
What he knew about theology he owed chiefly to certain
eastern theologians, and his writings do little more than
repeat their ideas in a form adapted to the western church.
In this he was typical, for most of the western theology of his
day was simply a reproduction in Latin of the theology of
the east. He took over from Philo and the Alexandrian
Fathers the allegorical method of interpreting the Bible and
employed it on a large scale. As Origen had done, he used it
not only to discover the so-called deeper meaning of Scripture, but also to remove the difficulties that arose for the
Christian faith when the Old Testament was interpreted
literally. He did more perhaps than anyone else for the
spread of allegory in the western church against which
Jerome protested in vain.

Among the more famous of his exegetical writings was the
Hexæmeron dealing with the six days of creation. It was
based upon and in considerable part translated from a work
with the same title by Basil, the Cappadocian Father, for
whom Ambrose had a great admiration. It became the
model for many other works of a pseudo-scientific character
produced in the west. In his De fide, maintaining the deity
of Christ against the Arians, and in his De Spiritu sancto,
defending the deity of the Holy Spirit, Ambrose also echoed
Basil and other eastern Fathers.

In the doctrine of sin and grace, on the other hand, he was

in the western tradition and followed Tertullian rather than the Greek Fathers. He wrote no work upon the subject, but in certain of his commentaries he expressed himself freely on one or another aspect of it. In contrast with Lactantius he accepted the doctrine of original sin, interpreting it in agreement with Tertullian as guilt not mere corruption, and he went beyond Tertullian in emphasizing the necessity of prevenient grace without which no one can turn from evil to good. He was not altogether consistent in his utterances and what he has to say on the subject is of no great importance, but it is of interest because it shows that the way was already prepared for the Augustinian doctrine of sin and grace which will be dealt with in the next chapter.

The most interesting of Ambrose's writings is his work on the duties of the clergy,[1] which in spite of its title is really a general treatise on ethics intended not for the clergy alone but for the laity as well. Like his theological treatises it is almost wholly lacking in originality and is neither philosophical nor profound, but it is full of good sense and practical sagacity. It has no such sweep of vision as Clement's magnificent portrait of the ideal Gnostic in the seventh book of his Stromateis, and it is far less original than the ethical portions of Lactantius' Institutes. The author was more conventional than either of them and his ethical ideas were more completely in harmony with the prevalent ideas of the age outside as well as inside the church.

The work was based on Cicero's De officiis and follows it very closely. It was Ambrose's intention to show the superiority of Christian to Ciceronian ethics, not to identify the two. But in spite of his protests the most striking thing about his work is the resemblance between its ethics and that of Cicero, which was nothing else than the common

[1] *De officiis ministrorum.*

Stoic ethics moderated and brought into harmony with the practical temper of the Roman world. In fact the ethical teaching of Ambrose, at any rate as contained in this particular treatise, is genuinely Ciceronian.

There are differences, to be sure, but they are neither as many nor as important as might have been expected. This appears, for instance, in connection with the four cardinal virtues of Greek tradition : prudence, justice, fortitude, and temperance. Ambrose took them over from Cicero and subsumed all the duties of Christians, both clergy and laity, under one or other of the four.[1] Of his interpretation of prudence, the first of the four, I shall speak a little later. His discussion of justice is almost identical with Cicero's even in detail. Like him he insists that justice must be observed in war as well as in peace, but war itself is not condemned, as it was for instance by Lactantius. As a matter of fact more is said in condemnation of war and in praise of peace in Cicero's work than in that of Ambrose.

There is a difference between Ambrose and Cicero in the matter of retributive justice. Cicero maintains that we owe a duty even to those who have wronged us and that retribution should not be carried too far but should aim only to bring the offender to repentance and deter others from wrong doing,[2] but Ambrose like Lactantius repudiates it altogether.[3] To be sure he is much less emphatic than Lactantius and takes the matter much less seriously. He even treats the forgiveness of injuries as a counsel of perfection instead of an elementary Christian duty,[4] showing how much farther he was from the spirit of Christ.

Ambrose follows Cicero in associating beneficence with

[1] *Ibid.* I. 27 ff.

[2] Cicero, *De officiis*, Bk. I. § 33.

[3] *De officiis ministrorum*, I. 28. Cf. III. 4, where he maintains that a Christian should not even defend himself against a robber.

[4] *Ibid.* I. 48.

justice, recognizing them as coördinate parts of one social virtue which binds human society together.[1] Justice, Ambrose says, seems to him the loftier, kindness the more pleasing of the two, a sentiment wholly in accord with Stoic ethics, but in striking contrast with the ethics of Jesus. According to Jesus not justice but love, kindness and mercy should control our dealings with our fellows. He repudiated the principle of an eye for an eye and a tooth for a tooth and would have a man renounce his rights, turn the other cheek, give his cloak also to him who took his coat. He did not associate justice and beneficence, as Cicero and Ambrose did and as it has been the fashion to do throughout the Christian centuries. Leaving justice wholly to God he put beneficence in its place, thus upsetting the whole structure of classical ethics whether Greek or Roman.

In speaking of courage, the third of the cardinal virtues, Ambrose was at one with Cicero in putting moral courage on a higher plane than physical, but he differed with him in emphasizing passive courage, or the patient endurance of suffering, of which he declares that the Christian martyrs were the great exemplars.[2] Both here and elsewhere he departed from Cicero in drawing his examples of eminent virtue from the Bible, particularly the Old Testament, instead of from Greek and Roman history. This makes the two works look more unlike than they really are. The truth is, though the persons referred to are different, the principles they illustrate and the virtues they exemplify are for the most part identical.

In dealing with the fourth cardinal virtue, temperance or self-control, Ambrose still follows Cicero very closely. But he adds a chapter particularly addressed to the clergy,[3] in which he speaks of the special requirements laid upon them to abstain from wine and from all sexual intercourse, and he

---

[1] *De officiis ministrorum*, I. 28.   [2] *Ibid.* I. 41.   [3] *Ibid.* I. 50.

applies to them the saying of Christ that whoever looketh on a woman to desire her hath committed adultery with her in his heart. It is interesting to notice that Ambrose specifically confines what he has to say on these matters to the clergy and gives no hint that he thought of ascetic practices of any kind as meritorious in the laity. Nor has he anything to say about the monastic life. This is surprising, for we know from some of his other writings that he set high value on virginity and was one of the leading champions of monasticism in that age. The omission may not be significant, but it illustrates in a striking way the fidelity with which he followed Cicero.

Much has been made by historians of the disparity between the moral ideals of the classical world and those of the Christian church. The latter's emphasis on humility and self-abnegation has been contrasted with the pagan emphasis on independence, self-confidence and self-reliance; the Christian emphasis on love with the pagan emphasis on justice; the Christian emphasis on modesty and personal purity with the widespread disregard of these virtues in the Roman world. But whatever may be true in general (and the difference has been greatly exaggerated) no such contrast is to be discovered between the ethics of Ambrose and the ethics of Cicero. Cicero as well as Ambrose denounced pride and arrogance, and insisted on humility, modesty and personal purity. He also emphasized beneficence and kindness and maintained that they were a part of justice not opposed to it. And if he made more than Ambrose did of civic virtue and the duty of the citizen to take part in affairs of state the latter at any rate could say that it was a nobler thing to labor for one's country than to lead a life of leisure.[1]

Though, as has been said, the works of Cicero and Ambrose

[1] *Ibid.* III. 3. Cf. also I. 27, where he follows Cicero in putting duty to one's country next after duty to God.

were almost identical in their ethical teaching, there was nevertheless a great difference between them. In turning from Cicero's treatise to that of Ambrose the reader seems to be entering another world. The tone and atmosphere of the two treatises indeed are quite unlike. While Cicero's is wholly naturalistic that of Ambrose is permeated with religion. Cicero, for instance, praises solitude because it affords an opportunity for converse with oneself, Ambrose because it affords an opportunity for communion with God. In another passage in dealing with justice Cicero declares, "The foundation of justice is faith, that is truth and fidelity to promises and agreements." Ambrose, on the other hand, quotes the words, "The foundation of justice is faith," [1] and then goes on to say that this means Christ as the foundation of the church, for Christ is the object of faith to all — an excellent example of the way in which he seized every possible occasion for religious edification.

The difference between the two men appears also in their treatment of the first cardinal virtue, prudence or wisdom, which Cicero understands in traditional fashion as knowledge of the true and the right, while Ambrose interprets it as piety, the giving to the Creator all devotion and reverence.[2] Piety toward God, he says, is the beginning of understanding and the foundation of all virtues, and throughout his work he continually refers to God and to man's duty toward him. To be sure in discussing justice Cicero says that "our first duty is to the immortal gods; our second to country; our third to parents; and so on in a descending scale to the rest" [3] — a statement which Ambrose reproduces literally except for the substitution of God for the gods.[4] But what is exceptional in Cicero's work is constant in that of Ambrose and the latter bears in consequence a very different

[1] Ambrose, I. 29; cf. 50.
[2] Cf. Cicero, I. § 18, 19 with Ambrose, I. 27.
[3] Cicero, I. § 160.
[4] Ambrose, I. 27.

aspect. Closely connected with his emphasis on piety was the other-worldliness of Ambrose's point of view. For him as for Lactantius and the Christian Fathers in general the chief good lay not in this life but in another. So to live as to inherit a blessed immortality should be the main concern of every man.

Following Cicero Ambrose divided his work into three books, the first dealing with the right, the second with the expedient, and the third with the conflict between the two. But while with Cicero the expedient was that which makes for happiness or welfare in this life, with Ambrose it was that which makes for eternal blessedness.[1] Only virtue or godliness does this. Earthly advantages and comforts are hindrances rather than helps and should not be sought after. Thus the traditional conflict between the right and the expedient, with which Cicero dealt at considerable length, disappears. The right and the expedient are one. The right alone makes for future blessedness and hence it alone is expedient in any and all circumstances.[2]

To be sure Cicero too denied any conflict between the right and the expedient and denounced in unmeasured terms the notion that a thing may be morally right and not expedient, or expedient and not morally right.[3] But he based his identification of the two not on any consideration of a future life but on the belief that human civilization depends on coöperation and mutual helpfulness. This being so, virtue, which leads us to treat all men with justice and beneficence, promotes their confidence and goodwill and thus makes for our happiness, prosperity and influence in this life as no wrongdoing possibly could. Thus the alleged conflict between the right and the expedient was only apparent not real for Cicero as well as for Ambrose, and both of them substantiated their

---

[1] Cf. *ibid*. II. 5 ff.   [2] *Ibid*. II. 6 ff.   Cf. also III. 2.
[3] Cicero, II. § 3.

thesis by a large number of instances drawn in the one case from Greek and Roman history, in the other from the Bible.

I have said that Ambrose interpreted the expedient as that which makes for eternal blessedness, but in spite of this he devoted a considerable part of his second book, just as Cicero did, and doubtless under his influence, to the usefulness of certain virtues in promoting confidence and goodwill on the part of others and thus increasing one's reputation and influence in this life. In this connection he had many sensible and wholesome things to say which he applied particularly to the clergy as Cicero applied them to the man in public life.

Historically it is a fact of the greatest moment, it may be said in conclusion, that Ambrose's work on the Duties of the Clergy followed Cicero so closely and put the stamp of approval upon so large a part of his ethical teaching. The treatise came to be regarded in the west as the official manual of Christian morals and during the greater part of the Middle Ages it was widely read and had tremendous influence. It is due to it more than to any other single work that the ethics of Stoicism rather than the ethics of Jesus has prevailed so widely within the Christian Church.

In certain respects more interesting than Ambrose, though historically of less importance, was his contemporary Jovinian, who is known chiefly for his opposition to monasticism. In the latter part of the fourth century monasticism was spreading rapidly in the west and was coming to be recognized by increasing multitudes as the ideal Christian life. There were some however who looked upon its spread with deep concern and here and there voices were raised in protest. About 380 Helvidius, a Christian layman living in Rome, attacked both monasticism and Mariolatry in a work on the perpetual virginity of Mary, a favorite doctrine both in east and west. He was opposed to the doctrine because it meant, as he was convinced, a superstitious veneration of Mary and also, and particularly, because it was widely appealed to in support of the belief that celibacy is better than marriage, a belief he had no patience with. His work is lost, but we know something of its contents and of the exegetical arguments employed in it from a reply written in 383 by Jerome, the great champion of Mariolatry and monasticism.[1] Jerome's reply is very bitter and represents in its sophistry, and in its substitution of vituperation for argument, the worst type of Christian polemics. In it he insisted upon the perpetual virginity of Mary as an article of faith. He also defended her worship and glorified virginity in the most extravagant terms, in such terms indeed as to make marriage seem no better than fornication. The truth is he carried the matter so far that even some of his best friends were outraged.

A few years later Jovinian took up the attack launched by Helvidius. He had lived some time as a monk in northern Italy, but becoming convinced of the falsity and unchristian character of the principles underlying monasticism he left the monastery and made his way to Rome, where he wrote several works and carried on an active propaganda for some years.

Still later Vigilantius, a presbyter of Aquitaine, wrote against the current veneration of saints and martyrs, denouncing it as no better than heathenism. He also protested against monasticism and asceticism in general. He was opposed to monasticism particularly because of its antisocial character. It deprived the churches, he complained, of pastors and the country of useful citizens, and it reduced

---

[1] Jerome's *De perpetua virginitate beatæ Mariæ adversus Helvidium* is in Migne, *Patrologia Latina*, vol. 23, col. 181 ff. Helvidius was denounced also by Augustine (*De hær.* 84) and by Gennadius (*De vir. ill.* 33).

the forces working in society for the overthrow of evil and the establishment of righteousness. He was replied to by Jerome as both Helvidius and Jovinian had been and in the same bitter temper.[1]

Of the three men, Helvidius, Jovinian and Vigilantius, Jovinian was the most important and significant. Indeed he was one of the most interesting figures in the ancient church. His writings, to be sure, have perished, like those of the other two, but we know a good deal about him not only from Jerome but also from Ambrose, Augustine, Julian of Eclanum and others.[2] Like Helvidius he opposed the doctrine of the perpetual virginity of Mary, at least he is reported to have done so by Ambrose, though Jerome says nothing about it probably because the matter was not discussed in the writings known to him. Jovinian also attacked monasticism, or more accurately the underlying belief that virginity is on a higher level morally and is more meritorious in the sight of God than marriage. He did not condemn virginity itself but only the assumption that there is special merit in it.[3]

In his work against Jovinian Jerome quotes four theses maintained by the former, the first that baptized virgins, widows and married women, if they do not differ in other respects, are of equal merit in the sight of God.[4] Similarly with regard to fasting, in the third of the four theses attributed to him by Jerome Jovinian asserted that there was no difference between abstaining from food and eating with thanksgiving; all things were made for man's sake and should be received with gratitude. It is the part of

---

[1] Jerome's *Liber contra Vigilantium* (Migne, *ibid.* col. 337 ff.) appeared in 400.

[2] Jerome's *Libri duo adversus Jovinianum* (Migne, *ibid.* col. 211 ff.) was published about 392. He attacked him also in his Epistles, 48, 49 and 50. Haller (in his *Jovinianus*) prints the fragments of Jovinian's writings which have been preserved by Jerome and others.

[3] Jerome, *Adv. Jovinianum*, I. 33 (Haller, § 13).

[4] Jerome, *ibid.* I. 3 (Haller, § 3).

the true Christian not to reject God's good gifts but to recognize them as coming from him and to use them as he intended.

In opposing the belief that virginity and fasting are especially meritorious Jovinian went further and rejected altogether the common notion that one can gain merit by good works and that in heaven some will enjoy a greater reward than others because they have laid up greater merit here. The last of Jovinian's four theses, according to Jerome, was just this, that he taught that in heaven there is but one reward for those who have preserved their baptism intact. As in Christ's parable all the laborers in the vineyard were paid an equal wage, though some had borne the burden and heat of the day while others had worked only a single hour, so all the saved will receive the same reward and inherit the same crown. A man's character, Jovinian insisted, depends not on his particular acts or on the abundance of his good works, but on his will or disposition. It is not the fruit that makes the tree good or bad but the tree the fruit. There are but two classes of persons, the good and the bad, or the sheep and the goats as Christ called them, and the difference between them is due ultimately not to man but to God. When asked, "Why should the righteous labor in peace or in persecutions if there be no profit and no greater rewards?" Jovinian replied, "Not that he may deserve more but that he may not lose what he has received." [1] With this accords the statement of Jerome that Jovinian held there was no difference in merit between virginity and marriage "because baptism makes a new man." In other words the contrast between the good and the bad, the sheep and the goats, is due to a divine gift received in baptism. Because of this the Christian is a new creature altogether, and whether he shall follow one way of life or another is unimportant. He

[1] *Ibid.* II. 18 (Haller, § 24).

is unlike other men not in what he does, but in what he is, and that he owes to God.

Jerome quotes Jovinian as saying, "The Lord says, 'He that eateth my flesh and drinketh my blood abideth in me and I in him.' As therefore Christ is in us without any difference in degree so we are also in Christ without any difference. 'Everyone that loveth me will keep my word and my Father will love him and we will come to him and make our abode with him.' Whoever is righteous loves. If any one loves, the Father and the Son will come to him and abide in his house. Where such a tenant dwells nothing, I think, can be lacking to the host." [1] With this agrees the second of the four theses attributed to Jovinian by Jerome: "Those who with full faith (plena fide) have been renewed in baptism cannot be subverted by the devil." [2] Later Jerome puts it more concisely: "Those who have been baptized cannot be tempted by the devil." [3]

"That he might not seem to be speaking foolishly," as Jerome expresses it, Jovinian added that if any were tempted they showed that they had been baptized with water only and not with the Spirit. In other words he ascribed the power to resist Satan not to the mere formal rite of baptism, but to the divine gift for which it stood, a gift whose bestowal was conditioned on the faith of the recipient. In support of his position he appealed to the words of I John: "Everyone that is born of God sinneth not because his seed remaineth in him, and he is not able to sin because he is born of God. And in this are manifest the sons of God and the sons of the devil."

It is evident that we are moving here in the Pauline and Johannine world of ideas. The contrast with the common thought of Jovinian's day, which had prevailed ever since

---

[1] Jerome, *Adv. Jovinianum*, II. 19 (Haller, § 27).   [2] *Ibid*. I. 3 (Haller, § 3).
[3] *Ibid*. II. 1 (Haller, § 19). In this sweeping form the sentiment was certainly not Jovinian's, for he clearly recognized that baptism without faith had no efficacy.

the first century, was enormous. It is interesting to notice
that Jerome makes almost no comments on Jovinian's second thesis. The other three theses he dwells upon at length,
but this one he leaves with hardly a word of protest. It was
apparently so foreign to his way of looking at things and to
that of his contemporaries that he could make nothing of it.
And probably he contented himself with the reflection that
it was its own refutation, or that in any event it was without
practical importance. As a matter of fact its connection with
the rest of Jovinian's teachings, as reported by Jerome, is
not at first apparent. Only when it is recognized as a part
of the Pauline doctrine that the Christian life is the divine
life in man, is its significance understood and appreciated.
The Christian, according to Paul and John as well, is a holy
being because the life he lives is not his own but Christ's.
With this mystical doctrine Jovinian was in full agreement.
Not that the Christian never sins — for he recognized his
continued need of repentance [1] — but that he is not overcome by Satan and thereby separated from Christ.

Jovinian agreed with Paul also in rejecting the idea of
meritorious works, and apparently it was his belief in the
indwelling Christ that enabled him to do so. He was thus
a genuine Paulinist in much of his thinking. To be sure, so
far as we can judge from our fragmentary sources, he made
less of faith than Paul did. It was not faith he emphasized
in contrast with works but the indwelling Christ, and Christ's
indwelling he believed was due to baptism or to baptism and
the eucharist. It is true he insisted that baptism has efficacy only if accompanied by faith, but neither for the inception nor for the continuance of the Christian life does faith
seem to have had so exclusive a value for him as it had for
Paul. As a matter of fact we do not know just how far his
Paulinism went or how thoroughgoing it was. But we know

[1] Cf. *Ibid.* II. 37 (Haller, § 39).

enough about it to signalize him as an exceptional figure in his day and for many a day to come.

In speaking of Jovinian reference has been made to his bitterest opponent Jerome, and it will not do to bring this chapter to a close without saying something about this most doughty champion of monasticism who was at the same time the greatest scholar of his day. There is not much to say about him, it is true, in a history of Christian thought, for in spite of his scholarship he was no great thinker. As a theologian, indeed, he was not of importance. Characteristic of him was his letter to Pope Damasus in which after protesting that hypostasis means substance, and that there is only one substance in the Godhead, he urged Damasus to decide whether one hypostasis should be spoken of or three, and declared that he would confess either three or one as the Pope might direct.[1] He wrote several polemic treatises which show his lifelong hatred of heresy and his uncommon power of invective, but betray at the same time a singular lack of conscience and a deplorable failure to understand the theological issues involved.

If he was not much of a theologian, as a literateur Jerome surpassed all his Christian contemporaries. We have from his pen a large number of letters dealing with all sorts of subjects and throwing a flood of light upon the life and culture of the day. Both in matter and in style some of them are amongst the most brilliant bits of writing that have come down to us from the ancient church. He possessed a genuine love of the classics and a wide acquaintance with them. To be sure he early had twinges of conscience over the matter, and even went so far on one occasion as to take a vow that he would leave profane literature altogether alone for

[1] Ep. XV. See also Ep. XVI. (likewise addressed to Damasus); and Zöckler, *Hieronymus*, pp. 70 ff.

the rest of his life.   He was driven to this step by a dream, in which he appeared before the judgment seat of Christ and was condemned because he was a Ciceronian instead of a Christian [1] — an interesting reflection of the common attitude on the subject.

That Jerome should have shared this attitude at least for a time is not surprising in view of his general notion of Christianity and the Christian life.   He early became a monk not from the desire to secure quiet and leisure for reading and study, as was true of many another, but because of his fear of hell, as he informed one of his correspondents.[2]   And it was for the same reason that he practised the most rigorous austerities, striving in the spirit of a genuine ascetic to save his soul by crucifying his body.   In the circumstances the extraordinary thing is not that he turned his back upon his classical studies but that, in spite of his vow, he returned once more after a few years to his early love.

It is not as a litterateur however that Jerome chiefly shone, but as a scholar, for he was without question the greatest scholar of the age.   It is true that even his scholarship left much to be desired.   He was apt to be hasty and careless in his work and was frequently guilty of inexcusable blunders, particularly in his historical writings.   The contrast in this respect between him and the great church historian Eusebius of Cæsarea upon whom he drew extensively is very marked. He was at his best as a biblical scholar.   As an exegete he was head and shoulders above his contemporaries, and as a translator he had no peers.   He knew Hebrew as well as Greek — a rare accomplishment in those days — and was fond of calling himself a trilinguist.   The famous Latin version of the Bible, known as the Vulgate, was his work ; and

---

[1] "Asked what I was I replied, 'I am a Christian.'   And he who presided said : 'Thou liest.   Thou art a Ciceronian not a Christian ; for where thy treasure is there is thy heart also.'"   (Ep. XXII. 30).

[2] Ep. XXII. 7.

in spite of the protests of Augustine he made the Hebrew text rather than the Septuagint the basis of his translation of the Old Testament, thus departing from the common custom and setting a new standard of biblical scholarship. Though he insisted himself on going back to the original, his example was rarely followed by those that came after him. All through the Middle Ages the Vulgate was the standard Bible in the west as it has been ever since among Roman Catholics. It was treated as the authoritative text and to appeal from it to the original tongues was considered then as now quite unnecessary. Thus in spite of the exiguousness of his theological endowments, Jerome did not a little to determine the theological vocabulary and even to some extent the theological ideas of the western Catholic church. That church indeed has not gone altogether wrong in counting him with Ambrose, Augustine and Gregory, as one of its four great doctors.

CHAPTER IV

AUGUSTINE

In his Confessions, written at the age of forty-five, Augustine gives an interesting but inadequate and in certain important respects misleading account of his intellectual and religious development. As a matter of fact the work is not and was not intended to be an autobiography in the ordinary sense. It was written rather to show forth, or "confess," the goodness and greatness of God as illustrated in certain phases of Augustine's own career. His purpose to glorify God led him also to describe briefly in the course of the work the lives of his friend Alypius and his mother Monnica, in which he found similar evidences of God's controlling grace. Augustine wrote the work after he had been a member of the Catholic church for thirteen years, and a bishop for five, and his Catholicism led him to see many things in a distorted light. The work is accurate enough in its reflection of his mood and state of mind at the time he wrote it, for it is as frank and probably as sincere as any such production can be. But it must be read with caution and with large allowance for the author's desire to make his career religiously edifying. Fortunately we have many writings from his pen besides the Confessions. His literary activity covered a period of more than forty years, and during that time he wrote not only sermons, Biblical commentaries, apologetic, doctrinal, polemic, and practical works, but also a vast number of letters more than two hundred of which are still extant. In fact no other ancient Father is as intimately known to us as Augustine.

With great intellectual gifts he combined a vivid emotional nature and a profoundly religious temperament. He had also an uncommon talent for expression and wielded a facile and tireless pen. He was a philosophical thinker of high rank and he made important contributions in psychology, particularly in connection with the primacy of the will. At the same time he was a theologian of great importance, the most famous and commanding of all the Latin Fathers. He entered into the heritage of western Catholic thought and can be understood only in its light. But though most of his ideas had found expression before his day he made them thoroughly his own, brought them into a larger and more imposing setting, and so worked them over in the light of experience and observation as to give them new significance and an influence far wider and more lasting than would otherwise have been possible.

He was born in 354 of a heathen father and a Christian mother at Tagaste, a small town in the province of Numidia. By his mother he was instructed in the Catholic faith as she understood it, a very crass and superstitious kind of faith, and would have been baptized as a boy had she not persuaded him to wait until mature years that the healing virtue of baptism might not be destroyed by the lusts of youth. In his Confessions he speaks of his mother in terms of filial devotion and says that he owed everything to her. She was a pious woman and her affection for her son was very real, but for all her piety she was controlled by decidedly worldly motives where he was concerned. For instance, when with a tardy sense of justice and decency he wanted to marry his mistress, the mother of his son, with whom he had been living for years, it was his mother that dissuaded him on the ground that the marriage would interfere with his prospects, and it was she who found him a wealthier fiancée. Religious-minded as she was Augustine undoubtedly had better stuff in him than she had, and we may fairly believe that he owed more to his father than is commonly supposed.

As a youth he was no worse and perhaps no better than his fellows, but he was richly endowed and early came under the dominance of an absorbing intellectual passion which he called the love of truth. This made him a hard student and an omnivorous reader, and kept him from many excesses to which his temperament made him easily liable. His reading was confined almost exclusively to Latin authors. Greek he studied as a boy, but he soon dropped it and was never able to use it with comfort. Some Greek writers, but not many, he knew in Latin translations. On the other hand, with Latin literature — Cicero, Varro, Sallust, Virgil, Lucretius, Seneca, and the North African Apuleius — he was very familiar. Cicero was his great admiration, and he ranked him above all other ancient writers, as was the fashion of the day. It was the reading of Cicero's Hortensius, when he was eighteen, that awoke in him for the first time an interest in philosophy. He had hitherto been engaged wholly in the study of rhetoric and literature in preparation for teaching. Now he became convinced, so he tells us many years later, that happiness was to be found chiefly in the pursuit of wisdom, which demanded contempt for wealth and worldly pleasure and the rooting out, or at any rate the rigid control, of the bodily passions. This youthful conviction he retained to the end of his life.

Soon after reading Cicero's Hortensius he joined the Manichæans. This may seem surprising in a student of rhetoric just awakened to the love of philosophy, but it must be remembered that he was a Christian, not a pagan, and it was natural that he should expect to find truth within, not without, Christianity.

Manichæism, though like Gnosticism of independent origin, yet adopted many elements of the Christian faith, and in Augustine's time claimed to be a higher form of Christianity, superior to the Catholic system because of its more rational and philosophical character. The Catholics were accused of resting wholly on authority, while Manichæism was built on reason and appealed to demonstration rather than faith.[1] The Manichæans recognized Christ as a divine Saviour, but maintained that his teaching had been falsified by the Catholic church, and that they themselves were in reality the only genuine Christians. While they accepted considerable parts of the New Testament they rejected the Old altogether, delighting to point out its inconsistencies, its inaccuracies and its scientific and philosophical absurdities. Upon the basis of a radical dualism between good and evil and light and darkness they built up a vast and complicated system of cosmogony, cosmology, astronomy, astrology, geology, physics, and history. In accordance with their dualistic principles they were ascetic in their ethics, insisting upon celibacy and vegetarianism, at least for the inner circles of the elect, and recommending a similar way of living to all their adherents. They were particularly opposed to the procreation of children, regarding mankind as the offspring of the devil.

It is not strange that Manichæism, which was strong in North Africa in Augustine's time, should have appealed to a youth of his temper and talents. Its claim to intellectual superiority, its ascetic attitude toward life, and its dualistic explanation of the origin of evil, an explanation in striking contrast with the seemingly irrational belief of Catholic Christianity that everything had come from the hand of God, united to win his respect, and while he never joined the inner circle, being deterred by his unwillingness to give up his worldly career, he became a member of the sect and for nine years was a zealous adherent and a stout champion.

[1] See Augustine, *De utilitate credendi*, 2.

Becoming a Manichæan he did not abandon Christianity; he simply exchanged what seemed to him a superstitious and vulgar for a higher and more intellectual form of it. As he put it himself many years later he joined the Manichæans "for no other cause than that they said that the terrors of authority being removed they would lead to God by pure and simple reason those who were willing to listen to them and would free them from all error. For what else constrained me to scorn the religion which had been implanted in me as a child by my parents and to follow those men for nearly nine years and listen diligently to them except that they said we are frightened by superstition and are required to have faith before reason, while they on the other hand urge no one to believe until first the truth has been discussed and made plain."[1]

Gradually Augustine's studies, which covered a wide range of subjects, including dialectics, ethics, and physics, led him to a growing dissatisfaction with the teachings of the sect. Astrology he wholly lost confidence in, and his intellectual development reached the point where much of the boasted wisdom of the Manichæans seemed only folly and pretence. After a protracted period of indecision, he finally broke with them altogether, and fell into scepticism, abandoning his effort to reconcile science and faith, and losing his earlier confidence in the power of human reason.

"I had a suspicion," he says in his Confessions, "that those philosophers whom they call Academics were wiser than the rest in thinking that we ought to doubt everything, and that no truth can be comprehended by man."[2] "And so after the manner of the Academics, doubting everything, and fluctuating among all, I decided that the Manichæans must be abandoned, judging in that very time of doubt that I

---

[1] *De utilitate credendi*, 2.
[2] *Confessions*, Bk. V. chap. 10 (19).

ought not to remain in a sect to which I now preferred some of the philosophers." [1]

Augustine's scepticism, however, was far from radical. It was modelled upon Cicero, to whom he owed his acquaintance with the principles of the Academy, and it went no further than his, if as far. He tells us, for instance, that he never ceased to believe in God and providence, but he did have doubts as to the immortality of the soul, and his general attitude was moderately agnostic, in striking contrast with the dogmatic confidence of his Manichæan days.

From this scepticism, which lasted two or three years, and made him very unhappy, for his was one of the minds that cannot long endure anything less than complete certitude, he was rescued by Platonism, or more accurately by Neoplatonism. He had probably long known Plato's Timæus, widely current in a Latin version, and possibly some other Platonic dialogues, but he was helped out of his scepticism not by Plato himself, but by the writings of Plotinus, which had recently been put into Latin by the North African Victorinus. He found in Neoplatonism much to attract him: the conception of a realm of spiritual being altogether different from the realm of things, the notion that all visible objects are but the types or expressions of invisible ones, the belief in the immateriality and immortality of the soul and in man's possession of a spiritual sense by which he may know God and the realities of the unseen world. Most of all he was influenced by the Neoplatonic solution of the problem of evil, the fundamental problem of the Manichæans. According to Plotinus, evil is in itself nothing, it is simply the absence of good. Augustine had heard this suggested long before, so he tells us,[2] but it had made no impression on him. Now it came like a new gospel and encouraged him

---

[1] *Confessions*, Bk. V. 14 (25).
[2] It is found both in Clement of Alexandria and Gregory of Nyssa.

to think that truth might not be wholly inaccessible after all and to resume feverishly the search which he had abandoned in despair.

The almost immediate and at first blush extraordinary result was his conversion to the Catholic church. The result, however, was not as strange as it seems. The kinship between Platonism and Christianity had long been recognized by the church Fathers, both east and west, and Victorinus himself, the translator of Plotinus, had died a Christian. Once released from the radical dualism of the Manichæans, which made the Catholic belief in divine creation impossible, and enabled by the Neoplatonic allegorical method of interpretation to explain away the difficulties of the Old Testament, which had led the Manichæans to reject it, Augustine swung back naturally to the Catholic church. Platonism and Catholic Christianity, he believed, were at bottom really one. Both of them laid emphasis on the contrast between the visible and the invisible worlds, both interpreted man and the universe in similar ways, both recognized a divine Logos, and both had a doctrine of the Trinity.[1] Platonism, as he understood it, seemed to Augustine only the philosophical expression of what in Christianity appeared in popular and unphilosophical form. Plato he thought of as the Christ of the philosophers, Christ as the Plato of the masses.

The new situation in which Augustine found himself was a counterpart of the old. What really happened was that after a brief period of scepticism he accepted Neoplatonism with the same confidence with which he had once accepted Manichæism. It seemed to him the highest philosophy, as Manichæism formerly had. But while Manichæism and Catholic Christianity were mutually exclusive, Neoplatonism

[1] The Neoplatonic Trinity, suggested already in Plato's *Timæus*, was the supreme good or one, the reason or word, and the soul of the world.

and Catholic Christianity were not, and hence whereas he had been obliged to withdraw from the Catholic church when he became a Manichæan, he could now return to it. And returning he found in its authority the complete certitude he craved — certitude not for the peculiar doctrines of the Christian faith, which he was not then seeking, but for the truth common to Platonism and Christianity, particularly the truth about God and the soul.

It was no great step from Platonism to Christianity as he understood them, and the step requires no labored explanation. Later, from the standpoint of a more developed orthodoxy, the step seemed to him as it has to the readers of his Confessions greater than it really was. It is commonly assumed that the dramatic account of the scene in the garden contained in the eighth book describes his conversion to Christianity. In fact, as is shown by the context, what it actually describes is his decision to abandon his profession and devote himself exclusively to the pursuit of philosophy and to the knowledge of God which always seemed to him the chief end of philosophy. He had long believed what he had learned from Cicero's Hortensius, that the happy life (vita beata) is the contemplative life, but he had hitherto lacked the resolution to act upon his belief. The step was now made easier by pulmonary trouble, which threatened in any event to prevent him from continuing the work of teaching, and by the encouragement and support of his friends who apparently supplied the funds to enable him to live without a profession.

Even so he fought against the step and did not take it without great agony of spirit. To abandon fame and all the emoluments of the brilliant career upon which he was already well started was no light matter. That he should have been unable to do it until fortified, as he believed, by a direct divine communication was only natural, his frame of mind being what it was. Inasmuch as he shortly thereafter joined the Catholic church it was not strange that later when he was a bishop and when his Neoplatonism had long been overshadowed by his Christian faith he should identify the emotional crisis, through which he passed in making up his mind to turn his back on the world and live the contemplative life of a philosopher, with his conversion to Christianity. As already said the step from Platonism, as he understood it, to Christianity, as he then interpreted it, was so easy and natural as to need no crisis to account for it. Looking back, however, from the vantage ground of his developed Catholic faith the distance seemed immense and the step to be explained only by direct divine interposition. Augustine was thus himself responsible for the misinterpretation of the crisis in the garden which he described with so much feeling and in such detail.

The decision to abandon his profession having been finally reached — and that it cost him a severe struggle is clear enough — he went into retirement with certain friends in a villa at Cassiciacum just outside of Milan where he had been teaching for some three years. Six months later in the spring of 381 he was baptized a Catholic Christian by Ambrose, bishop of Milan, for whom he had conceived a great respect. Afterward he spent a year in Rome and then returned to his native town where he lived in retirement until in 391, much against his will, he was made a priest in the Catholic church of the neighboring seaport of Hippo Regius. Here he remained for the rest of his life, giving himself wholly to the service of the church, for four years as priest, and then as bishop until his death in 430 at the age of seventy-five.

Augustine's earliest extant writings belong to the period immediately following his abandonment of his profession, when he was still in retirement at Cassiciacum. They clearly reveal his state of mind at the time and abundantly confirm what was said above. They are genuinely Neoplatonic and contain no reference to the crisis in the garden. In one of them, the Soliloquies, the name of Christ is not even mentioned. At the same time the work is profoundly religious, and is concerned with the problem of religious certitude and particularly with the knowledge of God. The question of immortality is also debated at considerable length. The discussion is carried on in the form of a dialogue between Augustine and Reason. A few quotations will reveal the state of his mind at the time and also give us a taste of his dialectic.

"*A.* Behold I have called upon God. *R.* What then do you wish to know? *A.* All these things that I have prayed for. *R.* Sum them up briefly. *A.* God and the soul I desire to know. *R.* Nothing more? *A.* Nothing whatever." [1] "*R.* You who wish to know yourself do you know that you are? *A.* I know. *R.* Whence do you know? *A.* I know not. *R.* Do you perceive that you are simple or manifold? *A.* I know not. *R.* Do you know yourself to be moved? *A.* I know not. *R.* Do you know that you think? *A.* I know. *R.* Therefore it is true that you think.[2] *A.* True. *R.* Do you know that you are immortal? *A.* I know not. *R.* Which of all these things that you have said you are ignorant of do you most desire to know? *A.* Whether I am immortal? *R.* Therefore you love to live? *A.* I confess it. *R.* When you have learned that you are immortal will that be enough? *R.* It will be a great thing but too little for me. *R.* But how much will

---

[1] *Soliloquia*, Bk. I. chap. II (7).

[2] In his *De civitate Dei*, Bk. XI. chap. 26, arguing against the scepticism of the Academicians who denied all certainty because of the possibility of self-deception, Augustine maintained that to be deceived was itself a proof of existence. "If I am deceived I exist. For he who exists not cannot be deceived; and on this account I exist, namely, if I am deceived." Cf. also *De trinitate*, Bk. X. chap. 10 (14).

you rejoice in it, small as it is? *A*. Very much. *R*. For nothing then will you weep? *A*. For nothing at all. *R*. What if that life shall be found to be such that in it you are permitted to know nothing more than you already know, will you refrain from tears? *A*. On the contrary I shall weep so bitterly that life will cease to be. *R*. Therefore you do not love to live for the sake of living but for the sake of knowing? *A*. I grant it."[1] "*R*. Sorrow not, the human mind is immortal. *A*. Whence do you prove it? *R*. From what you have already conceded. . . . If everything that is in the subject always abides, it is necessary that the subject itself should also abide. Every science is in the subject mind. It is therefore necessary that the mind always abide if the science always abides. But science is truth, and truth always abides, as was proved in the beginning of this book. Therefore the mind lasts forever, nor if dead is it to be called mind."[2]

Augustine became convinced at this time that there is no reality in changing things and that truth therefore cannot be discovered by the senses. Real knowledge is to be had only through the reason, the organ of access to the higher world of genuine reality. "The senses of the soul," he says, "are as it were the eyes of the mind." And again: "I, Reason, am the same in the mind as the act of looking is in the eyes."[3] Of this higher world the knowledge we attain through the reason is not speculative and doubtful but immediate and certain. Of the existence of God for instance the wise man is as sure as of any truth in mathematics.[4]

For some time after his baptism Augustine remained to all intents and purposes a Neoplatonist. But gradually he grew more orthodox and swung further and further away from Neoplatonism though he never ceased to feel its influ-

---

[1] *Soliloquia*, II. 1; cf. chap. XII. [3] *Ibid*. I. VI (12).
[2] *Ibid*. II. XIII (24). [4] Cf. *De ordine*, Bk. II. chap. VII (24).

ence. It is interesting to contrast with the Soliloquies his work On the Profit of Believing, written half a dozen years later, soon after he had become a priest in the church of Hippo. In this work he makes much of the authority of the church and insists that faith must precede knowledge, contrasting the Catholic attitude with that of the Manichæans who put knowledge before faith and emphasized free inquiry. Thus he says : "Rightly has it been ordained by the majesty of Catholic discipline that they who approach religion be first of all persuaded to have faith." [1] "True religion cannot be rightly entered upon unless we submit to authority and believe those things which afterward, if we live well and worthily, we shall attain to and understand." [2] With this may be compared the words from one of his sermons : " If you are not able to know, believe that you may know. Faith precedes ; the intellect follows." [3]

To the end of his life Augustine remained a devout believer in the authority of the Catholic church and found in it the assurance he could not get along without and could not find anywhere else. His earlier confidence that truth might be attained by human effort gave way to despair of the power of the reason and to an increasing dependence on revelation for whatever it was important to know. Ultimately he gave up altogether the hope of gaining full knowledge on earth and looked forward to the future for what could not be had here. Instead of being open only to the wise he then thought of the happy life as open only to the pious.[4]

Not only was there a marked change, after he joined the Catholic church, in his attitude toward authority, but also in

[1] *De utilitate credendi*, 29.
[2] *Ibid.* 21. Augustine had already shown a disposition to recognize the need of authority (see Holl, *Augustins innere Entwicklung*, p. 9), but had made much less of it than in his *De utilitate credendi* and later works.
[3] *Sermo*, 118 : 1.
[4] See *De vera religione*, 24, 25.

his thought on many other subjects. He began to study the Bible diligently, especially the Epistles of Paul, and his Christian ideas developed rapidly. By the time he became a bishop his theology was practically complete in its main lines. Thenceforth there was modification only in details, under the influence of his successive controversies with the Donatists and Pelagians which followed his initial controversy with his old co-religionists the Manichæans.

As time passed he became more and more of an ecclesiastic and devoted a large part of his thirty-five years' episcopate to the conflict with heretics, even invoking the arm of the law against the Donatists whom he found most troublesome of all. His polemic as a rule was bitter and unfair, as was the custom of his day, and he rarely did justice to his opponents, caricaturing them often in scandalous fashion. But in spite of all this, in spite too of his changed attitude in the matter of authority, he never lost his philosophical interest and was continually harking back to one or another problem that had attracted him in earlier days. Nor did he ever cease to feel the influence of Neoplatonism, though he accepted many beliefs that were diametrically opposed to it. His developed theology indeed was in considerable part a combination of Neoplatonic and traditional Christian ideas, a combination sometimes amounting to a real and vital fusion, at other times only to external juxtaposition. Because of this twofold strain a radical inconsistency runs through his system from beginning to end.

At the very centre of his thought was his doctrine of God. From one point of view this was simply his ontology phrased in religious terms. The warmth and moving quality of these terms, which have perhaps never been surpassed, have commonly obscured this fact. His piety is so vivid and vital that the philosophy is often overlooked. As a matter of fact, devout as the language is, it is singularly interpenetrated with reasoned thought. This appears clearly in such a passage as the following:

"How shall I call upon my God, my God and Lord? For when I call on him I call him into myself. And what place is there in me where God can come, where God can come who made heaven and earth? Is there anything in me, O Lord, my God, that can contain thee? Do the very heaven and earth which thou hast made and in which thou hast made me, contain thee? . . . I could not exist, I could not exist at all, O my God, unless thou wert in me. Or rather I could not exist unless I were in thee, from whom are all things, through whom are all things, in whom are all things. Even so, Lord, even so. Where do I call thee to, since I am in thee? Or whence canst thou come into me? For whither shall I go beyond heaven and earth that from thence my God may come into me who has said, 'I fill heaven and earth'? Do heaven and earth then contain thee because thou fillest them? Or dost thou fill them and does there yet remain something over because they cannot contain thee? And into what dost thou pour forth that which remaineth of thee when heaven and earth are filled? . . . As thou fillest all things, dost thou fill them with thy whole self? Or as all things cannot contain the whole of thee, do they contain a part, and do all at the same time contain the same part? Or do certain things contain certain parts, the greater the greater, the less the less? Is then one part of thee greater, another less? Or art thou wholly everywhere and does nothing contain the whole of thee?" [1]

Augustine's conception of God was at bottom Neoplatonic. Existence in itself is a good. He was so sure of this that he maintained it is better to exist even in misery than not to exist. And he insisted that the race as a whole agreed with

[1] *Confessions*, I. 2–3.

him and even animals and plants, all of which shun death by every means in their power. He thus recognized the will to live as a fundamental and universal instinct.[1] All being is good, "a great good if it cannot be corrupted, a small good if it can." [2] Non-being is evil; evil is merely negative, the loss of good (privatio boni).[3] "If things are deprived of all good they cease to exist. So long as they are, they are good. Whatever is is good. The evil then whose source I sought is not a substance, for were it a substance it would be good." [4]

God is the only real being, for he is the absolutely unchangeable and hence at the farthest remove from nonexistence. God is himself reality, and the only reality. All else is temporary and changing, and hence not truly real. Augustine thus interpreted reality, as all the Neoplatonists did, in the genuine Eleatic sense. "Other things that are called essences or substances," he says, "admit of accidents, whereby a change, whether great or of any size whatever, may be made in them. But to God nothing of this kind can happen. Therefore he who is God is the only unchangeable substance or essence, to whom assuredly being (esse) itself, from which comes the word essence, especially and most truly belongs. For what is changed does not preserve its being; and what can be changed, even if it be not changed, is able not to be what it was. Hence that alone which not only is not changed, but cannot be changed, may without scruple be most truly said to be." [5]

Being real and unchangeable God is eternal: "the only true and eternal substance." For the difference between eternity and time is not a matter of duration; eternity is not mere endless time. Where there is time there is change;

---

[1] Cf. *De civitate Dei*, XI. 27.   [3] *Ibid*. 11.
[2] *Enchiridion*, 12.   [4] *Confessions*, VII. 12 (18).
[5] *De trinitate*, V. 2 (3).

85

where there is eternity there is no change. Eternity thus belongs to a higher order of existence than time, as God belongs to a higher order of existence than the world, for time was created when the world was made.[1]

The contrast drawn by Augustine between time and eternity was not new; it was emphasized already by Plato. Moreover the objectivity of time and its complete independence of man was a commonplace in Greek philosophy from Plato's day on. But in the eleventh book of Augustine's Confessions (chapters 10–30) there is an extremely interesting and characteristic discussion of the matter in which he makes an important advance upon all his predecessors, suggesting that time has a subjective reference, that it exists in the soul of man alone and can be measured only there. To be sure this was a mere suggestion, or rather a query, on Augustine's part; he did not abandon the objective view of time, nor did he succeed in reconciling the two conceptions. But it is significant of his philosophical interest and insight that he was the first to raise the question whether time may not be subjective rather than objective, a question that has had so large a place in modern philosophy.

As God is the only real being, he is the only real good. Apart from him there is no reality and hence apart from him there is no good. Man's highest good is to depend upon God and cleave to him. It is the language of philosophy as well as of piety when Augustine says: "God, to turn away from whom is to fall; to turn back to whom is to rise again; to abide in whom is to stand fast. God, to depart from whom is to die; to return to whom is to come to life again; to dwell in whom is to live." [2] There is no such thing as independent goodness. The desire for independence indeed is the root of all evil. All this of course involves an extreme form of divine

---

[1] Cf. *De civitate Dei*, XI. 6; and Clement of Alexandria, *Stromateis*, VI. 16.
[2] *Soliloquia*, I. 1 (3).

immanence. Only as men and things are in God or he in them have they any existence.

But this is only one side of Augustine's thought. He also read God in terms of personality, or more particularly in terms of will. He could not do otherwise and be true to Hebrew and Christian tradition. The fact is he interpreted his own religious experience, as appears abundantly from his Confessions, not simply as oneness with the Absolute but as communion with a divine person. Increasingly as time passed he emphasized the personality of God, combining it in more or less consistent fashion with the Neoplatonic idea of God as absolute being. The two conceptions represent very diverse interests. When thinking as a philosopher, Augustine had the latter chiefly in mind; when thinking as a theologian, and especially as a practical Christian, he was concerned only with the former.

Augustine's interpretation of God as a person is seen clearly in his doctrine of the Trinity to which reference was made in the previous volume. He did not think of God, with the Cappadocians and other eastern Fathers, as a mere impersonal substance which is personalized in Father, Son, and Spirit. Rather he thought of him as one person who exists in three forms or manifests himself in three ways. The very analogies he employed in the effort to make the Trinity comprehensible are significant. Instead of comparing Father, Son, and Spirit to three men — Peter, James, and John — as Gregory of Nyssa did, he compared them to memory, under-standing, and will, or to memory, understanding, and love, making the human person an image not of one of the persons of the Trinity but of the triune God.[1] And not simply

---

[1] Cf. *De trinitate*, X. 12 (19); XIV. 8 (11); also IX. 2 (2) and XV. 6 (10). In Book V. chapter 9 (10) Augustine complains that the word person is im-properly used for Father, Son, or Spirit, but he can suggest nothing better. To speak of " three somethings " (tria quaedam) he recognizes would hardly do (cf. *ibid*. VII. 7 ff.).

this, his communion was not with the Father or the Son or the Spirit but with one God.

His interpretation of God in terms of personality, and particularly in terms of will, appears also in his doctrine of creation. Instead of thinking of God as the all-inclusive reality of which all that exists is only a part or a manifestation, Augustine thought of him as creator of the universe, an almighty Being who made the world of men and things not out of his own substance, or out of any other substance, but out of nothing. The world is not an emanation from God, or a necessary efflux from his infinite essence; it is due to God's voluntary act, an act of will. Being made out of nothing it tends to lapse again into nothingness unless constantly sustained by God. It is thus continually dependent on him, not only for its creation but also for its preservation. If God's thought of it and care for it were interrupted for a moment it would immediately cease to exist. It has no stability in itself, only such stability as God gives it, and this depends upon the unbroken exercise of divine power. God did not create the world and then leave it to itself, giving it the ability to go on alone; in a true sense he is creating it every instant, imparting to it afresh the reality which it can get only from him. Thus Augustine eschewed pantheism (the belief that all that is is God or a part of God) which was the natural corollary of the Neoplatonic conception of God as absolute being. Pantheism indeed was very offensive to him, both religiously and ethically.[1] By his doctrine of creation he was able to avoid it, while at the same time he remained true to his fundamental idea of God as the only genuine reality and of all else as always completely dependent upon him for its very existence.

The belief that God created the world out of nothing raised the problem of evil, always a cardinal problem with Augus-

[1] Cf. *e.g. De civitate Dei*, IV. 12–13.

tine, in another and more pressing form. Why should there be evil in a universe created out of nothing by a Being who is both good and all-powerful? Consistently with his Neo-platonic conception of evil as mere negation, as the loss or diminution of being, Augustine explained the evil in the world by the tendency of all created things to lapse again into the nothingness from which they came.[1] This tendency God alone can withstand. As he called the world into being so he alone can maintain it in being, that is he alone can keep evil out of the universe. The cause of evil is nothing positive. Evil is due rather to the absence of divine power which alone can sustain anything in existence, or in other words can alone create and conserve the good.

But why should God allow being to lapse and thus evil to enter the world? An answer to this question Augustine found in the Stoic notion of the universe as a harmonious whole made up of an infinite variety of parts. The charm of the world is due in some measure to the juxtaposition of opposites as language is embellished by antitheses; and even the presence of sinners enhances its beauty as shadows enhance the beauty of a picture.[2] In this connection Augustine criticized Origen for conceiving of the world only as a place of discipline for fallen souls instead of recognizing it as wholly good because created by a good God. From Augustine's point of view things that are evil when taken separately are seen to be good when considered in the light of the whole. Thus while he insisted that God is not the cause of evil he maintained that he permits evil, but always and only for the sake of a larger good.[3]

Similarly with the evil wills of men. Men, too, are created

---

[1] *De civitate Dei*, XIV. 11.

[2] *Ibid*. XI. 18, 23; cf. also XII. 4 f.

[3] In *De civitate Dei*, XIV. 11 Augustine says that evils are allowed to exist that it may be shown how the righteous foresight of God can make a good use even of them.

out of nothing and like everything else they tend constantly to lapse again into nothingness. This tendency reveals itself in their choice of the less instead of the greater, the choice of self instead of God, which is the essence of all sin. Only by the exercise of divine power, or the grace of God as Augustine calls it, can men be kept from sin, as only by his power can they be sustained in existence. God is not the author of sin as he is not the author of evil of any sort. He can prevent sin if he will, but he does not always choose to do so, for sin, like evil in general, may contribute to a larger good and it is never permitted without being overruled. Thus Augustine maintained the absolute power of God, whose will is never thwarted,[1] while at the same time he denied that God is the cause of evil or that the sins of men can be traced back to him.

Augustine's theory of evil was such that he did not need the fall of Adam to account for the universal sinfulness of the human race as Tertullian and Ambrose and others before him did. Quite apart from any act of Adam's, men are bound, if left to themselves, to choose self instead of God, that is they are bound to sin as Adam was. In spite of this, under the influence of Catholic tradition, Augustine accepted the doctrine of original sin and used it to explain the sins of Adam's descendants. The result was untold confusion.

In explaining Adam's own sin Augustine was true to his general theory of evil. Adam's sin, he maintained, was not due to the possession of a fleshly nature. He was created by God and his flesh as well as his spirit was good not bad. But created out of nothing as he was he tended to lapse again into nothingness, to turn from God to self and choose the lesser instead of the greater good. His fall was due to pride, the greatest of all sins, which means the putting of self before God and the denial of one's absolute dependence on him.

---

[1] "Nothing is done unless the Omnipotent wills it to be done, either by permitting it, or himself doing it." (*Enchiridion*, 95.)

All this is consistent. But when it came to connecting Adam's sin with the sins of his descendants Augustine fell into serious inconsistency. Adam's nature which was originally good was corrupted by his fall and its corruption expressed itself in fleshly lust. Transmitted to his descendants this corrupt nature became the incentive to sin in them. Thus for them the process was reversed. With Adam the choice of evil, that is of self instead of God, resulted in an evil nature; with them the evil nature with which they were born resulted in the choice of evil.

Even more inconsistent was Augustine's interpretation of original sin as guilt, in which he followed Tertullian and Ambrose as in many other matters. From the ontological point of view Adam's fall meant the loss of real being; he became mortal and hence potentially non-existent. From the ethical point of view his fall was a guilty act, an act of rebellion against his sovereign. Augustine combined the two ideas, apparently without realizing their disparity, and in agreement with Tertullian and Ambrose talked about the evil nature propagated from generation to generation as guilty and therefore punishable. Death which on his own principles was only the natural consequence of separation from God he interpreted in traditional fashion as punishment for sin and concluded that all human beings, even infants, are guilty, because all die.[1] At times he attempted to make the ascription of guilt to infants seem less arbitrary by asserting that everyone was actually in Adam and sinned with him and hence is as culpable as he was.[2] But this only shows the more clearly to what straits he was reduced by his effort to base all human sin on the sin of Adam when, with his underlying theory of the nature of evil, such an effort was wholly unjustified.

It was said above that, according to Augustine's doctrine

[1] Cf. Ep. 166, § 6. [2] Cf. *De correptione et gratia*, chap. x (28).

of original sin, the fleshly nature handed down by Adam to his descendants becomes in them the incentive to sin. But even so their free will is not destroyed. In opposition to Manichæism, which put the responsibility for man's sin on an evil principle in the universe, and in opposition to the astrologers, who made everything subject to fate, Augustine insisted that like Adam all his descendants are endowed with freedom of will in the ordinary sense of the term, in the sense namely that a man's acts are his own — that he is not a mere automaton — and that he has the power of choice between alternatives. This Augustine maintained not only in his early work De libero arbitrio, but also in his De civitate Dei, published many years later, where he argued at considerable length against the supposition that the freedom of man's will is circumscribed by the foreknowledge of God. Man's freedom indeed in all the affairs of life, including matters of right and wrong, is practically unlimited. He may elect at any time to do the better or the worse thing, to follow the dictates of conscience or to act in opposition to them. By the exercise of free will he may live righteously and grow steadily in virtue, or he may live wickedly and sink ever deeper into vice. But one thing he cannot do — and that the supreme thing — he cannot choose God and live for him instead of for self without divine help. And if he does not live for God all his deeds, even deeds high and noble in the sight of men, are in reality evil.[1] However humane and unselfish they may be, their motive is found in man not God and hence from the highest point of view is bad not good.

The divine help without which man cannot choose God and live for him Augustine called grace. As he interpreted it grace includes God's revelation of himself — for no one can choose God unless he know him — and also the persuasion of the will and the bestowal of power to enable a man to

[1] We are reminded again of the Stoics, who held a similar position.

turn from self to God.   From an early day divine grace had been understood not simply as the kindness and favor of God, shown especially in salvation, but also in an objective sense as something bestowed upon men or infused into them. The exact nature of this gift was uncertain.   Sometimes it was identified with the indwelling Spirit; oftener it was thought of in impersonal terms.   But of its substantial character there was little doubt, at any rate in the west, from Tertullian's time on.[1]   Augustine inherited the twofold idea and made divine grace, as a present indwelling power, given men for their renewing and strengthening, the very heart of his gospel.

At first and for several years afterward he assumed, in agreement with Ambrose, that grace is given only to those who have faith.   But later he insisted that faith, too, is a divine gift and that no one can believe in God unless moved thereto by his grace.   God bestows his grace freely and quite without regard to human merit either actual or foreseen. "He goes before the unwilling that he may will; he follows the willing that he may not will in vain," Augustine says in the Enchiridion;[2] and in the Confessions, "Give what thou commandest and command what thou wilt."[3]   As so often in his writings the language of theology and the language of piety are one.

Thus far Augustine's doctrine of grace can be explained on the Neoplatonic theory that God is the alone source of good and that there is nothing good in man apart from God, a theory with which his religious experience was in full agreement.   But he went further and declared that God's grace is irresistible.   Those whom he wills to save cannot prevent him even if they wish to do so.   "Who will be so

---

[1] See G. P. Wetter, *Charis* (1913), and N. P. Williams, *The Grace of God* (1930).
[2] *Enchiridion*, 32.   [3] *Confessions*, X. 29 (40).

foolish and impious as to say that God cannot change toward good such evil wills of men as he desires to, whenever and wherever he may desire?"[1] "It is not to be doubted that the will of God, who made all things that he would in heaven and earth and who also made those things that are to come, cannot be resisted by human wills so that he may not do what he will. For even with the very wills of men he does what he will, when he will."[2]

The basis of this conception was the notion of God as absolute or almighty will, an altogether different notion from that of God as the alone source of good. The former was no doubt due in part to the influence of Tertullian and Ambrose, but it had its philosophical basis and justification in Augustine's idea of God as absolute being. If will as well as being, God must be absolute will as he is absolute being. The natural conclusion might seem to be that as God is the only real being so he is the only real will and that finite creatures have no wills of their own. But against this Augustine's religious instinct revolted, for it would make God the author of sin. He therefore contented himself with recognizing God as absolute will in the sense of all-controlling rather than all-embracing, justifying himself as so often by appealing to the authority of Scripture. "Nowhere in Holy Scripture do we read 'There is no volition except from God.' And rightly is it not written because it is not true. Otherwise, if there be no volition except from him, God is the author even of sins, which God forbid!"[3]

Augustine's disciple, the Swiss reformer Zwingli of the sixteenth century, was less squeamish than his master at this point and declared that all the deeds of men, wicked as well as good, are done by God, the only real cause in the universe. But Augustine could not go so far. Not only was it a too

---

[1] *Enchiridion*, 98.   [2] *De correptione et gratia*, XIV (45).
[3] *De spiritu et littera*, XXXI (54).

flagrant contradiction of his belief in God as the alone source of good, but it also seemed to remove man's responsibility for sin and thus to undermine morality. Apparently it did not occur to him that it was equally demoralizing to take away man's responsibility for goodness. His failure to see this shows clearly enough that he was controlled, here as elsewhere, more by religious than by ethical considerations. His unwillingness to think of God as the author of sin was evidently due even more to respect for God than to fear of moral consequences.

Upon Augustine's idea of God as absolute will rested his famous doctrine of a double predestination, or the foreordaining of some to salvation and of others to damnation. Ordinarily he speaks only of predestination to salvation, apparently thinking of the wicked as left wholly to themselves, which of course means their death. But occasionally he goes further and refers to God as foreordaining men to punishment as well as to salvation. For instance: "He used the will of the creature who was opposing the creator's will, that he might carry out his own will, thus in his supreme goodness turning to good account even what is evil, to the condemnation of those whom he justly predestined to punishment and to the salvation of those whom he mercifully predestined to grace." [1] This does not mean that divine predestination was based on anything foreseen in men, that God chose the good for salvation and the wicked for damnation; on the contrary Augustine insisted over and over again that the ground of choice lay not in men but in God.[2] That some are saved and others not is wholly due to God's secret will which we are quite unable to fathom.[3]

---

[1] *Enchiridion,* 100; cf. also *De civitate Dei,* XXII. 24.

[2] God chooses men not because they have believed but that they may believe; not because they are holy but that they may become holy. Cf. *De prædestinatione sanctorum,* VIII (16).

[3] Cf. *De dono perseverantiæ,* chap. XVII (34).

To those whom God predestinates to eternal life he gives the gift of perseverance that they may endure to the end; none of the elect, of course, can permanently fall away and be lost. But this did not mean that all believers are certain to be saved, for some of them may abandon the faith and suffer everlasting condemnation.[1] Whether they shall persevere depends on God who may bestow the gift of perseverance or may withhold it without regard to their merit or demerit. Augustine's doctrine of perseverance was quite unlike that of the Protestant Reformers. They were interested in assurance — that the believer might be certain of his acceptance with God and live in perfect confidence instead of in constant fear. Augustine, however, regarded such confidence as extremely dangerous. "Men think," he says, "that all that appear to be good believers ought to be given perseverance to the end. But God has judged it better to mingle some that will not persevere with a certain number of his saints, that those for whom security from the temptations of this life is disadvantageous may not be secure. For many are restrained from harmful elation by the words of the Apostle: 'Let him that thinketh he standeth take heed lest he fall.' But by his own will he falls who falls; and by the will of God he stands who stands."[2] Elsewhere Augustine declares that nobody can know he is one of the elect, and hence be assured of salvation, except by a special revelation.[3] His attitude in this matter was shared permanently by the Catholics, and the Protestant reformers protested against it as a cardinal error.

According to Augustine unconditional predestination which determines the eternal destiny of men quite independently of any merit on their part is not unjust, even

---

[1] *De correptione et gratia*, vi–vii (10 ff.).
[2] *De dono perseverantiæ*, viii (19); cf. also *De correptione et gratia*, xiii (40).
[3] *De civitate Dei*, XI. 12.

though it may appear so at first sight, for justice does not mean treating everybody alike (it is no democratic thing as he pictures it any more than it was in Jesus' parable of the laborers), but treating everyone as well as he deserves. All are guilty, and therefore all deserve damnation; if any are spared they have cause to rejoice, but no one else has cause to complain. "In neither case do you see God unjust. For he would be righteous even though he punished both. Whence he who is saved has good ground for gratitude; he who is condemned has no ground for finding fault." [1]

Nor does divine predestination interfere in any way with human freedom, for the latter, Augustine maintains in this connection, in agreement with the apostle Paul, means not freedom from restraint, but freedom from evil, and he is most truly free who cannot do wrong. "For it was expedient that man should be at first so made as to be able to will both good and evil, not without reward if he willed good nor without punishment if he willed evil. But in the future life it will not be in his power to will evil. However he will not therefore be deprived of free will. On the contrary his will will be all the freer when it cannot become the slave of sin." [2]

"It must be considered diligently and carefully," Augustine says elsewhere, "how these pairs differ from one another: to be able not to sin and not to be able to sin; to be able not to die and not to be able to die; to be able not to forsake good and not to be able to forsake good. For the first man was able not to sin, was able not to die, was able not to forsake good. Shall we therefore say that he who had such a free will was not able to sin? Or that he was not able to die to whom it was said, 'If thou sinnest thou shalt die'? Or that he was not able to forsake good when he would forsake it by sinning and thus die? The first liberty

[1] *De dono perseverantiæ*, VIII (17).   [2] *Enchiridion*, 105.

of the will was to be able not to sin, the last will be much greater, not to be able to sin. The first immortality was to be able not to die, the last will be much greater, not to be able to die. The first was the power of perseverance, to be able not to forsake good, the last will be the felicity of perseverance, not to be able to forsake good." [1]

Had he chosen, God might by the exercise of his grace have prevented sin altogether without interfering in any way with human freedom, but he did not do so. On the contrary he permitted evil that good might come, that is that his attributes of justice and mercy might have opportunity for exercise.[2] This, however, does not make God the author of sin, or place upon him the responsibility for it. He gives men the ability to accomplish their evil purposes, but the purposes are theirs not his.

The number of the elect, according to Augustine, is unchangeably fixed and is the same as the number of the fallen angels, that the loss incurred by the defection of the latter may be made up. "That the number of the elect is certain and is to be neither increased nor diminished," he says, "is even more plainly indicated in the Apocalypse, 'Hold fast that thou hast, lest another take thy crown.' For if another is not to receive unless one has lost, the number must be fixed" [3] — an admirable example of the patristic method of Biblical interpretation. The curious combination in all this (in Augustine's doctrine of God and man and sin and grace) of mystical piety, Neoplatonic philosophy,

---

[1] *De correptione et gratia*, XII (33). This is a different idea of freedom from that referred to on p. 92 above, but the two ideas are not contradictory. The contrast between the present and the future, as Augustine envisaged it, has to do not with freedom but with character. In the future life freedom will not be curtailed, but character will be stabilized, so that the saved man while as free as ever to act according to his character will no more be able to do evil than God is.

[2] *De civitate Dei*, XXI. 12.

[3] *De correptione et gratia*, XIII (39); cf. *Enchiridion*, 29.

Manichæan dualism, Christian tradition, strained exegesis, rigorous logic, and glaring inconsistencies born of religious instincts and moral needs, can hardly be matched anywhere else in the history of human thought.

In his doctrine of predestination Augustine was out of line with the prevailing sentiment of the day, but in his interpretation of salvation and the Christian life he was much more at one with it, though even here there were significant differences. Salvation he thought of, in agreement with common Christian tradition, as a future not a present reality : it means the enjoyment of eternal blessedness in the life beyond the grave. In contrast with most of the Fathers he laid greater emphasis on the positive than on the negative aspect of salvation, on the enjoyment of eternal life than on escape from eternal death. At the same time his belief in everlasting punishment in a hell of material fire was as realistic as Tertullian's.[1]

Eternal life will involve two supreme blessings, the vision or enjoyment of God, an essentially mystical idea rooted in Neoplatonism, and perfect harmony with the will of God, an active and practical thing which served to limit and restrain the former. Of the vision of God the Christian may have a foretaste now and then in moments of mystic contemplation ; for the eternal harmony of one's will with God's will one may be trained by obedience here on earth. The necessity of obedience to the will of God as a condition of salvation had been widely emphasized. Augustine went further and made obedience, or the harmony of one's will with the divine will, not merely a means but an end. The influence of this on western thought was very great, tending always to keep the active and practical to the front and to prevent mysticism from running off into quietism.

[1] Cf. *De civitate Dei*, XXI. 9.

Of the process of salvation Augustine had a great deal to say. Consistently with his belief in God as the only source of good he insisted that men are saved wholly by grace, not by their own merits or achievements. Grace first arouses faith, the initial virtue of the Christian life. "No one," Augustine declares, "is sufficient of himself either to begin or to perfect faith." [1] "Therefore," he says elsewhere, "when in these ways God acts with the rational soul that it may believe in him — for it is not possible for free will to have faith unless there be some one in whom it is persuaded or invited to have faith — God certainly works in man the will to believe and in all things anticipates us with his mercy." [2] This was entirely in line with his Neoplatonic interpretation of God, according to which there is no good except from God. As faith is a good it must come from God and from God alone. Grace arouses faith not simply by revealing a god in whom one may believe, but also by acting directly on the will, for faith, according to Augustine, is an act of the will. In this connection appears, perhaps more clearly than anywhere else, his recognition of the primacy of the will and his subjection of the intellect to it. At this point he was in disagreement with the general tendency of ancient thought. His voluntarism was little understood and had scant influence, but it was prophetic of the thinking of a later day.

Faith is followed by forgiveness which is imparted freely and not in any sense as a reward. The believer is thus released from condemnation for his past sins as well as for the sin of Adam. But forgiveness is only preliminary and not of itself sufficient for salvation. It must be followed by one's change from an evil to a good, from a corrupt to a holy being. This change, too, is wholly the work of divine grace. It is not instantaneous, as in the thought of Paul, but grad-

[1] *De prædestinatione*, II (5).
[2] *De spiritu et littera*, XXXIV (60).

ual, and when it is complete the person so transformed is justified and saved.

The transformation is shown in the possession of love which is the greatest of Christian virtues. Without it faith is nothing. To create and nourish love in the heart of the believer is the supreme work of divine grace. Augustine even says that love goes before knowledge and that no one can know God or anyone else unless he loves him[1] — a profound psychological observation such as frequently illumines the pages of the great African.

Love as interpreted by Augustine means primarily love for God. This is so fundamental that without it there is no true virtue.[2] What seem to be virtues are only vices unless their motive be found in love for God and devotion to him. Virtue for virtue's sake, of which Greek and Roman moralists made so much, involves pride, the root of all evil.[3] Love for God manifests itself chiefly in submission to him and obedience to his will and in the performance of good works. These good works include prayer, in which the Christian expresses his surrender to God and dependence on him; fasting, which involves self-denial, abstinence from the things of this world, and the subjection of the lower to the higher nature; and the giving of alms, which likewise means the denial of self and in which love for the brethren also finds exercise. All these are commanded by God and are done out of love for him, the basis and justification of love both for self and for others.

Though Augustine has much to say about the Christian life his writings contain little that is new upon the subject. Ethics was only secondary with him, not primary, and he did

---

[1] *De diversis quæstionibus octoginta tribus*, XXXV. 2.

[2] Love for God Augustine sometimes interpreted as equivalent to love for truth, or for the higher and invisible world as distinguished from the world of sense.

[3] *De civitate Dei*, XIX. 25.

no creative work in it as he did in religion. His ethical thinking was marked by the same otherworldliness and the same
tendency toward asceticism as that of earlier Fathers. The
Christian life is a heavenly not an earthly life ; the Christian
is a citizen not of this world but of another and must govern
himself accordingly. But though Augustine believed in
otherworldliness and asceticism he was less extreme than
many. "God alone is to be loved," he says, "and all this
world, that is all sensible things, are to be despised ; but they
are to be used as the needs of this life require." [1] Moreover
his asceticism was due not, as was often the case, to the
notion that the flesh is evil and must therefore be crucified,
but to the conviction that only by living ascetically can one
give oneself wholly to the service of God and the pursuit of
higher things. In other words the value of asceticism, as
Augustine conceived it, was positive rather than negative,
and lay in the cultivation of love for God rather than in
mere abstinence from worldly employments and fleshly lusts.

At the close of the present life if Christian love has been
perfected and justification is complete the believer will go
directly to heaven. If there still remains something to be
done it is possible that he may be obliged to spend a season in
purgatory. "It is a matter that may be inquired into,"
Augustine says, "whether some believers shall pass through a
kind of purgatorial fire and in proportion as they have loved
more or less the goods that perish be more slowly or more
quickly saved." [2]

The whole process of justification by which love is perfected and the Christian transformed from a sinner to a saint
is in the hands of God. All is due to him, not to the man
himself ; the latter is quite without any worth or merit of his

[1] *De moralibus ecclesiæ catholicæ*, Bk. I. chap. xx (37) ; cf. also chap. xxvi
(48 ff.).
[2] *Enchiridion*, 69 ; cf. *De civitate Dei*, XXI. 26. In *ibid.* XXI. 13
Augustine speaks more positively on the subject.

own. And yet over and over again Augustine speaks of heaven in the common traditional fashion as a reward just as he speaks of hell as a punishment. This seems a flat contradiction, but he resolved it, at least to his own satisfaction, by declaring that God rewards his own merits, not man's. Thus he says: "When the Pelagians assert that the only grace not given according to our merits is that by which our sins are forgiven, but that the grace bestowed upon us at the end, namely eternal life, is rendered as a reward of merit they must be opposed. To be sure, if they so understood our merits as to recognize that they too are the gifts of God, their opinion would not deserve reproof. But because they preach human merits as due to man himself, quite properly the Apostle replies: 'Who maketh thee to differ? And what hast thou that thou didst not receive? But if thou didst receive it why dost thou glory as if thou hadst not received it?' To one who holds such views it is perfectly true to say: God crowns his own gifts, not your merits. If your merits are from yourself they are not from him, for if they are your own they are evil and God does not crown them. But if they are good they are the gifts of God, for, as was said by James the Apostle, 'Every good and perfect gift is from above and cometh down from the Father of lights.' . . . If therefore your merits are God's good gifts, God does not crown your merits as your merits but as his gifts." [1]

It is obvious that two inconsistent points of view are here combined. The idea of heaven as a reward — the whole idea of reward indeed — is out of place in such a system as Augustine's. And yet he was unable to break away from the common notion of this life as a probation for the life to come. In fact he seems to have been afraid to abandon the notion lest men should renounce the effort to live righteously, so imperfect was his confidence in his own doctrine

[1] *De gratia et libero arbitrio*, VI (15).

of predestination and so small was its effect on his ethical attitude. His retention of the traditional legal idea played havoc with his system and made it all the more impossible for his predestinarianism to find general acceptance. Not only was it out of line with the common Christian way of looking at things, and not only did it seem to cut the nerve of morals, it was also to all intents and purposes abandoned by its own protagonist when he came to deal with practical matters in which alone the mass of Christians had any interest.

In connection with Augustine's doctrine of salvation something should be said about his idea of Christ. It is significant that Christ had a comparatively small place in his system. In this he was different from most of the Fathers. His religious experience was an experience of love for God and communion with him, and he needed no mediator through whom to find his way to God. His doctrine of God as the only real being and the only real good, and as almighty and all-controlling will, was complete without Christ. He did not begin with Christ and discover God in him and through him, as so many primitive Christians did. On the contrary he began with God and his faith in Christ was secondary rather than primary. In his earlier works he had little to say about him. Later he made more of him and declared over and over again that he was the only way to God, but it is evident that his growing interest and emphasis were due rather to the influence of Christian tradition than to his own religious need. In general it may be said that when he came to reflect upon Christ he thought of him primarily as the head of the church which, as his body, enjoys the benefits of all he has done. Augustine's own communion with God was immediate and direct, but as a Catholic Christian he recognized the necessity of the church and the sacraments, and similarly he recognized the necessity of Christ the head of the church without whom neither church nor sacraments had any value. It may thus be said that Christ to Augustine was a part of the Catholic system which he took over when he returned to the Catholic church after his years of estrangement from it. Because he had grown up in that church and had learned the name of Christ from his mother in earliest childhood he did not realize how little the thought of Christ had to do with the religious experience (at heart Neoplatonic rather than Christian) which brought him back to the church and dominated all the rest of his life. He therefore unwittingly assigned Christ a larger part in his own religious development than really belonged to him.

Augustine had no consistent theory of the work of Christ. He reproduced at one time or another most of the things that had been said upon the subject by earlier Fathers, however inconsistent with his own thinking. Thus, in agreement with Irenæus, Athanasius, and others, he spoke of Christ's becoming incarnate that he might deify men and bring them immortality. "To make gods of those who were men," he says in one of his sermons, "he who was God was made a man." [1] And again : "For God wishes to make thee a god : not by nature, as he is whom he begat ; but by his own gift and adoption. For as he was made, by becoming man, a partaker of thy mortality ; so he makes thee, by exalting thee, a partaker of his immortality." [2] The idea was purely traditional with him and had no real place in his thinking. The same is true of his notion that Christ died to propitiate God, or to offer a sacrifice for sin, or to pay a price to the devil.[3] None of these ideas is carried out consistently or made part of a formal theory of the Saviour's work. To be sure Augustine was convinced that the remission of sins in baptism, without which no one can be saved, was due to Christ's death, but he was also sure that God might have saved men in some other way had he chosen.

[1] *Sermo*, 192 : 1.　　[2] *Sermo*, 166 : 4.　　[3] Cf. *De civitate Dei*, VII. 31 ; X. 24.

Christ seems to have been of value to Augustine chiefly as the most notable example of the grace of God, for to this was due his perfect holiness and all that he did and achieved. In the incarnation, moreover, in which the whole Trinity was concerned, not merely the Son or the Spirit,[1] Augustine found the supreme revelation of God's love for men. Christ came mainly, he says, that we might learn how much God loves us, and thus be moved to love him in return and also to love our neighbors at the command and example of him who was made our neighbor.[2] In addition Augustine saw in the incarnation the supreme example of humility, a virtue on which he laid the greatest possible emphasis, recognizing pride as he did as the root of all sin. In fact he made a great deal, after he became a Catholic Christian, of the human figure of Christ as a pattern and inspiration to Christians. More to him perhaps than to anyone else was due the separation of the divine and human Christ which meant so much for the piety of the western church of the Middle Ages in distinction from the piety of the east where the tendency was always toward monophysitism.

Historically of greater importance than his ideas about Christ was Augustine's theory of the church. It was largely traditional and was quite independent of the Neoplatonism and mysticism which controlled so much of his thinking. The brief period of scepticism through which he passed in early manhood left its permanent mark upon him. Thenceforth he was one of those who must have religious certitude

---

[1] See *Enchiridion*, 38. In one of his letters (Ep. 11:2–3) he voiced the difficulty he felt in speaking of Christ as the incarnation of the Son when Father, Son and Spirit are but one personal God and consequently must act together, not separately, in all they do. His effort to justify the apparent inconsistency was not altogether satisfactory even to himself. His attitude in the matter shows how different his interest was from that of Clement and Origen and how little he felt the philosophical difficulties that led to the development of the Logos Christology in the east.

[2] *De catechizandis rudibus*, chap. IV (8).

whatever else they lack. Of a profoundly religious temperament he could not do without religion; of a restless and inquiring mind he could not remain satisfied with any religion unless it were guaranteed by an authority to which he could bow. This he found in the Catholic church, a worldwide institution with a long history, an elaborate ritual, and an imposing system of revealed truth, an institution claiming to be the sole ark of salvation and the supreme authority on earth. To it he submitted, thus returning to the church of his youth after more than a dozen years of estrangement and disillusionment. He was baptized into its communion in his thirty-fourth year and remained a devout and loyal adherent until his death. His gratitude to the Catholic church which he always regarded as his spiritual mother was unbounded, and after a brief period of retirement, which he would have liked to prolong indefinitely, he gave himself wholly to its service for nearly forty years. To one who reads his Confessions with its glowing piety and the immediacy of religious experience to which it bears witness, it might seem as if an external institution like the Catholic church were quite superfluous. But the truth is the piety that came to expression in the Confessions moved wholly within the framework of that church. Though full of the spirit of Neoplatonism, it was nevertheless the piety of a devout Catholic who found the assurance that alone made it real and vital in the religious body to which he belonged. Apart therefrom, he was profoundly convinced, there was no true knowledge of God and no genuine communion with him.

At first Augustine seems simply to have taken the Catholic church for granted as the sole ark of salvation and the supreme authority on earth, but as a priest and later bishop in Hippo Regius he came into conflict with the Donatists, who were actually stronger there than the Catholics themselves, and was obliged to make a careful study of the claims of his own communion in order to defend it against the attacks of the rival sect.

The Donatist schism had originated in North Africa nearly a century before. Like the Novatian schism it was due to the desire to safeguard the holiness of the church, but the controversy from which it sprang concerned the sanctity of the clergy rather than of the membership at large. Early in the fourth century Cæcilian, a leader of the laxer party in the church of Carthage, was elected bishop to the scandal of the more rigorous spirits. On the ground that the bishops who consecrated him were traitors, as those were called who had given up the sacred books to be burned during the Diocletian persecution, his opponents refused to recognize him and seceded from the church, choosing a bishop of their own in his stead. This bishop, Majorinus, was soon succeeded by a more important figure, Donatus, from whom the new sect took its name. The sect spread rapidly, and within a few years was very strong throughout North Africa and had a foothold also in Southern Gaul and even in Rome itself.

The specific question at issue between the Donatists and the Catholics was whether clerical functions performed by unworthy clergymen were valid. The Donatists, following the more primitive opinion, denied that they were, insisting that their validity depended on the personal character of the minister. The Catholics, on the other hand, following the Roman principle, already widely accepted in North Africa, maintained that the personal character of the minister had no effect on his official acts. The interest underlying this principle is clear enough. If the validity of the sacraments were to depend on the character of the person administering them rather than on his official status the laity could have no assurance that they were actually receiving a genuine sacrament at his hands. Inasmuch as divine grace was generally believed to be confined to the sacraments such uncertainty as this must seem in the long run intolerable, and it is not surprising that the Roman view ultimately prevailed everywhere.

Augustine's controversy with the Donatists led him to write a number of works in which he set forth in greater detail than anyone before him the nature and functions of the church. A generation earlier another African bishop, Optatus of Milevis, had written an important treatise against the Donatists entitled De schismate Donatistarum. Augustine made large use of it, but worked the whole subject over more carefully and carried the matter still further. He took his stand on the ecclesiastical principles formulated by Cyprian and recognized both by Catholics and Donatists. The church of Christ is a hierarchical institution founded by the Apostles and ruled over by their successors the bishops. There is but one true church and outside of it there is no salvation. This the Donatists insisted on as strenuously as the Catholics. They did not claim to be another church in addition to the Catholic, but the only true church. There was no thought on either side of recognizing the claims of the rival institution ; one or the other must yield and give up all title to the Christian name. The Catholics, including Augustine himself, even went so far as to invoke the arm of the state and urge that the Donatists be suppressed by force.[1] In opposition to them the latter insisted that church and state should be wholly separate and that men should be left free to worship God in any way they chose.

In arguing the case of the Catholics against the Donatists Augustine set up four marks which must characterize the true church of Christ : unity, sanctity, apostolicity, and catholicity. The bonds of Christian unity are faith and

---

[1] Optatus had even urged the death penalty for them, but Augustine did not go as far as this. In later life, indeed, he opposed altogether the use of force against heretics. Cf. Epistles, 23, 93, 97, 100, 133, 139, 173, 185.

love.   Heretics violate the former; schismatics the latter. Augustine admitted that the Donatists were not heretics and had not broken the bond of faith; but they were schismatics and had broken the bond of love by abandoning the church to which they had belonged and setting up another institution in its stead.

The note of sanctity it was not so easy for the Catholic church to lay claim to, for it was this that the Donatists chiefly emphasized and it was the lack of it that led them to secede.   Following Optatus Augustine maintained that the sanctity of the church lies not in the character of its clergy or members, but in its possession of the sacraments whose validity is wholly independent of the personal worth of those administering them.   Turning upon the Donatists he accused them of destroying the sacraments altogether by making them depend on human merit rather than divine power.   The sacraments are of God not man, and no worthiness in the priest can enhance their efficacy and no unworthiness can hinder it.   The church is made up of bad and good, and among the clergy as well as the laity there are both pure and impure.

The recognition of this fact led Augustine to distinguish between the visible and the invisible church, between the external institution and the inner kernel of genuine Christians.   The former is a true church as well as the latter; it possesses the sacraments and is therefore a holy institution whatever the character of its members.   The former, indeed, is the one true church, for there are not two churches of Christ, and the inner kernel of genuine Christians is simply a part of the larger whole.   Moreover the visible church is identical with the kingdom of God and to it are to be applied all the New Testament passages referring to the kingdom. To be sure as a rule Augustine spoke of the kingdom of God as a future reality to be consummated in another world beyond the grave. But this did not prevent him from identifying it with the church on earth, the visible Catholic institution. "Now too," he says, "the church is the kingdom of Christ and the kingdom of heaven. Therefore the saints reign with him even now, but otherwise than they shall reign in the future." [1]

Thus, the church is an end in itself not a mere means. It does not exist for the sake of the kingdom of God which is one day to be established; it is itself the kingdom, for which all things have been made and in which the whole creation has its reason and its end. Both Hermas and the author of Second Clement nearly three centuries before had declared that the world was made for the sake of the church. Upon this belief Augustine built a grandiose structure of universal history, undertaking to show in his great work on the City of God how everything from the beginning of time was to be understood in the light of the church.

Again, in his controversy with the Donatists he insisted that the true church is an apostolic church. By this he meant that it was founded by the Apostles and is in possession of genuine apostolic writings and of sound apostolic doctrine. While the Donatists, as he admitted, shared with the Catholics genuine apostolic writings and sound apostolic doctrine, their church was not of apostolic origin, as was abundantly shown by the fact that they were not in communion with the local churches personally founded by Apostles, particularly the church of Rome.

Finally, Augustine insisted on the catholicity of the true church, by which he meant its universal spread. The Donatists, likewise, maintained their own catholicity, on the ground that they had all the sacraments and observed all the commandments of God.[2] But Augustine interpreted catholicity in a geographical sense. To this the Donatists could

[1] *De civitate Dei*, XX. 9   [2] See Augustine, Ep. 93 : 7.

lay no claim, for the sect was confined almost wholly to North Africa. Augustine therefore delighted to lay stress on this mark of the true church, and was never weary of calling attention to the world-wide extension of the Catholic institution as a signal evidence of its divine character. He found it particularly important to do this in view of the fact that not only in Hippo Regius itself but in many other towns of North Africa the Donatists were actually more numerous than the Catholics.

In emphasizing the universal extension of the Catholic church Augustine was not simply employing an effective argument against the Donatists; he was giving expression to a conviction which was very real to him, that in the long run the great mass of men must be right. This conviction helped to make him a Catholic and as a Catholic he always found comfort in it. He was no rebel spirit, delighting to be on the unpopular side. On the contrary, for all his intellectuality, he was instinctively a conformist and could never be quite happy unless the majority agreed with him or were on their way to do so.

In accordance with tradition the Catholic church, as has been said, was regarded by Augustine as the sole ark of salvation. As such it is provided with sacraments or means of grace without which no one can be saved. Of the sacraments Augustine had a great deal to say. His emphasis upon the need of divine grace was so great that the sacraments, without which grace could not be had, were proportionately magnified. At the same time he had no consistent theory of them and his writings contain many contradictory statements. He was moved by two diverse interests, the one spiritual, the other ecclesiastical, and as a consequence he emphasized at times the need of faith if the sacraments were to have effect, at other times their efficacy quite independently of the state of mind of the recipient.

He recognized many sacraments, using the term more or less loosely to signify various sacred rites and usages, but of baptism, the eucharist, and ordination he had most to say, and when he referred to the sacraments he usually had one or the other of these in mind. He spoke of the sacraments as "sacred signs"[1] and again as "visible signs of divine things,"[2] suggesting that faith in them and an understanding of their meaning was essential. But they were more to him than mere signs, for he believed that in and through them divine grace was actually given. He could therefore admit, as he did, the efficacy of infant baptism.

In harmony with traditional practice he acknowledged heretical baptism as valid but at the same time he denied salvation outside the Catholic church, justifying the seeming contradiction by claiming that baptism by whomsoever performed imparts an indelible character, and therefore is not to be repeated, but that grace follows only within the Catholic church and hence only when the one heretically baptized returns to the true fold. In the same way he justified also the recognition of heretical ordination.[3]

Augustine's insistence on the necessity of the sacraments was a severe limitation on his idea of the relation between God and man and seems inconsistent both with his own experience of direct communion with God, as recounted in his Confessions, and also with his doctrine of predestination. He met the latter difficulty by declaring that God predetermines means as well as ends and wills to save men only through the sacraments. The former inconsistency remained unresolved. The truth is, at this point as at certain others tradition proved too strong for him and led him to contradict his own deepest instincts and experiences. It

---

[1] *De civitate Dei*, X. 5.
[2] *De catechizandis rudibus*, chap. XXVI (50).
[3] Cf. *De baptismo*, Bk. I. chap. I.

was not Augustine the mystic, or the great religious genius, but Augustine the Catholic that spoke in his doctrine of the sacraments as in his doctrine of the church in general.

The Catholic church, according to Augustine, was not only the sole ark of salvation but also the supreme authority on earth. In the moral realm it has the power to declare God's will and the right to determine the conditions on which offenses against the divine law may be pardoned, a right exercised in the sacrament of penance. Its authority covers the intellectual realm as well as the moral. Men are responsible to it for what they believe not simply for what they do.

In treating the intellectual authority of the church Augustine followed common Catholic tradition, insisting that the church is infallible and that no one is a true Christian who doubts or questions its pronouncements on any subject. To be sure, he declared that he gave unhesitating assent only to the Scriptures,[1] but the Scriptures rested for him on the attestation of the church and had no validity apart from it. The church decides on the canon, interprets the books that compose it, and guarantees its authority, so that the church in Augustine's view is really above the Bible. The following passage from one of his works against the Manichæans is both interesting and illuminating. "If you met anyone not yet a believer in the gospel what would you do were he to say, 'I do not believe'? For my part I would not believe the gospel unless moved thereto by the authority of the Catholic church. Therefore, as I have obeyed those who told me to believe the gospel, why should I not obey them when they tell me not to believe Manichæus? Choose which you will. If you say, 'Believe the Catholics,' they admonish me

---

[1] *De natura et gratia*, LXXI (61). The infallibility of the Scriptures he asserted frequently: *e.g. De civitate Dei*, XI. 3; XVI. 9; *De genesi ad litteram*, Bk. II. chap. 5. Cf. also *Confessions*, VII. 7 (11).

to put no faith in you. Wherefore if I believe them I am unable to believe you. If you say, 'Do not believe the Catholics,' you cannot rightly use the gospel to force me to faith in Manichæus, for it was on the advice of the Catholics that I believed the gospel. But if you say, 'You were right in believing the Catholics when they praised the gospel but you were not right in believing them when they condemned Manichæus,' do you think me so foolish as to believe or not to believe as you like without due reason? For it is much fairer and safer for me, having once believed the Catholics, not to go over to you until, instead of commanding me to believe, you make me understand something most openly and clearly. If then you would convince me lay aside the gospel. If you hold to the gospel I will hold to those who commanded me to believe the gospel and in obedience to them I will not believe you at all. But if by chance you find in the gospel a clear testimony to the apostleship of Manichæus you will weaken my regard for the authority of the Catholics who command me not to believe you, and as a consequence I shall no longer be able to believe the gospel either, for it was through them that I got my faith in it. Thus nothing that you can produce from the gospel will avail with me. Wherefore if no convincing proof of the apostleship of Manichæus is found in the gospel I will believe the Catholics rather than you. But if you read there some clear evidence in his favor I will believe neither them nor you: not them, for they lied to me about you, and not you, for you quote to me that Scripture which I believed on the authority of those who lied to me." [1]

Though Augustine recognized the infallible authority of the church in the realm of faith, when it came to determining the organ of infallibility he found himself at sea. He admitted that bishops may err and councils too, œcumenical

[1] *Contra epistulam quam vocant fundamenti*, 5.

as well as provincial. "Who is ignorant," he says, "that the letters of bishops which have been written since the canon was completed, or are now being written, if there be anything in them that deviates from the truth may be confuted by the wiser discourse of some one who happens to be more expert in the matter than they, or by the weightier authority and greater knowledge of other bishops, or by the decisions of councils; and that the councils themselves, either local or provincial, yield without any doubt to the authority of plenary councils which are held for the whole Christian world; and that even plenary councils are often corrected by later ones?"[1] Thus, though he was confident that the Catholic church is infallible, and though he found in this confidence the religious assurance he needed to save him from scepticism, he failed to locate the church's infallibility and hence left the whole matter open to doubt whenever a crisis arose.

The authority of the Catholic church, Augustine maintained, is not confined to the intellectual and moral spheres. The church is not simply an infallible teacher of faith and morals; it is supreme over all the peoples and nations of the earth. In his great work known as The City of God, an apology for Christianity to which he devoted some fifteen years, he distinguishes between two societies, the civitas Dei and the civitas terrena, the city of God and the earthly city, the one sacred, the other profane, the one holy, the other corrupt. The former is made up of good angels and righteous men, the latter of devils and wicked men. They had their origin in the strife that broke out among the angels[2] and hence they antedate the creation of the world, but they are perpetuated on earth, the one in the communion of saints, or the fellowship of true Christians, the other in the rest of

[1] *De baptismo*, II. 3 (4).
[2] *De civitate Dei*, XI. 1.

mankind, and they have their visible embodiment, the former in the Catholic church, the latter in the Roman Empire.[1] Their identification with church and empire was beset with difficulties, for the Catholic church contained many that were not true Christians and did not really belong to the city of God, while the Roman Empire was not coextensive with the wicked. Indeed it contained Christians as well as heathen and in Augustine's own day was ruled over by Christian emperors and was at least nominally a Christian state. But these considerations did not prevent him from equating the civitas Dei with the Catholic church and the civitas terrena with the Roman Empire. However much confusion there might be in fact, in principle the two were totally diverse. The one was of heaven, the other of earth, and as Christians though in the world were not of the world, so the church though in the Empire did not belong to it, but to another and higher realm.

Augustine laid great emphasis upon the communal life of humanity — the normally social character of human existence — and the importance of maintaining it against all disintegrating influences.[2] In the Christian church, he insisted, communal life appears at its highest and best. In the world outside all sorts of things, not least the worship of many gods, promote division and war.[3] In the church, on the other hand, where one God is worshipped, where one Lord reigns, and where all are bound together by Christian love, everything makes for peace and concord here and hereafter.

Though Augustine said many harsh things about the civi-

---

[1] The civitas terrena, as Augustine envisaged it, was less definite and concrete than the civitas Dei, for it embraced the whole non-Christian world. The Catholic church was the only earthly representative of the civitas Dei, while the Roman Empire was but one of many representatives of the civitas terrena. The identity therefore between the latter and the empire was less close and exclusive than between the civitas Dei and the church and it was not made as much of by Augustine.

[2] Cf. *e.g. De civitate Dei*, XIX. 5 ff.   [3] Cf. Ep. 91 : 3.

tas terrena in contrast with the civitas Dei he was no unquali-
fied foe of the Roman Empire, or for that matter of earthly
states in general. On the contrary he had much to say in
their favor. They owe their existence to the providence of
God and without them ordered human life would be impossible.[1] The aim of all earthly states as of all human laws
and institutions is peace. They exist in order to promote and
conserve peace among their citizens, and in so far they are
good and are to be upheld by the church.[2] Christians are
not to condemn the state or rebel against it. They are to
obey its laws so far as they are not inconsistent with the laws
of God. The state is not an end in itself, but it is a means to
a higher end, and, under its protection and sharing the peace
and order it provides, the church may spread and prosper
and Christians be prepared for the life of the world to come.
Throughout history God has been educating the human race,
leading men on from earthly to heavenly things and fitting
them by life here for life hereafter.[3] Evil as well as good is
used by him for the carrying out of his plan. The sufferings
of men contribute to their spiritual growth; the persecutions endured by the church make for its strengthening; all
things work together for the one great end, the building of
the city of God.[4]

Augustine did not content himself with showing the superiority of the city of God and pointing out how all history
was but a preparation for it; he went further and claimed
that it is supreme over the civitas terrena. His sense of
the splendor and glory of the Catholic church in contrast
with the fast-decaying empire was such as to drive him to
the conclusion that the millennium, or the thousand years
foretold in the Revelation of John, had already dawned;
that it was not to commence with the second coming of Christ

---

[1] *De civitate Dei*, V. 1.
[2] *Ibid.* XIX. 17 *et passim.*
[3] *Ibid.* X. 14.
[4] *Ibid.* XVIII. 51.

on the clouds of heaven but had begun with his first appearance on earth as Saviour and Lord.[1] The first resurrection, spoken of there, Augustine identified not with the resurrection of the saints at the return of Christ but with regeneration or the new birth from death to life, making it spiritual only, not bodily, in distinction from the second resurrection at the end of the world. But in the millennium Christ and his saints, according to the Book of Revelation, were to reign over all the world. Augustine therefore concluded that Christ was now actually reigning through his church, and that as a consequence it was not simply another institution parallel with the Empire and independent of it but was in reality supreme over it and had the right to demand submission from it.

To be sure he did not follow up the suggestion, and nowhere indicated what the supremacy of the church involved or how and through whom it was to be exercised, so that the idea was wholly without practical significance. But later it took on tremendous importance, becoming one of the foundations upon which was reared the papal supremacy of the Middle Ages. The truth is Augustine's theory of the relation of the church to the world dominated the history of western Europe for well nigh a thousand years. Nothing in all his teaching, indeed, was fraught with greater consequences.

Before leaving Augustine it may be worth while to examine briefly his views of the physical universe, which influenced Christian thought upon the subject for many centuries. Fundamental was his belief that the world was not only created but is also sustained by God, and without his constant activity would lapse into nothingness. As already

---

[1] *Ibid.* XX. 6 ff. In chapter 7 Augustine says that he had once accepted premillenarianism but had afterward abandoned it as carnal and degrading.

seen, Augustine did not identify the world with God; but he insisted that it is completely dependent on him not only for its origin but also for its preservation. In a true sense God is creating the world every instant and imparting to it afresh the reality which it can get from him alone.

This means that the common distinction between the natural and the supernatural breaks down completely. The world is through and through supernatural. God is everywhere active in it and no part of it is independent of him or divorced from his control. Thus miracles need no special explanation. They are no more acts of God than are the ordinary phenomena of everyday experience. This idea of all-permeating and universally active divine power it is necessary to keep constantly in mind if we would understand the Catholic attitude toward the universe, for the idea became the permanent possession of theologians and controlled the thinking of the church at large for many a century.

Like most of his contemporaries both within and without the church Augustine believed in miracle on a large scale. There is nothing in the nature of things to bind God to a particular mode of working and he may at any time act in ways that seem to us miraculous, because unusual, without interfering with an established order or exercising any extraordinary degree of power. Moreover the world is peopled with invisible beings — angels and demons — creatures of God to whom he has given the ability to do many things men cannot do, and hence every age has been marked by strange and mysterious occurrences. Particularly in the time of Christ miracles were wrought to induce men to believe in him and they are still wrought with the same purpose but less frequently because less needed now that the whole world believes. Augustine's City of God, especially the twenty-second book, contains many accounts of contemporary miracles some of which he even claims to have seen with his own eyes, and in one passage he declares that those performed by a certain African martyr, Stephen, would fill many volumes.[1]

Augustine's belief in God's immediate presence and power did not prevent him from recognizing the play of natural forces. This is nowhere more evident than in his interpretation of the method of creation. God did not make all forms of life in the beginning, but produced the seeds from which various orders of living beings have come by a gradual process.[2] This evolutionary theory is enough to prove that there was in Augustine's mind no inconsistency between natural causation and the omnipresent power and activity of God. Because phenomena may be traced to natural causes they are no less due to divine activity, for God works in and through the ordinary forces of nature as well as independently of them.

Although with the instinctive curiosity of a vigorous mind Augustine was interested in physical phenomena he was constrained, as most of the Fathers were, by two considerations which prevented him from giving any study to the external world and did much to hinder the development of science during the Middle Ages. In the first place spiritual affairs seemed so important that he counted it a waste of time to turn his attention to other things. "It is customary," he says, "to inquire what the form and figure of the heavens are supposed to be according to our Scriptures. For many dispute much about subjects which with greater prudence our writers have omitted because they are of no profit to those who are learning the blessed life and what is worse consume much precious time which ought to be spent on

[1] *De civitate Dei*, XXII. 8.
[2] Cf. his *De trinitate*, III. 8–9. This notion, current among the Greek philosophers, was shared also by the eastern Fathers, Basil and Gregory of Nyssa.

matters pertaining to salvation. For how does it concern me whether the heavens enclose the earth on every side like a sphere, or cover it on only one side like a disc?"[1]

Augustine was not singular in his attitude. More than a century before Arnobius had expressed the same sentiment even more emphatically in a passage already quoted.[2] Arnobius' words and Augustine's represent the general attitude of the Fathers and for that matter of the leading thinkers of the age outside as well as inside the church. Even before the beginning of the Christian era, particularly under the influence of the later Platonism, there was a growing interest in the spiritual and ideal and a growing contempt for external fact. Natural science was becoming increasingly unpopular and symbolism and allegory were more and more absorbing attention. Into this heritage the Christian Fathers entered, and in them the tendency reached its highest development as a consequence of their overmastering sense of the nearness and eternal glories of the future life. Augustine was thus only giving voice to the prevailing sentiment of the age in declaring that the study of the physical universe was a waste of time and an unworthy occupation for serious-minded men.

But this was not all. In the second place, in common with many other Fathers, he insisted that the Bible contains an authoritative and infallible account of the world and its phenomena and that therefore any further study of them is superfluous. In spite of this he wrote books on the creation of the world, as Basil and Ambrose had done, with the aim particularly of showing the glory of God in his handiwork. And in his commentaries he made use often of such knowledge as he had of physical phenomena in the effort to elucidate the text of Scripture. But beyond this he thought it wrong to go. To what absurdities the notion might lead that the Bible is

---

[1] *De genesi ad litteram*, II. 9 (20).   [2] See above, p. 43.

to be taken as a text book on natural science is seen in the
Christian Topography of Cosmos Indicopleustes, an Egyptian
mariner of the fifth century who late in life became a monk
and wrote extensively on cosmography and the exposition of
Scripture. In the book referred to, taking Noah's ark and
the tabernacle of Moses as models of the world, he worked
out the form and dimensions of the earth in great detail,
maintaining that it is a flat parallelogram surrounded by
lofty walls surmounted by a cylindrical vault, the whole
being divided horizontally into three stories, the lowest
inhabited by the wicked dead, the middle by the living, and
the highest by the saints.

To such lengths Augustine did not go. Though his scientific views were crude enough they were not as crude as those
of many another. In disagreement with the general opinion
of his day he was inclined to think that the earth is spherical,
but even so, in common with the other Fathers, he denied
both on rational and Biblical grounds that its other side is
inhabited. If it be, people there walk with heads downward,
which is absurd, and the command to the Apostles to preach
the gospel to every creature has been disobeyed, for they
certainly never visited the antipodes; but disobedience on
their part is inconceivable. Astronomy Augustine denounced
because it pries into secrets which we are not intended to
know, and which would do us no good if we did. Anatomy
he abhorred as carnal and bloody. In general he set the
fashion for later generations, and was followed by Gregory
the Great, Isidore of Seville, the Venerable Bede and others.
Though in details they differed widely among themselves, in
their habitual attitude and in the principles that governed
them they were all much alike.

But this whole side of Augustine's thought was to him at
least of minor importance. He was a great religious genius,
and his interest always centered in religion. Whatever he

was as philosopher, psychologist, and theologian, he was above all a man of religion, and his overmastering influence in the western church was due chiefly to this fact. A considerable part of his theology was unpopular and was rejected as a dangerous novelty, but he remained for centuries a dominant and compelling figure and his name was used to conjure with even where his doctrines were least understood or accepted. Though he belonged himself to the ancient not the mediaeval world, it was due to him more than to any other single man that the spirit of classical antiquity gave way to the spirit of the Middle Ages. Man ceased to to be the centre of the universe and was displaced by the infinite and almighty God. In his hands all men are tools. They exist but to carry out his will. Their chief end is to glorify him. Their highest ambition is to serve him. Their supreme happiness is to enjoy communion with him. This spirit of course was not original with Augustine — the Psalms are full of it, Paul was controlled by it, Neoplatonism was built upon it. But of all the Fathers Augustine was most completely under its spell, and to him above all it owes its dominance in the western church. The moralism and legalism that marked the Christianity of Tertullian never lost their influence, but the centre of gravity was changed. What was before primary now became secondary, and nature and man were viewed only in the light of God from whom they came and whose purposes they served. This of course is only part of the story. The world of the Middle Ages was no more a unit than the world of antiquity, and within the church the variety of opinion was as great in the days of Thomas Aquinas as in those of Augustine himself. But of this later. In the meantime we must turn to the doctrinal development in the western church of the fifth and sixth centuries while theologians and ecclesiastics were trying to discover the true path between Augustine and his opponents.

CHAPTER V

PELAGIUS AND THE SEMI-PELAGIANS

At the opening of the fifth century there was living in Rome a British monk Pelagius, a man of high character, well known for his sanctity. He was profoundly interested in Christian conduct and devoted himself to the task of improving moral conditions in the local community which seemed to him in sad need of amendment. He had a large following and wielded considerable influence as a religious and moral leader. In accordance with the best Christian tradition he laid emphasis particularly on personal purity and abstinence from the corruptions and frivolities of the world. While he was not an extreme ascetic his teaching was rigorous and he made a strong appeal to the more serious-minded in the church.

Religiously and theologically he stood at the opposite pole from Augustine. The low tone of Christian morals, he believed, was largely due to the lack of a vivid sense of personal responsibility. The doctrine of original sin taught by Tertullian and Ambrose had fostered, so he was convinced, the notion of moral inability and had undermined the belief in human freedom without which virtue was quite impossible. Moreover, the growing emphasis on divine control was having the same effect. Christians were depending too much on God and on the church and too little on their own efforts. In a letter to a woman friend, Demetrias, Pelagius wrote: "Whenever I have to speak concerning moral instruction and holy living I am accustomed to point out first the force and quality of human nature and what it is able to accomplish and then to incite the mind of the hearer to many kinds of virtue, since it is not without profit to be summoned to those things which perhaps he has assumed are impossible to him. For we are by no means able to tread the way of virtue unless we have hope as a companion." [1]

Pelagius' sympathies were with Stoicism rather than Neoplatonism. His philosophy, if the term may be used in relation to him, was the common moral philosophy of the west to which Cicero had given clearest expression. His position was not in any way novel. He had no thought of heresy and for some time others had no thought of it in connection with him. He was a devout Christian and was generally recognized as a sound and competent teacher. To start a controversy or to stir up strife within the church was the last thing he desired. He wrote several works, most of which are now lost. One of the most important of them, fortunately still preserved, was a commentary on Paul's Epistles, the earliest extant work by a British author as it has been termed. This, together with his letter to Demetrias and many quotations from his writings in the works of Augustine and others, enables us to draw an adequate picture of his views. [2]

The doctrine of original sin he wholly rejected, insisting that sin is purely voluntary and individual and cannot be transmitted. Adam's fall affected neither the souls nor the bodies of his descendants. Their flesh comes from him but not their souls, and their flesh is good as everything made by God is good. So far as their nature and abilities go all human beings are in the same condition as Adam was in the beginning. They suffer, however, from the bad example of the

---

[1] *Ep. ad Demetriadem*, chap. 11. The whole letter should be read.

[2] For what follows see Pelagius' Epistle to Demetrias, his commentary on Romans, 5:7, 12, 15; 7:8; 8:3, 13; on Philippians, 4:19; Jerome's *Dialogus adv. Pelagianos*, Bk. I. chap. 28; and many passages in Augustine's writings, e.g. *De peccatorum meritis et remissione*, Bk. I. chap. IX; III. III (5); *De natura et gratia*, VII (8); XIX (21); XXXVI (42); XL (47); *De gestis Pelagii*, III (5); XI (26); XXXV (62); *De gratia Christi*, XXII (24); *De peccato originali*, XIII (14); XV (16).

race as he did not. In spite of this they are free, as he was free, and are able to choose either good or evil. Like Adam every man creates his own character and determines his own destiny. His character belongs to him and cannot be handed on to another. Moreover his character does not determine his conduct. Whatever course he may have pursued in the past he is able now to choose as he will with perfect freedom. In contrast with Augustine Pelagius' view of human nature was wholly atomic. According to the former if a man is bad he will do bad deeds; according to the latter if he does bad deeds he is a bad man.

Adam was created mortal and his death was not the result of sin or a punishment for it, but a natural event as it is for everyone else. It was with him, however, that sin began, and all men, or at any rate most of them, have followed his example. It is possible to live without sin but few have actually done so. Adam's sin was not due, and sin in his descendants is not due, to the possession of an evil nature. It is the result of yielding to one's natural desires which in themselves are innocent but when uncontrolled carry a person too far and lead to transgression. All have the power to do right, as Adam had, but they need light not only to tell them what is right but also to show them the results of wrong-doing and thus give them an adequate motive to follow the dictates of conscience.

The relation between God and man Pelagius interpreted in legal fashion. God is the great lawgiver who requires obedience and rewards the good and punishes the wicked everlastingly. As a consequence all men, or at any rate all that have sinned, need salvation and this is brought by Christ alone who reveals God's will and the rewards and punishments which he has promised and threatened. Pelagius made much of the saving work of Christ and also of his importance as an example and as an inspiration to Christian living. Those who believe in Christ and receive Christian baptism are forgiven for all their past sins. This initial forgiveness, which unless they fall again into sin means salvation, is given freely not on the basis of merit but of faith alone.[1] After they have been forgiven they are expected to live thenceforth without sin as they are well able to do. This belief in the possibility of Christian perfection was one of the principal grounds of offense to Augustine and other opponents of Pelagius, and the question was warmly debated on both sides. An extended defense of Pelagius' position by his follower Cœlestius contains as pretty a piece of dialectic as one could wish to see. A few sentences may be quoted by way of illustration. "Again it is to be inquired whether a man ought to be sinless. Without doubt he ought. If he ought he can ; if he cannot he ought not. And if a man ought not to be sinless then he ought to be sinful, and that will not be sin which it is admitted he ought to do."[2]

If Christians fail to live virtuously they must do penance. But as Pelagius emphasized the possibility of avoiding sin altogether, and as he was particularly concerned to enforce the doctrine of human ability he made less of penance than most Christians. In fact he was inclined to look askance at it as tending to encourage a too easy yielding to sin.

Though Pelagius made so much of human ability and independence he yet talked about the necessity of divine grace, insisting that without it no one can win eternal life.[3]

[1] Pelagius asserted this repeatedly ; see e.g. *Expositio in Rom.* 4 : 5 ; 5 : 1 ; *in Eph.* 2 : 8. Augustine's statement in his *Contra duas epistolas Pelagianorum*, Bk. III. chap. VIII (24), and *De dono perseverantiæ*, II (4) is therefore inaccurate.

[2] Cœlestius' discussion from which this passage is taken is found in Augustine's *De perfectione justitiae hominis*, chap. II ff ; the passage itself in chap. III. 5.

[3] For Pelagius' idea of grace see his *Expositio in Rom.* 6 : 14 ; and Augustine's *De spiritu et littera*, II (4) ; *De natura et gratia*, XXXIV (39) ; *De gestis Pelagii*, X (22) ; XXXV (61) ; *De gratia Christi*, II–X (2–11) ; XXXI (34) ; XXXV–XL (38–44).

He meant by grace, however, not some indwelling divine power or substance, but instruction and enlightenment, including the revelation of future rewards and punishments. The physical idea of grace as well as of sin he rejected altogether. "We are not by nature," he says, "but by imitation sons of God." [1] He even used the word grace in a still broader sense to denote free will and the gifts of reason and conscience with which all men are endowed. In the beginning these natural gifts were enough, but afterward bad habits and the influence of evil example made added light necessary. This was given first in the law and then in the gospel and is still given in ever larger measure to those who make the right use of the light they already have. It was this enlightenment, bestowed as it is needed, that Pelagius commonly meant when he spoke of the divine grace given to believers. But in view of the current idea of the word, the use of it in this sense was misleading and led to much confusion.

Equally confusing was the employment of the word regeneration, which meant, as Pelagius interpreted it, not the birth of a new nature but the forgiveness of sins in baptism, the illumination of the mind by the truth, and the stimulation of the will by divine promises. [2] Misunderstanding would have been avoided and clarity promoted had both words been abandoned instead of having their significance so transformed. But Pelagius simply did what most theologians do in similar circumstances.

Even more serious was the retention of infant baptism. [3]

---

[1] *Expositio in Ephesios*, 5 : 1.

[2] Whether the word regeneration (regeneratio) which is very common in Augustine was actually used by Pelagius is uncertain though it seems probable. At any rate he spoke of Christians as reborn (renati : *Ep. ad Demetriadem*, 8), and as renewed by the Holy Spirit in baptism (*Expositio in Titum*, 3 : 5). Cf. also Augustine's *Contra duas epistolas Pelagianorum*, Bk. II. chap. VI (11).

[3] Cf. Augustine's *De gratia Christi*, XXX (32) ; XXXII (35) ; *De peccato originali*, XVII (19) ; XIX (21) ; XXI (24).

As Pelagius denied original sin it would seem that there was no adequate ground for retaining the practice, except as a service of dedication or something of the sort. As it was he connected it in traditional fashion not only with forgiveness but also with the new birth, but, interpreting the latter as he did, he left no place for the regeneration of infants any more than for their forgiveness. To continue to baptize them therefore might well seem inconsistent. Apparently the practice of infant baptism had already so established itself in the affections of Christian people that it seemed better to retain it even at the risk of misinterpretation than to attempt to put a stop to it.

Pelagius supported his positions both by rational and Biblical arguments. Divine justice, he claimed, demands that men be rewarded only for their own independent merits; that all be given equal opportunities, and special favor be shown to none. Moreover if men are to be counted as moral beings, responsible for their acts, it is essential that they have free will and be able at any time to choose either good or evil. Biblical arguments he found in profusion.[1] Those passages in which men are exhorted to virtue and warned against sin and those that speak of the rewards of the righteous and the punishment of the wicked were especially useful to him.

On the whole Pelagius was a fairly though not wholly consistent exponent of the idea of Christianity as a moral system, an idea shared by Justin Martyr and certain other Fathers of the second century. It was a natural view and was in line not only with the common moral philosophy of Justin's day but also with the later Judaism, particularly the Judaism of the dispersion. But within the Christian church, as has been seen, it was commonly overlaid by or combined with ideas of an altogether different sort, ideas akin to those

[1] See especially Jerome's *Dialogus adversus Pelagianos.*

of the mystery-religions. The combination was effected in many ways and in varying proportions. In the east mystical ideas were apt to predominate, in the west moral. With Augustine the former came to the front, with Pelagius the latter. As a matter of fact they represented two radically different temperaments and types of experience. To the one divine activity was everything, to the other human; to the one God was the centre of interest, to the other man.

It was inevitable that two so sharply divergent interpretations of Christianity should come into conflict. When Pelagius first heard of Augustine is uncertain. His teaching was not due to reaction against the teaching of Augustine but was developed quite independently. Augustine informs us that when his own words, "Give what thou commandest and command what thou wilt," were brought to Pelagius' attention the latter was much offended by them,[1] but the date of this occurrence we do not know. In Pelagius' commentary on Paul's Epistles, which was published sometime before 410, there is no sign that he knew anything about Augustine. But in 411, when Alaric's invasion had made Rome difficult, he went to Carthage in company with one of his disciples, a lawyer Cœlestius, his leading champion and an even more radical exponent of Pelagianism than Pelagius himself, and there he could not fail to hear of him. In Carthage Augustine's influence was very great and here Cœlestius came into active controversy with his supporters. While Pelagius soon left for the east Cœlestius remained in Carthage and sought ordination to the priesthood in the local Catholic church. This however aroused the opposition of Augustine's followers and ordination was refused him and he was even condemned for heresy. He then followed Pelagius to the east and became a priest in the church of Ephesus, where he resided for some years. Pelagius in the meantime

---

[1] *De dono perseverantiæ*, xx (53).

made his home in Palestine. There he had many friends and enjoyed the support of John, bishop of Jerusalem. His views were more popular in the east than the views of Augustine, who never got a foothold in that part of the world.

Though Pelagius and Cœlestius had left for the east the controversy precipitated by the latter while he was in Carthage went on, and before long Augustine himself took a hand in it with a work on Merits and the Remission of Sins, which was followed by several other treatises in rapid succession. In fact after he had once engaged in the controversy he gave himself to it as vigorously as he had in earlier years to the conflict with Manichæans and Donatists. At first he treated Pelagius with respect and spoke highly of his reputation for sanctity, but later he denounced him in unsparing terms, accusing him not only of dangerous heresy but of dishonesty in pretending to be more orthodox than he really was.[1] In his anti-Pelagian writings Augustine's predestinarian views came to clear and vigorous expression. There was no change in his general attitude and in his doctrine of predestination as a whole, but at certain points he worked the matter out in greater detail and his statements frequently took on a harsher and more uncompromising cast than in earlier writings.

In 415 at the instigation of some of Augustine's followers, who were aided and abetted by Jerome, at that time living in Palestine, Pelagius was accused of heresy and was obliged to defend himself at two synods, one at Jerusalem and the other at Diospolis. He was acquitted on both occasions, but his acquittal only made his western adversaries more bitter and they carried the case to Rome. Here Pelagius had many supporters and the influence of Augustine was less dominant than in Carthage. As a consequence the Roman see found itself in difficulty. Pope Innocent I was finally

[1] Cf. *e.g.* his *De gestis Pelagii.*

induced to pronounce against Pelagius early in 417, but Zosimus, who succeeded him almost immediately, was at first inclined to take the other side. Soon, however, under heavy pressure from Carthage, where a synod attended by some two hundred bishops met in 418 and passed condemnation on Pelagius and his followers,[1] Zosimus abandoned him and confirmed the action of the synod. In the same year the Emperor Honorius was persuaded to intervene for the protection of the orthodox faith, and issued a decree of exile against both Pelagius and Cœlestius. At the general Council of Ephesus in 431, though most eastern theologians were more in sympathy with the Pelagians as they understood them than with Augustine and his supporters, the papal condemnation of Pelagius and his followers was confirmed in return for the condemnation of Nestorius in the west. Pelagianism is therefore officially a heresy both in east and west.

We lose sight of Pelagius in 418 and of Cœlestius not long afterward, but their cause was taken up by several bishops in Southern Italy under the leadership of Julian of Eclanum, who became the principal theologian of the movement and carried on a vigorous campaign for a number of years. With his death about the middle of the century the Pelagian controversy may be said to have come to an end. Julian was the most important thinker among the Pelagians. He was more of a rationalist than either Pelagius or Cœlestius and he drew the consequences of their teaching more consistently than they and with less regard to Catholic tradition. His opposition to Augustine was even more thoroughgoing than theirs and his polemic even more severe. It was against him that Augustine directed his most elaborate anti-Pelagian works.

---

[1] On the decisions of the Carthaginian Council see Hefele, *Conciliengeschichte*, vol. II. pp. 116 ff.

Though the followers of Augustine were chiefly instrumental in securing the condemnation of Pelagianism their victory did not mean the victory of Augustinianism. In condemning Pelagius and his associates the Council of Ephesus made no reference to doctrine, and the Council of Carthage of 418 simply denounced certain teachings ascribed to Pelagius without committing itself to the positions of Augustine. The canons of the latter council anathematize those who say that Adam was created mortal and that death was not a punishment for his sin ; that infants are not to be baptized or at any rate not for sin inherited from Adam ; that grace is only for the forgiveness of past sins and does not help us to avoid future sins ; that it gives only light not power and merely makes easier the keeping of God's commands which, by the exercise of our own free will, we are able to keep even without grace ; that it is possible for Christians to live without sin. Nothing is said about predestination, about the natural man's complete inability to good, or about prevenient or irresistible grace, all of which Augustine made much of. The document containing Pope Zosimus' approval of the condemnation of Pelagius is no longer extant, but it is certain that he went no further in the direction of Augustinianism than the Council of Carthage if as far.

The truth is, in spite of Augustine's great repute, his teaching was accepted in its entirety by comparatively few. It was generally recognized as a novelty and most theologians of the day were afraid of it because it seemed to destroy all human freedom and initiative. Their controlling interest was ethical, not religious as Augustine's was, and his doctrine of absolute divine control, whose motive was solely religious, was obnoxious to them as it must be to anyone to whom human character and conduct are the chief concern. That in spite of this they did not accept Pelagianism was due largely to ecclesiastical considerations. It is significant that what first attracted unfavorable attention to Cœlestius in Carthage was his attitude on infant baptism. As has been seen he did not reject it but he denied that it was for the remission of sins and why then it should be retained was not altogether clear. Similarly Pelagius' conception of grace as mere illumination, and his belief that Christians may live lives of perfect holiness and may conceivably do so even without divine help, tended to make the sacraments seem unnecessary and thus undermine the authority of the church and confidence in it as the sole ark of salvation. Pelagius and Cœlestius did not carry the matter as far as this. Both of them insisted that salvation is impossible outside the church, but it was easy to see that if their principles were generally adopted the church might suffer. It was therefore inevitable that they should be condemned, but it by no means followed that Augustinianism must be accepted.

Among the prominent theologians who regarded Pelagius as heretical but did not agree in all respects with Augustine was his contemporary Jerome. He was instrumental in bringing Pelagius to trial in Palestine and he wrote a work against the Pelagians,[1] but he never accepted Augustine's high predestinarianism and his doctrine of human inability and irresistible grace. There were many others of the same way of thinking and already before the latter's death some of them protested against his extreme views. His treatises On Grace and Free Will and On Rebuke and Grace were written to meet the difficulties particularly of certain monks of Hadrumetum in North Africa, who were perplexed by his teachings but held him in high esteem and wished to follow him if they could. Whether these two works, in which his extreme views appear with the greatest clearness and emphasis, put an end to their scruples we do not know, but at any rate they made no further trouble.

[1] *Dialogus contra Pelagianos.*

The opposition to Augustine's teaching was particularly strong in southern Gaul and ultimately gained the support of the leading theologians of that part of the world, including John Cassian, Vincent of Lerins, Hilary of Arles, Faustus of Riez and Gennadius of Marseilles. They accepted the doctrine of original sin and agreed with Augustine that without divine grace men are wholly incapable of good, but they differed with him in giving them some part in their own salvation instead of ascribing it entirely to God, and his doctrine of irresistible grace and unconditional predestination they rejected altogether. Because the movement had its centre at Marseilles it was called Massilianism, but it has been known since the seventeenth century as Semi-Pelagianism. The name, however, is unfortunate, for it seems to imply a connection with Pelagius which did not actually exist. The Semi-Pelagians represented the common sentiment of the western church which antedated both Augustine and Pelagius and was opposed to the latter as well as the former.

Augustine's attention was first called to the situation in Gaul by Prosper of Aquitaine and a certain Hilary, otherwise unknown, who is to be distinguished from the Semi-Pelagian Hilary of Arles. In two letters, preserved in Augustine's correspondence,[1] they give an admirably fair and clear account of the positions of Augustine's critics. According to them the Massilians recognized that all men are sinners because of Adam's sin and that no one can be saved unless regenerated by divine grace; that salvation is offered to all without exception and that it is in every man's power to determine whether he will accept the offered grace and be saved or reject it and be lost; that God helps the believer to live as he should but that the act of faith is a man's own and the initiative belongs with him not God :

[1] Eps. 225 and 226.

that predestination is based on God's foreknowledge of one's faith and perseverance and that therefore the number of the elect is not fixed. Augustine's doctrine of predestination and of man's inability even to take the first step toward salvation they rejected as a novelty and also because it made the church's preaching and care of souls vain and nugatory. The account given in these letters is confirmed by the writings of Cassian, particularly his Conferences which have considerable to say on the matters in dispute and may be taken as representing the general attitude of the group as a whole.

Upon receiving the letters of Prosper and Hilary, Augustine wrote two more brief works, On the Predestination of Saints and On the Gift of Perseverance. In them, while treating his critics with friendliness as Christian brothers he set forth his own extreme positions in clear and explicit fashion. The works were not calculated to conciliate his opponents and hostility to his views only increased. Augustine himself died within a year or two but controversy continued, the defense of his teaching being taken over by Prosper and others. They did not strengthen his case, for they emphasized his predestinarian views detached from the rest of his teaching and thus gave them an appearance of paradox and arbitrariness which, as an integral part of his religious view of the universe, did not really belong to them. It is unfortunate that the controversy should have confined itself so exclusively to a single aspect of his thought. The result was that Augustinianism came to be identified with predestinarianism, and the breadth and richness and controllingly religious character of his system as a whole were almost completely lost sight of.

Meanwhile Semi-Pelagian views spread rapidly throughout Gaul which as a consequence of the Vandal invasion of North Africa was beginning to assume the intellectual leadership of the western church.   It was against Augustine, though he did not mention his name, that Vincent of Lerins in 434 wrote his famous Commonitorium.   The purpose of the work was to set out the principles by which orthodoxy and heresy may be distinguished.   The standard of authority, according to Vincent, is twofold : the Bible and the tradition of the Catholic church.   The Bible is absolutely infallible and constitutes a perfect canon of truth, but it may be easily misunderstood and needs interpreting.[1]   The function of interpretation belongs to the Catholic church which speaks through general councils and also through the writings of the Fathers.   Only those Fathers are to be depended on who remained in the Catholic church until their death, and only that is to be regarded as orthodox which has been believed everywhere, always and by all.[2]   Not their private, esoteric and singular opinions are authoritative, but only those taught by all, or by most, with one consent, openly, frequently and persistently.[3]

The church only interprets the Bible and does not go beyond it at any point nor add anything to its teachings.   This might seem to make all progress impossible.   Vincent answers the objection in the following words : "But someone perhaps will say, Shall there then be no religious progress in the church of Christ ?   Certainly, the greatest progress.   For who is there so envious of men and so full of hatred for God as to attempt to forbid it ?   But on condition that it really be progress and not change of faith.   For progress means that a thing, though enlarged, remains itself, change that it is transformed from one thing into another.   The intelligence, the knowledge, and the wisdom of individuals as well as of all, of one man as well as of the whole church, ought

[1] *Commonitorium*, chap. II.
[2] In ipsa item catholica ecclesia magnopere curandum est, ut id teneamus quod ubique, quod semper, quod ab omnibus creditum est (*ibid.*).
[3] *Ibid.* III.

therefore in the course of ages and centuries to increase and make great progress, but only in their own kind, that is in the same doctrine, in the same sense, and in the same significance." [1]

Just how much was involved in the distinction drawn in this passage between progress and change it is impossible to say. The distinction, as a matter of fact, is more verbal than real. Probably the progress or development, envisaged by Vincent, was only the fuller and clearer enunciation, to meet new emergencies, of doctrines already generally believed. But the principle as stated is so elastic that it might be interpreted to mean much more — so elastic indeed as to be of little use as a guide to the faithful.

Although Vincent did not mention Augustine or his teaching, his purpose in writing the Commonitorium just at this time was clear enough, and there can be no doubt that the work had a good deal to do with undermining Augustine's influence in Gaul and spreading the conviction that his views were heretical because novel and singular. On Vincent's principles it was not necessary to prove that a man denied the official creed of the church or the decisions of a general council in order to count him a heretic; it was enough to show that his opinions were new or unusual and had not been held generally by the Fathers of earlier days. If this were the criterion to be applied there could be no doubt that Augustine was far from orthodox, at any rate at certain points which seemed of fundamental importance to his critics in southern Gaul as in many other quarters. Later, when Massilianism was in its turn outmoded and Vincent's use of his canon to discredit Augustine was discarded, the canon itself was still retained. As a consequence there remained little room for individual opinion or belief. Even if a council had not spoken the Fathers had. Thus a new

[1] *Ibid.* XXIII (28).

and elastic standard was erected and general councils were no longer necessary to determine the faith except in extreme emergencies.

In 473 the Councils of Arles and Lyons, whose acts are no longer extant, condemned predestinarianism as a heresy and commissioned Bishop Faustus of Riez to set forth the sound doctrine in opposition to it. This he did in a work on Grace and Free Will,[1] in which in substantial agreement with Gennadius and other Massilians he steered a careful course between Pelagianism on the one hand and Augustinianism on the other, insisting on the necessity of grace as an indwelling divine power but also on the coöperation of free will, and basing predestination on foreseen faith and merit. For some time the position maintained at the two councils was regarded in Gaul as alone orthodox, but in the early sixth century sentiment swung back toward Augustine, and under the influence of the famous preacher Cæsarius of Arles, a synod meeting at Orange in 529, and known as the Second Council of Orange, committed itself to a series of propositions of a more Augustinian character.[2]

According to this council Adam's fall brought not only on himself but on all his descendants the death both of body and soul. Even if he had not fallen human nature could not have preserved its integrity without divine help; much less can it regain it when lost. Free will, weakened and destroyed in Adam, can be repaired and restored only by the grace of baptism. Unmerited grace precedes meritorious works. Grace is not merely given when we ask for it, it is itself the cause of our asking as it is also the cause of our desire to be purified from sin. The same is true of faith which owes not simply its growth but its very beginning to divine grace.

[1] *De gratia Dei et humanæ mentis libero arbitrio libri duo.*
[2] For the decisions of the council see Hefele, *Conciliengeschichte*, vol. II. pp. 726 ff.

Christians are always in need of God's help if they are to live aright. In fact all good thoughts and deeds, including love for God, are his gifts. When men do evil they do their own will, when good the will of God.

The council was attended by only a few bishops and would have had little significance had not Cæsarius succeeded in securing the confirmation of Pope Boniface for its decisions, thus giving them an official standing in the west which they have never lost. They were treated by Gregory the Great, at the end of the century, as genuinely Augustinian and his influence had much to do with the permanent credit they enjoyed. Ever since Augustinianism has been orthodox in the western Catholic church, but an Augustinianism markedly different in its controlling interest from that of Augustine himself and lacking certain features regarded by him as essential. There is nothing, for instance, in the decisions of the Council of Orange about irresistible grace or unconditional predestination. Nothing at all, indeed, is said about predestination except to anathematize "with detestation" the belief that God predestines anyone to evil, a belief held by Augustine and emphasized by some of his followers.

On the other hand not only Pelagianism but Semi-Pelagianism as well was rejected by the council, the necessity of prevenient grace and man's dependence upon it for faith and salvation being asserted in unequivocal terms, and every form of independent human merit being totally repudiated. At the same time, as prevenient grace was identified with baptismal grace, and as infant baptism had become practically universal, what actually followed was that every man, his free will having been restored in infancy, was able when he came to maturity to believe or refuse to believe on his own initiative and additional or concomitant grace having been given him in response to his faith he could go on to live the Christian life or not as he chose. Thus the divine control which was absolute and complete according to Augustine was recognized as only partial, and the baptized person really determined his own destiny.

The doctrinal position of the Council of Orange is sometimes called Semi-Augustinianism to distinguish it from the Semi-Pelagianism which it displaced. But though it was more Augustinian than the latter, at least in its phrasing, and though the council did actually insist upon the necessity of prevenient grace, thus making faith itself impossible without divine initiative, it is clear that the controlling interest was identical with that of Semi-Pelagianism, namely, to conserve human freedom and responsibility and at the same time to keep men properly humble and wholly dependent on the church.[1] It was this double motive that led the council to identify prevenient with baptismal grace and to omit altogether irresistible grace and unconditional predestination, thus leaving it to a baptized person (the unbaptized was of course lost) to determine his own fate instead of putting it wholly in God's hands.

The real line of distinction was not between Augustine and the Council of Orange on the one side and Pelagius and the Semi-Pelagians on the other, but between Augustine on the one side and the Council of Orange, the Semi-Pelagians and the Catholic church as a whole on the other. With Augustine the dominating motive was religious, with Pelagius moral. With Semi-Pelagians and Semi-Augustinians alike, and after them with most Catholic theologians, it was both moral and ecclesiastical, to preserve human freedom and responsibility and yet to restrain human pride and insure man's absolute dependence on the church. The ecclesiastical interest to be sure was in a sense religious — the church was a divine institution and to make men dependent

[1] On the supreme importance of humility see Cassian's *Institutes*, Bk. XII. chaps. 9 ff.

on it was supposedly to make them dependent on God. As a consequence the Catholic opponents of Pelagius in his own day and ever since have believed themselves, in contrast with him, to be religiously motivated, but certainly their religious motive was profoundly different from Augustine's. With him God was everything; with the others man and his welfare occupied the foreground and God was important chiefly because through his church he makes man's salvation possible. However the difference may be phrased it is profound and fundamental. In the one case God is end, in the other means. Augustine's genuine descendants were not the anti-Pelagian theologians of the fifth and following centuries but the mystics of the Middle Ages. Unlike him as they were in many ways, they were one with him in making God the centre and circumference of their thought and life.

CHAPTER VI

GREGORY THE GREAT

BORN not long before the middle of the sixth century of a wealthy patrician family, Gregory became bishop of Rome in 590. His family had been Christian for several generations and among his ancestors was Felix, bishop of Rome in the fifth century. His parents were sound Catholics, noted for their piety, and Gregory was brought up in a devoutly religious atmosphere. Already before his day the spread of monasticism in the west had completed the break with antique culture which remained always wholly alien to Gregory. He had the habit of mind not of a converted pagan but of a Catholic born and bred.

He was trained as a lawyer, was a member of the Roman Senate, and held for a time the post of prefect of Rome. After his father's death, however, he abandoned his civil career and entered a monastery, one of seven built and endowed out of his own funds. Here he practised extreme austerities, acquiring a reputation for sanctity which spread far and wide. He was not the only one of his family to embrace the monastic life. Two of his aunts had already done so and upon the death of her husband his mother followed their example.

His austerities, carried so far as permanently to ruin his health, suggest that in turning to the monastic life he was moved in part at least by other aims than Augustine. This impression is confirmed by what he says of himself in the introduction to his Dialogues. Augustine's motive in abandoning his career and going into seclusion was controllingly

144

intellectual — to find time and leisure for philosophical reflection and discussion — and he surrounded himself with kindred spirits interested in the same pursuits. Gregory, too, wished to escape the cares and distractions of the world but rather for the sake of religion than philosophy; not only that he might think more uninterruptedly of divine and heavenly matters but also that he might show his devotion and win the favor of God by denying himself the pleasures of the flesh and practising the most rigid asceticism. His attitude was that of most monks. It was more typical, indeed, than Augustine's, as he himself was nearer the common man.

Though he spent only a few years in the monastery, Gregory was controlled until his death by the monastic ideal, which continued to dominate his thinking and living. Always he counted the life of contemplation higher than the active life and celibacy higher than marriage, and always he regarded complete separation from the world as alone fully consistent with the requirements of Christian discipleship. In spite of this he passed the greater part of his life, much against his will, immersed in public affairs and was obliged to content himself with celebrating the glories of monasticism and doing what he could in various ways to promote its credit and influence.

By Pope Benedict I he was appointed a deacon and entrusted with important administrative duties. Under Benedict's successor, Pelagius II, he served for several years as papal ambassador at Constantinople and later as papal secretary at Rome. In 590 he succeeded Pelagius as bishop of Rome, and held the post until his death in 604. He was the first of his name to occupy the see and early became known as Gregory the Great. The appellation was well deserved, for none of his predecessors was his equal and few, if any, of his successors have surpassed him either in ability or in achievements. He had great force of character, was endowed with executive gifts of a high order, and was a born leader of men.

That the bishop of Rome was the divinely appointed head of the church Gregory was profoundly convinced and he did much to make his primacy a reality. He also did a great deal for the spread of Roman Christianity beyond the borders of the empire. For years he had wished to go as a missionary to Britain and at one time actually started upon the venture, but at the insistence of the Roman people he was recalled by Pelagius and was obliged to content himself with sending the monk Augustine[1] thither some years later after he had himself become Pope.

He was a noted preacher and also something of a theologian. As a matter of fact he is known with Ambrose, Jerome and Augustine as one of the four great doctors of the Latin church. He produced no system of theology, but he expressed himself largely on doctrinal subjects and in such a way as to be easily understood. For some time he was the most widely read of all the Fathers and his influence was tremendous, all the greater no doubt because he was not an original thinker and gave his readers only the common thought of the church. We have from his pen, in addition to more than eight hundred letters on all sorts of subjects, the Pastoral Rule, a work on the office of bishop which was used for centuries as a handbook of pastoral theology; a series of homilies on Ezekiel and on the Gospels; the Dialogues, an immensely popular work filled with monastic tales of miracles and prodigies; and the Moralia.

The Dialogues[2] are taken up largely with the adventures and experiences of monks, the second book being devoted wholly to the career of Benedict of Nursia. The following

---

[1] This Augustine was prior of one of Gregory's monasteries in Rome.

[2] *Dialogorum libri IV de vita et miraculis patrum Italicorum et de aeternitate animarum.*

tale is a fair sample of the sort of thing the work abounds in. "A certain Sclavonian, who was a monk and lived with me here in this city in my Monastery, used to tell me that at such time as he dwelt in the wilderness, he knew one Peter, a monk born in Spain, who lived with him in the vast desert called Evasa: which Peter (as he said) told him how, before he came to dwell in that place, by a certain sickness he died, and was straightways restored to life again, affirming that he had seen the torments and innumerable places of hell, and divers, who were mighty men in this world, hanging in those flames; and that as himself was carried to be thrown also into the same fire, suddenly an Angel in a beautiful attire appeared, who would not suffer him to be cast into those torments: but spake unto him in this manner: 'Go thy way back again, and hereafter carefully look unto thyself, how thou leadest thy life': after which words his body by little and little became warm, and himself, waking out of the sleep of everlasting death, reported all such things as happened to him: after which time he bound himself to such fasting and watching that though he had said nothing, yet his very life and conversation did speak what torments he had seen and was afraid of: and so God's merciful providence wrought in his temporal death that he died not everlastingly." [1]

In the fourth book there is considerable theology drawn from Gregory by the questions of his interlocutor, another monk named Peter. The latter often raises objections very much to the point which Gregory finds it difficult to answer. But he grapples with them manfully and in such a way as doubtless to meet the needs of his readers of that age if not always of later times. At any rate this part of the work

---

[1] *Dialogues*, Bk. IV. chap. 36 (quoted from the seventeenth-century translation edited by E. G. Gardner). Gregory was anticipated particularly by Jerome and Cassian in the telling of monastic tales.

testifies to his honesty and sincerity and shows that traditional though he was in his theology, he was no mere narrow-minded bigot.

Most important of all Gregory's writings is his Moralia,[1] an elaborate treatise on theology and ethics in the form of an exposition of the Book of Job which is interpreted allegorically and thus made the medium for whatever Gregory thought it important to teach. It is not a systematic treatise, but it contains his views on a wide range of theological and ethical topics and its influence in the Middle Ages was very great. In fact for some centuries it was the principal text-book of theology in the western church.

Gregory is important to us chiefly for two reasons: first, because he set out more clearly and comprehensively than anyone else the common faith of the western Catholic church of his day, and secondly, because he was the principal medium through which the teaching of Augustine was handed down to subsequent times.

Though not a systematic theologian he dealt in one or another form with practically the whole range of theology.[2] Moreover he treated the questions involved in a simple and practical way not too abstruse or difficult for the average mind. His writings were also enlivened and made interesting by all sorts of tales of a nature to appeal to the piety and credulity of the common people outside as well as within the monasteries. His ecclesiastical position and his reputation both as bishop and saint increased his influence, and it is not surprising that he became an instructor in religion and morals for practically the whole west.

He was also a devout disciple of Augustine and an eager

---

[1] *Expositio in beatum Job, seu moralium libri XXXV.* An English translation in four volumes is contained in *A Library of Fathers of the Holy Catholic Church.*

[2] On Gregory's theology see particularly F. H. Dudden's *Gregory the Great* Part III.

student of his writings and he did his best to interpret him and commend him to his fellow Christians. To be sure his understanding of the great African Father was very meagre. He was brought up in a world vastly different from that of Augustine. Of Neoplatonism he knew nothing, and classical literature, which formed the staple of Augustine's education, was wholly unfamiliar to him. In the training of Catholic youths Christian writings long before his time had widely taken the place of pagan, and Gregory grew up believing that no Christian should have anything to do with the latter. They could only corrupt his morals and undermine his faith in Christ, and were to be avoided at all hazards. To be sure this was not the universal opinion. Boethius, Cassiodorus, and other champions of classical learning had their followers in Gregory's day, but they were a dwindling minority, and the immense authority of Gregory himself was thrown on the other side. In a letter to Bishop Desiderius of Vienne, he called him sharply to account for applying himself to secular literature, admonishing him that "the praises of Christ do not belong in the same mouth with the praises of Jove." [1]

As already said, though a devout disciple of Augustine and an eager student of his writings, Gregory understood him but imperfectly. Often he used Augustine's language without in the least comprehending what it meant. He not only lacked the background of a general classical education but was also quite without philosophical gifts or training; he had no interest in and no capacity for theological speculation; his beliefs were traditional only and his aim wholly practical, namely, to bring Christian doctrines to bear on Christian living. In the process he popularized and vulgarized Augustine to an extraordinary degree. Those of Augustine's ideas that were in line with the common thinking of western Christendom he chiefly emphasized, while

[1] In the collection of Gregory's epistles, Bk. XI. Ep. 54.

those in which the great North African Father was most original and farthest from the church at large he minimized or omitted altogether. At the same time considerable parts of Augustine's thought lived on in Gregory's writings and became the possession of many who would otherwise have known little or nothing of him.

Gregory's doctrine of God is a capital example of the way he combined the language of Augustine and some of his ideas with the beliefs generally prevalent among western Christians. God, he declared, is the only true being. All else has been created by him out of nothing and tends to lapse again into nothingness.[1] The world was not made by God and then left to run of itself like a machine. He is always present, sustaining and preserving it by his ever active power.[2] God is the only true good and nothing else is good except as it partakes of him. Evil is nothing; it has no positive reality. On the contrary it is only the defect of being or of good.[3] Evil is not due to God, but he permits it for his own wise purposes and overrules it for good.[4]

All this is genuinely Augustinian, but it was taken over by Gregory without any understanding of its Neoplatonic background and with little appreciation of its implications. He combined it with and subordinated it to the common notion of God as a lawgiver and judge, whose great function it is to condemn sin and punish the sinner. "The Lord," he says, "by no means spares the offender, for he leaves no fault without taking vengeance on it."[5] Gregory called God Father, to be sure, but this meant that, while kind to the obedient, he is very stern with the disobedient and exercises the strictest discipline. It was authority, in fact, more than love that the term Father connoted to Gregory

---

[1] *Moralia*, XVI. 45.
[2] *Ibid.* II. 20; XVI. 12; XXVII. 35.
[3] *Ibid.* XXVI. 68.
[4] *Ibid.* VI. 28 ff.
[5] *Ibid.* IX. 54.

as was true of the Roman world in general. God he interpreted chiefly in legal terms and Augustine's Neoplatonic
conception had little influence with him. His real thought
of God, indeed, was much nearer Tertullian's than Augustine's.

In his doctrine of man Gregory stood midway between
Augustine and the Semi-Pelagians, following closely the
teaching of the Second Council of Orange. Adam's fall has
affected all his descendants, weakening but not destroying
their freedom of will. Because of it they are quite unable
to will the good or even to take the first step toward it without prevenient grace, or in other words without being moved
thereto by God.[1] Having received grace they may coöperate
with it and thus win merit for themselves by their good
works which are the joint product of divine grace and human
will. In rewarding them therefore God rewards not merely
his own merits, as Augustine insisted, but their merits as well.[2]

Though grace is prevenient it is not irresistible. In spite
of his disagreement at this point Gregory followed Augustine in declaring that the number of the elect is irrevocably
fixed, it being God's intention that they should make good
the defection of the fallen angels.[3] How this could be when
men retain the power to accept or reject grace as they please
he did not explain. Predestination is to salvation only,
but whether it is unconditional, as Augustine taught, or
depends upon foreseen merit in man Gregory was uncertain.
This and many other questions, indeed, he left undecided,
declaring that to seek to answer them was to strive to be
wise above what is written, or in other words was to yield
to curiosity, a most dangerous disease and the root of all
heresy. In contrast with it humility — the willingness to
be ignorant about many things — is alone truly Christian.[4]

[1] *Moralia*, XXIV. 24; XXXIII. 40; cf. VIII. 19, 51.
[2] *Ibid*. XVI. 30.   [3] *Ibid*. XXXI. 9.   [4] *Ibid*. XX. 18.

Prevenient grace is given in baptism and has both a negative and a positive effect, bringing forgiveness and remitting the punishment of all pre-baptismal sin, both original and actual, and at any rate in the case of those baptized in mature years, inspiring them to will what is good. The good they will, they are then enabled to accomplish by the assistance of coöperating grace.[1] Unbaptized persons, whether dying in infancy or in maturity, are punished eternally.

Though those baptized are freed from guilt they still possess the corrupt nature inherited from Adam and will inevitably sin again. In baptism forgiving grace is granted freely without any merit on men's part, but for sins committed after baptism atonement must be made by penance, which is simply a form of punishment inflicted by the man himself instead of by God. "For either man himself by penance punishes sin in himself, or God taking vengeance on him smites it." [2] Penance involves repentance, which must be sincere and of the heart, and also confession and meritorious works. Repentance springs first from fear, that is, fear of eternal punishment, and then from love, which means love for the joys of heaven.[3] Confession should be free and full and should be made both inwardly to God and outwardly to the bishop. If one tries to conceal one's sins, and is unwilling to acknowledge them, repentance is not genuine and one cannot expect to be forgiven.

The meritorious works without which penance is not complete are deeds involving sacrifice or suffering, such as almsgiving, ascetic practices and the like. The greater our sins the more must we do to make up for them, and the more careful must we be to avoid them in the future. Whether we have done enough to atone for them we cannot know until after death. Over and over again we must do penance in the hope that we may make it unnecessary for God to pun-

[1] *Moralia*, XXII. 20.   [2] *Ibid.* IX. 54.   [3] *Dialogues*, III. 34.

ish us and may thus escape hell, but we can never be sure of success. Constant anxiety is the only safe attitude until life is over and temptation past. Assurance of salvation and the feeling of safety engendered by it are dangerous for anybody and would not be desirable even if possible.[1] Gregory made large use of the motive of fear to keep Christians from falling away and neglecting to do penance. In his Moralia he returns to the subject again and again and insists upon the matter repeatedly in practically identical language.[2]

For those who have not done enough in this life to atone for their sins purgatory is provided. This is a place of purification and suffering, not for those who die with serious offenses still charged against them, but for those who are not as yet altogether righteous. At death the perfectly holy go at once to heaven and the wicked to hell, while those of an intermediate character, who still have minor sins for which penance must be done, spend a season in purgatory. Only those who by good works in this life have been made worthy will enjoy the privilege of enduring the temporal pains of purgatory and thus escaping the eternal pains of hell.[3] The belief in purgatory was much older than Gregory. Indeed it was current in certain ethnic cults (e.g. Orphism) long before the time of Christ. It was common among the Christians of North Africa in Tertullian's day and by the fifth century was widespread in the west. Augustine, as has been seen, was not altogether sure about the matter, but in Gregory's mind there was no uncertainty. He emphasized the belief and did much to clarify it and give it a permanent place in Catholic doctrine.

Of the work of Christ Gregory had a great deal to say,

---

[1] See the interesting letter to a Constantinopolitan woman quoted by Dudden, *op. cit.* vol. II. p. 425. The letter is in the collection of Gregory's epistles, Bk. VII. Ep. 22.
[2] Cf. *e.g. Moralia,* V. 21; VII. 58; XXIV. 32; XXV. 13; XXVIII. 20.
[3] Cf. *Dialogues,* IV. 39.

and though he did not reach complete clearness in the matter he was more definite and more consistent in his teaching than Augustine, partly because his controlling conception of God was in line with the common traditional notions of Christ's work while Augustine's was not. Though the great avenger of sin God is also merciful and through Christ has made it possible for men to escape the consequences of his wrath. By Adam's fall the human race came under the control of the devil. This meant that all were doomed to death and must certainly perish unless in some way his mastery could be broken. He was within his rights in keeping the entire race in bondage, for the race is sinful and death, according to divine decree, is the penalty of sin. But if he overstepped his right and claimed more than was his due, he might justly be deprived of it altogether. With this in mind Christ came into the world with the aim of inducing Satan to lay hold of him as he was laying hold of other men. As Christ was the Son of God and a perfectly holy being, Satan had no rights over him, and if he tried to take him captive he would not only be defeated but would forfeit his claim to the rest of mankind. If Satan knew what Christ was he would not be so foolish as to attempt his subjugation. Consequently by taking on flesh and subjecting himself to the limitations of humanity Christ deceived him into thinking he was only a man. And so Satan caused him to be betrayed and crucified, but in doing so put himself in the wrong and lost forever his right to the children of Adam. Thus it became possible for God to forgive repentant sinners without violating the principles of justice.

As seen in the previous volume the grotesque notion that Christ practised deceit upon the devil, and thereby accomplished his redemptive purpose, appeared in a somewhat different form in the writings of Origen. But Gregory worked out the theory in even greater detail and apparently took it much more seriously than Origen had done. It was of a sort indeed to prove very congenial to the Roman Christians of his day.[1]

Gregory also taught, though only in a vague and fragmentary way, that Christ satisfied the justice of God by suffering and dying in the place of sinners.[2] Not that the suffering and death of Christ were necessary; God who made man out of nothing could have restored him, Gregory says, without exacting any conditions. But Christ became what we were, and suffered in our behalf, out of his great love for us. And not merely did he suffer for us, his whole life was a sacrifice which he is continually offering to God on our account.[3] This side of Gregory's thought is lacking in clearness. Evidently he was struggling with an idea that seemed valuable, but was unable fully to understand it or see the bearing of it. On the other hand with the common notion that Christ saved men by revealing God to them and setting them an example of holy living he had no difficulty and emphasized it frequently, as Augustine had done before him.[4]

More important than anything Gregory had to say about the work of Christ was his interpretation of the eucharist as a repetition of Christ's sacrifice for sin.[5] Cyprian anticipated Gregory in this, but the latter made much more of it and permanently established the doctrine in the thinking of the church. The eucharist is not only a sacrifice, it is also a communing with Christ whose body and blood, according to Gregory, are really present in the elements. Feeding upon them we nourish and strengthen our spiritual life. But it is of greater significance that when the eucharist is admin-

[1] On this theory of Christ's work see Dudden, *op. cit.* vol. II. pp. 337 ff.
[2] *Moralia*, XVII. 46.
[3] *Ibid.* I. 32 ; XX. 69.
[4] Cf. *e.g. Moralia*, XXI. 11 ; XXX. 69.
[5] Cf. *Dialogues*, IV. 58.

istered Christ's sacrifice is repeated by the priest for the sins of men. The sacrifice is not, as was the death upon the cross, for the sins of all men, or of all the elect, but only for the sins of the participants, or of those for whose benefit it may be specifically offered. For all such it has the same effect as penance, taking the place of a certain amount of suffering which they would otherwise have to undergo because of their sins. It may benefit the dead as well as the living, that is the dead in purgatory not in hell. If offered for anyone in purgatory it will hasten the time of his release.

The following tale, related by Gregory in his Dialogues, shows his belief with sufficient clearness. After telling of the death of one of his monks who had been found guilty of hoarding money and had been severely punished, he continues: "Thirty days after his departure I began to take compassion upon him and with great grief to think of his punishment, and what means there was to help him. Whereupon I called again for Pretiosus, Prior of my Monastery, and with a heavy heart spake thus unto him: 'It is now a good while since that our brother which is departed remaineth in the torments of fire, and therefore we must show him some charity, and labor what we may to procure his delivery: wherefore go your way and see that for thirty days following sacrifice be offered for him, so that no one day pass in which for his absolution and discharge the healthful sacrifice be not offered'; who forthwith departed and put my commandment in execution. In the meantime, my mind being busied about other affairs so that I took no heed to the days how they passed: upon a certain night the same monk that was dead appeared to his brother Copiosus; who seeing him inquired of his state in this manner: 'What is the matter, brother? and how is it with you?' To whom he answered thus: 'Hitherto have I been in bad case, but now I am well, for this day have I received the communion';

with which news Copiosus straightways coming to the Monastery told the monks; and they diligently counting the days found it to be that in which the thirtieth sacrifice was offered for his soul; and so, though neither Copiosus knew what the monks had done for him, nor they what he had seen concerning the state of his brother, yet at one and the same time both he knew what they had done and they what he had seen, and so the sacrifice and vision agreeing together, apparent it was that the dead monk was by the holy sacrifice delivered from his pains." [1]

The doctrine was very prominent in the western church from Gregory's time on and helped to give its peculiar tone to the piety of the Middle Ages. The same is true of the doctrine of angels and demons about whom he had a great deal to say. He reflected much upon the nature and character of the angels, assigning them their several functions and their relative rank with great care. He gave them an important place in the government of the world and in the control of human affairs. Demons, too, and Satan their chief received considerable attention from him. His Dialogues are enlivened with many tales of their plots and chicaneries, especially against monks and nuns. In most of these tales they appear grotesque rather than terrible, mischief makers rather than awesome powers of darkness. The stories, indeed, are just such as have been current among the common people in all ages and in all religions. It is difficult to believe that Gregory can have given them credence, but he seems to have done so, and he seems also to have seen in them excellent nourishment for Christian faith and life, in all of them the machinations of the demons being frustrated by the saints. Augustine was credulous enough but Gregory went far beyond him in his acceptance of supernatural marvels and in his liking for them. Nothing indeed

[1] *Dialogues*, IV. 55 (quoted from the seventeenth-century translation).

seemed too weird or too trivial to engage his attention and command his assent if it could be made use of for edification. The significance of Gregory's treatment of the whole subject is not that he had anything new to impart but that he gave the popular belief in angels and demons in all its crudities and absurdities the support of his authority and thus raised it to the dignity of a part of the doctrinal system of the church.

Of the invocation of the saints and of their intercession in behalf of sinners he also had much to say. "If you had a case to be tried on the morrow before some great magistrate you would surely spend the whole of today planning for it; you would seek a patron and would beg him earnestly to become your defender. Behold the severe judge Jesus is about to come; the terror of that mighty council of angels and archangels is at hand. In that assembly our case will be tried and yet we are not seeking patrons who will then come to our defense. Our holy martyrs are ready to be your advocates; they desire to be asked, indeed if I may say so, they entreat that they may be entreated. Seek them as helpers of your prayer; turn to them that they may protect you in your guilt; for the judge himself wishes to be importuned that he may not be obliged to punish sinners." [1]

The notion of Christ's character revealed in this passage is illuminating. From an early day he had been thought of not only as saviour but also as judge. It was but natural that where the awfulness of the judgment was made much of, as it was particularly in the west, the severity of the judge should be taken for granted [2] as also the need of advocates to represent the interests of the accused. The belief in the intercession of the saints and the custom of appealing to

---

[1] *Homilia in evangelia*, XXXII. 8; cf. *Moralia*, XVI. 64.

[2] The notion of Christ as a severe judge finds its most striking expression long after Gregory in Michael Angelo's painting of the last judgment which accurately reflects the common opinion both early and late.

them to use their influence with Christ did not originate with Gregory; both the belief and the custom were much older than he. But he emphasized them and gave them too the weight of his authority.

Though Gregory cheapened and vulgarized much of Augustine's thought the latter's theory of the church he took over practically unchanged. The Catholic church is the one true church and outside of it salvation is impossible. Outside of it indeed there are no good works, no forgiveness of sins, no true worship, no effective sacrifices, no genuine martyrdom, no saving truth, no real faith and charity.[1] Heretics are without the pale because they violate the bond of faith; schismatics because they violate the bond of love.[2] The church is the authoritative teacher of divine truth. Unlike the heretics she is humble and recognizes that there are many things that cannot be known, that there is much, in fact, that she cannot herself understand, but she hands on what has been committed to her without alteration or abridgment. For all her teachings she demands unquestioning faith. Whether they can be rationally comprehended or not they are to be believed on her authority.[3] Faith indeed is the only proper attitude in all religious affairs. The things of God are open only to the believer. The human reason cannot explain them and cannot justify the ways of God to men, and should not attempt to do so.[4] Faith alone is acceptable to God and the merit of faith lies above all in accepting what the reason cannot grasp. "We must understand," Gregory says, "that if a divine work were comprehended by the reason it would not be wonderful. Nor is faith meritorious to which the human reason furnishes proof."[5] A position taken by Augustine only under the

---

[1] *Moralia*, XIV. 5; XXV. 13, 33.   [3] *Ibid*. IV. 19; XIV. 32; XX. 2.
[2] *Ibid*. XVIII. 42.   [4] *Ibid*. XVI. 81.
[5] *Homilia in evangelia*, XXVI. 1.   Compare the words of Tertullian quoted above, pp. 15 f.

pressure of emergency and particularly when he was dealing with certain difficult doctrines and acts of God, Gregory seems to have found entirely congenial and he committed himself whole-heartedly to it.

The sources from which to learn the teaching of the church are the Bible (including both the Old Testament and the New) and tradition. Gregory did not attempt to define and delimit tradition as Vincent of Lerins had done, but speaking generally it included the decisions of the four œcumenical councils of Nicæa, Constantinople, Ephesus, and Chalcedon, whose authority was unquestioned, and the writings of the Fathers. Just what Fathers he had in mind and in what circumstances their teachings were to be taken as binding he failed to indicate. Apparently it did not occur to him that there would be any difficulty at this point, and very likely there was none in his circle. The councils and the Fathers, it was assumed, had simply reproduced and elucidated the truth already found in the Bible and had not altered it in any way or added anything new to it. Tradition was thus, as Gregory viewed it, not an independent organ of divine truth, but only confirmatory and explanatory of the Scriptures.

In his exposition of the Scriptures, both Old Testament and New, Gregory followed the common allegorical method of the age, carrying it even further than most. He insisted, to be sure, as others did, that the literal historical sense must not be neglected and that type and allegory must be built upon it, not elaborated independently of it. But in practice this principle was often, perhaps usually, disregarded, so that he was able to draw from almost any part of the Bible anything he desired. In the Book of Job, for instance, as already seen, he found practically the whole of his theology.

The importance of Gregory in the history of western Catholic thought can hardly be exaggerated. Not in any sense an original genius he contributed no new ideas and created no epoch in theology. But he formulated the common faith of his day and handed it on to the Catholic church of the Middle Ages, including within it not merely the official pronouncements of the councils and the teachings of the Fathers, but also the notions of the illiterate populace, often crude and superstitious to the last degree and very largely pagan. To this mass of material he gave the support of his authority and as a consequence it became an integral part of the faith of the western church, of theologians and ecclesiastics as well as of monks and laity. The thinking of the Middle Ages cannot be understood without Gregory. Back of it is not simply the theology of the great Fathers, east and west, but the beliefs and practices of the monks and of the uneducated and uncultured masses outside the monasteries. Of all this, as has been said, Gregory was the authoritative formulator and guarantor.

It is worth while in this connection to call attention to the contrast between the eastern and the western church of Gregory's day. In spite of a large range of belief and practice in which the two were one, the difference between them was very great. Most important of all was the fact that in the east Christianity was commonly thought of as a mystical religion bringing salvation by uniting man to God and transforming him from a corrupt to an incorrupt, from a mortal to an immortal being; while in the west it was generally interpreted in legal terms as a religion requiring obedience to law and offering men the opportunity to escape from the consequences of disobedience by sacrifices and good works. There was legalism also in the east and there was mysticism also in the west, but the ruling tendencies in the one and in the other were diverse. In the east the spirit of the mystery-religions was in control and the Christianity of Paul and John and Ignatius prevailed; in the west the spirit of later

Judaism which was akin to that of Rome was dominant and here the Christianity of James and Clement and Hermas was chiefly current. Of this Christianity in its earlier stages Tertullian was an admirable example. Augustine was too much of a Platonist to be a representative westerner, but in Gregory the temper of the west came again to clear and characteristic expression, perhaps clearer and more characteristic than in any other figure of the ancient church.

BOOK FOUR

CHRISTIAN THOUGHT IN THE WESTERN CHURCH OF THE MIDDLE AGES

CHAPTER VII

JOHN SCOTUS ERIUGENA

THOUGH convenient, and too well established in common usage to be abandoned, the term Middle Ages is unfortunate, for it suggests that there was a period in European history whose chief significance, as distinguished from other periods, was its transitional character. All ages are transitional. It has not made for a sound understanding either of past or present that one age alone has been singled out for the honour or the obloquy of being known principally as a bridge between two others. A natural consequence of viewing it thus has been the tendency to see the period in question as a single homogeneous and undifferentiated whole, and to overlook the originality and creativeness, the freshness and variety that characterized it in many ways. In reality it was a time of growth and change on a large scale and the greater part of it was marked by uncommon intellectual activity.

Because the Humanists and the Reformers condemned it and harked back to classical or Christian antiquity the modern world, at least the Protestant world, has inherited a prejudice against it which historians have found difficult to eradicate. To call a thing ancient is not necessarily to disparage it; to call it mediæval is to hand it over to widespread contumely. A sympathetic appreciation of the period is consequently not easy even for those who have learned to recognize its importance. Unhappily this is particularly true of historians of Christian thought.

Notwithstanding the variety displayed by the Middle Ages there was also a large degree of unity. The chief symbol and agent of this unity was the Catholic church, an international or better a supernational institution which embraced the whole of western Christendom. Though primarily a religious institution it was also much else and it made its influence felt in many fields. To the church it was due in no small part that there developed during the Middle Ages a common European civilization so that despite all political divisions and all local differences western Europe became in a real sense one whole.

In the educational sphere the church was not only influential but dominant. There were lay schools as well as clerical, but at any rate north of the Alps the latter predominated and the majority of schoolmasters came from the ranks of the clergy. It was out of the old cathedral schools that the great universities, Paris, Oxford, and the rest, developed in the twelfth and following centuries. The language of the schools, from the lowest to the highest, was Latin which every educated man must know. It was the medium of communication among the cultured all over the western world. Its prevalence meant a great deal for mediæval theology as for law and philosophy and other branches of learning. It broke down walls of division and made possible the free interchange of ideas. At the same time the use of an acquired tongue rather than every man's vernacular tended to set theology — not to mention other subjects — apart from the ordinary affairs of life and to make it wholly inaccessible to the masses. Unlike the east, where Greek was the language of both learned and unlearned and where the people were often as interested in the shibboleths of the theologians as were the latter themselves, theology in the west was generally regarded as the employment only of a privileged class. Its connection with religion (which alone was the affair of all) seemed at any rate to the common man more remote than ever. Doubtless because of this a larger measure of freedom was enjoyed by theologians than might otherwise have been theirs. As in other times the chief danger dreaded by the authorities whether of state or church was disturbances among the masses. Anything that threatened to stir up popular excitement, or to start great popular movements, was apt to be put down with a strong hand — witness the treatment accorded the Albigenses and the Waldenses. But theological speculation confined to the circles of the initiate and inaccessible to the rank and file was as a rule allowed a large measure of license. Now and then there were theologians that took seriously all divergencies from accepted doctrine, even the most trivial, and tried to crush those guilty of them, but the ecclesiastical powers were usually content to let such persons alone and meddled with them only when driven to do so by pressure from others.

The existence of the Catholic church conditioned in important ways the Christian thinking of the Middle Ages. It meant for one thing that continuity with the thinking of the past was maintained unbroken. The Middle Ages inherited the doctrinal system of an earlier day as formulated in the east and modified and supplemented by the Latin Fathers. Theologians moved within the framework or at any rate against the background of a common faith handed down from another age, a common faith that was never forgotten and seldom questioned.

The existence of the Catholic church meant also that the theologians of the Middle Ages, wherever born and bred, were fellow-citizens of one great commonwealth which transcended all national boundaries. That they came from Italy or France or Germany or England, though it might affect to some extent their culture and their literary style, was less important for their theological development and their theological achievements than that they were Catholics. Theology in the Middle Ages overleaped all communal and national limitations. It was the work of a class apart and did not feel the influence of local situations, or of political, social, and economic conditions, in any marked degree. In this respect it resembled modern science whose intellectual equivalent it was. The period was marked by great changes in almost every department of life. Theology reflected these changes little if at all. It was not a time of stagnation in theology — far from it — but the activity went on for the most part aloof from other interests in what might almost be called a timeless world of the spirit. In this connection it should not be forgotten that most mediæval theologians were monks. It is true that if other influences counted for little, the influence of philosophy was profoundly felt as will be seen. But philosophy too, like theology, had its roots elsewhere than in contemporary and local conditions.

During the century and a half succeeding the death of Gregory the Great there was comparatively little theological activity in the western church. Theology shared, however, in the intellectual renaissance and in the awakened interest in the antique, which marked the Carolingian period, and in the centuries following there was considerable theological discussion and a good deal of heated controversy. Even now, to be sure, there was not much original or creative thinking; theologians were almost exclusively engaged in appropriating the heritage of the past and adapting it to the needs of the new age. But one man stood out from his contemporaries as a speculative genius of the first rank. In the entire history of Christian thought there are few more striking figures than John Scotus Eriugena. His interests were largely unlike the prevailing interests of his day and he had little influence either in his own century or in the centuries immediately following, but his writings were preserved and later he came into his own.

Born in Ireland early in the ninth century he made his way to France where he enjoyed the friendship of Charles the Bald and became the most famous scholar and teacher of the day. In Ireland where culture was at a relatively high level he received an education better than fell to the lot of most. His knowledge of Greek and his acquaintance with Greek philosophy and with certain eastern Fathers not well known in the west gave him a great advantage over the scholars of the continent. It is not surprising that his restless and brilliant intellect, working with materials largely unfamiliar to his contemporaries, should lead him to opinions out of line with theirs and should create the impression that he was an exceedingly dangerous teacher. The fact is he was a bold and venturesome thinker, and while he recognized the authority of the Scriptures and the Fathers, he put reason first and insisted that it must be followed at all costs. Though authority is earlier in time than reason, the latter is by nature older than the former and superior to it. Authority comes from reason not reason from authority, and while reason needs no support from authority, authority must have the support of reason.[1] The Fathers found truth by the use of reason and we must find it in the same way. To follow reason, however, does not mean to break with authority, since both come from God and cannot contradict each other. "True authority does not oppose right reason, nor right reason true authority. For it is not to be doubted that both come from one source, namely, the divine wisdom."[2] Eriugena made large use of the Fathers and as a rule

---

[1] Eriugena, *De divisione naturæ*, Bk. I. chap. 69.
[2] *Ibid.* I. 66.

quoted them with approval, but he did not hesitate to differ with them on occasion and in one passage, after giving the opinions of some of them on a certain subject, he declared that no one should be urged to believe what seemed to him incredible.[1] The truth of the Bible he did not question, but he was not hampered by its authority, for he took it for granted that it was to be read allegorically, not literally.

"Do not be alarmed," he says, "for now we must follow reason which investigates the truth of things, and overpowered by no authority and in no way shackled, sets forth and proclaims openly what it has studiously examined and laboriously discovered. To be sure the authority of Holy Scripture must be followed in all things, for in it we have the truth as it were in its secret haunts. Nevertheless, it is not to be understood literally as if in making the divine nature known to us it always called things by their own names. On the contrary, condescending to our infirmity it uses figurative and symbolical language, encouraging our as yet immature and infantile senses by simple doctrine."[2]

Eriugena was primarily a philosopher and as such he is dealt with in most histories of philosophy. But in his hands philosophy and theology were one, and the historian of Christian thought can ill afford to neglect him. At the beginning of his work on predestination he declares that philosophy and religion are identical. "What else is it to treat philosophy than to expound the principles of true religion by which God, the highest and chief cause of all things, is both humbly worshipped and rationally investigated? We conclude then that true philosophy is true religion and conversely that true religion is true philosophy."[3] The identification was not merely verbal; Eriugena meant

---

[1] *Ibid.* V. 8; cf. also IV. 9.   [2] *Ibid.* I. 63–64.
[3] *De prædestinatione*, chap. I. § I.

it to be taken seriously as appears clearly enough from his principal work. Evidently his religion was a genuinely intellectual affair, speculative rather than practical, a matter of philosophy more than of devotional exercises and good works. He did not stand alone in this. But more perhaps than has been true of most theologians he was engrossed by philosophical speculation to the exclusion of all else.

Eriugena owed much to Neoplatonism and found himself most in sympathy with those Fathers that had felt its influence. The so-called Dionysius the Areopagite was especially congenial to him. He translated his writings into Latin and in his chief work drew largely upon him, speaking of him often in extravagant terms. Maximus the Confessor, the chief commentator of Dionysius, he also quoted frequently,[1] as he did certain works of Gregory of Nyssa. Among western Fathers he made most use of Ambrose and Augustine, especially the latter.

Though Eriugena was largely influenced by earlier thinkers his system of philosophy or theology — for it may be called either — was truly his own and surpassed in originality and profundity anything produced in the western church for many a century. It is set forth boldly, and considering the difficulty of the theme is discussed with exemplary clearness though with considerable repetitiousness, in his principal work On the Division of Nature (De divisione naturæ). The work is in five books and is in the form of a dialogue, but as the interlocutors are teacher and pupil it is easier than in many dialogues to recognize the opinions of the author himself, which he had little hesitation in avowing. The term Nature as used in the title of the work includes both God and the universe, everything indeed that can be thought about whether existent or non-existent. "Nature," Eriugena says, "is the general name for all that is and that

[1] He also translated Maximus' *Ambigua in S. Gregorium theologum.*

is not." [1]   Nature therefore is simply another name for the all — the all of thought as well as of things.

Under the influence of Neoplatonism, and particularly of Pseudo-Dionysius, Eriugena emphasized the transcendence and incomprehensibility of God.[2]   God is above all being.   He is wholly unknowable and can be neither perceived nor conceived.   We can know that he is but not what he is.   The affirmative theology which ascribes to God all perfections is symbolical only.   When we declare that God is omnipotent, omniscient and the like, we are only trying to say in figurative language that he is greater than can be said or thought.   The only true theology is the negative theology which denies that God is, not because he is below being but above ; and which denies that he is powerful and wise and beneficent, not because he is less but more than all these, so much more that none of them can be truly said of him.[3]

But though Eriugena followed Dionysius and the Neoplatonists in emphasizing the transcendence and unknowability of God his real interest lay elsewhere.   He remarked in one passage that he did not like to hear existence denied to God, for the denial seemed to imply that God was less than being instead of more ; [4] and he was careful not to allow any reader to misunderstand the significance of the negative theology in this respect.   Though influenced largely by Dionysius he was not a mystic and was not concerned with the practical question of how men may be brought into oneness with God.   While he gave his conditional approval to the negative theology, he apparently cared nothing about the via negativa, by which alone, according to Dionysius, men may reach mystical union with the divine.   Nor was he interested in priests and sacra-

---

[1] *De divisione naturæ*, I (beginning).
[2] Cf. *e.g.* I. 3 ff; 66 ff.
[3] I. 14 ff; 39.
[4] III. 5.

ments and means of grace. Indeed the entire range of thought covered by Dionysius' Ecclesiastical Hierarchy seems to have been alien to him.[1]

Eriugena's interest, I have said, lay elsewhere. Not the transcendence but the immanence of God was his fundamental postulate, immanence amounting to genuine pantheism.[2] The divine nature embraces everything; apart from God or outside of him there is nothing. He is Being unlimited and undifferentiated; the world is Being circumscribed and divided.[3] The unity between God and the creature is complete; he is in all things and is the being of all. When we say that God created everything, we mean that he is in everything as its essence, the common substance of all that is.[4] He cannot be seen in himself but only in the things that he inhabits.[5] Spirits and bodies, all things that exist are but manifestations of him; each is a genuine theophany.[6] And not only is God in everything, he is identical with all that is, for God and the creature are not two but one and the same.[7]

Language could not well go further than this. But though Eriugena asserted unequivocally that God is in all and is the essence of all and that he and the creature are one and the same, he yet declared that God is at the same time above all, as man is above as well as in the world of things.[8] Eriugena's pantheism was therefore not thoroughgoing. In spite of his strong statements he did not identify God and the world completely and without qualification. But it was on the identity rather than the distinction that he laid stress

---

[1] He is reported, to be sure, to have written a work on the Eucharist (now lost) in which he maintained the symbolical view of the elements in agreement with Pseudo-Dionysius. But the report is probably unfounded.

[2] The very use of the term Nature in the title of his principal work to include God as well as the world is significant of his general attitude.

[3] I. 12; III. 17.

[4] I. 72.

[5] I. 10.

[6] III. 4.

[7] III. 17.

[8] *E.g.* III. 20; IV. 5.

and the pantheistic character of his system as a whole is abundantly evident.

With the conception of God as an individual separate from other individuals and ruling them as an earthly sovereign rules his people — a conception generally prevalent in the west — he had no patience. It was partly no doubt because of his hostility to the anthropomorphism of current thought that he made use, as has been already seen, of the negative theology of Pseudo-Dionysius, involving the incomprehensibility of God and his unlikeness to all that can be seen or thought. Inconsistent as it seems with the doctrine of divine immanence, in which he was chiefly interested, it is yet one with it in its denial of all anthropomorphism and particularly of the common western reading of the universe in legal terms.

I have said that Eriugena's fundamental tenet was the immanence of God, or rather the oneness of God and the universe. But this is only half the story, for his philosophy was not simply pantheistic, it was also dynamic. With the idea of divine immanence he combined the idea of evolution. The universe is not static or at rest, it is continually developing. Out of God, the great All, all things come and back to him they all find their way. Everything, Eriugena says, tends naturally to return to its source and the universe which comes from God tends naturally to return to him. The process of evolution and involution in reality goes on within the divine nature itself, for God is all and the universe is but an expression or manifestation of him. In the unfolding of the divine essence the world comes into existence — a phenomenal universe in space and time — to return ultimately to the source whence it came.

In the evolutionary process there are no new or extraneous factors.   In the cause all its effects are already present. God is the one and only source and all comes from him.

When it is said that he created all things out of nothing, it is meant that he created all things out of himself,[1] the phrase ex nihilo being used to indicate not that which is below but that which is above being. The process of evolution is not a matter of choice with God. Creation is not an accident, something that might or might not have been ; creation is a necessity and God could not have refrained from it if he would. His nature is such that it must unfold itself, must express itself in the world of ideas and in the world of space and time. It has within itself the potentiality which means the actuality of an endlessly developing universe.[2] We are dealing here, evidently, not with a static but with a dynamic pantheism, the pantheism of a Hegel rather than a Spinoza. It is true that occasionally Eriugena used the language of geometry, as Spinoza did, and pictured the relation of God to things as that of the centre to the radii of a circle.[3] But such utterances are to be interpreted in the light of his system as a whole, and are not to be understood as in Spinoza's philosophy. God, he insisted, is not quiescence but activity, ceaseless and all embracing.[4]

In his work On the Division of Nature, Eriugena, with a sweep of imagination seldom equalled, set himself to expound the eternal process of evolution and involution, in which all being is embraced. At the beginning of the work he

[1] Cf. III. 19–23. This is in striking contrast with the position of Origen and many others who distinguished "made from the nature of God" (as Christ is) and "made out of nothing" (as the universe is).

[2] III. 6.

[3] Cf. e.g. III. 1

[4] In this connection it is interesting to notice that Eriugena (in I. 12) derives the word θεός from θέειν (to run). In the same passage he asserts that God is self-moving but not moved by anything outside. Elsewhere he declares that motion and activity do not belong to God (e.g. I. 71 ff) ; but there he is speaking in terms of the negative theology which denies everything, even being, to God, because he is more than can be said or thought. The denial of motion to him therefore does not contradict the dynamic character of Eriugena's theism.

divided nature, or the all, into four parts : first, that which creates and is not created, namely, God ; second, that which is created and creates, namely, the world of ideas or pri-mordial causes ; third, that which is created and does not create, the phenomenal world in space and time ; and fourth, that which is neither created nor creates, the return, that is, of all to God from whence all came. This fourfold division gave its title to the work and formed its main theme. In it not only Eriugena's philosophy but also his theology and religion came to completest expression. The division had to do not with substance but with process. Not that the all is made up of four parts, but that it passes through four stages, from the primeval oneness through the world of ideas and the world of things back again to the primeval oneness, or God, from unity through multiplicity back to unity.

In the first book of his De divisione naturæ Eriugena deals with God, the one who creates and is not created. As already seen he reproduces the negative theology of Diony-sius and the Neoplatonists, denying all being and attributes to God, but he does not stop there. With Dionysius he goes on to the affirmative theology, and asserts many things of God, for instance that he is all-wise and all-power-ful and particularly that he is all-beneficent. Goodness, indeed, is God's principal attribute from which all others flow. It was goodness that led him to create ; in fact the whole process of evolution roots itself in the divine benefi-cence. "God is properly called love because he is the cause of all love and is poured through all things and gathers all things into one and returns into himself in an unutterable way and brings to an end in himself the loves of every creature." [1] It was said above that Eriugena interpreted creation out of nothing as meaning that all things come

[1] I. 74.

from the nature of God ; but he interpreted it also as meaning that all things come from the divine goodness, for there is no distinction between the two.[1] That creation is due to the goodness of God does not make it any the less necessary ; goodness is not a matter of will with God but of nature. He could not be otherwise than good, and he could not do otherwise than supreme and eternal goodness demands.[2]

The second stage of being, that which is created and creates, Eriugena in agreement with Augustine and the Neoplatonists identified with the world of ideas, or primordial causes. This contains the prototypes of all existing things, the forms according to which the actual world was made.[3] Eriugena was a genuine idealist. Everything exists in idea before it exists as an external fact. In the idea, indeed, is the essence of the fact. Objects have their existence, so far as they exist at all, in the ideas of them, and only in the divine idea of the world and of man do the latter have true reality. God does not know an object because it is ; it is because he knows it.[4] The ideas of things are implanted in us by God.[5] They are not our own creation nor are they caused by the things themselves, for the ideas precede the things both in God and in man. The senses were not given us that objects might be perceived, but objects were made for man's sake, that his senses might have whereon to exercise themselves.[6]

Eriugena was also a realist, in the Platonic and mediæval sense, for the universal, he believed, exists before the particular and all things are but expressions of a larger whole.[7] The process of evolution is from the general to the particular.

[1] III. 19 ff.
[2] A considerable part of the first book of the *De divisione naturæ* is taken up with philosophical questions such as the nature of being, different modes of existence, space and time and the other categories of Aristotle. While there is much in these chapters to interest the historian of philosophy they need not detain us here.
[3] II. 34.   [4] II. 28.   [5] IV. 7.   [6] IV. 10.   [7] III. 1.

Individual things come into existence through the unfolding of universal being, and the degree of reality is in inverse proportion to the degree of individuation — the nearer to being in general the more real, the farther from it the less real. From universal being through its divisions into visible and invisible, spiritual and material, animate and inanimate, through genera and species to individual persons and things, the process of differentiation goes on, and all along the line reality depends on the connection of each member of the series with the larger whole of which it is a part. Individuals are not propagated, only species; for individuals have no independent existence but are simply manifestations of the species to which they belong and apart from which they have no reality. In Eriugena's day the conflict between realism and nominalism, which occupied the attention of so many thinkers of the Middle Ages, had not yet broken out, but there is no question that he would have been on the side of the realists as all pantheistically minded naturally are.

The world of ideas, according to Eriugena, exists in the divine Son or Logos.[1] It is eternal as he is eternal and represents, as from another point of view he represents, the first stage in the unfolding of the Absolute. The connection of the world of ideas with the Logos shows the influence of Christian tradition. In this part of his work Eriugena was philosophically not theologically interested, and there was no apparent reason why he should bring in the Logos except to attach his system to the historic belief of the church and secure for it the sanction of Christian faith. He did not begin with the Logos, as many earlier thinkers had done, and find in philosophy a justification and application of the Logos doctrine; he began with philosophy and used the Logos only to give his philosophy Christian standing. By his reference to the Logos or Son in connection with the eternal world of

[1] Cf. II. 21; III. 6 ff; IV. 7.

ideas he set the Christian seal upon his speculations, while at the same time he remained true to Plato who, as already remarked, identified the world with the Son of God.

The next stage in the process of the divine unfolding, or manifestation of God, was the creation of the sensible world including angels as well as men and things. It had its cause in the world of ideas and took its pattern therefrom, but it exists in space and time as the world of ideas does not. Space and time, indeed, came into existence with the sensible world which can be and can be known only in the space and time relation.[1] The sensible world is composed of matter, but matter is made up of immaterial elements,[2] the nature of which Eriugena, in contrast with our modern physicists, did not attempt to describe.

In the beginning the world was an undifferentiated whole : there were no genera, no species, no sex. The oneness of man's nature was so perfect and the unity between him and the world so complete that he knew everything immediately and by intuition and had no need to reflect or draw conclusions.[3] But in consequence of human sin all was changed, simplicity became complexity, homogeneity heterogeneity, identity difference, and all the ills of a divided existence were visited upon the universe.[4] Not that the divisions arose after the fall ; they were there from the beginning. For God foreseeing the fall created with man himself the consequences wrapped up in his disobedience : a material and mortal body subject to growth and decay, the distinction between male and female, the need for such things as food and drink and sleep.[5] Though by his fall man disrupted the original oneness of the physical world, he is yet in his nature a reconciler of all differences, for he is made up of spirit and body, the highest and lowest things in the universe. He is indeed a microcosm of the whole creation both visible and invisible.[6]

[1] I. 39.　　[2] III. 14.　　[3] IV. 25.　　[4] II. 6–10.　　[5] IV. 14.　　[6] II. 3 ff.

Not only was the world made for his sake that he might rule and control it, in a sense the whole world truly exists in him, for it is his idea of it that gives it reality as it is God's idea of him that gives man reality.[1]

Eriugena's system provided, as we have seen, not simply for the coming of all things from God but also for the return of all things to God. To this, the most difficult part of his task, as he pronounced it, he devoted the fifth and longest book of his great work. It is not surprising that he found the subject difficult, for here even more than elsewhere he felt himself obliged to make a place in his system for traditional beliefs quite alien to it.

The tendency of everything, so he maintained, is to seek its source. In the end all being, having come from God and having passed through multiplicity and diversity, will return to the original unity whence it came.[2] The return will include the whole creation, not men and angels alone but brutes as well, and all things animate and inanimate. The process of evolution, or the unfolding of the divine, was from higher to lower: first the eternal world of ideas, then the phenomenal world of space and time, and in the latter first angels, then men, then animals, and so on down the scale. In the return to God the process will be reversed. The lower creation will be absorbed in man and with him will ascend to the world of ideas or primordial causes, and this in turn with all that has come from it — space and time, matter and spirit, the visible and the invisible — will make its way back to God, gathering up everything in him until he becomes finally all in all again as he was at the beginning.

In this grandiose vision Eriugena's religion came to expression as well as his philosophy. And his religion took the form of Christianity, for he found in Christ the one in and through whom the return is accomplished. In the earlier

[1] IV. 7; cf. II. 9.   [2] V. 1 ff.

books of his work there is little specifically Christian, but in the fifth book Christ is given a controlling place. Having by his incarnation become a part of the created universe he prefigures and foreshadows by his resurrection the return to God not of some men alone but of the whole human race and of the entire universe as well.[1] From Eriugena's point of view the incarnation and the resurrection were the important matters; other events in Christ's career he had little interest in.[2] To have connected Christ, the incarnate and risen Word with the return of all things to God, as he had connected the eternal Word with the creation of the universe, seemed to him enough to guarantee the Christian character of his system. Beyond this he was not concerned to go, at any rate in this particular work.

The return to God, as has been said, will include the whole creation. Nothing that God has made will ever be destroyed, for all of it partakes of his nature. No part of the universe will pass into nothingness, nor will anything be left outside the all-inclusive unity.[3] But this raises the question of the fate of the wicked. Eriugena's system was such that the final salvation of all men seems its natural conclusion, and certain passages suggest that this was his real conviction as it was Origen's.[4] But in Eriugena's day the doctrine of everlasting punishment was too firmly entrenched in the belief of the church to be rejected and hence he was obliged to make a place for it. It is interesting to see the straits in which he found himself and the way he was driven to moderate and reinterpret the doctrine in his effort to bring it into harmony with his system as a whole. For one thing he read the future life in exclusively spiritual terms. Heaven and hell are not places but states of mind.[5] When the world

[1] V. 22, 38.
[2] What he says about Christ's death in V. 38 and elsewhere is wholly perfunctory.
[3] V. 14 ff. [4] *E.g.* V. 35. [5] V. 29, 35, 36.

has passed away space and time will pass with it and there will be no possibility of a localized heaven and hell. Both bad and good will have spiritual bodies composed of one and the same substance, for sin does not change the nature of man. And they will all be with God, not separate from him or outside the common unity. But the bad will suffer unceasingly as they realize how completely they have failed to achieve their aims, and they will be plagued with remorse as they remember the false ideas which they took for true and by which they lived.[1]

Eriugena pictured the suffering of the wicked in many ways, but he always insisted that it was mental only, that it affected in no degree their constitution or status, that it deprived them of none of the natural advantages and privileges enjoyed by the good, and that it did not banish them from the presence of God or from association with the righteous. The many mansions spoken of by Christ are for the bad as well as the good, for all will dwell forever in God's house.[2] This was a remarkable position for any theologian to take and illustrates anew the unconventional character of Eriugena's thought.

The subject of future punishment led Eriugena to discuss the problem of evil. It is significant that he dealt with it here instead of in connection with the goodness of God, as Dionysius had done. His interest in it was evidently more philosophical than religious. Not so much to justify the ways of God as to prevent the breakdown of his system he grappled with the age-old problem. His solution, as might have been expected, was that of Dionysius and Augustine who took it from the Neoplatonists. Evil is negative not positive. It is not a substance; indeed it is nothing at all. Being and good are one; evil is simply the absence of being or of good. Nothing is good except as it

[1] V. 31, 32.   [2] V. 36.

partakes of being or of God, and evil, which is nothing at all, partakes of neither. Being nothing it has no cause, for to speak of a cause of nothing is absurd. Now and then, to be sure, Eriugena refers to the cause of sin, finding it in the freedom or changeableness of the will. But this was out of line with his general attitude and is not to be pressed. Freedom of the will is itself a negative thing, the absence namely of determination or control, and on Eriugena's own principles it could not properly be called the cause of anything. Sin, he maintained, is simply the failure to rise to higher things. The failure is due not to something positive (he rejected altogether the notion that the seat of sin is the flesh) but to the absence of the requisite desire and effort. To seek its cause is to seek the cause of nothing. The same view of evil appears also in Eriugena's earlier work on Predestination, written against the monk Gottschalk who was teaching the doctrine of predestination both to salvation and to damnation, to the great scandal of most of his contemporaries. Among the other arguments, almost exclusively philosophical, urged by Eriugena in favor of predestination to good alone was the contention that evil is nothing and as such can neither be foreknown nor predestined by God.[1]

Evil being nothing, Eriugena goes on to say in his De divisione naturæ, will not disturb the harmony of the final consummation. Harmony is heightened by contrasts and the misery of the wicked, not in some distant world but side by side forever with the happiness of the saved, will but enhance the beauty of the whole. Evil indeed will entirely disappear.[2] There will be no more sinning and no more desire to sin even on the part of the lost, and the suffering which they endure in their consciences, as they reflect upon the past, will be recognized by them and by everybody else as just, and will serve to exhibit in greater splendor both the

[1] Cf. *De prædestinatione*, chap. x.   [2] *De divisione naturæ*, V. 28.

righteousness and the mercy of God, who preserves the saved and the lost alike.

In the future consummation all will enjoy the blessing of God's presence, but for those who have lived for the highest things — the saints and holy ones of earth — a still loftier privilege is reserved. They will be deified, becoming completely one with God and enjoying forever the contemplation of the truth, the greatest of all felicities in Eriugena's opinion.[1] We are reminded here of the choice souls referred to by Dionysius who rise by way of ecstasy to mystical union with God and complete absorption in him. But it is significant that ecstasy has no place in Eriugena's picture, which thus lacks the characteristic feature of Neoplatonic mysticism.

Eriugena's was the first great philosophical system of the Middle Ages and for some centuries there was no other to compare with it. Indeed for sweep of imagination and breadth of vision it has seldom been approached in ancient or modern times. The system was too profound to be commonly understood and much of Eriugena's thinking was too adventurous and too unlike the current thought of the age to be generally acceptable. His great ability was recognized but his soundness was doubted and he had few disciples. Through his translation of the writings of Pseudo-Dionysius and his commentaries upon them he had considerable influence in mystical circles, particularly in the later Middle Ages. But his other works were generally forgotten until the twelfth century when his De divisione naturæ was rediscovered and widely read. It was condemned early in the following century by Pope Honorius III and was almost wholly lost sight of until late in the seventeenth century, when it appeared for the first time in print. Since then its importance has come to be recognized among philosophers and certain schools of thought have owed it much.

[1] V. 21, 25, 36, 38.

CHAPTER VIII

ANSELM

A THINKER of an entirely different type was Anselm, Archbishop of Canterbury. He came of a noble family of Lombardy and was born in 1033 at Aosta in Piedmont. He was a devout and studious youth, and ascetic in his habits even from boyhood. Meeting with opposition in his wish to become a monk he early left home and after travelling for some years found his way to the monastery of Le Bec in Normandy where his countryman Lanfranc, the most famous teacher of his age, was prior. Here he devoted himself eagerly to the study of philosophy and theology and when Lanfranc left to become abbot of another monastery Anselm took his place. Later he was made abbot and finally left Le Bec only to succeed Lanfranc as Archbishop of Canterbury in 1093.

As Archbishop he had a troubled career. He was a high churchman and a loyal papist and supported with great energy the extravagant claims of Gregory VII and his successors. For several years he was at swords' points first with William Rufus and then with Henry over the question of investiture and the relative authority of church and state in England. Twice he was exiled, but peace was finally patched up and he died at his post in 1109.

Throughout his life Anselm was devoutly religious and whether as head of the monastery of Le Bec or as Archbishop of Canterbury was deeply concerned for the spiritual welfare of those under his care. We have from his pen a number of

ascetic and devotional tracts, some of them of a high order.
We are interested in him here, however, rather as a theologian
than as an administrator and pastor. As such he was one of
the most interesting and influential figures of the Middle
Ages, important particularly for his theological method and
for his confidence in the rationality and demonstrability of
Christian truth. He was an orthodox believer, accepting
without question the traditional Catholic faith. There was
nothing of the sceptic about him and he had no inclination
to criticize received doctrines. Saving faith he believed
involved the sincere and humble acceptance of the truth
taught by the Catholic church. But faith must be followed
by love and knowledge; it must bear fruit both practical
and theoretical. Without love faith is dead; without knowledge it is immature and imperfect. As it should be the aim
of every Christian to go on from faith in God to love for him,
it should be his aim, in such measure as his endowments and
training permit, to go on from faith in God to an understanding of him and his truth. "No Christian," Anselm says,
"ought in any way to dispute the truth of what the Catholic
church believes in its heart and confesses with its mouth.
But always holding the same faith unquestioningly, loving it
and living by it, he ought himself as far as he is able to seek
the reason for it. If he can understand it let him thank God.
If he cannot let him not raise his head in opposition but bow
in reverence." [1]

As a theologian Anselm took his motto from Augustine of
whose writings he was an eager student. Not "I know that
I may believe," but "I believe that I may know." [2] He
insisted that all Catholic doctrines are true because divinely
revealed, and that the Christian must accept them on the

[1] *De fide trinitatis*, 2.
[2] "Neque enim quaero intelligere ut credam, sed credo ut intelligam."
(*Proslogion*, chap. 1.) Augustine's words are "credimus ut cognoscamus."

authority of the church, but he maintained that they are also rational, meaning thereby that they may be understood and may be proved true, without recourse to revelation, by the use of the reason alone. The theologian therefore has a double task, to explain and elucidate the truths of revelation for the sake of believers and to prove them true for the sake of unbelievers. In this connection it is interesting to notice that Anselm made little use of the customary authorities in his theological works. As a matter of fact most of his writings are singularly free from references to the Bible and the Fathers.

Anselm was an accomplished dialectician and insisted that a thorough training in logic was indispensable to the theologian. He was also something of a philosopher, but philosophy interested him not for its own sake but only for the sake of theology. If one's philosophy were unsound one's theology was bound to be the same. He was a genuine realist of the Platonic type and was convinced that unless a theologian recognized the reality of universals he could not be an orthodox believer. His realism was not merely implicit but explicit and deliberate. It appears clearly in his little dialogue On Truth in which he maintains that there are not many truths but only one, that truth is unchanging and eternal, that it has real existence, and that things are true only because they partake of it.[1]

His realism appears also in his work on the Trinity which was written against Roscellin, Abbot of Compiegne. "Those dialecticians, or rather dialectical heretics, of our time," he says, "who think that universal substances are nothing but words (flatum vocis), and are unable to distinguish color from bodies or the wisdom of man from his soul, should be wholly excluded from the discussion of spiritual questions. For in their souls reason which ought

[1] Cf. *De veritate*, 13, where Anselm summarizes his position.

to be the ruler and judge of all that is in man is so involved in corporeal images that it is not able to escape from them or to discriminate between them and the things that should be contemplated by reason simply and alone. For how can he who does not yet understand that many men are in species one man comprehend how in that most lofty and mysterious nature a plurality of persons, each of whom singly is perfect God, are one God?" [1] Anselm was entirely right in believing that the orthodox doctrine of the Trinity presupposed philosophical realism, and it was historically of great importance that he pointed this out so clearly. Otherwise his brief treatise was of no special significance.

Roscellin's work on the Trinity is lost, but he was evidently a nominalist — one of those "heretical dialecticians" who maintained that individuals alone are real and universals nothing but words. Applying his nominalism to the doctrine of the Trinity he claimed that the three persons (Father, Son, and Spirit) were real but that the common divine nature which they were supposed to share had no actual existence. Anselm consequently accused him of tritheism. "Either he wishes to confess three gods or he does not understand what he says. If he confesses three gods he is not a Christian ; if he says what he does not understand he is not to be trusted." [2] To be sure, according to Anselm, Roscellin taught that the three persons of the Trinity are one in will and purpose and equal in power, but they are not one in essence or substance. Indeed they could not be, for there is no such thing as divine essence or substance. In his emphasis on the threeness, in which he went so far as to liken the persons of the Trinity to three angels or three men, Roscellin resembled the Cappadocian Fathers but he differed with them radically in denying to the three persons a common divine nature.

[1] *De fide trinitatis*, 2.   [2] *Ibid.* 3.

Anselm was not a systematic theologian and did not attempt to cover the whole range of Christian doctrine. His theological writings, all of them short and concise, deal only with subjects that happened to interest him or were forced upon him by controversy. They are, however, by no means casual in character and content. Their author had evidently thought the Christian system through in the most thoroughgoing fashion and in all of them his fundamental principles clearly appear.

His earliest theological treatise, the Monologium or Soliloquy,[1] reveals the twofold purpose referred to above, the apologetic and the religious. In it he undertook in the first place to demonstrate the existence of God on the basis of reason alone without appealing to authority. Since there are many goods of various kinds it is necessary to believe that there is one supreme good through which they are all good. In the same way we are compelled to recognize that there is one being greater and higher than all others through whom they all exist. An infinite regress, Anselm claims, is unthinkable and we must therefore assume an original self-existent being to which all else is due. This is the familiar cosmological argument from contingent to necessary being, though phrased, it must be admitted, in somewhat awkward fashion. There is a great show of logic in the discussion but the logic is largely verbal and the argument is full of unfounded assumptions. For instance, it is impious, Anselm says, to suppose that the supreme Being is liable to change or corruption, but why there is no attempt to show. The truth is the absolute unchangeableness of God had been a theological axiom for generations. Anselm therefore simply took it for granted and felt no need of arguing about it.

Having proved to his satisfaction the existence of God Anselm devoted the remainder of the work to a consideration

[1] *De divinitatis essentia monologium.*

of his nature, thus carrying out the second purpose of the treatise. The original self-existent Being, through which all others exist and to which they owe such excellence and such greatness as they possess, must be the greatest and best of all beings. "It is necessary that it be living, wise, powerful and all-powerful, true, just, blessed, eternal, and similarly whatever is better than all that is not it."[1]

But it is not enough to say that the supreme Being is just, wise, powerful and the like, for one is just through participation in justice, wise through participation in wisdom and so on, and this would mean that the supreme Being is not this or that of itself but because of something else.[2] We must, therefore, say that the supreme Being is justice and wisdom and power. The just man is not justice, but possesses justice; the supreme Being is justice itself. "It is supreme being, supreme life, supreme reason, supreme safety, supreme justice, supreme wisdom, supreme truth, supreme goodness, supreme greatness, supreme beauty, supreme immortality, supreme incorruptibility, supreme immutability, supreme blessedness, supreme eternity, supreme unity, which is nothing else than to be supremely, to live supremely and the like."[3]

Though the supreme Being is all these he is nevertheless simple and indivisible, not made up of parts; he is wholly everywhere at all times; he is above space and time, not contained in them as things are. Things are not simply present in space and time, they are bounded by them as God is not. We may say that God is everywhere but in another sense than things. We may say with equal truth that he is nowhere.[4] This does not mean that Anselm involved himself in the paradoxes of the negative theology of Dionysius and the Neoplatonists. As a matter of fact he was quite free

[1] Chap. 15.
[2] The realism of all this is interesting.
[3] Chap. 16.
[4] Chap. 23.

from that sort of thing. It only means that he was trying to say that God's relation to space and time is very different from that of men and things.

The supreme Being, Anselm goes on to say, is without beginning and end; he is immutable; he may be called substance, for the essence of anything is usually called substance; but he is different from all other substance and far above it, and he exists in such a manner that other things in comparison with him can hardly be said to exist at all. They are not wholly non-existent to be sure, for through the supreme Being they have been made something from nothing.[1] The moderation of Anselm's statements in contrast with those of many other theologians is noticeable. Though his doctrine of God, in the Monologium at any rate, was more philosophical than religious he did not indulge in the speculative flights for instance of an Eriugena. The truth is he had no such grandiose conception of the universe as Eriugena had. So far as he philosophized he did so within the limits of the traditional thinking of his day.

Having dealt with the nature of God Anselm turns next to God's expression of himself, the divine Word through whom all things were created. An amusing example of his habit of rationalizing accepted doctrines is his explanation of why it is fitting to speak of God and his Word as father and son rather than mother and daughter. The first and principal cause of offspring, he says, is in the father, and the son is always more like his father than the daughter is, "Hence it is most true that the supreme spirit is father of his offspring," and "that his offspring is not a daughter but a son." [2]

The supreme Being loves himself, and this love Anselm identifies, in traditional fashion, with the Holy Spirit. Though he discusses the doctrine of the Trinity at some length and tries to rationalize the distinction of the three

[1] Chaps. 17–28.　　　　[2] Chap. 42.

persons (or substances as he prefers to call them) by comparing them with human memory, intelligence and love,[1] he admits finally that the mystery is incomprehensible and that the most one can do is to accept the truth of the doctrine, which is beyond all question.

Man was created to love the supreme Being above all other things, indeed nothing else at all except because of him, for he is good in himself and nothing else is good unless through him. But love is possible only where there is knowledge, and hence it is man's duty to devote all his powers to knowing God. Man was also created to love God everlastingly; hence he must be immortal. If he loves God he never dies. And God gives to the one that loves him not some lesser good or some lesser blessedness but himself, the supreme goodness, to be enjoyed through all eternity.[2] On the other hand the soul that despises the supreme good will suffer eternal misery. Annihilation is not bad enough for such a one, for reason demands that the guilty person shall not be as well off as if he had never existed and had never despised God.[3]

After writing his Monologium, which Anselm says was made up of many arguments, he began to ask himself whether there might not be found a single proof of the existence of God which would require no other for its support.[4] The result was his famous ontological argument, a contribution of his own, which he set forth in a treatise entitled Proslogion or Address.[5] The Proslogion is even briefer than the Monologium and the greater part of it is devotional rather than argumentative in character and takes the form of an address to God after the style of Augustine's Confessions. The argument is contained in the second

---

[1] As Augustine had done before him. See above, p. 87.
[2] Chaps. 68–70. [3] Chap. 71.
[4] As a matter of fact the *Monologium* contains only one general argument for God's existence though phrased in different forms.
[5] *Proslogion seu alloquium de Dei existentia.*

chapter and runs as follows — to give Anselm's summary of it in his own words. "Even the fool is convinced
that there is something, at any rate in the understanding,
than which nothing greater can be conceived, for when he
hears this he understands it, and whatever is understood is in
the understanding. And certainly that than which a greater
cannot be conceived cannot exist in the understanding alone.
For if it be in the understanding alone, it is possible to conceive it as existing in reality, which is greater. If therefore
that than which a greater cannot be conceived is in the understanding alone, that very thing than which a greater cannot
be conceived is one than which a greater can be conceived.
But this assuredly cannot be. Without any doubt therefore
there exists something both in the understanding and in
reality than which a greater cannot be conceived."

Anselm's argument called forth a brief reply from a contemporary, the monk Gaunilo of Marmoutier, who took up
the cudgels in behalf of 'the fool who says in his heart
there is no God.' In answer to his objections Anselm repeated his argument at greater length and expounded it in
some detail in his Liber apologeticus contra Gaunilonem.
There is nothing however in the expanded version of it that
needs comment here. The original form in the second
chapter of the Proslogion remains the best and clearest
statement of it that exists.

Though Guanilo's reply was acute and of a sort to throw
suspicion on all argumentation from idea to reality it did not
touch the heart of Anselm's argument that to exist both in the
understanding and in reality is greater than to exist in the
understanding alone. It was not until Kant indeed that the
unsoundness of this cardinal assumption was fully exposed.[1]
But though no adequate answer was forthcoming for seven
hundred years the argument did not generally commend

[1] See my *Rise of Modern Religious Ideas*, pp. 55 ff.

itself and was used by none of the great schoolmen of the Middle Ages.

Except for its early chapters containing the ontological argument the Proslogion is taken up with a description of God similar to that in the Monologium though more devotional and less apologetic and argumentative in form. It is interesting that although, as remarked above, Anselm did not go with the Neoplatonists and certain of the Fathers in denying all attributes and even being itself to God, he did assert that God is passionless (passion being a form of weakness) and drew the conclusion that he does not feel pity for those that suffer but only treats them as if he did. "How art thou at the same time compassionate and impassible? For if thou art impassible thou dost not feel pity; if thou dost not feel pity thy heart is not made miserable by sympathy with the miserable, which is what it means to be compassionate. But if thou art not compassionate whence do the miserable receive so great consolation? How then, Lord, art thou both compassionate and not compassionate, unless because thou art compassionate from our point of view but art not compassionate in thyself? Thou art so indeed in our sense and not in thine. For when thou lookest upon us miserable men we experience the effect of compassion, but thou dost not experience the feeling. Thou art therefore both compassionate because thou savest the miserable and sparest those that sin against thee, and not compassionate because thou art not affected by sympathy with misery." [1]

This is characteristic of Anselm's general attitude. For all his piety, which was both deep and genuine, and for all his emphasis on loving God as well as knowing him, God was conceived chiefly in philosophical terms and was thought of as the supreme Being, than whom no greater can be conceived, rather than as a loving father. That Anselm himself

[1] *Proslogion*, 8.

felt the difficulty is suggested by such a passage as the following: "Hast thou found, my soul, what thou didst seek? Thou didst seek God and didst find him to be that which is highest of all, than which nothing better can be conceived. And thou didst find that this being is life itself, light, wisdom, goodness, eternal blessedness and blessed eternity and that he is everywhere and always. For if thou hast not found thy God, how is he this being which thou hast found and which thou hast conceived him to be with so sure truth and so true certitude? If indeed thou hast found him wherefore dost thou not feel that thou hast found him? Why, Lord God, doth my soul not feel thee if it hath found thee?" [1] The contrast between Anselm and Augustine at this point is very marked. There was no such fusion in Anselm of the theologian and the religious devotee as in Augustine. Knowledge of God there might be and love for him, but despite the devout language of the Proslogion it testifies only to an intellectual conception of God not to an immediate experience of him. And the same is true in large measure even of the devotional tracts and of the meditations and prayers in which Anselm's piety came to beautiful and often moving expression. Whatever else he was, and however profound his religious emotions, he was not a mystic in any genuine sense. He belonged, in fact, rather in the native Latin tradition than in the tradition of Dionysius and the Neoplatonists.

The only other work of Anselm's that needs mention is his Cur deus homo, the most famous of all. In it, again with unbelievers in mind, he undertook to show the necessity of the incarnation by the use of reason alone without appealing to authority as he had undertaken in the Monologium and Proslogion to demonstrate the existence of God. The work, which is about the same length as the Monologium,

---

[1] *Proslogion*, 14.

is divided into two books and is in the form of a dialogue between Anselm himself and one of his pupils. Though the reasoning is for the most part acute the work is repetitious and ill-arranged and contains many digressions which interrupt the course of the argument. Anselm's general theory, however, is clear enough and may be summarized as follows.

Every rational creature is bound to obey God. If he always paid God what he owed him he would never sin. To sin is nothing else than to withhold from God his due. But this is to rob and dishonour him.[1] Justice (justice both to God himself and to the general order of things) demands either that God be repaid for the loss he has incurred or that the offender be punished. In either event his authority over the creature is maintained and thus his honour vindicated. But to punish all men everlastingly — and justice demands that the punishment of the wicked be everlasting as the reward of the good is — would defeat the divine purpose in creation, for man was made to be eternally happy in the enjoyment of God. Consequently, for his own sake, quite apart from any consideration for the human race, God must save at least some men, enough at any rate to make up for the number of fallen angels. This he can do only if adequate satisfaction be given. Man cannot give it, since all men are sinners and one sinner cannot justify another. Indeed a man cannot even atone for his own sins, for all the self-denial and asceticism he may practise in the effort to do so he owes in any event to God who rightfully demands of him all that he has and is and can become.[2] Moreover, even the least of sins is greater than can be compensated for by the whole world or by an infinity of

[1] Bk. I. chap. 11. The argument begins with this chapter.
[2] I. 20. This really undermines the assumption on which the whole theory of penance is based, but there is no sign that Anselm drew the application

worlds. Only a being superior to all that is not God, only God himself in fact, is great enough to render satisfaction even for the smallest sin. But it is man that owes it, for he is the offender. Therefore only one who was both God and man, that is, Christ alone, could render the needed satisfaction and he could do it in no other way than by offering God something that he did not owe him and that God could not demand as his right. But God justly demands of every rational being complete obedience to his will. Christ therefore owed him obedience on his own account and could not atone for others' sins even by a life of perfect holiness. One thing, however, he was under no obligation to do and that was to lay down his life, for as he was not a sinner death had no claim upon him.[1] Consequently by dying he could make satisfaction for human sin and he could do it in no other way. As his life, the life of the God-man, was of infinite value, his death was sufficient to atone not for some sins merely but for the sins of all the world and even infinitely more. In order that his sacrifice of himself might be efficacious it was necessary that he be not only sinless, and hence under no obligation to die, but also omnipotent and hence able not to die. In other words he must die not under compulsion but of his own free will. As a reward for freely offering up his life all are saved that accept him and are his. His death does not avail for the reconciliation of Satan and the fallen angels; they could be reconciled only by the death of a God-angel, not of a God-man.

Thus Anselm undertook to prove that the incarnation and death of the Son of God were necessary and grounded in the very nature of things. In this he went beyond all

---

[1] Though Christ took on human nature he was not a sinner, for Mary was purified from sin before his birth (II. 16). Cf. Anselm's *Liber de conceptu virginali et originali peccato*, chap. 8 ff.

his predecessors. Some of his ideas were anticipated by others, but the notion that God must have saved man in this particular way and in no other was wholly new and was typical of Anselm's general attitude. His theory was important also among other things because it excluded the old notion shared even by Augustine that Christ by his death paid a price to the devil and thus made it possible for God to release men from his control. Anselm attacked the notion directly [1] and the whole weight of his theory was against it.

It is to be noticed that, according to Anselm, Christ was not punished for the sins of men but rendered satisfaction for them. The interlocutor Boso objected that for the innocent to bear the punishment of the guilty was not just [2] — an objection often brought against the Anselmic theory. But the objection, as Anselm showed, is misplaced. For though according to the traditional Protestant doctrine of the atonement, often wrongly called the Anselmic, this is exactly what happens, according to Anselm Christ did not bear the punishment of the guilty but gave his life as a satisfaction for their sins and thus made punishment unnecessary. The theory is of a piece with the Catholic doctrine of penance and was based upon the same presuppositions. Every sin is an affront to God and must be punished or made good in some other way: according to the doctrine of penance by penitential acts of one or another sort, according to the Anselmic theory of Christ's work by the payment of his life. Already by Augustine and Gregory Christ's death had been connected with penance, but the matter was left vague and indefinite as was the whole subject of his part in the salvation of men. Anselm was the first western theologian to bring clearness out of obscurity and to frame a consistent and coherent theory. The contrast with the

[1] Cf. I. 7.   [2] I. 8.

theory of Irenæus which underlay all eastern thought upon the subject is very striking. While with Irenæus the emphasis was on the incarnation, with Anselm in spite of the title of his work the emphasis was on the death ; and while Irenæus thought chiefly in physical and mystical terms, the thinking of Anselm was controllingly ethical and legal.[1] The two theories are genuinely typical, the one of the eastern, the other of the western way of looking at things.

It has been maintained by certain scholars that the principle on which Anselm's theory was built — the assumption, namely, that every sin must be followed either by punishment or by satisfaction — was taken over from German law and represents something new in Christian thinking. The fact is the principle referred to underlay the whole penitential system and dates from primitive days. All that Anselm did was to make the relation between God and man presupposed by it the basis for a carefully wrought-out theory of Christ's work which, in accordance with his wonted practice, he claimed could be rationally demonstrated. The premises of his argument were ancient not mediæval ; the method of argumentation was characteristically his own and proved acceptable to few.

It has also been contended that Anselm's theory reveals the influence of feudalism and is thus an example of the way Christian thinking is controlled by the social and political environment.[2] It is difficult, however, to see anything peculiarly feudal in the theory. If the emphasis on the honour of God may seem congenial to the age of

[1] In this connection attention may be called to Anselm's statement (*De fide trinitatis*, 4) that in the incarnation man was brought into union not with the divine nature but with a divine person, the Son of God. "For he who rightly understands his incarnation, believes that he took man up into a unity not of nature but of person." The difference of emphasis between this and the eastern idea of salvation through deification is very marked.

[2] For instance by Shailer Mathews in his book, *The Atonement and the Social Process* (1930), chap. VIII.

chivalry (as suggested by Menegoz) it should be noticed that such emphasis was not new. Tertullian, for instance, made much of the divine honour, as was seen in an earlier chapter. The truth is, Anselm's theory is an example less of the influence of contemporary conditions than of the application of logic to traditional beliefs and customs. The Cur deus homo is thus of a piece with the Monologium and the Proslogion and like them is an illustration of Anselm's general theological method.

Anselm's fame as a theologian rests chiefly on his ontological argument for the existence of God and on his theory of the atonement. But even more important, at any rate for the thinking of the Middle Ages, was his claim that the accepted doctrines of the Catholic church, including even such as the incarnation and death of Christ, could be demonstrated without recourse to revelation, by the use of reason alone. The claim engaged the attention of most of the theologians of the next few centuries and their varying attitudes toward it form an important chapter in the history of western Catholic thought. That the claim could be taken seriously even by those who did not approve it, or approved it only in part, is one of the most striking differences between that age and our own.

CHAPTER IX

ABELARD

"HE that believes quickly is light minded." These words from Ecclesiasticus may fairly be taken as the motto of the present chapter. They were quoted by Abelard in his so-called Introduction to Theology and they admirably represent his general attitude. Born in 1079 at Le Pallet in Brittany, the eldest son of a noble house, he early turned his back on the career of a feudal lord and gave himself to the pursuit of learning. With a high regard for his own powers and a contempt for the abilities of others he combined a contentious temper which kept him constantly at war. He delighted in measuring wits with his teachers and exposing their weak points and when he disagreed with them no feelings of piety restrained him from attacking them publicly and in the most contemptuous terms.

He was a pupil for a time of the nominalist Roscellin, who was then teaching in Brittany, and later of the famous realist William of Champeaux, head of the Cathedral school in Paris. He broke with both of them, however, and they were for many years among his bitterest foes. His own doctrine of universals — in effect a moderate Aristotelian realism — is set out with sufficient clearness in his Glosses on Porphyry,[1] the best example of his dialectical method. He repudiated William's realism, denying that universals exist before particulars and independently of them, but

[1] Aristotle's *Categories* and Porphyry's *Isagoge*, both translated into Latin by Boethius, were the principal text-books on logic in Abelard's day.

he also rejected the extreme nominalism of Roscellin who maintained that universals are mere words and devoid of all reality. Among his contemporaries he was known as a nominalist and his position was actually nearer Roscellin's than William's. With the former he recognized the individual as alone real in the strict sense, holding that there is no general substance but only particular substances. But he maintained that a genus or species has reality in a secondary sense, in that the individuals that constitute it are bound together by the possession of identical qualities which actually reside in the things themselves and are not merely the products of our imagination.

Abelard early set up for himself as a teacher of philosophy, that is particularly of dialectics or logic. In that age logic was widely regarded as the principal road to truth, the chief way by which we may pass from the known to the unknown. With intellectual men it had the same standing as the scientific method has now. It was generally believed that being and thought are in such a sense consonant with each other that by sound thinking objective reality may be discovered and its nature known. The laws of thought therefore were studied with the utmost diligence, and throughout a considerable part of the twelfth century they made up the burden of philosophical discussion and instruction.

Abelard's success as a teacher was immediate and extraordinary. Owing to the influence of William, whose authority was supreme in Paris, he was unable to get a foothold there, but he established himself in the immediate vicinity where students flocked to him from far and wide and in ever increasing numbers. He soon became the most celebrated teacher and the most formidable dialectician of his generation and as his fame grew William's steadily declined. Ambitious to try his powers in what was generally recognized as the highest intellectual pursuit he turned finally to theology, studying for a brief period with a certain Anselm of Laon, not to be confounded with his greater namesake of Canterbury. Though Anselm of Laon was the most famous theological teacher of the day Abelard speedily decided that he was unworthy of his high reputation and treated him with his usual disdain. Years later he wrote of him: "He was wonderfully fluent in his use of words, but poor in matter and empty of reason. When he kindled a fire he filled the house with smoke, he did not adorn it with light." [1] By his contemptuous attitude he won Anselm's hostility and made lifelong enemies of some of his pupils, a circumstance, as the event proved, of tragic consequence for Abelard himself.

As a teacher of theology he repeated his earlier success, this time in Paris, William meanwhile having left to become Bishop of Châlons sur Marne. Abelard's tragic love affair with Heloise, which drove him humiliated and disgraced into a monastery, while it destroyed all hope of high preferment, did not put an end to his career as a scholar or his influence and popularity as a teacher. His most important theological work was done after he became a monk and his reputation as a theologian grew apace. Theology was now his chief concern and, though at the urgent request of his students he still taught dialectics, he used philosophy, as he says, only as a bait for religion.[2] Though it was not religion that made a monk of him or a nun of Heloise, in course of time he became deeply pious, and rigorous and ascetic in his ethical principles. He was indeed a different man in many ways, but he still remained primarily a scholar and teacher and his critical temper underwent no change.

From the time he became a monk his career was a troubled cne. He was almost constantly in difficulties and was seldom able to remain long at peace. In the famous abbey

---

[1] *Historia calamitatum*, 3.   [2] *Ibid.* 8.

of St. Denis near Paris, where he began his monastic life, he made permanent enemies of his superiors and his fellow monks by throwing doubt upon the identity of its patron saint with Dionysius the Areopagite, convert of the apostle Paul. At the monastery of St. Gildas in Brittany where he was later abbot, he was so unpopular with the inmates because of the rigor of his discipline that he was finally obliged to abandon the place altogether. In 1121 at the Council of Soissons, as the result of a campaign instituted by two pupils of Anselm of Laon, his work on the Trinity, possibly his first theological production, was condemned and he was compelled with his own hand to consign it to the flames. But in spite of all his troubles he continued to teach as opportunity offered, part of the time in Paris or its neighborhood, part of the time elsewhere, and always his courses were thronged by eager students, even when given in the most inauspicious surroundings.

In later years he was unfortunate enough to incur the animosity of Bernard of Clairvaux, ecclesiastically the most influential man of the day and religiously of an altogether different type from Abelard. It was due chiefly to Bernard that Abelard himself was condemned as a heretic at the Council of Sens in 1141 and that Pope Innocent II approved the decision of the Council. To be sure the sentence was not carried out. Abelard still had his friends and supporters and found a refuge at the famous monastery of Cluny where he was highly honoured and was given charge of the studies of his fellows. The following year, however, he died a disillusioned and broken man.

In an autobiographical sketch entitled Historia calamitatum he ascribes most of his troubles to the envy of other scholars and theologians who for years, according to his own account, did all they could to destroy him. At the same time he admits his own pride and arrogance and recognizes that the ill-will which he inspired was in part at least his own fault. The truth is while personal animosity had something to do with the harsh treatment accorded him by the ecclesiastical authorities his general theological attitude was chiefly responsible for it, that is, not so much heretical views on particular doctrines as the rationalistic tendency and temper which marked much of his work and seemed to many to threaten the very foundations of the faith. He was not indeed a sceptic, as was widely thought, nor even a rationalist in any thoroughgoing sense. But the common habit of believing in religious matters whatever one was told to believe without asking whether it was reasonable he had no patience with. Though the words "intelligo ut credam" often ascribed to him are not really his they fairly represent his position. That one should fully understand a doctrine before accepting it he did not assert, but he maintained that one should at least have some perception of its meaning and should be convinced that it was not irrational if one were to give it his assent. He did not contend that belief must wait upon proof and that no doctrine was to be accepted until it had been rationally demonstrated — Anselm's conviction that the tenets of the Christian faith can be shown to be necessary, and are therefore demonstrable in the strict sense, he did not share. But he was sure they must be in harmony with reason or they could not be true.[1]

Abelard opposed all compulsion in matters of faith. Belief, he maintained, should be free and no one should be forced to accept what seemed to him untrue or condemned for not accepting it. His individualism at this point was of a piece with his individualism in ethics.[2] Freedom of investigation and discussion he championed over and over

[1] Cf. *e.g.* his *Introductio ad theologiam*, Bk. II. chap. 3. For Abelard's ideas touching the relation of faith and reason, see particularly Deutsch, *Peter Abälard*, pp. 116 ff.

[2] See below, p. 215.

again and not always merely in his own interest. Even heretics he insisted should be reasoned with, not subjected to force. To be sure his denunciation of Roscellin as a heretic to the Bishop of Paris was hardly in accord with this principle, but he was moved in that case by personal animosity and by the report that Roscellin was about to treat him in the same way.

Though he insisted on the application of reason to the doctrines of the Christian system he was not, as has been already said, a thoroughgoing rationalist, for he believed in a divine revelation and recognized the authority of the Scriptures. What was plainly written in the Bible, he maintained, was to be accepted without question. He deprecated, however, the practice of reading into the sacred text all sorts of things that were not there, and his own exegesis was as a rule uncommonly sober and restrained. Moreover he had a broad view of inspiration. It was not confined, so he held, to the biblical authors, but was shared by philosophers and sages of many lands. And it did not consist in external control or in the imparting of truth from without, but in such enlightenment of the mind as enables a man to discover truth for himself. This inspiration the biblical writers had in large measure — some to be sure in larger measure than others — and as a consequence they could speak with peculiar authority.

Abelard's view of inspiration was very modern, but it did not lead him to doubt the full authority of the Bible.[1] At this point he was one with the common sentiment of the church. On the other hand he disagreed with the church at large in his estimate of the Fathers whose writings were generally recognized as authoritative, and whose opinions were supposed to be binding on the conscience of all Chris-

---

[1] He recognized, it is true, that some of the biblical writers might conceivably have erred but he nowhere treats this possibility as an actuality.

tians. Though he made large use of them and was as glad as anyone else to claim their support when he found himself in harmony with them, he did not regard them as infallible. He was well aware that they differed with each other in many and important matters and he made it his business to point out their disagreements in order to undermine the belief in their infallibility, which he was convinced tended to destroy all independence and make the free use of reason in religion impossible.

His famous work entitled Sic et non (Yes and No) was compiled with this end in view. In the prologue he declares that many seeming discrepancies among the Fathers are apparent only. Sometimes they are due to a corruption of the text, sometimes the fault is ours. For instance we may misunderstand their statements, may interpret figurative language literally, may ascribe to them heretical opinions which they quote only to refute, or may commit other similar blunders. The consequence is that they often seem farther apart than they really are. But if after all allowances are made contradictions still remain we ought not to accuse the Fathers of sin but only of ignorance. In so vast a mass of writings it is not strange that there are mistakes and we should not be troubled by them, for we are under no obligation to follow the Fathers as we are to follow Scripture. On the contrary we are at liberty to pass judgment upon their opinions and to reject those that seem erroneous.

The work Sic et non itself is made up wholly of patristic quotations so arranged as to show the disagreements of the Fathers, real or apparent, on a large variety of topics, theological, ethical, ecclesiastical, historical and the like. The topics are phrased in the form of propositions, of which there are no fewer than a hundred and fifty-eight. Among them are such as the following, to quote only a few at random: That we should believe in one God; that he is

triune; that he is the cause of evil; that Christ became
flesh; that he was ignorant; that the creature is to be
worshipped; that all the Apostles had wives except John;
that Peter and Paul and the other Apostles are equal; that
James the Just, the brother of the Lord, wrote the first of
the seven canonical epistles; that without baptism no one
can be saved; that the works of the saints do not justify a
man; that lying and killing are permitted; that Cain was
not damned. Under each of the headings utterances of the
Fathers are quoted first in support of the proposition and
then against it. Thus the first section is headed: "That
faith must be supported by human reasons, and the contrary," [1] and quotations pro and con are then given from
Gregory, Augustine, Ambrose, Jerome, Isidore, Hilary,
Bede and others.

Some of the propositions are such that differences of
opinion concerning them might be thought of little consequence; others have to do with the very foundations of
the faith or with the official dogmas of the church. A lack
of harmony on such matters could seem nothing less than a
scandal. To be sure the quotations from the Fathers are
not always as contradictory as the phrasing of the proposition suggests. Sometimes the divergencies are slight and
concern only minor details; occasionally no negative
utterances at all are quoted. But the general impression
is that of serious disagreement over a wide range of subjects more or less vitally connected with the Christian faith.
No solutions are offered and no attempt is made to reconcile the differences. The quotations are simply left to
speak for themselves. Abelard says in the prologue that
he compiled the work in order that young readers might be
incited to search out the truth and might be made more

---

[1] "Quod fides humanis rationibus sit adstruenda, et contra." This is the
regular form but sometimes "et non" is substituted for "et contra."

acute by the searching. "For by doubting," he goes on, "we come to inquiry, by inquiry we discover the truth" — a general statement which he fortifies by a quotation from Aristotle. However sound the pedagogical principle the very suggestion that the disagreements among the Fathers be exploited for the purpose of training the minds of the young shows how far Abelard was from sharing the common reverence for them. It is abundantly evident indeed that the real purpose of the work was to demonstrate that the Fathers were fallible and were not to be followed without question.

In spite of his attitude toward them it was not Abelard's wish, as many of his contemporaries supposed, to undermine Christianity or to get rid of the supernatural element in it. He was an apologist for Christianity not an opponent of it. Like many a modern liberal he simply desired to make it more acceptable to intelligent men and with this end in view he undertook to show its rationality and where necessary to interpret it in such ways as to bring it more fully into accord with the best thinking of the age. His brief treatise on the Trinity,[1] which was condemned at the Council of Soissons in 1121, admirably illustrates his general interest. It was not intended as an attack on the Trinitarian dogma. On the contrary it was written at the request of his students to make the doctrine more comprehensible and thus strengthen rather than weaken faith. In support of it he quotes from the Bible, both Old Testament and New, from the Fathers, and even from pagan philosophers.[2] With the evident

---

[1] *De unitate et trinitate divina;* discovered and published by R. Stölzle: *Abaelards 1121 zu Soissons verurtheilter Tractatus de unitate et trinitate divina* (1891).

[2] He refers particularly to Plato's doctrine of the anima mundi and to ideas of the Logos current among the Greeks. His quotations from pagan writers came to him chiefly by way of Augustine and Lactantius. His knowledge of Greek, as he elsewhere confesses, was meagre and his acquaintance with Greek authors limited.

intention of justifying himself for appealing to the philosophers he declares that they taught faith and immortality and
virtue and he emphasizes the nobility of their lives and their
contempt of the world which contrast favorably with the
conduct of many Christians.[1]

After quoting testimonies in the first book in support of
belief in the Trinity Abelard appeals in the second book to
reason. He begins with an attack on the "sophists" or those
"professors of dialectics" who abuse the art instead of
making the proper use of it, and who oppose the established
doctrine. Among these dialecticians he evidently had his
old teacher Roscellin chiefly in mind though he does not
mention him by name. While attacking the dialecticians he
commends dialectics in strong terms, appealing to Augustine
and others in its behalf. All knowledge is good even the
knowledge of evil. Without it we cannot avoid sin and
without a knowledge of heresy we cannot guard ourselves
against the false teachings of the heretics.[2] Pride and
arrogance, to be sure, are to be avoided and the notion that
everything can be discovered by human reason. We must
recognize that all true knowledge comes from God and that
we cannot know him unless he reveals himself. It is profitable
indeed to believe what cannot be explained, for according to
Gregory "faith that is supported by human reason has no
merit." But because many will not listen to authority and
demand reasons before believing we will answer the foolish
according to their folly and endeavor to conquer them with
their own weapons.[3]

After thus clearing the way for the use of dialectics Abelard
employs it freely in the remainder of the work, undertaking
to show that the oneness and the threeness of the Godhead if
properly understood do no violence to sound reason. His

[1] *De unitate et trinitate divina*, Bk. I. chap. 5 (p. 15 ff.).
[2] *Ibid*. Bk. II. p. 22.   [3] *Ibid*. p. 27 ff.

own interpretation of the doctrine was similar to Augustine's though not identical. The three persons he represented not as individual beings or substances, and not as persons in the ordinary sense, but as attributes or properties of the one individual and simple substance God. The Father is power, the Son wisdom, the Holy Spirit beneficence or goodness.[1] God is triune in that he is all powerful, wise and good. If omnipotence or wisdom or goodness be lacking he is not truly God; only as his power is directed by wisdom and used for beneficent ends is it divine power. Thus God is necessarily triune. Unless he be at once powerful, wise and good, that is unless he be at once Father, Son and Spirit, he is not God. "In these three, namely, power, wisdom and benignity, the entire perfection of the good consists and whichever of them is without the other two must be thought little of. For if he that is powerful know not how to do wisely what he is able to do, his power is pernicious and deadly. If on the other hand he be wise and discreet in action but has little power, he is ineffective. While if he be powerful and wise but without benignity, he is the more liable to do harm because his power and wisdom enable him to accomplish what he will." [2] "Two things make us obey God, fear and love. Power and wisdom inspire us chiefly with fear, for we know that he is able to punish errors and that nothing can be hidden from him. But his benignity leads to love so that we love him best whom we find most benevolent." [3]

Abelard's interpretation of the Father as power, of the Son as wisdom and of the Spirit as goodness did not mean that he thought of the Father alone as powerful, of the Son alone as wise and of the Spirit alone as beneficent. On the

---

[1] In speaking of the Holy Spirit he uses the words benignitas, caritas and bonitas. It is interesting that goodness or love is made the characteristic mark not of the Father but of the Spirit, fatherhood being taken to connote power rather than affection.

[2] *Ibid.* Bk. I. chap. 2 (p. 3).　　　　[3] *Ibid.* p. 4.

contrary, though power is the characteristic mark of the Father, wisdom of the Son, and goodness of the Spirit, it is the one God who is powerful and wise and beneficent all at once.[1]

In his Historia calamitatum (chapter 9) Abelard tells us that he was accused at Soissons of teaching tritheism. Certainly there is no sign of anything of the kind in his treatise on the Trinity. On the contrary it looks rather in the direction of Sabellianism and we are not surprised to learn that some criticised it on that account. The accusation of tritheism was probably due to the fact that Abelard was known to have rejected the traditional realism and to the consequent assumption that he must agree with his teacher Roscellin, the famous nominalist, who had been attacked by Anselm of Canterbury and whose "tritheism" had been condemned at an earlier council of Soissons. The truth of the matter is that Abelard agreed neither with Anselm nor with Roscellin. He did not conceive of God as a universal divine substance which is individualized in three persons, Father, Son and Spirit, but as a unique, single and individual substance which is possessed of three properties: power, wisdom and goodness. Thus he avoided the tritheism of Roscellin without adopting the realism of Anselm.

Abelard was really as sound on the doctrine of the Trinity as Augustine and there was no reason why he should have been accused of heresy, at any rate for anything said in his extant treatise, unless because he tried to penetrate, as Augustine and many Fathers before him had done, the mysteries of the faith, and to make more comprehensible and thus profane a doctrine which multitudes of devout Christians believed should be accepted without investigation or elucidation. It is significant that when his opponents at Soissons tried to show his work heretical they were unable to do so

[1] *Ibid.* Bk. II. chap. 5.

and that it was finally condemned only because it had been issued without ecclesiastical license.[1]

Already in this little work there appears Abelard's interest, which he never lost, in the moral character of God. It was his desire to ethicize the idea of God through and through. Anything like pantheism — the identification of God with nature — was abhorrent to him. It was in part because of its pantheistic tendency that he opposed the realism of William of Champeaux. Always he insisted on the personality of God, his uniqueness and individuality, his freedom, his independence of the world, and the control of all his activities by moral ends.

A similar ethical interest appears very clearly in his doctrine of Christ's work which he set forth in his notable commentary on Paul's Epistle to the Romans.[2] In agreement with Anselm, whom however he did not mention, he repudiated the traditional notion that Christ by his death paid a price to Satan, but he also rejected Anselm's own doctrine. Instead of following him in teaching that the purpose of Christ's incarnation and death was to make it possible for God to forgive human sin without impairing the divine honour, Abelard maintained that there was nothing in the nature of God to hinder the free exercise of forgiveness and that the only impediment to it was in men not in God. Christ took on flesh and lived among men and died on the cross in order to reveal the love of God and thus arouse in them an answering love which is their reconciliation and redemption. The harmony of this with Abelard's general conception of God's character is apparent and it shows, in its contrast with Anselm's theory, how thoroughly he had ethicized the conception of God and how completely he had

---

[1] Cf. *Historia calamitatum*, 9.
[2] Ep. ad Romanos, Bk. II. chaps. III and v.   (Migne, vol. 178, cols. 831 ff. and 859 ff.)

freed it from all bondage to natural law or metaphysical determinism.

Some time after Abelard's tractate On the Divine Unity and Trinity had been condemned at Soissons he issued a revised edition of it under the title Theologia christiana,[1] a large work in five books which until Stölzle's discovery was supposed by many to be the work condemned at the council. It is more than four times as long as the original treatise, the expansion being due in part to the multiplication of quotations from the Bible, the Fathers and pagan writers, and to the fuller treatment of certain topics, in part to the addition of a long section (the whole of the fifth book) on monotheism, a subject not discussed in the earlier work. There are also many changes, mostly however of a minor character. Both the additions and the alterations were intended in the main to emphasize and clarify the points made in the earlier treatise, or in some cases to meet the criticisms that had been passed upon it. But in spite of them the tone and temper of the work as a whole remain unchanged as also the general line of argument.

The work on the Trinity exists in still a third edition, a considerable part of the Theologia christiana being reproduced in a somewhat abbreviated form in a general treatise on theology to which Abelard himself refers simply as Theologia, but which is commonly though incorrectly called Introductio ad theologiam.[2] At the beginning of the work he says that human salvation depends on three things: "fides, caritas et sacramentum," and he divides the work accordingly, thus departing from Augustine who in his Enchiridion had treated Christian doctrine under the three heads: faith, hope and love. Abelard's division was more practical and much truer to the existing situation, for the sacraments had as

---

[1] In Migne, vol. 178, cols. 1123–1330.
[2] Under the latter title in Migne, vol. 178, cols. 979–1114.

important a place in the life of the Christians of that age as faith and love, and demanded equal recognition.[1] The omission of hope he justified by remarking that faith includes hope as a genus a species, for faith may refer to both good and bad things, and to the present and past as well as the future, while hope has as its object only what is desirable and is yet to come. Faith he calls a judgment or opinion (existimatio) about things unseen — a definition that scandalized Bernard. Love is represented as primarily love for God, which is the sole ground of love both for one's neighbor and oneself and which should be the motive for all one does. Sacramentum is defined in agreement with Augustine as "a visible sign of the invisible grace of God." [2]

After these preliminary definitions Abelard turns to the subject of faith which is prior to both love and the sacraments and is "the foundation of all good things." The extant portion of the work, which breaks off abruptly before the conclusion of the third book, deals only with faith (the Catholic faith "without which no one can be saved")[3] and chiefly with the doctrine of the Trinity. The treatment of the doctrine though somewhat briefer is substantially identical with that in the Theologia christiana and the same is true of the discussion of monotheism that follows. But in one respect there is a marked difference between the two works. Whereas in the Theologia christiana as in the earlier Tractatus de unitate et trinitate divina Abelard had emphasized the importance of faith and the duty of accepting on authority even what one cannot understand, in the present work he laid chief stress on the need of knowledge and denounced at considerable length a faith that was quick to believe without understanding.[4] It was in this connection

[1] See Hugo of St. Victor's *De sacramentis*, I. 8 : 1.
[2] *Introductio ad theologiam*, Bk. I. chap. 2.
[3] *Ibid*. Bk. I. chap. 4.   [4] *Ibid*. Bk. II. chap. 3.

that he quoted from Ecclesiasticus the saying "He that believes quickly is light minded," a quotation lacking in the Theologia christiana. It was in this connection too that he undertook to show that the words of Gregory, "Faith that is supported by human reason has no merit," which he had quoted with approval in the earlier work, must not be employed to discredit the use of reason in religion. What had occurred to cause this change of emphasis — for it was chiefly a matter of emphasis — we do not know. But as time passed Abelard seems to have become increasingly aware, probably as a result of his own unhappy experiences, that the truth had more to fear from orthodox traditionalists than from heretics and outsiders; from a too easy faith than from a too rigorous rationalism. The impression is confirmed by his famous Dialogue, the latest, or at any rate one of the latest, of his writings and the most radical of them all.

The loss of the latter part of Abelard's general work on theology, covering presumably the Christian life and the means of grace, is compensated for in a measure by the preservation of a portion of his treatise on ethics, which was written some time later.[1] The work reveals his controlling moral interest in its sharp attack on indulgences and his relative indifference to ecclesiastical requirements in its statement that while the forgiveness of sins is ordinarily conditioned on repentance, confession and satisfaction, only repentance is really essential. The same interest appears also in his emphasis on human freedom and independence, an emphasis more in the spirit of Pelagius than of Augustine. Characteristic too is the insistence that virtue depends wholly on intention; not on the character of the deed done, but solely on the motive that prompts it.[2] To be sure there

[1] *Ethica seu liber dictus scito te ipsum* (in Migne, vol. 178, cols. 633–678). The *Theologia* is referred to in chapter 23. [2] *Ethica*, chaps. 3 ff.

is no sin if the will does not come to expression in action ; to desire a woman is not wrong but only to yield to the desire. But when desire bears fruit in deed it is the intention with which the deed is committed not the deed itself that determines moral character. No act is sinful unless it be against the conscience. Abelard even went so far as to declare that the persecutors did not commit sin when they put the martyrs to death as long as they thought they were doing right.[1]

Rarely has subjectivity in ethics been carried further than in this work of Abelard's. When virtue is thus interpreted wholly in terms of personal merit, and as a matter of conscience alone, the dynamic which should reside in Christianity for the betterment of society is all too apt to be wanting. It is one of the most astounding and lamentable failures of historic Christianity that there has been so little advance in ethical ideals, and in the means for realizing them, since Christianity came upon the scene. But this is to wander from our subject.

I referred above to Abelard's Dialogue,[2] the most radical and probably the latest of all his works. Like most of his writings it exists only in an incomplete form. Whether it was never finished or has lost its conclusion is not certain, but the former seems more likely, for the work is referred to by none of Abelard's contemporaries and had it been published it could hardly have helped attracting wide attention. The participants in the dialogue are a philosopher, a Jew, and a Christian who appear to Abelard in a dream and debate the subject of religion in his presence that he may pass judgment upon the relative merits of the faiths they severally profess. In reply to his question why they have come they

[1] *Ethica*, chap. 13.
[2] *Dialogus inter philosophum, Judæum et Christianum* (in Migne, vol. 178, cols. 1611–1682). Cf. Deutsch, *Peter Abälard*, pp. 433 ff.

answer : "We are men belonging to diverse religious sects. To be sure we all alike profess ourselves worshippers of one God, but our service differs both in faith and life. One of us, a Gentile, of the number of those whom they call philosophers, is content with the natural law. The other two, of whom the first is a Jew and the second is called a Christian, have scriptures. After conferring and contending with each other for a long time concerning our different faiths we have come to submit the question to your judgment."

After Abelard has consented to act as judge the subject is debated at considerable length, first between the philosopher and the Jew, then between the philosopher and the Christian. As the philosopher does not recognize the validity of the Jewish and Christian Scriptures, it is agreed that the final appeal shall be to reason rather than authority, and the debate is carried on with that understanding. The Dialogue was not written primarily to promote religious tolerance, as is often said, or to show that all religions are at bottom one, and to liken it to Lessing's Nathan der Weise is wholly to misunderstand it. To be sure it is remarked in the introduction that there is good as well as bad in all religions and attention is called to the fact that all three of the interlocutors worship one God. But the main purpose of the work lay elsewhere, to show how in spite of its large measure of oneness with them Christianity transcends and surpasses both Judaism and natural religion. The Dialogue as a matter of fact is a genuine apology for Christianity conceived in a broad and tolerant spirit and with a full recognition of the excellences of other faiths, but none the less with the conviction that Christianity is better than they and that they find their true fulfilment in it. In its extant form the work breaks off abruptly without recording Abelard's decision, but already the narrowness and unphilosophical character of Judaism have been exposed by the philosopher, and he in his turn has been won by the Christian to an acknowledgment that Christianity is superior to the religion of nature and an advance upon it. To be sure it is not the common Christianity of the masses whose superiority is recognized. It is a Christianity reinterpreted and divested of many of its carnal features, such for instance as a local and literal heaven and hell. These are offensive to the Christian interlocutor as well as to the philosopher. Heaven, the Christian says, is communion with God and hell is separation from him.

The philosopher finally agrees with the Christian that the chief good (the summum bonum) whose meaning they have been discussing at length is not virtue but communion with God to which virtue leads, and in this definition of it Abelard himself evidently saw the fundamental difference between Christianity and natural religion. In other words, with all his approval of the philosopher's insistence on virtue he believed that in religion there was more than mere virtue and that this more was to be found in Christianity.

Not only the nature of the chief good was to have been discussed by the philosopher and the Christian but also the way to it. The Dialogue, however, as we have it, breaks off before this matter is reached. We are thus left in ignorance as to what Abelard would have included, or actually did include, as essential to final blessedness over and above virtue. In view of his sublimation of the common notions of the future life, one may fairly doubt whether he would have insisted on belief in the Trinity and the incarnation and other traditional elements of the Christian system elsewhere treated as fundamental. It may be that faced with this question, which might well seem to demand an altogether different answer in an apologetic work where the appeal was to reason rather than revelation, he found himself in such difficulties that he left his work unfinished and refrained from publishing it. This of course is mere surmise. But the very question suggests that there was need of a more thorough-going analysis and comparison of the rational and superrational elements in the Christian system than had yet been attempted. At this point as at many others the great schoolmen of the next century made important contributions.

In spite of his many enemies and his condemnation by both council and pope Abelard was enormously influential. His career indeed marked an epoch in the development of Christian thought. Among his pupils were several who later attained high place in the western church, theologians, bishops, cardinals, and even a pope (Alexander III). But his influence was not confined to his pupils. Many who had never heard him lecture, and many even who had never read his books, felt the impact of his ideas and looked at things differently because of him. This was true both of friends and foes. It was difficult in fact for anybody to escape his influence. Consciously or unconsciously, willingly or unwillingly, Christian thinkers for generations to come were affected both by his achievements and by his failures. His general way of looking at things, the problems he raised and the methods he employed in dealing with them, all helped to transform the intellectual climate of the age and to determine its interests.

More specific and definite was the effect of his general treatise on theology (commonly known as Introduction to Theology) and of his Sic et non. The former opened the way for a long series of systematic works which not only gave a peculiar tone to the Christian literature of succeeding centuries, but determined in no small degree the character and direction of Christian thinking. The latter, with its massing of authorities pro and con, became the standing model for the treatment of theological questions and had much to do with the shape they assumed and the solutions they received.

More general but of still greater moment was Abelard's influence in certain other lines. His attitude toward faith and reason brought the question of their relationship to the front and it remained for some time the central problem in theology. His attack on the realism of William of Champeaux and the nominalism of Roscellin forced a compromise which prepared the way for the ascendency of Aristotle in the west, and weakened permanently the age-long unity between Plato and the Catholic faith. Of all this there will be occasion to speak further as we go on. It is enough here simply to have called attention thus briefly to Abelard's exceptionally important place in the history of mediæval Christian thought.

CHAPTER X

BERNARD OF CLAIRVAUX AND FRANCIS
OF ASSISI

In the previous chapter I referred to Bernard of Clairvaux as an opponent of Abelard and a foe of all heresy, but he was much more than that. He was the greatest religious genius of the twelfth century and the principal figure in a religious movement which profoundly affected the life of the western church, and was not without its influence on the development of Christian thought.

As in theology the formal acceptance of the traditional system was followed ultimately by its rationalization and subjective appropriation, so in religion objective rites and ceremonies and means of grace ceased wholly to satisfy the growing spiritual needs of the western world and piety was becoming more and more a matter of inner experience rather than of mere external observance.[1] In the eleventh century this inner personal religion found frequent and sometimes deeply emotional expression in the writings of Peter Damiani, Othloh, Anselm and others, and in the twelfth century it spread rapidly and became widely dominant. Bernard was its most famous and in some respects its most important representative.

A younger contemporary of Abelard he was wholly unlike him in temper and attitude. Born of a noble family near Dijon in eastern France, he entered while still a youth the neighboring monastery of Citeaux, the parent house of the

[1] Cf. Seeberg, *Dogmengeschichte*[3], vol. III, p. 119.

Cistercians, taking with him his brothers and several friends. Here he showed himself so devout and zealous that he speedily gained a reputation for peculiar sanctity and before long was sent out to found a sister monastery at Clairvaux (Clara Vallis) whose abbot he remained for the rest of his life, wielding a growing influence in the church until he became the most commanding figure in western Christendom. During the later years of his life (he died in 1153) his authority was very great, not only in the monastic world but also in the church at large, and in governmental circles both ecclesiastical and civil.

He was an indefatigable letter writer and his correspondents included most of the leading personages of the day: crowned heads, nobles, popes, cardinals, archbishops, bishops and abbots. More than four hundred of his letters are still extant and constitute an important source for the history of the period. They show that he had always upon his conscience the duties of others as well as his own. They are filled with advice, often unsolicited, and with exhortations and warnings. He was quite without fear of those in high places and admonished them as freely as his equals or inferiors. Sometimes he was unpleasantly censorious and fault-finding; again his mood was gentler and more amiable. Several of his letters are delightful reading, others quite the opposite. Often he urges upon those that have been over severe a more lenient treatment of offenders and he frequently has wise things to say about the efficacy of sympathy and kindness rather than harshness and cruelty in the training of children. In disagreement with many of his contemporaries he opposed the persecution of the Jews; [1] but when there was any hint of heresy among Christians, or any suspicion of novelty in theological opinion, he could be bitter and uncompromising enough. Certain letters attacking Abelard show

---

[1] Cf. Eps. 363, 365.

his temper in this respect.[1] He was not content simply to denounce him or to show him wrong, he did all he could to organize a regular campaign against him. He was especially outraged by Abelard's presumption in appealing from the decision of the council of Sens to the Pope, and he urged his correspondents to bring pressure to bear upon the holy see to secure his condemnation.

A quotation or two may not be amiss in this connection. "His life, his conversation, and his books prove that Peter Abelard is a persecutor of the Catholic faith and an enemy of the cross of Christ. Outwardly he is a monk, but inwardly a heretic, having nothing of the monk about him save the name and the garment. His inexperienced auditors who have been but newly weaned from dialectic, and if I may say so are scarcely able to bear the first elements of the faith, he introduces to the mystery of the Trinity, to the holy of holies, to the chamber of the King, and to him who has made darkness his habitation.[2] Finally, with Arius our theologian distinguishes grades and steps in the Trinity; with Pelagius he prefers free will to grace; with Nestorius he divides Christ and excludes his human nature from the fellowship of the Trinity.[3] Thus traversing almost all sacred subjects he boldly attacks them from end to end and disposes of each in a damnable manner."[4] "Is there none among you to grieve on Christ's behalf, to love justice, to hate iniquity? If the mouth of him that speaks wicked things be not stopped, he will see and judge who alone has a care for distress and sorrow."[5]

In addition to his letters we have from Bernard's pen a large number of sermons and a few brief treatises on practical

[1] E.g. Eps. 187–193; 330–338.
[2] Elsewhere (Ep. 192) he complains that Abelard saw nothing through a glass darkly.
[3] This sentence reappears in several letters.
[4] Ep. 331.　　　　　[5] Ep. 332. Cf. also Eps. 333 and 338.

and doctrinal subjects. One of the treatises entitled De consideratione was addressed to Pope Eugenius, who owed his position in no small measure to the Abbot of Clairvaux, and contains the boldest and frankest kind of advice touching the duties and responsibilities of his office. Among the sermons are eighty-six on the Song of Songs, constituting one of the most striking series of discourses in existence. The Hebrew love poems are interpreted in traditional fashion as an allegory of the relation between Christ and the church, or more especially between Christ and the individual Christian.

Preached in the chapel of the monastery of Clairvaux the sermons were intended primarily for the monks, but they are of much wider application. Fanciful and often extravagant in their use of allegory and sometimes, as might have been expected in the circumstances, unpleasantly sentimental or morbid in tone, they reveal nevertheless great spiritual insight and an extraordinary knowledge of the human soul, and they contain many eloquent and beautiful passages. For the most part they are wholly practical in purpose, dealing in an intimate way with the religious and moral life of Christians and shedding much light on its problems and difficulties; but a few of them, particularly of the later ones, are prevailingly theological in character. It is amusing to see that some of the monks complained of these and that Bernard had to apologize for departing from his usual custom.[1]

Though he expressed himself often on theological subjects, Bernard was not a theologian. He was essentially a pastor and preacher, concerned first of all for the personal religious life of the monks under his care but also profoundly interested

---

[1] Cf. *Sermo in cantica canticorum*, 80 : 1. Unless otherwise indicated the sermons quoted or referred to in this chapter are from this series on the Song of Songs.

in the welfare and peace and purity of the church at large. He was firmly convinced of the truth of the whole Christian system and bitterly opposed to heresy and theological novelties of every kind, but his attention was centred in life rather than doctrine, in religion rather than theology. His attitude was that of the devout and unquestioning believer, accepting whatever was handed down as true, and refraining from inquiring too closely either into its credentials or its meaning. Unlike Anselm he had no zeal to penetrate the mysteries of the faith, and to understand what he believed. "The eternal and blessed Trinity," he remarked in one of his sermons, "I believe though I do not comprehend, and I hold by faith what I cannot grasp with the mind." [1]

That Bernard did not attempt to rationalize his beliefs argued no lack of confidence on his part. To understand what one believed was not in any degree to increase one's assurance of it. The certitude of faith was as complete as the certitude of knowledge, indeed more complete than that of the knowledge gained by the senses.[2] Abelard's notion of faith as opinion Bernard violently repudiated. "God forbid that in our faith or hope we should think, as he does, that anything depends on doubtful opinion and not rather, all of it, on sure and valid truth; being divinely supported by oracles and miracles, established and consecrated by the birth from a virgin, by the blood of the Redeemer, by the glory of the resurrection. The credibility of these testimonies is beyond all question. If it were less so we have, finally, the Spirit itself which bears witness with our spirit that we are sons of God. How then can anyone dare to call faith opinion unless it be one that has not yet received the Spirit or is ignorant of the gospel or esteems it a fable? 'I know whom I have believed and am certain,' exclaims the

---

[1] *Sermo*, 76 : 6.
[2] Cf. *Sermo*, 28 : 8.

Apostle.   And wilt thou hiss at me that faith is opinion? . . .
Faith is not opinion, but certitude." [1]

Elsewhere, speaking of knowledge, faith and opinion in
relation to divine things, he says: "Knowledge rests on
reason, faith on authority, while opinion is obliged to content
itself with a mere semblance of the truth.   The first two
have assured truth, but faith has it hidden and wrapped up,
knowledge has it unveiled and manifest.   Opinion, on the
other hand, being devoid of certainty, instead of apprehend-
ing the truth searches for it among probabilities." [2]

Though faith meant a great deal to Bernard, it was but a
part and the less significant part of his piety.   Not so much
what he believed as what he experienced was vital to him.
In religious matters the intelligence, he remarked, understands no more than is given in experience.[3]   The word
experience was a favorite with him.   His religion was not
merely a traditional thing; it was intensely personal, his
own in a very real sense.   The Christian, he insisted, should
not only believe that there is a God, and accept the truth
revealed by him, he should live in intimate touch with God
and know for himself what direct converse with him means.
Neither on faith, nor on reason, but on union with God
assurance is ultimately based, a union which illumines the
whole range of life and makes truth self-witnessing and self-
evident.

Bernard's piety was of a genuinely mystical type, but his
mysticism was not as extreme as that of Dionysius and many
another.   For one thing the union with God, of which he
had a great deal to say and which he regarded as the aim of
all religion, involves neither here nor in the future an identity

[1] Ep. 190 : 9.   Cf. *Sermones in vigilia nativitatis Domini*, 3; *Sermones de
diversis*, 45.

[2] *De consideratione*, Bk. V. chap. III (5).

[3] *Sermo*, 22 : 2 ; cf. 85 : 14.   In *Sermo*, 6 : 9 he speaks of himself as instructed
by the magistra experientia.

of nature or substance between man and God, but only a oneness of will and affection. He maintained, it is true, that God dwells in man and man dwells in God. Moreover man's union with God at its highest is an ecstatic union in which he loses consciousness of self and is conscious of God alone.[1] But he does not cease to be a man and is not absorbed into the divine nature. After speaking of the oneness of essence between the Father and the Son Bernard goes on to say, "But we are of the opinion that God and man, because both their wills and substances are distinct, abide in each other in an altogether different way, that is, their substances are not fused but their wills are in harmony. And this union is for them a communion of wills and an agreement in love."[2]

Bernard's mysticism differed from that of Dionysius also in that it meant not simply union with God but union with Christ, or with the divine Word. In the following passage he draws a distinction between union with the Father and union with the Word. "What is it for the Word to come into the soul? To instruct it in wisdom. What is it for the Father to come? To incite it to the love of wisdom so that the soul can say 'I am become a lover of her beauty.' To love is of the Father and therefore the coming of the Father is proved by the infusion of love. What is the effect of learning without love? Pride. What is the effect of love without learning? Error."[3] But as a rule in speaking of union with, or of abiding in the divine, or of the divine indwelling, Bernard refers indifferently to God or the Word or Christ without distinguishing one from the other.

The practical and moral effects of the divine indwelling, as conceived by Bernard, appear in the following vivid bit of autobiography. "I confess, I say it in my folly, that the Word has visited me and that many times. And though

[1] Cf. *Sermo*, 52 : 5; 85 : 13.   [2] 71 : 10.   [3] 69 : 2.

he has often entered into me I have never known when he came. I have felt his presence, I remember that he has been present, and sometimes I have been able to foretell his entrance, but never to perceive his coming or his going. For whence he came into my soul or whither he went on leaving it and how he entered and departed I confess I am still ignorant. . . . He did not enter by the eyes, for he is without color, nor by the ears, for he is without sound, nor by the nostrils, for he is not mingled with the air but with the mind, and he made the air, he did not impregnate it. Nor did he enter by the mouth, for he is not food or drink, nor did I detect him by touch, for he is impalpable. How then did he enter? Or can it be that he did not enter because he did not come from without, not being of those things that are without? But neither did he come from within, for he is good and I know that in me there is no good thing. . . . How then you ask, when his ways are thus altogether unsearchable, could I know that he was present? Only by the movement of my heart have I been aware of him. In the flight of vices and the restraint of carnal affections I have perceived the power of his virtue. In the examination and reproof of my secret faults I have admired the profundity of his wisdom. In the amendment, however small, of my ways I have experienced his goodness and gentleness. In the renovation and reformation of my mind and spirit, that is of my inner man, I have seen the fashion of his beauty. And as I have reflected on all these things I have been overwhelmed by his greatness." [1]

Historically even more important than Bernard's emphasis on the divine Christ and mystical union with him, was his emphasis on the human Christ and his constant insistence that the Christian life lies in imitating him. One of his chief aims as a preacher, and he was the greatest preacher of the

[1] *Sermo*, 74 : 5–6.

age, was to make him real to others and to bring them under the spell of his personality. To be sure, in all his emphasis on the man Jesus he never lost sight of the divine Christ. "He who dwells among the lilies reigns above the stars." [1] It is in Christ's humanity, indeed, that his divinity is most patently displayed. But quite apart from this Bernard was profoundly interested in the human figure of Jesus, in his character and conduct and the principles that governed his life, and he never wearied of preaching him as an example to be imitated by all his followers.

Curiously enough there is little about the imitation of Christ in earlier Christian literature. He was thought of so controllingly as the second person of the Trinity, or as the Christ present in the eucharist, that the man of Nazareth was largely lost sight of and little or no use was made of his example to guide and inspire Christian living. Whether the Crusades, in which Bernard was deeply interested and which served to bring the human Jesus vividly before the mind of the western world, had anything to do with it or not, at any rate Bernard was the first to put the imitation of Christ in the forefront of his preaching, and from his day on it was made much of. The figure of Jesus was enshrined in the hearts of the Christians of the west and increasingly as time passed their thoughts and emotions gathered about him.

The traits which Bernard chiefly emphasized in Jesus were humility and love. In these, he insisted, the imitation of Christ principally consists. Of humility, "the mother of salvation" as he called it, he had a great deal to say, coming back to it over and over again in his sermons on the Song of Songs.[2] There are two kinds of humility: the one has its seat in the intellect, the other in the affections.[3] The former is involuntary — we are driven to it as we see our own imper-

[1] 70 : 2.   [2] Cf. *e.g.* 37 ff.   [3] 42 : 6.

fections. The latter is voluntary and is the fruit of love which leads us to humble ourselves as Christ humbled himself and took on the form of a servant for our sakes. "It is not enough to be subject to God, unless you are subject also to every human creature for God's sake; whether to the abbot as ruler or to the priors appointed by him. I say more: Be subject to your equals and even to your inferiors. For thus it becomes us to fulfil all righteousness. If you wish to be perfect make advances to him that is less than you; defer to your inferior, bow down to your junior. . . . He whom truth compels to be humble cannot attain this, for his humility is for himself alone and is not suffered to go forth and delight those without."[1]

Bernard, as I have said, made much of humility, but he made even more of love. He was to his age the great apostle of love, at least in word if not always in deed. "I have read that God is love," he says, "not that he is honour or dignity. . . . Honour and glory indeed are due to God and to him alone, but he will accept neither of them if they be not preserved in the honey of love. Love is sufficient of itself; it pleases by itself and on its own account. It is itself merit and is itself its own reward. Love seeks no cause beyond itself and no fruit. It is its own fruit, its own enjoyment. I love because I love; I love that I may love. Love is a great thing provided it recurs to its beginning, returns to its origin, and draws always from that fountain which is perpetually in flood. Of all the feelings and affections of the soul love is the only one by which the creature, though not on equal terms, is able to respond to the creator and to repay what it has received from him. . . . For when God loves us he desires nothing but to be loved. He loves for no other reason, indeed, than that he may be loved, knowing that by their love itself those who love him are blessed."[2] This emphasis

[1] *Sermo*, 42 : 9.   [2] 83 : 4.

on love for its own sake links Bernard with the romanticists of all ages.

The road to God is through the affections, not the intellect; we come to know God by love rather than by learning. "God's love creates love in the soul and God's attention to the soul makes the soul attentive and his solicitude makes it solicitous in return. For by some affinity of nature, I know not what, when once with unveiled face the soul has been enabled to see the glory of God it is of necessity made forthwith like him and is transformed into the same image." [1] In his brief treatise On Loving God Bernard speaks of four stages of love: first, loving ourselves for our own sake; second, loving God for our own sake, because we look for blessings from him; third, loving God for God's sake, because we recognize his loveliness; and fourth, loving ourselves not for our own sake but for God's sake alone that he may do with us what he will and make such use of us as he can. To the last stage, the perfection of love, we can fully attain only in the future life.[2]

Bernard did not stop with love for God or Christ, he insisted also that the Christian must love his neighbors including even his enemies. Not necessarily that he must feel affection for them — that is not always possible in this life, though it will be in heaven — but that he must treat them as love dictates, doing always for others what he would that they should do for him.[3] While the category of neighbor includes one's enemies it does not include everybody. There are some, according to Bernard, who are to be hated rather than loved. "You therefore," he says, "who love yourself only because you love God, love as yourself all those that love him as you do. As for an enemy, because he is nothing in that he does not love God, you cannot love him as your-

---

[1] 69:7.　　[2] *De diligendo Deo*, chap. VIII ff.　Cf. also *Sermones* 20 and 83.
[3] *Sermo*, 50:7.

self who do love God. Nevertheless you should love him that he may love. It is not the same thing however to love him that he may love and to love him because he loves. . . . As for him who it is clear will not return to the love of God it is necessary that you think of him not as almost nothing but as nothing at all, since he is nothing for all eternity. With the exception, then, of such a one who is not to be loved at all, but is to be held in hatred according to the word : 'Shall I not hate those, Lord, who hate thee, and be consumed with anger at thine enemies?' — with the exception of such a one love does not permit you to deny some measure of affection, however small, to anybody even your worst enemy." [1]

Whether his appeal to Scripture was only a salve to his conscience or he really believed, as he may well have done, that it was his duty to hate those whom he counted enemies of God, at any rate Bernard suited the action to the word in his treatment of them. For all his praise of love he was a violent hater. He expressed delight at the sudden death of the antipope Anacletus and hoped other foes of the church might meet a like fate ; [2] and his language about Abelard's disciple, the social and political radical Arnold of Brescia, was far from kindly.[3] Heretics, he said in one of his discourses on the Song of Songs, should be taken by argument not by force of arms, but if they prove obdurate, they should be placed under restraint.[4] And in a later sermon he declared that it would be better to put them to death than to allow them to lead others astray.[5] But in spite of all this there can be no doubt whatever that Bernard took seriously the injunction to love one's neighbors as well as to love God and that his emphasis upon it meant much for the

---

[1] *Sermo*, 50 : 7.
[2] Ep. 147.
[3] Cf. Eps. 189, 195, 196.
[4] *Sermo*, 64 : 8.
[5] 66 : 12.

centuries that followed. As a monk and a true Catholic he combined with love not only humility, but also contempt for the world, in his ideal of the Christian man, but he gave love the supreme place, insisting that no one should live for himself alone and that even the joys of spiritual contemplation should if necessary be sacrificed for the good of others.[1]

It may be worth while before turning from him to quote his summary of the character of the ideal Christian. "Give me a man who before all things loves God with his whole soul; who loves himself and his neighbor in so far as they love God, his enemy also as one who may sometime love him; who loves his relatives according to the flesh in a brotherly fashion by reason of nature, his spiritual instructors more abundantly by reason of grace, his love for other things being thus regulated by his love for God; who despises the earth and fixes his mind on heaven; who uses this world as not using it and distinguishes by a certain inner taste the things that are only to be used from those that are to be enjoyed, so that he troubles himself for transitory things only temporarily, while and in so far as there is need of them, and embraces eternal things with desire eternal."[2]

The imitation of Christ, preached so eloquently by Bernard of Clairvaux, was lived even more eloquently by Francis of Assisi. He was born some thirty years after Bernard's death and though profoundly different from him in character and ideals he became the greatest religious force of the thirteenth century, as Bernard was of the twelfth. One of the most fascinating and winning figures in the history of the church, his influence lay in the sphere of life rather than of thought and I can do no more here than refer to him briefly in passing. We have scarcely anything from his pen. He wrote very little and what still remains would fill at most

[1] Cf. *Sermo*, 41:6.   [2] 50:8.

but a few pages. For our knowledge of him we are obliged to rely chiefly on the reports of others, particularly his disciples.

He was not in any sense a theologian. He had no theological education, little formal education indeed of any kind, and he was wholly without interest in theological questions. For that matter he may be said to have been largely without intellectual interests of any sort. A poet and a romantic, endowed with a vivid imagination and an exquisite fancy and fond of all sorts of quaint conceits, filled with the joy of living, imbued with the spirit of chivalry, ambitious to do splendid deeds and to shine among his fellows, yet singularly free from selfishness and self-consciousness, a lover of outdoors, a brother of sun and moon and stars, the friend of all living creatures, men and beasts and birds, with a whimsical regard for the welfare even of inanimate things, it is not easy to think of him as a monk. As a matter of fact when he abandoned the world he joined none of the existing monastic bodies, and though he became the founder of a brotherhood of his own which soon developed into a regular order and received the sanction of the pope, it was very different from the others in many respects at any rate as long as he lived.

Francis' supreme ambition was to follow Christ and become truly one with him. And this meant, as he understood it, to love and serve his fellows as Christ did. Love was the heart of his Christianity. Not love for God or even love for Christ, though he made a great deal of the latter, but love for human beings. Bernard, too, emphasized love, but like many another he put love for God first and made love for men only a corollary of it. But Francis was less sophisticated and more simply human in this matter. His heart overflowed with sympathy and charity and he did not need to justify his attitude. It was no mere matter of words with him and no mere kindly sentiment. To help those in want or sickness or sorrow he was not only willing but eager to spend himself to the uttermost, to sacrifice time and strength and health and everything he had.

Francis' love for others was without limits. Bernard's hatred for the enemies of the Lord he did not share. There was, indeed, nothing of the hater about him. He had no desire to attack or to take vengeance on anybody, heretic or evil-doer. He would have the wicked reformed by good example rather than by denunciation and punishment. He was utterly without censoriousness and to condemn others whose ideals and practices differed from his own was wholly foreign to him.

His ideal of Christian love he did all he could to impress upon the brotherhood. It was not contemplation, or the cultivation of their own spiritual natures, that he would have them make their chief concern. Rather it was a life of active service in imitation of Jesus Christ. It was, therefore, not his plan that they should settle down quietly and permanently in any one place, but that they should go about doing good : mingling with the people, sharing in their tasks, preaching repentance and peace, and trying in every way they could to convert the masses to more Christian ways of living. It is interesting to notice that as soon as he had a little group of followers he sent them out like the Apostles two by two and laid upon them injunctions similar to Jesus' own. As long as he lived he emphasized this kind of peripatetic service.

This explains his attitude toward asceticism. Unlike the ordinary monastic founder he made little of it. He believed in it, to be sure, as most devout Christians did, and he regarded it as an essential part of the monastic life. But he did not count it an end in itself. On the contrary he deliberately subordinated it to the service of others. He directed the members of his order to eat what was set before them, asking no questions for conscience' sake, and though he often practised the severest austerities himself, he warned the weak and the poor in health against too strenuous fasting and other ascetic exercises.

To serve one's fellows in the spirit of Jesus Christ was not the whole of Francis' ideal. If one were to imitate Christ as he was eager to imitate him, one must divest oneself, so he believed, of the goods of this world and live in complete poverty. The son of a rich merchant of Assisi, generous and free-handed from boyhood up, when he turned his back upon the pleasures and adventures in which he had been a leading spirit the first thing he did was to give away everything he had. This was no uncommon step for one who had determined to abandon the world for religion's sake. But Francis invested it with the poetry and romance that attended all he did. Every knight must have a lady and he chose Lady Poverty for his. From this time on he counted the possession of any kind of property a curse. Like the Waldenses and other similar brotherhoods whose influence he very likely felt, he had a special horror of money which seemed to him the root of all evil in a sense not true of any other kind of goods. To get rid of money altogether and bring back primitive conditions of barter was the ideal of many a radical of the day with whom Francis may well have sympathized. The members of his order, he insisted, were to work for their daily bread and for shelter when shelter was needed, but they were never in any circumstances to receive money for their labor.

Still further he insisted on complete poverty not only for himself and his associates but also for the group as a whole. Unlike the regular monastic orders the community was to own no property: no lands, no houses, no goods of any sort. This principle of poverty, corporate as well as individual, Francis made one of the corner stones of his order.

He was continually emphasizing its importance and warning his followers against abandoning it after he was gone.

Closely connected with the ideal of poverty was that of humility. Poverty indeed, as Francis conceived it, was but a form of humility. The two belonged together and neither could be divorced from the other. There was nothing new in his emphasis on humility. It is one of the oldest Christian virtues, cherished particularly in monastic circles. But Francis gave it a picturesque and dramatic quality as he did everything else. The ideal was embodied in the very title of his society, for he named it the Order of Lesser Brothers (Ordo fratrum minorum). No one ever went further than he in the practice of humility. To humble himself not merely before God but before men as well, to engage in the most menial employments, to associate familiarly with beggars and outcasts, to share the living conditions of the lowest classes — all this he delighted in. To turn the other cheek to the smiter, to accept insult without anger, to endure contradiction without retort, to bear misunderstanding and calumny without complaint — this seemed to him only the Christian's duty and he always met duty more than half way.

With humility went obedience and of this too Francis made a great deal. Like humility it was one of the traditional monastic virtues, but to Francis it was much more than this. He counted obedience not simply a duty but a delight. If he could be obeying someone he seemed particularly happy. He had a general of the order appointed in his place and also a special guardian of his own that he might have two superiors to obey. The imitation of Christ in that age often meant hostility to the church and the ecclesiastical authorities, but it did not mean this for Francis. On the contrary there was never a more loyal son of the church and a more devoted servant of the pope than he.

It was a great thing for thirteenth-century Catholicism that the two mendicant orders, the Franciscan and the Dominican, founded both of them almost at the beginning of the century, put themselves unqualifiedly at the service of the church. The Franciscans worked chiefly among the lower classes, the Dominicans among the higher. The Dominicans, known as the Order of Preachers, gave themselves chiefly to the defense of the Catholic faith against infidels and heretics; the Franciscans to the spread of the gospel of repentance and the promotion of Christian living. Between them they worked wonders.

In Francis mediæval piety attained its clearest and loftiest expression. He represented the very best in the life of the Catholic church. To be sure he represented only certain aspects of it. Its culture and its learning, its intellectual life in general, found no response in him. He did not like learning and directed that if a person could not read when he joined the brotherhood he was not to be taught. With many another he had a distaste for theology and a distrust of it, but he did not attack it, as some did, and though he had a horror of heresy, he never felt called upon to expose it, or to pursue and denounce the heretic. Science, too, lay beyond the confines of his interest and literature as well. Reading he indulged in very sparingly and he discouraged it in others, maintaining that the breviary and the Psalter contained all that anybody needed. The contrast in all this between him and Dominic is very striking.

Religion and religion alone was Francis' affair — religion interpreted above all else as the imitation of Christ and union with him in his life of unworldliness and brotherly love. It was due largely to his influence, together with that of the order which he founded and of the lay brotherhoods which sprang up everywhere in response to his message and example, that the thirteenth century represented the high-water mark religiously and ethically in the life of the western church.

As has been said Francis himself was opposed to learning, but already within a generation after his death there were important theologians among the Franciscans, who disputed the leadership of the theological world with the great Dominican doctors. In the hands of these two orders the theological development chiefly lay for generations to come. To that development it will be necessary to turn later.

CHAPTER XI

HUGO OF ST. VICTOR AND PETER LOMBARD

BERNARD of Clairvaux, as I have said, was not a theologian, but his friend and fellow-mystic Hugo of St. Victor was. Though Hugo was half a dozen years younger than Bernard the latter owed much to him. It was he, indeed, rather than Bernard who was the real fountain head of the Catholic mysticism of the twelfth and following centuries. He was not a preacher, as Bernard was, and he took no part in ecclesiastical affairs but devoted himself wholly to teaching and writing. A native of Saxony he found his way at an early age to the recently established monastic school of St. Victor in Paris, where he remained for the rest of his life, first as pupil, then as teacher, and finally as principal. He was a prolific writer and though he died in his early forties he left many important works, exegetical, dogmatic, and mystical. He wrote an admirable style, clear, concise and vigorous, and his writings are interesting and impressive above most that have come down to us from the Middle Ages.

He was something of a universal genius and taught a wide range of subjects. We have from his pen an introductory work on philosophy (Eruditio didascalica) which contains brief prolegomena to the study of all the current disciplines — mathematics, music, astronomy, physics, agriculture, navigation, medicine, logic and the rest — as well as to the study of the Scriptures. But his chief work was in the field of theology and his principal theological production, the most important of all his writings, was his De sacramentis christianæ fidei, which deals not with the sacraments alone but with the whole Christian system, all the works of God being sacraments for the religious-minded. Religion includes the creation, the fall, the work of redemption, and the joys of the saved, all of them forming one connected and inter-related whole. Redemption is the heart of Christianity. To it everything else is related as condition or consequence.

Although the principal subject of the Bible is man's restoration, nevertheless to treat of this adequately, Hugo says, it is necessary to recount briefly the beginning of things. "For it could not rightly be shown how man was restored unless it was first told how he fell; nor could his fall be fittingly recounted unless it was first explained in what condition he was originally placed by God. But to understand the spiritual state of man the creation and constitution of the whole world must be set forth, for the world was made on account of man, the spirit for God's sake, the body for the spirit's sake, and the world for the body's sake, that the spirit might be subjected to God, the body to the spirit and the world to the body. Therefore sacred Scripture first describes the creation of the world which was formed on man's account; then it tells how man was made and placed in a state of righteousness and discipline, after-wards how he fell, finally how he was restored." [1]

Hugo's work is divided into two books, the first covering the period from the beginning of the world to the incarnation, the second from the incarnation to the final consummation. The first book deals with the creation of the world, the knowledge of God, the divine will, angels, the formation of man, the fall, original sin, the restoration of man, faith, and the sacraments both of the natural and of the written law, [2]

---

[1] *De sacramentis christianæ fidei*, Bk. I. prologue, chap. 3.
[2] Hugo wrote a separate work in the form of a dialogue entitled *De sacramentis legis naturalis et scriptæ*.

that is the whole of God's redemptive work before Christ came. The second book deals with the incarnation, the unity of the church which is the body of Christ, clerical orders, the dress of the clergy, the dedication of church buildings, baptism, confirmation, the eucharist, minor sacraments and sacred rites intended not for salvation but for edification, simony, marriage, vows, vices and virtues, confession, penance and forgiveness, the end of the world and the future life.

The work thus covers a wide range of topics. It was indeed the most comprehensive system of theology produced in the west up to Hugo's time. It resembles in some ways John of Damascus' Exposition of the Orthodox Faith but it is far more original and independent and differs from it in emphasizing the practical doctrines of Christianity and making more of soteriology than of Christology which was John's chief interest. It differs from John's work, too, in that it is dominated by one great controlling principle, the economy of redemption, to which everything else is made tributary. Such a principle John's work altogether lacked. It was therefore a mere compendium of doctrines while Hugo's was a genuine system, an organic whole.

Hugo was an orthodox believer and accepted without question the traditional Catholic faith in its entirety. Though he took the Scriptures rather than the Fathers as his authority he did not distrust patristic teaching nor exploit its inconsistencies as Abelard did. At the same time, while a devout and orthodox believer, he was not opposed to the use of reason in religion as Bernard was. He saw no necessary inconsistency between faith and reason. On the contrary he emphasized the importance of the latter and made large use of it in his theological writings. His spirit closely resembled Anselm's, though his confidence in reason was less complete, for he believed that few Christian doctrines were rationally demonstrable. As a matter of fact he divided truth into three classes : that which is from reason (ex ratione), according to reason (secundum rationem), above reason (supra rationem). "Some things," he says, "are from reason, others according to reason, others above reason ; and besides these there are things contrary to reason. Those from reason are necessary, according to reason probable, above reason wonderful, contrary to reason incredible. The two extremes indeed do not admit of faith. For that which is from reason is fully known and being known cannot be believed. Similarly that which is contrary to reason can in no way be believed, for it is altogether irrational, nor does reason ever consent to it. Therefore that which is according to reason or above reason can alone be the object of faith." [1]

In those truths that are according to reason faith and reason coöperate and strengthen each other, revelation confirming and making certain what reason makes probable. On the other hand those above reason are known only through revelation and are grasped by faith alone. In connection with such truths reason's only function is to assure us that what purports to be revealed is not irrational, for if it were it could not possibly be true. Hugo had no doubt, however, that the Christian system was true in all its parts, and that the whole of it was to be accepted even though it contained much that could neither be rationally proved nor fully understood, much therefore that must be taken on trust.

Theology he divided into natural and revealed, or as he called them mundane and divine theology.[2] The former includes both things that are "from reason" and "according to reason," the latter things that are "above reason."

[1] *De sacramentis*, I. 3 : 30.
[2] *Commentary on the Celestial Hierarchy of Dionysius*, Bk. I. chap. 1.

To the former belongs the creation with all pertaining thereto, including the doctrine of God as one and triune, which, so Hugo maintained as Abelard did, was known quite independently of revelation and to heathen as well as Jews and Christians. "Divine theology" on the other hand has to do with redemption. This is above reason and can be known only through revelation. It includes the incarnation, the church, the sacraments and so on, that is all the matters covered in the second book of the De sacramentis.

Unfortunately Hugo's distinction between mundane and divine theology lacks clearness and consistency. For, as seen above, he recognized that revelation covered more than redemption, that God's creative activity, with its conditions and implications, had also been revealed because the restoration of man could not be understood without it. The category of revelation, as he understood it, was thus broader than redemption and the contrast between the two kinds of theology was consequently obscured. Confusion was caused also by his acceptance of the Neoplatonic notion that all knowledge is based upon divine inspiration or illumination, a notion that tended to destroy the distinction between the natural and the revealed. However, in spite of the confusion, his sharp differentiation of truths "above reason" from those "according to reason," and his insistence that a part of the Christian system falls under the former category, a part under the latter, marked an advance toward clarity and was of the greatest consequence for the development of theology.

As there is much in Christianity, according to Hugo, that is above reason, much in other words that can be neither rationally proved nor fully understood and must therefore be taken on trust, there is large room for faith on the Christian's part. In the first book of the De sacramentis there

is an admirable discussion of faith, one of the best in mediæval literature.[1]   Faith is an act both of the intellect and
of the will.   Intellectually it lies between opinion and
knowledge; it is higher than opinion but lower than knowledge.   There may be in it the same degree of assurance as in
knowledge but it is an assurance based on the testimony of
others, or on indirect evidence of some sort, rather than on
the presence of the thing itself.   But faith is not merely
intellectual, not merely an imperfect or incomplete form of
knowledge, it is also the voluntary commitment of oneself to
some person or cause.[2]   Faith may be more or less comprehensive, covering a larger or smaller range of truth, that
is, its content may vary.   It may also be firmer or weaker,
the will being more or less fully enlisted, that is, it may be
of one or another quality.   It is its quality alone that determines its merit; for there is merit only where free will is
involved.   Not how much a man believes is the important
question, but whether he is firm and constant in his belief.

There are three stages of faith: the first when we simply
accept the teaching of the church without reflecting upon it
or understanding why it is worthy of belief; the second when
our reason approves our faith; the third when we experience
inwardly what we have believed.   The third passes over into
mystic contemplation which for Hugo was highest of all.
We may have a foretaste of it now and then in the present
life, but it can be realized in its fulness only in the life beyond
the grave.   Of this mystic contemplation Hugo had much
to say in certain of his writings.   In it the Christian comes
into perfect union with God, a union mediated by both love
and knowledge.[3]   For this union Hugo used the figure of

---

[1] *De sacramentis*, I. 10; cf. also II. 18 : 17.

[2] In his emphasis on the voluntary character of faith Hugo was in line with
Augustine rather than with Abelard.   Against Abelard's interpretation of faith
in exclusively intellectual terms he revolted as Bernard did.

[3] Cf. Hugo's *De arca Noe morali*, Bk. I. chap. 2.

marriage, as Bernard did, but the marriage he referred to was not between the soul and Christ but between the soul and God.[1] Of Bernard's Christ-mysticism, so far as I am aware, he made no use.

In one passage in his De sacramentis [2] Hugo says that man originally had three organs of vision : the eye of the flesh, the eye of reason, and the eye of contemplation. With the first he saw the external world, with the second the internal world, with the third God and the things of God. The first was left unaffected by the fall, the second was weakened, the third was wholly destroyed. Faith therefore became necessary. The eye of contemplation, however, Hugo frequently refers to as if it were still in active use, at least on the part of Christians, having been restored apparently by divine grace. But only in the future, as already indicated, will it regain full strength.

Thus Hugo made a place for mysticism in his theology and for theology in his mysticism. Faith, reason, mystical vision : the acceptance of the Catholic system, the understanding of it so far as possible by means of reason, and finally the realization of God and divine things that comes from complete oneness with him. When the matter is thus conceived rational theology ceases to be an alien in the Christian commonwealth, an enemy to be distrusted and thrust out. It has its place in the progress from faith to vision and may therefore legitimately be studied by the most pious Christian. The combination of rationalism and mysticism thus achieved was of incalculable significance for the generations that followed.

Hugo was historically important not only because he combined mysticism and rational theology but also because he produced in his De sacramentis an elaborate and carefully articulated system of theology which became the model for

---

[1] Cf. his *De amore sponsi ad sponsam.*   [2] *De sacramentis*, I. 10 : 2.

many others in the twelfth and following centuries. His
example in this respect was followed by theologians both
of a mystical and of a non-mystical type. The works of
the former were as dialectical, or as scholastic (to employ
a familiar if somewhat vague term), as those of the latter.
Not only Hugo but others after him have made it abundantly evident that mysticism and scholasticism are not
necessarily exclusive the one of the other as has often been
assumed.

In addition to the De sacramentis there is printed among
Hugo's works another and briefer system of theology entitled Summa sententiarum. After a few introductory
chapters on faith, hope, and love, it deals in the first book
(or tractatus) with the Trinity, predestination, the will of
God, and the incarnation; in the second with the angels;
in the third with man (his creation and fall, original sin,
free will and so forth); in the fourth with the sacraments
in general and with the decalogue; in the fifth, sixth, and
seventh with the individual sacraments. The arrangement
is very different from that of the De sacramentis and there
is no controlling principle binding the whole together as in
the larger work. So far as its style and contents are concerned it might have been by Hugo and it is maintained
by some scholars that he was its author. But it was early
ascribed to one of his pupils, Odo of St. Victor, and the
ascription is probably correct. Whether by Hugo or not
the work is important and is mentioned here because it was
evidently known to Peter Lombard and influenced the
composition of his famous text-book, Sententiarum libri
quattuor.

In the previous chapter I spoke of Abelard's work on
theology of which we have a fragment in the Introductio ad
theologiam. It was divided into three parts — faith, love,
and the sacraments — the first dealing with doctrine, par-

ticularly the doctrine of the Trinity, the second presumably with ethics and the Christian life, the third with the means of grace. Several of Abelard's pupils, among them Roland of Bologna, who later became Pope Alexander III, wrote compends of theology in which Abelard's teaching was reproduced with greater or less fidelity.[1] In these works his threefold division was adopted, though in the order faith, sacraments, love, the last being treated as the product of faith and the sacraments.

More important than any of these was the compend of another of Abelard's pupils referred to just above, the Sententiarum libri quattuor of Peter Lombard, the famous Magister sententiarum as he was called. Born in Lombardy, he studied in Paris and taught theology there for many years, becoming finally Bishop of Paris shortly before his death. At the beginning of the compend on which his fame rests, he followed Augustine in drawing a distinction between things and signs (res et signa). The former have their end in themselves, the latter point beyond themselves to something else, and are valuable chiefly or solely because they do. Instead, however, of dividing his work, as might have been expected, into two general parts, the first dealing with things, the second with signs, Lombard divided it into four books: the first on the Trinity, together with the knowledge of God, divine providence and predestination; the second on the creation, including both angels and men, the fall, grace, and free will; the third on the incarnation, embracing the person and work of Christ, and followed by a discussion of faith, hope, love, virtue and vice; the fourth

[1] See Denifle, *Die Sentenzen Abelards und die Bearbeitungen seiner Theologie vor Mitte des 12. Jhs.* (in *Archiv für Litteratur-und Kirchengeschichte d. Mittelalters*, vol. I). Among these compends is the *Epitome theologiæ christianæ*, first published by Rheinwald in 1835 and printed among Abelard's works in Migne's edition.

on the sacraments and eschatology. Of these only the fourth has to do with signs and that not exclusively. Evidently Lombard found the Augustinian distinction between things and signs too general to be used as a principle of classification in a theological text-book.

The fourfold division actually adopted was apparently suggested by John of Damascus' Exposition of the Orthodox Faith which had been recently translated into Latin. In other respects, however, Lombard's work follows Abelard and Hugo instead of John and reproduces the teaching of the western rather than the eastern church. Abelard's influence is seen particularly in the method of treatment. For one thing dialectics is used on a large scale to elucidate the doctrines presented, to define and clarify the problems involved, and to clear up difficulties. Moreover, as in Abelard's Sic et non, authorities are quoted extensively both for and against the propositions under discussion. Lombard took his quotations not only from the Bible and the Fathers but also from creeds and conciliar decisions and, especially in the fourth book, from Gratian's Decretum.[1] The Greek Fathers, except for John of Damascus, he drew upon rarely and only indirectly. The Latin Fathers, on the other hand, he quoted copiously, particularly from Augustine on. There are over a thousand citations from Augustine alone, more than twice as many as from all the others combined. The quotations pro and con are not left to speak for themselves as by Abelard. In most cases inconsistencies are reconciled and seeming contradictions explained, though occasionally the solution is left to the reader.

Abelard's Sic et non was only a collection of sources. In Lombard's work the sources are made use of to illustrate and throw light on the questions under discussion or to

---

[1] On the sources of Lombard's work see O. Baltzer: *Die Sentenzen des Petrus Lombardus.*

determine the conclusions to be drawn. And whereas the effect of Abelard's work was to create doubt in the infallibility of the Fathers, the effect of Lombard's was to restore confidence in them and to encourage the belief that all inconsistencies could ultimately be explained. The method was admirably fitted, not to be sure to forward the discovery of new truth, but to promote an understanding of a body of doctrines handed down from the past. It is, therefore, not surprising that it was followed by all the great schoolmen of the thirteenth century.

The author, as has been said, was a disciple of Abelard but he was less radical than his master and more fully in sympathy with traditional beliefs. While he followed Abelard as far as he could he did not hesitate to disagree with him on occasion. At many points he found Hugo's positions more to his liking. The work indeed, at least in content if not in form, shows the latter's influence almost as much as Abelard's, though there is no trace in it of Hugo's mysticism.

Lombard was not interested in philosophical and psychological problems; at any rate they have no place in his compend. Nor did he concern himself with such fundamental matters as the nature of faith, the relation of faith and reason, and the limits of authority in religion. He ignores all these preliminary questions and simply takes up the traditional doctrines one by one and independently of each other. There is no general principle binding everything together as in Hugo's De sacramentis. The work consequently is not an organic and articulated whole, but for the most part a collection of distinct and unrelated beliefs — a circumstance not without its influence upon the Catholic theology of subsequent centuries.

Though Lombard was not a philosopher or an original thinker he had a remarkable gift for gathering up and presenting in clear and systematic form the thought of others freed from irrelevant and unimportant details. While containing little or nothing that was new the compend, for all its limitations, was an extraordinarily convenient summary of the Catholic faith of the day, all the more useful because of its lack of originality. It was no accident that it became very soon and remained for centuries thereafter the great theological handbook of the west. It was, indeed, one of the most successful text-books the world has ever seen. Teachers of theology made it the basis of their lectures and discussions, and commentaries without number were written upon it. For some time it was looked upon askance by the conservatives both because Lombard was a disciple of Abelard and reproduced many of his ideas and also because of its large use of dialectic. But the opposition was gradually overcome and in the thirteenth century the work won its way to general acceptance. As a consequence many of Abelard's opinions became ultimately the common property of the western church.

Before bringing this chapter to a close, it may be worth while to say a few words about mediæval symbolism, to which both Hugo and Lombard bear witness, and of which the former was a notable exponent. Symbolism is common in all religions, and Christianity is no exception to the rule. The allegorical interpretation of the Scriptures, current among theologians from the very beginning, is a striking example of it. Not the literal meaning of the text is the important matter, but the spiritual truths which have been hidden beneath it by the divine author, and which it is the duty of the devout interpreter to discover, if he would know the true value of Scripture and give the word of God its rightful influence. To what lengths allegory could be carried was illustrated by many a Father as by many a mediæval schoolman. Practically no one was free from it, though some were more sober than others in their treatment of the sacred text. Allegory was employed not simply in connection with the Bible. Other sacred objects — sacred because ordained by God and connected in some way with man's salvation — early received the same kind of treatment. Noah's ark was used by Bishop Callixtus of Rome in the third century as a figure of the church, and in the twelfth century in his two treatises De arca Noe morali and De arca Noe mystica, Hugo worked out its symbolism in detail.

The following passage will serve as an illustration : "The length of three hundred cubits denotes the present age. This includes three periods — of the natural law, of the written law, and of grace — through which the holy church moves from the beginning of the world to the end, from the present life to future glory. The width of fifty cubits signifies all believers who are established under one head, namely Christ. For fifty is made up of seven sevens, that is forty-nine, a number that stands for the totality of believers, and one more, meaning Christ who is the head of the church and the consummation of our desires. On which account he is epitomized in one cubit. The height of thirty cubits signifies the thirty books of divine Scripture, that is, twenty-two of the Old Testament and eight of the New in which is contained the sum of all things that God either has done or will do for the sake of his church." [1]

The various institutions and activities of the church were also allegorized on a large scale. What might be made of the hierarchy, the sacraments, and other ecclesiastical rites and ceremonies was seen in the chapter on Dionysius the Areopagite, and he was but one witness to a tendency that increased with the passing of the centuries. Every portion of the cultus, every appurtenance of the services,

[1] *De arca Noe morali*, I. 4.

every part of the sacred buildings was given its symbolical significance. Cathedrals were not simply places of worship, but sermons in stone. The nave, the aisles, the choir, the columns, the windows, all had their figurative meanings and invited the worshippers to the contemplation of things unseen and spiritual.

Christian symbolism was not confined to so-called sacred objects, like the Bible, the sacraments, the church and its accessories. Already at an early day we find references here and there to the representative quality of this or that natural object, and in the Middle Ages nature-symbolism flourished on a large scale. As was said above, according to Hugo all the works of God are sacraments for the religious minded, that is, the religious man sees everywhere signs of divine activity and types of divine realities. The world, it was generally believed, was created for the sake of man, not simply for his use but for his instruction as well; and every part of it had some spiritual meaning given it by God. Nature, Vincent of Beauvais declared, is a book written by the finger of God.[1] This, of course, meant that like the Scriptures it was to be read allegorically. According to Thomas Aquinas, nature is not important in itself, but because it points beyond itself to a supernatural world. Things are not simply what they seem, they are revelations of divine truth, and it is in this their value chiefly lies.

From an early day the heavenly bodies were favorite objects of symbolical interpretation. John of Damascus saw in the orderly arrangement of sun and moon and stars an emblem of the diversities in human rank and a proof that the latter are grounded in the very nature of things. In the west the sun and moon were commonly held to represent church and state, and the dependence of the latter

[1] According to Eicken, *Geschichte und System der mittelalterlichen Welt-anschauung*, p. 637.

on the former was argued from the dependence of the moon on the sun for its light.

Precious stones, plants, animals and even the human frame itself were also allegorized and made vehicles of spiritual truth. That man has his eyes in front and his ears at the side signifies that God should be first with him and his neighbors second. The vine was a standing emblem of Christ, the olive of divine love, the lily of chastity, the cypress of humility, the palm of victory over death. The lamb and the unicorn signified the Saviour, the pelican his atoning death, the dove the Holy Spirit, the cock penitence, the stag the soul thirsting for salvation, the phœnix the resurrection, the lamb purity and innocence ; while human vices were typified by swine and other unclean beasts, and Satan by the dragon and the serpent.[1] In a mediæval clavis wrongly attributed to the Apologist Melito of the second century, there is given a list of hundreds of natural objects, animate and inanimate, with their figurative meanings.[2] Appended to the writings of Hugo of St. Victor (in Migne, vol. 177) is a work by a certain Hugo of Folieto entitled De bestiis et aliis rebus, the first part of which is an elaborate treatise on the symbolism of birds.

Many symbols, particularly those suggested in the Bible, were early stereotyped and became the common possession of Christians everywhere. Others were of later origin and had only a limited circulation. Allegorists vied with one another in discovering new meanings in visible things. Sometimes they found credence for the products of their fancy, sometimes not. But whether this or that particular interpretation was regarded as sound or unsound, the general

---

[1] Often qualities of the symbolic object were carried over to the being or truth symbolized and the latter was modified accordingly. This is illustrated for instance by the effect the use of the lamb as a symbol of Christ has had on the interpretation of Christ's character.

[2] See Pitra, *Analecta Sacra*, vol. II. pp. 3 ff.

principle was commonly accepted, that all visible things have their spiritual reference which it is the privilege or duty of theologians to discover if they can.

The religious significance of mediæval symbolism can hardly be exaggerated. With the whole world recognized as a revelation of God, and with visible objects on every side testifying to the unseen and spiritual, it was not easy for a person to forget religion altogether and to become wholly absorbed in material things. Reminders of the divine were everywhere, and he must be callous indeed who paid no attention to them.

Mediæval symbolism had effects also in the scientific realm. The figurative aspect of phenomena was believed to be an inherent and essential part of them. To understand a thing therefore it was not enough to acquaint oneself with its physical properties and its relations to other external objects, its spiritual meaning and its place in the divine purpose must also be discovered. Its natural qualities were not denied nor the importance of knowing them in order to be able to carry on intelligently the ordinary business of life. But as the spiritual world was counted higher and more important than the material, the symbolic reading of nature tended to overshadow the literal, and science seemed to many to have its chief value in its investigation of the former rather than the latter. If the notion of Arnobius and Augustine and many others that the study of nature is to be eschewed because it distracts a man from looking after the salvation of his soul, tended to undermine natural science, the mediæval belief in symbolism had an equally unfortunate though more subtle effect, resulting as it did in a pseudo-science which proved one of the chief obstacles to the rise and development of the genuine science of modern times. It was no accident that for long the latter seemed to devout believers wholly profane and unworthy the regard of religious men.

CHAPTER XII

THOMAS AQUINAS

With the thirteenth century a new period opened in the history of western thought, a period distinguished from the preceding by the controlling influence of Aristotle. Except for his treatises on logic, known collectively as the Organon, Aristotle's writings were inaccessible to the Christians of the west until late in the twelfth century, when they began to find their way across the border from Spain where they had for some time been diligently studied by the Arabian scholars of that part of the world. In the late twelfth and in the thirteenth century Latin translations of his physical and metaphysical writings appeared in increasing numbers and before long the Christian scholars of Europe were in a turmoil about them. The first reaction to them was hostile. Out of line as they were in many respects with the common Christian ideas of the day it was widely felt that they could only do harm. They were therefore attacked bitterly by many theologians. The ecclesiastical authorities also took a hand in the conflict and in 1210 forbade instruction in Aristotle's physics and metaphysics at the University of Paris, a prohibition renewed more than once during the next half century.

At the other extreme was a relatively small group of convinced and thoroughgoing disciples of Aristotle of whom the interesting and somewhat enigmatic figure Siger of Brabant, professor in the University of Paris, is the most famous.[1]

[1] See Mandonnet, *Siger de Brabant, et l'Averroïsme latin au XIIIème siècle,* 1899 (2nd ed., 2 vols., 1908, 1911).

They were known as Averroists because in their interpretation of Aristotle they followed more or less closely his great Arabian commentator Averroes. With him they asserted the eternity of the world and denied divine providence and foreknowledge of contingent events, and some of them at least rejected both free will and personal immortality. In spite of the disagreement at these and other points between their Aristotelianism and current Christian belief they seem not to have been troubled by it and they apparently made no effort to adjust the differences or to bring Aristotle and Christianity into line with one another. They were condemned by the Bishop of Paris in 1277 and Siger himself was compelled to spend the closing years of his life under arrest at the curia. Between these two extreme groups, those who rejected Aristotle altogether and those who followed him loyally and even slavishly, there were others who recognized his importance and welcomed the recovery of his writings, but at the same time were genuinely orthodox in their acceptance of the traditional Christian faith and were not minded to throw it over at the behest of any system of philosophy. Chief among these were Albert von Bollstädt, or Albertus Magnus as he is commonly called, and his pupil Thomas Aquinas.

Albert was one of the most learned men of the Middle Ages, interested alike in philosophy, theology and natural science. Attracted particularly by Aristotle the scientist he did much to popularize his scientific ideas. He produced several treatises based upon the writings of the Stagyrite and embodying observations of his own which in certain fields were both penetrating and extensive. He was also a theologian and attempted to bring Aristotle's scientific ideas as well as his philosophy into harmony with the Christian faith. In this, however, he was less successful than his pupil Thomas and the effort may best be studied in the writings of the latter.

Thomas was born about 1225 of the noble family of Aquino in central Italy and got his early education at the neighboring monastery of Monte Cassino, the parent house of the Benedictines. In spite of bitter opposition from family and friends he joined while still a youth the newly founded mendicant Order of Preachers (the Dominican Order) and later made his way to Paris to study with Albert, the greatest scholar of the day and the leading light of the Dominicans. Subsequently he accompanied Albert to Cologne and continued his studies under him there, becoming finally a teacher on his own account and carrying on his work in Paris, Naples and elsewhere. He died before he was fifty on his way to attend the Council of Lyons in 1274. He was extraordinarily productive and left a surprising amount of writing for one whose life closed so early. We have from his pen many philosophical and theological works, including commentaries on Aristotle, on the Scriptures, and on the Sentences of Peter Lombard. For our purpose the most important of his writings are his Summa contra gentiles and his Summa theologiæ, the latter a vast system of theology on which his fame chiefly rests.

Like Albert, Thomas was a modernist and his great effort was to reinterpret the Christian system in the light of Aristotle, or in other words to form a synthesis of Christian theology and Aristotelian philosophy. He was convinced that Aristotelianism had come to stay and was bound in the end to be generally accepted by intelligent men. Christianity therefore must make terms with it, so he believed, if it were not to lose the confidence of the educated classes. At the same time he was a devout and orthodox believer and the last thing he wanted was to sacrifice Christian truth to the demands of Aristotelianism or any other philosophy. His attitude was similar to that of many a liberal theologian of the nineteenth century who undertook to reinterpret Christianity in the light of Darwinism, not for the purpose of undermining and destroying Christianity, as their orthodox opponents thought, but to make it possible for the two to live harmoniously together.

Aquinas' problem was to effect a reconciliation, or better a combination, of Christian faith and Aristotelian philosophy which should leave the former intact and yet make room for the principles, methods and points of view of the latter. As already remarked, western theology from the time of Augustine was dominated to a considerable degree by Platonism or more especially Neoplatonism. Among the many differences between Plato and Aristotle the most significant for our present purpose was epistemological. Plato and even more emphatically the Neoplatonists assumed that a knowledge of unseen realities is possible quite apart from individual things, that man has a faculty of direct vision by which he can see God and the spiritual world ; while Aristotle insisted that all human knowledge comes through the senses alone and is the result either mediate or immediate of sensible experience. Nothing could well be more opposed than these two views. They represent indeed two radically different philosophical tendencies. It is evident at a glance that such a theory of knowledge as Aristotle's was out of line with traditional Christian ideas. How on such a supposition could the Christian know God and come into communion with him? In spite of the difficulties Thomas combined Aristotelianism and Christian theology and he did it by drawing two sharp distinctions : the one between natural and revealed theology and the other between the conditions of knowledge in this life and in the next.

As seen in the previous chapter, Hugo of St. Victor, a century before Thomas, had clearly distinguished mundane from divine theology, the former accessible to natural reason, the latter not. Thomas followed him ; but he interpreted the category of natural theology in the light of Aristotle's theory of knowledge instead of by such general and more or less vague notions of reason as were current in the western church of Hugo's day. Natural theology or philosophy begins with the creature and ascends to God; revealed theology, or theology as Thomas calls it in distinction from philosophy, begins with God and descends to the creature. Natural theology or philosophy comprises all those truths concerning God and his relation to man and the world that may be deduced from sense-experience, a priori reasoning and so-called innate ideas being altogether excluded. In other words natural theology includes those truths and only those about God and his relation to man and the world that may be discovered on Aristotelian principles.

Thomas, it should be said in passing, was no slavish adherent of Aristotle. At many points his Aristotelianism was limited and modified by the influence of Neoplatonic or Augustinian ideas. He was primarily interested not in Aristotelianism as a philosophy but in its reconciliation with the Christian faith and its use as an apologetic for the latter. But in spite of his many disagreements, in the fundamental matter already indicated he fully accepted Aristotle's teaching, recognizing sense-experience as the source of all human knowledge. "The origin of our knowledge," he says, "is in sense, even of those things that are above sense." [1] Upon this he always insisted. At this point he remained a convinced and consistent Aristotelian.

It is interesting and instructive to see the shape that natural theology took when derived from sense-experience alone. Thomas set forth his interpretation of it in what is in some respects the greatest, as it is certainly the most original, of all his writings, his Summa contra gentiles.[2]

---

[1] *Summa contra gentiles*, Bk. I. chap. 12.

[2] *Summa contra gentiles sive de veritate catholicæ fidei contra errores infidelium libri quattuor.* In the Leonine edition of Thomas' works, vols. 13–15.

The work, of which an autograph copy still exists, is in four books. The first three contain an elaborate exposition and defense of natural theology, the fourth a summary account of revealed theology which supplements and completes the former.

In Book One, dealing with God, Thomas undertakes first to prove his existence and then to show of what sort he is. In disagreement with those theologians who maintained that God could not be proved but could only be believed, he insisted that it was possible rationally to demonstrate his existence and that it was the business of the philosopher to do so. Rejecting, in accordance with his Aristotelian theory of knowledge, Anselm's ontological proof from the idea of the most perfect being, rejecting also the notion that the idea of God is inborn or that it is self-evident and needs no proof, he confined himself to the a posteriori argument from effect to cause. We cannot perceive God but we can know that he exists as we observe in the world about us the effects of his activity. Among these effects is motion which can be accounted for, so Thomas maintains in agreement with Aristotle, only by tracing it back to an unmoved mover, it being assumed on grounds given at great length, that objects are not self-moved but remain at rest unless moved from without, and that an infinite regress from effect to cause is impossible.

Thomas refers briefly to other arguments for the existence of God : from the existence of things to a first cause to which they owe their being, from the existence of beings of various degrees of perfection to a supreme Being who is absolutely perfect, and from the order in the universe to an intelligent governor. All of these are but variations of the one general argument from effect to cause and he evidently regarded the first form of it, from motion to an unmoved mover, as the most cogent. It should be noticed in this connection, that according to Thomas, even though it were assumed that the world is eternal still the theistic argument would be valid. Even then it would be necessary to account for motion by an unmoved mover. If this were not so the theistic argument would rest upon a doctrine of faith, for it cannot be proved but can only be believed on the basis of revelation that the world is not eternal. In that event the existence of God being undemonstrable by human reason would cease to be a truth of natural religion — a conclusion which Thomas rejected.

The arguments from effect to cause employed by Aquinas led not to an immanent God (or a God in any way in present contact with the world), nor to the great All embracing everything that is, but to a first cause with which the existing system of cause and effect had its inception. At least this was true of all except the familiar argument from order in the universe to an intelligent governor, and that Thomas dismissed in a brief paragraph. It was not that sensible phenomena lead us to assume a living being whose deeds they are — no supernatural forces or agencies are introduced to account for them — but that the natural order of which they are a part must have had a beginning and that this beginning must have been due to a cause other than itself.

Having shown how the existence of God may be proved on Aristotelian principles Thomas turned next to the nature of God. Of what sort is the God to whom we are led by our observation of the world in which we live? To call him the unmoved mover leaves him little better than a bare abstraction hardly worthy of the name of God. But Thomas insisted that we know much more about him than this. We know, for instance, that he is eternal, for there is time only where there is change and the unmoved mover therefore transcends time.[1] He is also necessary not contingent, for

[1] In support of each proposition touching the nature of God Thomas urged several arguments, but as it is out of the question to reproduce them all here *I*

contingency presupposes necessity; otherwise we should have to assume an infinite regress from contingent to contingent. Being eternal and necessary God has no admixture of potentiality as all other beings have, but is pure actuality. This means that he is simple, not compound, and is therefore incorporeal, for all corporeal things are compounded and divisible into parts. There cannot be two necessary and simple beings, for if there were they would be distinguishable from each other only in case one of them had added to it some differentia which the other lacked, that is only if one or both of them were composite not simple. God therefore must be one.

Again God is perfect, for imperfection implies potentiality which does not attach to God. Being perfect God is good, since goodness is included in perfection; and being perfect he is perfect goodness and the supreme good (summum bonum).[1] As perfect and as pure actuality with no admixture of potentiality God is infinite: infinite in goodness, power and essence. He is also intelligent, not only because infinite perfection includes intelligence but also because the intelligence in the world requires an intelligent author, it being assumed that an effect can contain nothing not already in its cause and that it can in no way rise above its cause. To the divine intelligence Thomas devoted many chapters,[2] dealing with it more fully than with any other topic. God's knowledge is immediate and intuitive, not reasoned or discursive, for there is only actuality not potentiality in him. All things are eternally present to him, or in other words all

have contented myself in each case with a single one which will serve to illustrate his dialectic method. It will be noticed that as a rule he did not argue, as he might have been expected to, from the existence of certain qualities in the universe to their existence in God (though he did at times) but reached his results by a logical analysis of the conception of the unmoved mover. In this, however, he but followed his master Aristotle.

[1] Thomas did not indicate the content of the divine goodness. As he used the word it was practically synonymous with perfection.

[2] I. 44–71.

things are present to him in an everlasting now. Primarily God knows only himself, but in knowing himself he knows all things, for he is the cause of all. Perfect knowledge of a cause involves a knowledge of all its effects, since there is in the effects nothing that is not already in their cause. As his essence is infinitely perfect while all else is imperfect God is greater than the sum of all that is and hence his knowledge reaches not only to things that are but also to things that are not. Knowing what is not he also knows evil (though he is not the cause of it), for evil is only the lack of perfection and is therefore in reality nothing.

God is also will, understanding and will being inseparable. A mind that knows the good must will it. The will indeed is nothing else than the understanding embracing that which it sees or believes to be good. God's will, like the will of every other intelligent being, is, therefore, controlled by his understanding. He wills nothing arbitrarily. What he wills is not good because he wills it, but he wills it because it is good. He cannot will what is opposed to his nature or character, or what is impossible or self-contradictory, but he wills all that is, for all that is is good.

Again, God has no passions, both because he is pure actuality without any mixture of potentiality, and because passions are rooted in the sensitive appetites which God, as an incorporeal being, is wholly without; at the same time he knows joy and delight and happiness. Happiness is the proper good of God, as of every intelligent being, and is such a being's greatest perfection. God indeed is his own happiness. And as he is the most perfect of beings he is happiest of all — happy because he is sufficient for himself and in want of nothing, happy in his contemplation of himself and other beings, and happy in his government of the whole universe. "According to Boethius," Thomas says, "happiness consists in five things: pleasure, riches, power, dignity, and fame.

But God has a most excellent delight in himself and a universal joy in all good things without the admixture of anything of a contrary sort. For riches he has in himself a complete sufficiency of all goods. For power he has infinite strength. For dignity he has the primacy and rule over all beings. For fame he has the admiration of every intelligence that in any way knows him." [1] It is worth observing that Thomas has nothing to say here about the good of others, or about the opportunity to bless them as a reason for God's happiness.

In the second book Thomas deals with the creation and particularly with God as creator. The method of argumentation employed is similar to that of the first book. As it has already appeared with sufficient clearness it is unnecessary to illustrate it further. I shall therefore give only a brief summary of the conclusions reached. As in the first book Aristotle is quoted or referred to in almost every chapter, often several times in a chapter. [2] God, Thomas asserts, and every assertion he fortifies with an elaborate argument, is the cause of being to all that is. All things were created out of nothing. Creation was instantaneous not successive. All matter and all species were produced at once and have not had to be renewed. [3] God's relations to things are external to himself and the act of creation has not changed or affected him in any way. Creation was not necessary to him, but was an act of free will motivated by goodness and controlled by wisdom. As he never acts arbitrarily, so he did not in this case, but had regard to a supreme end for which all things were made. [4]

[1] I. 102.
[2] Thomas seems somewhat less bound by Aristotle's authority and departs from him more frequently than in the first book. The argumentation, moreover, is somewhat less closely knit and often less cogent.
[3] II. 15–16; 19 ff. The contrast with Augustine at this point is interesting. Thomas' not Augustine's was the common view.
[4] II. 23 ff.

Whether the world was created in time or has existed from eternity cannot be proved or disproved. In this Thomas disagreed with Averroes and other Arabian philosophers who thought it could be proved that creation was eternal, as also with many Christian theologians of the day who thought it could be proved that it was not. In opposition to both of them Thomas argued at great length that there are no adequate reasons to be urged on either side, and that therefore if one rejects the eternity of the world, as he himself did, he must do it on the basis of faith alone.[1]

Still further, Thomas maintained that the immense diversities among creatures are not due to the existence of two primary powers, a good and a bad, or of a plurality of creating agents. Nor are the inequalities in human conditions and fortunes a consequence of the pre-mundane merits and demerits of men, as Origen held. God was under no obligation to make all creatures equal, for creation was not an act of justice which bound him to treat all alike, but an act of generosity which left him free to treat everyone as he pleased. The reason for the variety among creatures was God's wish that his likeness might appear in the creation in all possible forms and degrees. On this account the multiplication of species was more important and a greater addition to the good of the universe than the multiplication of individuals within a species.[2]

The second book contains a long discussion of the human soul and of human intelligence and will, the freedom of the will being stoutly insisted upon.[3] The relation of the soul to the body is also dealt with at length and it is maintained, in agreement with Aristotle rather than Plato, that man is both soul and body, not a mere soul inhabiting a body.[4] Personal immortality, nevertheless, is asserted, and it is claimed that it can be demonstrated on rational grounds

[1] II. 40.   [2] II. 41–44.   [3] II. 48.   [4] II. 57.

without an appeal to revelation. Among the arguments urged in its support is the contention that since nature does nothing in vain it is impossible to suppose any natural desire permanently frustrated.[1] It is interesting to observe that Thomas also made the existence of angels (intelligent beings without material bodies) a part of his natural theology, arguing that when there exists a compound of two substances such as man who is both soul and body, and when one of these substances and that the lower of them is found alone, as in material things, it may be assumed a fortiori that the other also, namely mind, will be found alone.[2]

The first book having dealt with the nature of God and the second with his power, the third treats of his dignity and authority as the final end of all things and the ruler over them. Referring to God as the end of all things Thomas maintains that it is the chief end of every intelligent being to understand God, that the happiness of such a being lies in the understanding, not in the will, and that his highest happiness consists not in bodily pleasures, in wealth or glory or power or even virtue, but in the contemplation of God.[3] He maintains also that the knowledge of God which brings true happiness is not the fruit of demonstration or of faith but of direct vision, a vision not to be had in this life but only in the life to come when we shall be rid of our corporeal natures and be able by God's help to look directly upon him, and when in knowing him we shall know all things so far, at least, as they may be grasped by human intelligence.[4] Thomas has been called a mystic because he taught a direct vision of God, but it is to be noticed that the vision of which he spoke is to be had only in the future life, not in this. Here a man's knowledge is indirect only — a knowledge due to demonstration or faith — and can never be

---

[1] II. 55, 79. [2] II. 91. [3] III. 25 ff.
[4] For Thomas' discussion of the vision of God see III. 37–63.

anything more. In his reading of the present life, therefore, Thomas was far from mysticism. He was very devout and pious, a spiritually-minded man in the best sense, but he was not a mystic and to pronounce him one, as many are doing, is to misunderstand both Thomas himself and his influence upon the Catholic church.

In speaking of the vision of God Thomas went far beyond Aristotle. They agreed in making the chief end of man knowledge and in putting the happiness of an intelligent being in the understanding rather than the will, but of seeing God Aristotle had nothing to say, or of a future life in which he could be seen. Anything like a direct vision of God indeed was quite out of line with his general theory of knowledge. It is significant that in this connection Thomas appealed to the Bible rather than to Aristotle and clinched the matter by declaring that the denial that man may see God "contradicts the authority of Holy Scripture" and "is to be rejected as false and heretical." [1]

By confining the vision of God to the future life when we shall be freed from our corporeal nature, Thomas remained true, so far as this life is concerned, to Aristotle's epistemological principles, and kept his natural theology within the bounds of knowledge derivable from sense-experience. But what about revealed theology? The fact that he accepted divine revelation and recognized it as the source of a knowledge about God and divine things inaccessible to the natural reason seems to contradict his Aristotelian principle that all human knowledge has its origin in the senses. But here a distinction is to be drawn between the prophet who receives the revelation and other men who accept it on the authority of the prophet, as they accept any other fact which they have not themselves witnessed on the authority of one who has. For the ordinary man, that is

[1] III. 54.

for everyone since the time of the Prophets and Apostles — for Thomas believed there had been no divine revelation since their day [1] — the knowledge of the truths of revealed theology which he gains by hearing or reading is as much a fruit of sensible experience as anything else. In accepting such truths his mind works in the same way as in accepting any other truths on the authority of one who knows.

On the other hand, with the prophet himself (whether of Old Testament or New) the situation was different, as Thomas makes very clear in his discussion of prophecy in the second part of his Summa theologiæ.[2] The psychology of the prophet was not that of the ordinary man. As in the future life when we are freed from our bodies our way of knowing will be entirely different from now, so the prophet's way of knowing was different from that of others. He was under supernatural control, his mind was illuminated from above, and truth was communicated to him, sometimes when he was in an ecstasy and wholly oblivious to the sensible world, sometimes not, but in either case quite without the medium of the senses through which knowledge is ordinarily gained. His experience was a foretaste of that of the blessed in the future life, but was not as perfect, for the revelation was mediated by angels not given directly by God himself and the prophet did not see the divine essence, though Moses, the greatest of the old dispensation, and Paul, the greatest of the new, actually did.[3] Thus Thomas provided for divine revelation without contradicting his Aristotelian theory of knowledge so far as men in general are concerned. But when it came to the prophet he broke with his Aristotelian principles altogether and treated him

---

[1] Cf. *Summa theologiæ*, Part I. Qu. 1: Art. 8.

[2] *Ibid.* IIb. 171–175. The second part of the *Summa theologiæ* has two sub-divisions, known respectively as *Prima secundæ* and *Secunda secundæ*. For convenience' sake I refer to the former as IIa and to the latter as IIb.

[3] *Ibid.* IIb. 175: 3.

as if he were a disembodied spirit like the angels and the saints in heaven.

Having completed what he had to say in his Summa contra gentiles about God as the last end of all things and the supreme object of human knowledge, Thomas turned to divine providence, or God as the ruler of the world. In showing the connection between the two subjects he remarks : "When things are ordained for a particular end all of them are subject to the government of him to whom the end principally pertains, as appears in an army. For all the parts of an army and their works are ordained for a final end, namely, *the good of the commander which is victory*. And therefore it belongs to him to govern the whole army." [1] Thomas then goes on in the usual way to prove that God rules the world, that he preserves all things in being, that he is everywhere and in all things, that he is the cause of all activity, that his activity is not inconsistent with the presence of evil in the world, with contingency and freedom, or with prayer, that he rules through subordinate agents, both angels and men, and acts ordinarily by means of secondary causes, but that he may act directly if he pleases, or in other words, may work miracles.

Men, like other rational creatures, are cared for and governed by God for their own sakes, but lower creatures only for the sake of man, who may use them in any way he chooses. If cruelty to them is forbidden, it is not on their account but on man's own, lest it cause loss to someone or encourage cruel treatment of human beings.[2] In this estimate of the brute creation Thomas, like the apostle Paul, was simply reflecting the common sentiment of his age. Francis of Assisi's attitude is all the more striking by contrast.

---

[1] *Summa contra gentiles*, III. 64. The words I have italicized throw an interesting light on Thomas' idea of God.
[2] III. 112.

God has given a law for the government of men's lives, a law to which are attached rewards and punishments both temporal and eternal.[1] By law in this case Thomas meant not the Mosaic or any other revealed law, but what is ordinarily called the law of nature. Its end is love for God, and it requires love for one's neighbors, worship of God, and right belief as well as right conduct. In this connection Thomas argued on rational grounds for the sanctity and indissolubility of marriage,[2] while at the same time he defended on similar grounds chastity, poverty and the like, or in other words the abandonment of lower goods for the sake of higher.[3]

The third book closes with several chapters on divine grace. Thomas justified himself for dealing with this subject in a treatise on natural theology by appealing to the fact that, unlike other creatures, man's final end, namely, the vision of God, is above his natural powers and hence he needs divine assistance in order to attain it.[4] There will be occasion to speak of Thomas' view of grace later and it is unnecessary to say anything on the subject here.

In the fourth book Thomas turns to revealed theology which supplements and completes natural theology. Already at the beginning of the first book he had emphasized the importance of divine revelation without which God could not be adequately known, and had maintained that a revelation had actually been given in Christianity, as was proved by miracles both physical and spiritual and also by the fulfilment of prophecy.[5] "Man may have a threefold knowledge of divine things," he says at the beginning of the fourth book. "The first is what he gains by the natural light of reason when he ascends through creatures to God. The

---

[1] III. 114 ff., 141 ff.
[2] III. 122.
[3] III. 131.
[4] Cf. III. 50 ff.
[5] IV. 6.

second is when divine truth exceeding human understanding descends to us by way of revelation, not as it were proved to sight but offered for belief. The third is when the human mind is raised to a perfect insight into the things that are revealed." [1]

It is with the second kind of knowledge that Thomas deals in the fourth book. Revelation, to be sure, covers truths that are discoverable by reason as well as those that are not, for there are few persons that have the ability and the leisure to theologize for themselves and hence even the truths of natural religion would remain unknown to most were it not for revelation. But over and above these God reveals truths that are quite inaccessible to the natural reason even of philosophers. Though above reason such truths are not contrary to it, for reason and revelation cannot contradict each other. But their proof must be found wholly in revelation and the most that reason can do is to show that they are not irrational and that there is some probability in their favor. "Since reason," Thomas says, "ascends through created things to the knowledge of God, but the knowledge that comes from faith descends by way of revelation from God to us, the way of ascent and descent being the same, it is proper to proceed by the same way in dealing with the things of faith that are above reason, as was followed in our rational inquiry concerning God. Hence we shall treat first of the truths above reason that are to be believed concerning God himself, for example the doctrine of the Trinity; secondly of the deeds above reason performed by God, like the work of the incarnation and its consequences; thirdly of the events above reason that are to be expected at the end of human history, as for instance the resurrection and deification of the body, everlasting blessedness and the events connected therewith." [2] Following this outline

[1] IV. I.   [2] *Ibid.*

Thomas discusses the Trinity, the incarnation, including original sin and the sacraments, and eschatology, including the resurrection, the future life and everlasting rewards and punishments. It is not necessary to dwell upon his treatment of these familiar themes.[1] The significance of the work we have been examining lies not in the fourth book but in the first three, which contain the clearest and most consistent presentation and defense of natural theology to be found in mediæval literature.

The only other work that needs attention in this chapter is the Summa theologiæ,[2] the largest and most famous of all Thomas' writings. It constitutes a general system of theology covering the whole range of Christian truth, but in spite of its formidable proportions it was intended, at least according to Thomas' preface, for beginners in theology and was meant to serve as an introduction to the subject. "It is our purpose in this work," he says, "to treat of those matters that pertain to the Christian religion in a way fitted to the instruction of beginners. For we are of the opinion that neophytes in this science are much impeded by what has been written by various authors, partly because of the multiplication of useless questions, articles and arguments ; partly because those things which they need to know are taught in a way required not by the subject itself but by the nature of the book or the form of the argument ; and partly because their frequent repetition gives rise to distaste and confusion in the mind of the reader. Therefore studying to avoid these and similar faults we shall attempt, trusting in divine help, to present those things that pertain

---

[1] It is significant that the reason Thomas removed the Trinity from the truths of natural theology, among which it was reckoned by some theologians, was that in creation we observe the work of God as God and not the work of the separate persons of the Godhead and therefore can argue back only to one God, not to the Trinity (cf. *Summa theologiæ*, I. 32 : 1).

[2] In the Leonine edition of Thomas' works, vols. IV–XII.

to sacred doctrine briefly and clearly, so far as the subject permits."

As a matter of fact the argumentation in the later Summa is as a rule less abstruse and less strictly philosophical than in the earlier. In the one Thomas evidently had philosophers chiefly in mind, in the other theologians and theological students; and in the one he was addressing himself primarily to unbelievers, in the other to Christians. The work is divided into three parts, the first treating of God, the second of the rational creature's approach to God, and the third of Christ, the way to God. Each part is divided into a large number of "Questions" and each question into several articles. Taken all together there are more than six hundred questions and more than three thousand articles. Every question is handled according to a fixed scheme which is followed without variation throughout the work. First there is a general statement of the subject to be dealt with; then the subdivisions of the subject are treated in successive articles. Each of these contains, first, opinions with which Thomas did not agree, or agreed only in part. These counter opinions are commonly called Objections, as for instance in the English translation, but they bear no title in the original. Sometimes there are several of them, sometimes only one or two.[1] There follows a paragraph to the opposite effect (introduced with the words Sed contra) which is usually in the form of a quotation from the Bible or the Fathers, particularly Augustine, occasionally from Aristotle or some other philosopher. Thomas' own solution, which constitutes the body of the article, is then intro-

---

[1] There are approximately ten thousand of these so-called "Objections." It was evidently Thomas' desire to meet every objection that had been or possibly could be brought against the opinions he adopted. The persistence with which he runs them down and the frankness with which he states them are very impressive even though his answers are not always as satisfactory as might be wished.

duced with the words Respondeo dicendum, and the article is concluded with answers to the objections cited at the beginning. Occasionally these answers are omitted as unnecessary.

Unlike the Summa contra gentiles, the Summa theologiæ gives the system of Christian doctrine as a whole instead of natural and revealed theology separately. The two, to be sure, are often distinguished in the discussion of this or that topic and it is shown what may be derived from reason and what only from revelation. Nevertheless the entire system is treated as one and all its parts as belonging to a common body of faith, though Thomas' conclusions are often only tentative and not intended to be binding upon Christians. In general, while the method of treatment is different, the later Summa deals with much the same subjects as the earlier and the conclusions reached are as a rule identical. Its greater size is due in part to the divergent opinions cited so abundantly, in part to the larger amount of space devoted to the doctrines of revealed theology, in part to the extended treatise on ethics which fills more than half the work.

It is unnecessary to go over the contents in detail. It is enough to call attention to certain points of special interest or importance. Sacred doctrine, Thomas recognized, is both speculative and practical. But he departed from the common opinion of the day in regarding it as more largely the former than the latter because it has to do chiefly with God and is primarily concerned with divine things rather than human. It deals with creatures, indeed, only in so far as they are referable to God as their beginning or end.[1] Sacred doctrine does not attempt to prove its principles but assumes them as certain on the basis of revelation and then goes on to draw conclusions from them. Thomas' method of reaching these conclusions is similar to that

[1] *Summa theologiæ*, I. I : 3, 4.

employed in the Summa contra gentiles where the materials were drawn from sense-experience. Whether the materials come from thence or from divine revelation they are treated as the basis for theological conclusions of wide range and reach. "As other sciences do not argue in support of their principles," Thomas says, "but from those principles go on to prove other things, so this doctrine does not argue in support of its principles, which are the articles of faith, but from them goes on to prove something else. . . . In this doctrine it is particularly fitting to argue from authority, for its principles are given by revelation and hence should be believed on the authority of those to whom the revelation was made. Neither does this detract from the dignity of the doctrine, for although an argument from authority based on human reason is very weak, an argument from authority based on divine revelation is most efficacious." [1] "Our faith," he continues, "rests on the revelation given to the apostles and prophets who wrote the canonical books and not on the revelation given to other doctors if there was any such." At the same time the doctors of the church and philosophers as well may be appealed to for instruction in matters with which they were familiar, even though their authority is not to be taken as final.

After his introductory discussion of the nature and extent of sacred doctrine Thomas turns to the subject of God and our knowledge of him. His position is the same as in the Summa contra gentiles. By natural reason drawing conclusions from sense-experience we may be sure that God exists. [2] In this life we can know him only indirectly either through his works or on the authority of his revelation to prophets and apostles. Even the latter gives us no more than an indirect knowledge of him. We have no special

[1] I. 1 : 8.
[2] I. 2 : 3. Thomas uses the same arguments employed in the earlier *Summa* and also adds the familiar proof from contingent to necessary being.

faculty by which we can see him and come into immediate communion with him. Only in the future life when freed from the limitations of the body shall we look directly upon him and enjoy the vision of him as he is.[1] That in the Summa theologiæ Aquinas should take the same position as in the earlier work shows how convinced he was in this matter.[2]

Thomas' account of the nature and attributes of God is also substantially identical with that of the earlier Summa. God is a simple not a composite being, incorporeal, perfect, good and the supreme good, infinite, immutable, eternal, one; he has will as well as intellect; he is omniscient, omnipotent, and supremely blessed; he is a God of love, of righteousness, and of mercy; and he is the creator and providential ruler of the world.

All things, not simply the germs of things as Augustine maintained, were created by God directly. Divine creation Thomas interpreted, in agreement with common Christian tradition, as creation ex nihilo. To be sure he spoke of it as emanation (emanatio),[3] but this does not mean that he thought of creatures as sharing in the nature of God. On the contrary he insisted that they were made out of nothing. Anything like pantheism was altogether abhorrent to him. The contrast at this point between him and Eriugena is very striking.

In connection with divine providence Thomas discussed in some detail the subject of predestination. At this point he followed Augustine in teaching that predestination is not conditioned on anything actual or foreseen in man and that it includes both election and reprobation. The latter

---

[1] I. 12.

[2] In some of his earlier tracts written before his Aristotelianism was fully developed there are passages that look in the direction of mysticism, but they do not represent his mature attitude.

[3] *Summa theologiæ*, I. 45 : 1.

to be sure he phrased in terms of permission rather than of positive decree.[1] Even so his doctrine of predestination was much more Augustinian than the common opinion of his day, which was of a decidedly Semipelagian cast. With Augustine he taught also that except in special cases no one is permitted to know whether he is one of the elect, lest he fall into despair, or feel himself secure and so relax his vigilance. Apparently Thomas was no more troubled than Augustine had been by the inconsistency into which practical interests thus betrayed him.

In dealing with the creation and government of the world Aquinas was led to speak at considerable length of angels,[2] the loftiest creatures of God, to whom he had referred more briefly in his earlier Summa. "The perfection of the universe," he says, "requires that there be intellectual creatures. To know cannot be the act of a body or of any corporeal power, for every body is limited to here and now. Hence it is necessary to assume for the perfection of the universe the existence of some incorporeal creature."[3] Various questions are then raised in regard to angels: whether one of them can be simultaneously in different places, whether several angels can be in the same place at the same time, whether in passing from one place to another an angel passes through intermediate space, how angels know and what is the extent of their knowledge, whether they have free will, whether they are eternal, whether they need divine grace, whether they talk with one another, whether they can work miracles, whether they influence the lives of men, and so on. Thomas' conclusions, which are some-

---

[1] "Since men are ordained by divine providence to eternal life, it belongs also to divine providence to permit some to fail of that end. And this is called reprobation . . . As predestination includes the will to confer grace and glory, reprobation includes the will to permit a person to fall into guilt and to visit upon him the punishment of damnation for his guilt" (I. 23 : 3).

[2] *Summa theologiæ*, I. 50–64; 107–114.

[3] I. 50 : 1.

times expressed positively, sometimes only tentatively, are based partly on reason, partly on authority, both the Scriptures and the Fathers (particularly Pseudo-Dionysius) being quoted profusely. Much of the discussion seems futile in the extreme, but the subject had for thinkers like Thomas not simply the curious interest that attaches to it in the minds of the uncultured but also a speculative interest in the nature of spiritual being. In man we have the spiritual and the corporeal united. What must the spiritual be when it is without the limitations, physical and intellectual, entailed by its union with a body? How does it gain its knowledge when it is without sense-perception? Given the belief in the existence of angels, which was universal in Thomas' day, and which he regarded as well grounded in reason quite apart from revelation, the questions as to their nature and faculties were as engaging and as important to speculative philosophers as similar questions touching the nature and faculties of man.

The second part of the Summa theologiæ deals with ethics and constitutes the most elaborate treatise on the subject produced within the Christian church up to Thomas' time. As in the Summa contra gentiles, man's last end is declared to be happiness, which consists in the vision of God and is to be attained only in the future life.[1] Although this happiness cannot be achieved by man himself but must be divinely bestowed, it is granted only as a reward for works of virtue, and consequently it is necessary to consider in detail the acts by which he obtains it.[2] Thus Thomas brought ethics into connection with theology and justified himself for dealing with it in his Summa theologiæ. The study of morals, he says, should include first general principles and secondly matters of detail. Accordingly, in the first subdivision of Part II (Prima secundæ), he treats

[1] *Summa theologiæ*, IIa. 2:8; 3:8.   [2] IIa. 5:5–7; 6:1.

such subjects as man's last end, the will, good and evil, the passions, habits, law and grace; in the second subdivision (Secunda secundæ) particular virtues with their corresponding vices: first those pertaining to all men and then those pertaining to special classes such as monks and bishops.

Law he divides into eternal law, namely the absolute principles of wisdom according to which God governs the universe; natural law, or eternal law so far as it applies to the conduct of men; human law, or the enactments of earthly governments, which are sometimes in harmony with the principles of eternal law and sometimes not; and finally divine law which has been revealed by God in its two historic forms, the Jewish and the Christian. The Christian law is not primarily a written law like that of the Jews, but an inward law having to do with the attitude and disposition.[1] To be sure it prescribes certain external things, as for instance the sacraments, and the decalogue remains permanently binding upon Christians. In general, however, it confines itself to the heart and leaves outward acts to be regulated in such ways as may best express the spirit of love for God, the essence of the law. Since much is left free in it, in contrast with the law of the Jews, and since the controlling motive is not hope of reward or fear of punishment but love for God, which means love for the good, it is rightly called a law of liberty. To live Christianly is not to keep the law because it is a law and demands obedience, but because we love God from whom the law came and love the good to which it gives expression.[2]

Though Thomas dealt with virtues and vices in great detail and had much to say about the proper conduct of

[1] IIa. 106.
[2] IIa. 107:1. Thomas found another reason for calling the Christian law a law of liberty in the evangelical counsels which offer Christians an opportunity to do things well pleasing to God but not required by him.

Christians in all possible relations of life, he always laid chief emphasis on the inner disposition and insisted that no formal correctness of life and no mere legal righteousness made up for the lack of love for God and devotion to him. To be sure the virtue of an act depends not merely on the motive with which it is done but also on the nature of the act itself and on the attendant circumstances. But even so, apart from the inner disposition the external deed is without moral quality.

As in the earlier Summa the section on law is followed by one on grace.[1] "The most powerful thing," Thomas says, "in the law of the New Testament and that wherein its whole virtue consists is the grace of the Holy Spirit, which is given through faith in Christ."[2] And again, "Grace joins man to the highest good which is God."[3] This, however, is not to be taken in a mystical sense as if it meant a real participation in the nature of God.[4] So far as the relation between God and man was concerned Thomas thought in ethical rather than physical terms, and that too though he conceived of grace not simply as a personal influence but also as a substance. The notion of grace as a substance he shared with those that went before him. It was interwoven with the idea of the sacraments which were generally believed not simply to symbolize grace but to contain and convey it.[5] The inevitable confusion in his thought was no greater than in that of others before and since his day, and he was more consistent than most of them in reading the relation between God and man, notwithstanding his disparate conception of grace, in strictly personal and moral terms.

[1] IIa. 109 ff.
[2] IIa. 106 : 1.
[3] IIa. 112 : 4.
[4] The grace of adoption, Thomas says, does not bring about a union of nature but of affection (III. 50 : 1); cf. also IIa. 110 : 4.
[5] Cf. III. 62 : 1.

In speaking of the effects of grace Thomas has some interesting things to say about justification. He identifies it with the forgiveness of sin, which is an instantaneous act on God's part and the first step in the salvation of the sinner. Justification is by faith alone : not a mere empty or barren faith such as is denounced in the Epistle of James but faith informed with love. This faith which includes the belief that God justifies sinners through Christ is the fruit of divine grace infused into the heart and leads to good works. Justification, however, is not based on good works either actual or foreseen, but on faith alone. It cannot be earned but is given freely.[1] Nor do we merit justification by our faith, for justifying faith is a gift of God, not a meritorious work of our own. Though justification is thus by faith alone it is not, according to Thomas, identical with salvation, as later to Luther. Eternal life is granted only to him who having been freely justified goes on to do good works not in his own strength but with the help of divine grace.

In the second subdivision of Part II (Secunda secundæ) Thomas turns to particular virtues. These he divides into natural and theological. The former are within a man's own power and while they may serve to bring him a certain measure of happiness they cannot lead to eternal blessedness. For that only supernatural virtues beyond the ability of the natural man are adequate. These are called theological, for they have God as their object and are revealed and communicated by him.[2] Thus Thomas made room in ethics as well as in theology for the two subdivisions, natural and revealed. Moreover, as revealed theology does not contradict but supplements natural theology, so the theological virtues do not displace but crown the natural virtues. Grace, according to Thomas, perfects nature rather than

[1] IIa. 114 : 5.　　　　　　　[2] IIa. 62 : 1.

destroys it, and this principle he maintained consistently both in ethics and in theology.

The theological virtues are three in number: faith, hope and charity. Faith, Thomas says, assents only to what is revealed by God and only because it is revealed.[1] But divine revelation, as shown in the Summa contra gentiles, includes both things that are above reason (as for instance the Trinity) and also things that are demonstrable by reason (for instance the existence of God), and therefore faith is not confined to the former but is directed toward the latter as well.[2] The substance of the faith remains always the same, but its articles increase as time passes, what was only implicit being made explicit to meet the needs of later times.[3] Faith is meritorious and unbelief is the greatest of sins, though not every act of unbelievers is necessarily sinful as Augustine maintained. But whenever they do anything as a result of their unbelief they sin.[4] Thomas' attitude in this matter illustrates his general sanity and moderation. He was uncommonly free from extreme views and was seldom carried away by the seeming logic of his positions.

Concerning the treatment to be accorded unbelievers and heretics he speaks at some length and with great care. Unbelievers may, as a rule, be tolerated and Christians may be allowed to associate familiarly with them if they are strong enough in the faith to resist temptation and perhaps even to convert them to Christianity.[5] But with heretics the situation is different. With regard to them Thomas says there are two points to be observed. "So far as they are concerned they have merited by their sin not only ex´ communication but also death. For it is much worse to corrupt the faith through which the soul lives than to coun-

[1] IIb. 1:1.
[2] IIb. 11:4.   The same reasons are given as in the earlier Summa.
[3] IIb. 1:7.   [4] IIb. 10:4.   [5] IIb. 10:9 ff.

terfeit money which supports the temporal life. But if counterfeiters and other malefactors are with justice sum‧marily executed by secular princes, much more heretics when they have been convicted of heresy may with justice not only be immediately excommunicated but also slain. On the other hand, there is mercy in the church for the conversion of the erring. Hence she does not condemn at once but only after a first and second admonition, as the Apostle directs. Later, if the offender persists, the church, abandoning hope of his conversion, provides for the safety of others by excommunicating him and finally gives him up to the secular judge that he may be put out of the world by death." [1]

Though faith is the first of the theological virtues the greatest of them is charity (caritas), without which no true virtue is possible. [2] Charity means primarily friendship with God and love for him : God is to be loved as the last end to which all other things are referred. [3] Charity means secondarily love for one's neighbor not for his own sake but for the sake of God. The command to love God includes love for our neighbor and the latter need not have been specifically required. But because of the ignorant who might not have understood that love for others is involved in love for God it was given the dignity of a special enact‧ment. [4] Love for God embraces also love for sinners and en‧emies and for angels as well, but it stops short of demons and irrational animals. Moreover, love for God implies love for oneself. Indeed Thomas insists that a man should

---

[1] IIb. 11 : 3.

[2] IIb. 23 : 6–7. Caritas is the theological virtue which includes or is the source of love in the ordinary sense (amor or dilectio) from which it is not always sharply distinguished. In one passage Thomas speaks of caritas as a kind of love (caritas amor quidam est : IIb. 24 : 1). Elsewhere he refers to dilectio as the principal act of caritas (IIb. 27).

[3] IIb. 44 : 4.

[4] IIb. 44 : 2.

love himself even more than his neighbor; not for his own sake, to be sure (that would be only selfishness), but for God's sake. That a man should love himself more than any other person, Thomas says, "is evident from the very reason for loving. For, as was said above, God is loved as the principle of good on which charity is founded. But a man out of charity loves himself for the reason that he is a participant in the aforesaid good; while his neighbor is loved because he is a companion in that good. Association, however, is a reason for love in proportion to the degree of union with God. Therefore as unity is stronger than union, that a man himself participates in the divine good is a stronger reason for loving than that another is associated with him in this participation. Hence a man out of charity should love himself more than his neighbor. And the sign of this is that a man ought not to commit any sin which will hinder his own participation in blessedness in order to free his neighbor from sin." [1]

After dealing with the theological virtues Thomas turns to the four cardinal virtues (prudence, justice, fortitude and temperance) traditional in Christian thought ever since Ambrose. To these he devotes even more space than to the former. Under the general head of justice he defends the right of private property, but he recognizes that the right is relative only, not absolute, for it is founded not on natural law which taken by itself makes for a community of goods, but on positive law, that is on human agreement which in this case does not contradict but supplements natural law. He also insists that while private property is lawful it should not be held as if it were one's own but as if it were common and hence should be freely used for the relief of those in want.[2] In accordance with this principle he even goes so far as to declare that while theft is always a sin it is not

[1] IIb. 26:4.   [2] IIb. 66:2.

theft when in extreme need one takes another's property either openly or secretly for the purpose of supporting one's life or aiding a destitute neighbor.[1]   It is interesting to notice, it may be remarked in passing, that Thomas pronounces religion a virtue and includes it too under the general head of justice to cover what we owe God or our duties to him.[2]   As already in Ambrose's work On the Duties of the Clergy the classical interpretation of the cardinal virtues is considerably modified by Christian ideals and the quadrilateral framework is frequently strained to include virtues that found little or no place in antique ethics, as for instance humility, unworldliness, virginity, fasting and the like. As a matter of fact Thomas' treatment of the subject of ethics betrays even more than his treatment of theology the influence of diverse forces.   The fourfold classification is crossed by Aristotle's tenfold classification,[3] as also by his general division of the virtues into intellectual and moral, the former including wisdom, knowledge and understanding.[4]   Aristotle's definition of virtue as the mean between two extremes (for instance, courage as the mean between rashness and cowardice and truthfulness as the mean between the assertion of a falsehood and the denial of a truth) is adopted, though it accords ill with Thomas' general idea of virtue, and has no application, as he recognizes, to the theological virtues: faith, hope and charity.[5]

In spite, however, of its inconsistencies, and the confusion that besets it at many points, Thomas' treatment of the subject of ethics is extraordinarily sane and practical and uncommonly free from paradox and from extremes of every

[1] IIb. 66 : 7.
[2] IIb. 81 ff.
[3] Fortitude, temperance, liberality, magnificence, magnanimity, love of honour, clemency, friendship, truthfulness, urbanity. Cf. Thomas' *Summa theologiæ*, IIa. 60 : 5.
[4] IIa. 57–58.
[5] Cf. IIa. 64.

kind. Nothing, indeed, could be better adapted to the needs of a great institution like the Catholic church to which people of all classes and all degrees of culture look for moral guidance. The influence of this part of Thomas' work has been enormous, perhaps greater than that of any other part, for moral conduct is of practical concern to every Christian layman as well as theologian.

The third part of the Summa theologiæ deals with the incarnation, with the work of Christ, and with the sacraments, that is with the means ordained for the salvation of men; as also with the resurrection and the future life. Thomas did not live to complete the Summa. He finished what he had to say on the incarnation and the work of Christ, on the nature and purpose of the sacraments in general, and on baptism, confirmation and the eucharist in particular.[1] When he laid down his pen he was in the midst of the sacrament of penance. After his death the work was brought to a conclusion by a disciple on the basis of his early commentary on the Sentences of Lombard.

Of Aquinas' doctrine of the incarnation and the work of Christ it is worth while to speak in some detail, both because of its historical importance and also because it admirably reveals certain aspects of his theological method. At the beginning of Part III he discusses the rationale of the incarnation. In the fourth book of the Summa contra gentiles he had already dealt with the matter at considerable length. There he had cited no less than twenty-six objections to the incarnation and eight reasons in its favor. Among the latter were the following: As beatitude consists in the vision of God it was fitting that it should be shown possible by the union of God and man; to arouse men's love for God the best means was to exhibit God's love for them by the incarnation; as blessedness is the prize of virtue, an example

[1] On Thomas' doctrine of the sacraments see below, Chap. XIV.

of virtue was needed such as only a God-man could furnish; if man is to attain salvation he must have his sins forgiven and this is possible only if satisfaction be rendered by one who is at once God and man.[1]

In the corresponding passage in the Summa theologiæ the subject is handled in similar fashion but more briefly. Here the principal reason for the incarnation is represented as the goodness of God to which it belongs to communicate itself to the creature in the highest way possible. What is said of the incarnation, however, must be supplemented by what is said later of Christ's passion and death,[2] a matter not referred to in the earlier Summa. Taking the two together we get a comprehensive and adequate view of Thomas' doctrine of the work of Christ which has been generally normative in Catholic theology ever since. In agreement with Augustine but in disagreement with Anselm he maintained that it was not necessary, in the strict sense, that Christ should have suffered and died. God might have chosen some other way to save men, though none so fitting as the way he actually chose, for by means of it many other things were accomplished besides man's liberation from sin.[3] Thus, from Christ's death we learn how much God loves us and so are incited to love him; in it there has been given us an example of obedience, humility, constancy, justice and other virtues which are necessary to salvation; by dying Christ has not only freed us from sin but has also won for us justifying grace and future glory; again, being bought with so great a price, there is the more reason why we should keep ourselves free from sin; and as man was conquered by Satan and brought into subjection to death it makes for human dignity that a man should over-

---

[1] *Summa contra gentiles*, IV. 53–55.
[2] *Summa theologiæ*, III. 46–50.
[3] III. 1 : 2 ; 46 : 1–3.

come Satan and by dying should vanquish death. "It was therefore more fitting," Thomas concludes, "that we should be set free by the passion of Christ than by the will of God alone." [1]

Later, in speaking of Christ's death, he says it was appropriate that he should die, first to render satisfaction for sin by submitting to the penalty deserved by men; secondly to show the reality of his human flesh; thirdly to deliver us from the fear of death; fourthly to set us an example of dying spiritually unto sin; and fifthly that by rising from the dead he might give us the hope of a resurrection. [2] His passion, according to Thomas, was more than enough to atone for human sins. "He properly atones for an offense who offers to the offended one what the latter loves as much or more than he hated the offense. But Christ by suffering out of charity and obedience offered God something greater than was needed to compensate for all the sins of the human race. First, because of the greatness of the charity which led him to suffer; secondly, because of the dignity of his life which he offered as atonement, for it was the life of God and man; thirdly, because of the amplitude of the passion and the greatness of the sorrow which he endured, as already said. Therefore Christ's passion was not only a sufficient but a superabundant satisfaction for the sins of the human race." [3]

The benefits of Christ's passion are enjoyed by all that are his. For grace was bestowed upon him not as an individual but as the head of the church, that it might overflow from him to his members. [4] These benefits are, first, the forgiveness of sin; secondly, deliverance from the power of Satan; thirdly, release from punishment; fourthly,

[1] III. 46:3.
[2] III. 50:1.
[3] III. 48:2. Cf. III. 48:3-4.
[4] III. 48:1.

reconciliation with God; and fifthly, the opening of heaven's gates.[1] In a section on Christ as mediator between God and man Thomas remarks that it belongs to Christ to unite men to God by giving them precepts and gifts, by rendering satisfaction, and by interceding with God for them.[2] And later, in speaking of Christ's resurrection, he declares that it is the cause both of our resurrection and of our justification, that is of the resurrection both of our bodies and of our souls. For the resurrection of the latter is nothing else than our justification.[3]

As the incarnation, with the suffering and death and resurrection of Christ, while more fitting than any other way of saving men, was not the only way that might have been chosen, it belongs, according to Thomas, not to natural but to revealed theology. It cannot be proved to have been necessary; it can only be accepted on the authority of revelation. But having been revealed its appropriateness may be demonstrated, as he abundantly shows.

Thomas was the first theologian to do justice to Anselm's theory of the work of Christ, but he both modified and enlarged it. While denying the necessity of the incarnation, emphasized so strongly by Anselm, he went beyond him in teaching that the satisfaction rendered by Christ included not the mere laying down of his life but also his sufferings, and that his work had positive as well as negative value, resulting not simply in the forgiveness of human sin but in the bestowal of the divine life and the quickening of man's love for God and devotion to him. Thus Thomas combined in his doctrine of Christ's work both the negative and positive and both the objective and subjective elements, all of which had had their place in previous thought about Christ but had not before been brought together in a doctrine at once so rich and so consistent. I have dwelt on

[1] III. 49: 1–5.   [2] III. 26: 2.   [3] III. 56: 2.

the matter at such length because it illustrates as almost nothing else the catholicity and comprehensiveness of his thought and the way he gathered up and utilized all the thinking of the past that had any relevancy to the subject in hand.

It is unnecessary to say more about Thomas' Summa theologiæ. Its comprehensiveness, its sanity and moderation, the thoroughness with which each subject is treated, the pertinacity with which every problem is traced to its source, the fairness and exhaustiveness with which all possible objections are stated and the care with which they are answered, the very sameness in order and method of treatment — all contribute to make it the most impressive system of theology of the Middle Ages if not of any age. It is no wonder that it soon took a foremost place among works of the kind and has retained it ever since.

It has seemed worth while in view of Thomas' historical importance and of his position at the beginning of a new period in the development of Catholic thought to deal with him in greater detail than with many another. Several aspects of his thought have been left unnoticed, but enough has been said to make his general attitude clear. Of greatest moment was his combination of Aristotelianism and Christianity. There are some sections of his theology, it is true, where the influence of Aristotle was almost or altogether lacking, and where the influence of Augustine remained undisturbed, but these do not affect the significance of the synthesis which was carried through with extraordinary thoroughness and persistency over wide ranges of thought. The synthesis was most patent in the sphere of natural theology. Indeed Thomas' creation of a natural theology on the basis of the Aristotelian philosophy was his greatest intellectual achievement and its historic importance cannot be exaggerated. In his treatment of revealed theology he was much more under the influence of Christian tradition and included many things not because they had significance for him but simply because they were a part of the Catholic faith. With a fine impartiality he treated them with the same respect as other items of the common heritage and endeavored to justify and explain their presence in the system. Though he recognized and emphasized the impossibility of proving the doctrines of revealed theology as distinguished from those of natural theology, he was never content to leave them supported by mere authority. To rationalize them at least in some degree and to show that they were reasonable if not demonstrable was his constant effort. God, he was sure, was never arbitrary and whether in theology or morals revealed nothing and commanded nothing without good reason. To show what his reasons were, so far as they could be discovered, and thus to justify his ways to men Thomas conceived to be the theologian's paramount duty. His discussion of the work of Christ recounted above is an excellent example of the kind of thing he tried to do.

Thomas' theology was a combination of all sorts of disparate tendencies and an aggregate of a large variety of ideas. But it was a genuine system worked into a consistent whole by a great dominating principle, the doctrine of God, to which everything was made tributary and in the light of which all things were viewed. The combination included, as has been seen, both natural and revealed theology. Here also it was no mere juxtaposition of two disparate systems that Thomas accomplished. On the contrary he brought the supernatural into organic relation with the natural. The principles of reason he recognized as identical in God and man and insisted on the rational character of the whole range of truth, revealed as well as natural. The notion of a double truth (that something could be true in philosophy which was false in theology and vice versa), though it was becoming widely current, was utterly abhorrent to him.

As was said at the beginning of the chapter, Thomas was an innovator and represented the modernist tendency in the thirteenth century. As a consequence he was looked at askance by the conservatives of the day and was attacked with vigor. Within three years after his death many of his teachings were condemned as heretical by the archbishops both of Paris and of Canterbury. Before long, however, the opposition of the conservatives, who included members of his own order as well as others, was largely overcome, and in 1323 he was canonized by Pope John XXII. Thenceforth his orthodoxy was not questioned and he was everywhere recognized as one of the great doctors of the church.

In spite of the criticism showered upon it, and in spite of the party differences that long divided Thomists and Scotists, Thomas' great enterprise, the synthesis of Aristotelian philosophy and Christian theology, proved increasingly popular. Its lasting success was due above all to the fact that it offered new and from the point of view of that age scientific support to the Christian system. Its apologetic value at a time when apologetic was becoming increasingly important was the real secret of its victory. It is interesting that a theologian who was in his day a modernist should bear the reputation of being one of the leading conservatives in the history of the church. As a matter of fact, notwithstanding the transformation that he wrought, indeed largely because of it, he proved actually a conserver not a destroyer of the Catholic system.

CHAPTER XIII

DUNS SCOTUS AND WILLIAM OF OCKHAM

HOSTILITY to Thomas Aquinas was not confined to the conservatives. In the Franciscan Order, the great rival of the Order of Preachers, opposition was widespread and was shared by liberals as well as conservatives. Among the latter, Bonaventura, like Hugo of St. Victor both mystic and theologian, was the most notable. He disagreed with Thomas on various subjects, but was chiefly opposed to him because he denied the possibility of knowing God directly in this life — a denial which seemed to Bonaventura as to many others to cut the very nerve of religion. He was not a mere conservative. Like his teacher Alexander of Hales, the first great theologian of the Franciscan Order, he felt the influence of the newly discovered Aristotle at several points. But neither he nor Alexander drew from Aristotle the conclusion that all human knowledge is based on sense-experience. On the contrary he still retained with most of the early Franciscans Augustine's notion of divine illumination and remained true to the Augustinian Neoplatonic mystical tradition.

More significant than Bonaventura's attitude was that of Duns Scotus, founder of the younger Franciscan school and himself a genuine modernist like Thomas. With the latter he accepted the philosophy of Aristotle, at least in large part, and undertook to read the Christian system in its light. He was, however, essentially a critic, not a constructive thinker, and he was much more concerned to expose the errors of others than to set forth his own views. Thomas was not the only object of attack. Duns criticized without fear or favor theologians of various schools, not sparing even members of his own order. But Thomas came in for his full share, and it is Duns' relation to him that chiefly interests us here. Born probably in Scotland about 1265, Duns was educated at Oxford and taught both there and in Paris and finally at Cologne where he died in 1308. He was known as "The subtle Doctor" (Doctor subtilis) and had the reputation of being the keenest dialectician and the most penetrating critic of his day. Though, like Thomas, he died in early middle life he left a large body of writing. His principal works are his elaborate commentary on Lombard's Sentences, commonly called the Opus Oxoniense, and another and smaller one known as the Reportata Parisiensia.[1] In addition we have from his pen a brief work on natural theology entitled De primo principio.[2] Of the many other writings attributed to him most are either certainly or probably spurious.[3]

Except for the brief De primo principio he produced no systematic work like the Summa contra gentiles or the Summa theologiae of Thomas, and his views have to be gathered for the most part by the way in connection with his comments on the opinions of others. As a matter of fact it is often impossible to tell what his own views were because his statements on this or that subject varied accord-

[1] The *Opus Oxoniense* is contained in volumes 8–21 of the Vivès edition of Duns' works; the *Reportata Parisiensia* in volumes 22–24. The difference in size is not so great as it appears, for a considerable part of volumes 8–21 is filled with commentaries on Duns' work by other Franciscans.

[2] Printed in the Vivès edition, vol. 4.

[3] On the authenticity of the works ascribed to Duns see especially Longpré, *La philosophie du B. Duns Scot*, in *Études Franciscaines*, vol. 34, pp. 448 ff. Longpré regards as certainly genuine the *Opus Oxoniense*, the *Reportata Parisiensia*, the *De primo principio*, the *Quæstiones* on Aristotle's *Metaphysics*, and the *Quæstiones quod libetales*. The *De rerum principio* and the *Theoremata*, which have been drawn upon largely by historians and biographers, Longpré, in agreement with other recent scholars, regards as certainly spurious.

DUNS SCOTUS

ing to the positions he was combating. At the same time his general attitude and his conclusions on most important matters can be gathered with sufficient accuracy if one has the patience to read him. The truth is he is not easy reading. His style, in contrast with that of Thomas, is labored and obscure. And not only that, the hair-splitting dialectic that marks his works, the fine-spun distinctions, the excessive dividing and subdividing of the questions under discussion, the insignificance of many of the problems dealt with at greatest length, make his works tedious to the last degree. To read Thomas is a delight; to read Duns is a weariness to the flesh.

Duns was an adept at discovering logical fallacies and exposing the inconclusiveness of others' demonstrations, but when he argued in his own turn he was apt to be no more convincing than they. A capital illustration is his elaborate and complicated discussion of the evidence for the existence of God.[1] With Thomas he denied the possibility of a direct or intuitive knowledge of God and confined himself to a posteriori proofs drawn from sense-experience. The Aristotelian argument, however, from motion to an original unmoved mover, which Thomas had chiefly emphasized, he rejected as inconclusive on the ground that the major premise — every moving object must owe its motion to something outside itself — is fallacious. His exposé of the weakness of this celebrated proof was very acute and searching. But he then went on to employ other forms of the a posteriori argument, including that from contingent to necessary being and from the different degrees of perfection in the world to the existence of an absolutely perfect, as if they were not equally open to criticism.

Duns' historical importance has been much exaggerated. As already said he was essentially a critic not a constructive

[1] *Opus Oxoniense*, Bk. I. Dist. 2 : Qu. 2 (§§ 5 ff.).

thinker, and his contributions to the development of Christian thought were relatively slight. Upon the basis of certain works now generally recognized as spurious he was formerly supposed to have been more of an innovator than he actually was. The opinions of some of his followers were wrongly ascribed to him and he was represented as having broken completely with the past and inaugurated a new period in the history of mediæval thought. This, however, was to misunderstand him. The notion that he exposed the irrational character of Christian truth and destroyed the existing connection between philosophy and theology is entirely erroneous. Philosophy and theology, he always insisted, cannot contradict each other. He had the same confidence as Thomas in human reason, and his respect for philosophy was as great as his.[1]

Though a critic he was not a sceptic and he did not save himself from scepticism by appealing to authority as Ockham later did. Nor was he a mystic, though mysticism was widespread within the Franciscan Order. On the contrary he was an Aristotelian like Thomas and belonged as he did among the modernists of the age. Though critical of Aristotle as he was of everyone else he recognized him as the greatest of philosophers and undertook to reinterpret Christianity in the light of his philosophy. His differences with Thomas concerned details rather than principles. He agreed with him as to the relation of faith and reason ; he shared with him the Aristotelian theory that all human knowledge is based upon sense-perception ; and with him he rejected the Augustinian notion of divine illumination of which Bonaventura and others made so much. Like him too, as we have already seen, he denied all intuitive knowledge of God, and used only a posteriori arguments for his existence. He also made the same distinction

[1] Cf. *Opus Oxoniense*, Prologue, Qu. 1 and 3.

between natural and revealed theology and showed equal confidence in both.[1] To be sure he drew the limits of natural theology somewhat more narrowly than Thomas. For instance while he believed in immortality on the basis of divine revelation he denied that it could be proved.[2] But this involved no change of principle. It meant only that he was more critical of the rational arguments for immortality and found them less cogent than Thomas did.

There were differences, to be sure, between Duns and Thomas, but they were for the most part differences only in emphasis and were by no means so thoroughgoing or important as has been widely thought. Thus, for instance, much has been made of Duns' voluntarism, so-called, and its contrast with the intellectualism of Thomas. It is true that his constant emphasis on the will gives his writings a different tone from those of Thomas. It is true too that he actually taught the primacy of the will, maintaining in disagreement with the older theologian that it is the highest faculty both in God and man.[3] But this did not mean as much as has been generally supposed. It did not mean, for instance, that the will either in God or in man acts arbitrarily and without motives. Duns recognized as fully as Thomas did that all God's actions are controlled by his goodness and that men's characters and habits largely determine their choices. To be sure he insisted that while the will is influenced by motives it is itself (and not any motive or complex of motives) the ultimate cause of its own acts. But Thomas, too, maintained the same thing.[4] Both

---

[1] The notion that he anticipated Ritschl's rejection of the category of natural theology is unfounded. This step was taken by William of Ockham.

[2] *Opus Oxoniense*, IV. 43 : 2.

[3] For passages in Duns' writings pointing in another direction see Longpré in *Études Franciscaines*, vol. 36, pp. 32 ff.

[4] Cf. Thomas' *Summa theologiæ*, I. 83 : 1.

he and Duns in fact were concerned to avoid such determinism as should make freedom impossible and so destroy
morality and reduce man to a mere machine. In doing so
they expressed themselves differently. Thomas emphasized
the intellectual side of the act of choice ; Duns, feeling that
the older theologian had not sufficiently safeguarded the
freedom of the will in which they were both interested,
emphasized the voluntaristic side. But the difference,
though psychologically interesting, was not particularly
significant either philosophically or theologically. Duns
was not, as commonly thought, an indeterminist in contrast
with the determinist Thomas. From one point of view
they were both alike indeterminists ; from another they were
both determinists.

It is interesting to notice in this connection that the
freedom on which Duns insisted was freedom not from divine
control but from subjection to the world-machine. Man is
free in the sense that he is more than a mere cog in the
mechanical order, that he is a creative force and can act
upon nature from without. This freedom is an immediate
datum of experience. It is impossible to prove it ; but it
needs no proof, for we know it beyond all peradventure.
Any theory that makes such freedom impossible is indubi-
tably wrong. Man's freedom, however, does not remove
him from God's control. To be subject to a being higher
than oneself is no limitation upon one's liberty, only to be
subject to that which is lower than oneself [1] — a good Augustinian doctrine. Though not always consistent in this
matter — though at times he struggled to give man a
larger measure of independence — Duns was in reality as
much of a determinist and predestinarian as Thomas.
Nothing else, indeed, would have harmonized with his doc-

---

[1] Cf. *Opus Oxoniense*, IV. 49 : 6 (§ 15).

trine of God's absolute will, a fundamental tenet of his theology.[1]

Duns carried his doctrine of God's absolute will so far as to declare, as Tertullian had done centuries before, that the sole ground of right and wrong is the will of God. A thing is good because God has willed it ; he does not will it because it is good.[2] This again is emphasized by many historians as a fundamental difference between Duns and Thomas. But it is to be noticed that Duns also gave expression to the opposite doctrine. Thus he declared that the goodness of an act depends on its consonance with right reason, and that an evil act is not made good by being commanded.[3] It is evident that there is an inconsistency here, an inconsistency which he seems to have done nothing to resolve. Apparently when thinking theologically, with the idea of God's absolute will in mind, he emphasized without reserve God's independence of all natural principles of right and reason. But when thinking ethically, with the moral character of God and man chiefly in mind, he emphasized the inherent rightness of all God's purposes and precepts. Of the latter, indeed, he was just as sure as Thomas was in spite of the many utterances that seem to point in the opposite direction. That he did not attempt to reconcile these divergent positions, as he did divine determinism and free will, may have been due to the fact — for it is a fact, strange as it seems in view of his emphasis on theology as a practical science — that he was not so much interested in ethics as in theology and that moral questions intrigued him far less than metaphysical. There is nothing, for

---

[1] On this whole subject of the relation of divine determinism to human freedom in Duns see Seeberg, *Die Theologie des Johannes Duns Scotus*, pp. 86 ff., 156 ff.

[2] *Opus Oxoniense*, III. 19 : qu. unica (§ 7).

[3] *Rep. Par.* II. 22 : qu. unica (§ 3) ; IV. 28 : qu. unica (§ 5). Cf. Harris, *Duns Scotus*, vol. II. p. 332.

instance, in any of his writings to be compared with the elaborate treatise on ethics that fills the second part of Thomas' Summa theologiæ.

Closely connected with Duns' emphasis on the will was his contention that the supreme good of man lies in the love of God. At this point he seems to have been in disagreement with Thomas who made the supreme good the vision of God. It is to be noticed, however, that Duns did not deny that beatitude includes the vision of God. It consists, so he maintained, in the perfection of both will and intellect. It involves the whole man and includes the beatific vision as well as the fulness of love which it inspires. Thus he says: "It is impossible that a nature should be perfectly happy and perfectly at peace unless it be wholly at peace and not only in part. Therefore the will cannot be at peace without the intellect, nor conversely, for each is a power of the one undivided nature. Consequently beatitude consists in the perfection of both powers." [1]

On the other hand, so far as Thomas is concerned, it should be noticed that in calling the vision of God the supreme good he was contrasting it not with love for God but with the indirect knowledge of God which is alone possible in this life, a knowledge drawn from the data of sense-experience or based upon the testimony of others. It was not so much Thomas' intellectualism that spoke in his identification of the supreme good with the vision of God as his piety, his yearning for direct communion with God which could be had only in the future life. To contrast him with Duns at this point, and to regard him as less practical than the latter, is, therefore, to misunderstand him as Duns himself seems to have misunderstood him. He would hardly have found fault with Duns' assertion that the supreme good is to love God, for he was sure that no one could enjoy the

[1] *Rep. Par.* IV. 49 : 3. On this whole subject see *ibid.* IV. 49 : 3-4.

vision of God without loving him supremely, that perfect love and perfect knowledge are but two sides of one experience, the experience of eternal beatitude.

As Duns differed with Thomas in his phrasing of man's supreme good, he differed with him also in his definition of theology. While Thomas spoke of it as primarily a speculative science because it had to do chiefly with God, Duns, following the common tradition, pronounced it a practical science.[1] By this he did not mean, as some have supposed, that its organ is the practical reason, as Kant maintained, and that the speculative reason has no place in it. On the contrary he made as large use of the latter in his theology as Thomas did. Like Thomas, as we have seen, he recognized natural as well as revealed theology and employed rational proofs for the existence of God. To interpret Duns as anticipating in any way the Kantian revolution is, therefore, to misinterpret him. All that he meant when he called theology a practical science, or at any rate all of importance, was that it has a practical purpose. In metaphysics we are moved only by the desire to know; in theology we wish to know in order to be or do. Theology is a science which enlarges and clarifies our knowledge like any other science. But in it we learn about God not simply out of curiosity, as we learn about the stars in astronomy, but that we may do his will and be conformed to his likeness. With such an estimate of the practical value of theology Thomas could have had no quarrel. To him it was a practical science in this sense as much as to Duns, as his Summa theologiæ abundantly shows. But this did not make it any the less true that theology has to do primarily with God, and reads everything in the light of God, as Thomas insisted and as Duns agreed. Again the difference between them is seen to be more verbal than real.

[1] See *Opus Oxoniense*, Prologue, qu. 4.

Summing it all up we may say that while there were marked differences of emphasis between Duns and Thomas they were due to no real divergence in principle. Fundamentally the two men were substantially at one. Duns inaugurated no new period in the history of Christian thought. He endeavored to refine and improve upon Thomas and to correct what seemed to him mistaken and dangerous in the Thomistic synthesis of Aristotelianism and the Christian faith. But he believed as fully as Thomas did in the possibility and necessity of such a synthesis and the last thing he desired was to sever the bond between philosophy and Christianity. With his extraordinarily acute mind he often saw differences where they were quite invisible to others and drew distinctions too fine for any but himself to appreciate. Small divergencies were magnified, and many matters of minor importance took on a significance in his eyes that hardly belonged to them. In many quarters all that was remembered of him was his hair-splitting logic and his endless discussion of questions that no one else cared about. It is one of the amusing ironies of history, that the word "dunce," used originally for a Scotist or follower of Duns, should have come to mean a sophistical person and finally a dull wit or ignoramus.

All this, however, should not lead us to belittle the importance of the man. Though he was not a great constructive genius, though he was no innovator and opened no new period in the history of thought, he was one of the keenest minds of the Middle Ages and he made a tremendous impression on his contemporaries. His followers who were known as Scotists, in distinction from the followers of Aquinas, or Thomists, were very numerous and devoted. They regarded Duns as the most illustrious theologian of the Franciscan Order and acclaimed him as the greater rival of the Dominican Thomas. For some centuries there were

Scotist theologians as well as Thomist in the faculties of the leading universities and the controversy between the two schools made a great noise in the theological world. The differences between them increased with time and as was natural were magnified by the contestants on either side. As was also natural the tendency was to read back into Duns himself the opinions of his followers and to attribute to him not only ideas but also writings that were not his. It is due to this that we have so many spurious works handed down among his genuine productions.

Historically more important than Duns was another Franciscan, the Englishman William of Ockham.[1] Born toward the end of the thirteenth century at Ockham in Surrey he was educated at Oxford and taught there for a time. The tradition that he studied under Duns has no foundation; he was probably but a lad when the older theologian died. In 1324 he was summoned to the papal court at Avignon to answer charges of heresy.[2] After being held there for some time he escaped and made his way to Italy and afterward to Munich, where he spent the latter part of his life and where he died probably in 1349. As a member of the stricter party within the Franciscan Order and a champion of the principle of absolute poverty, corporate as well as individual, he came into conflict with Pope John XXII who supported the other party. John denounced as heretical the claim that Christ and his apostles had no possessions, either individually or in common, and that absolute poverty was therefore the real evangelical way of

[1] As I have not had access to Ockham's principal works I have been obliged to depend for my account of him almost wholly on the writings of others and on their quotations from him.

[2] See Pelzer: *Les 51 articles de Guillaume Occam censurés en Avignon en 1326* (*Revue d'histoire ecclésiastique*, 1922), where the text of the articles is given. They have to do chiefly with questions of logic and ontology and the bearing of the latter on certain dogmas, particularly transubstantiation.

life. Ockham wrote a number of works against him, declaring him in error and appealing from him to the Scriptures. In the long struggle between the pope and Louis of Bavaria he took the side of the latter, attacked, as many others were doing, the political power of the papacy, and defended the theory of the State's complete independence of the church.[1]

Ockham is commonly spoken of as a disciple of Duns and is supposed to have upheld and carried on his teaching. The truth is he was rather his critic than his follower. As Duns' teaching developed largely from his criticism of Thomas, Henry of Ghent and others, Ockham's developed in the main from his criticism of Duns. At the same time though not a disciple in any true sense Ockham was a Franciscan and his thinking was inevitably dominated to some degree by the great Franciscan theologian whose reputation within the order was unrivalled in the early fourteenth century and who was also, like Thomas the chief glory of the Dominican Order, a modernist in theology. Nor was Duns' influence over Ockham wholly negative. While at some points the younger theologian was diametrically opposed to the older, in other matters he was at least in partial agreement with him. But even in these, though he may have got his suggestions from Duns, he commonly went beyond him and drew conclusions quite alien to Duns' own. Almost never were the two wholly at one. Several of the innovations usually ascribed to Duns were really due to Ockham, a fact of which he was fully conscious. He was fond of emphasizing his own independence of other thinkers, particularly of Duns, and in at least one passage declared that he did not regard the latter as an authority.[2]

Philosophically the principal difference between the two men lay in Ockham's nominalism. Both Thomas and Duns

[1] See below, pp. 346 ff.
[2] See Longpré: in *Études Franciscaines*, vol. 35, p. 584.

were moderate realists of the Aristotelian type, asserting the objective reality but denying the independent existence of universals. The latter exist not before or apart from individuals but in them (universalia in rebus). Ockham on the other hand denied their objective reality altogether, maintaining that they are mere concepts built upon the observed likenesses of things (universalia post res). The contrast between Ockham and Duns in this matter was very marked. Duns insisted that nominalism destroyed not only metaphysics but also science and faith. If individuals alone are real all connections and relations disappear and the world becomes purely atomistic.[1] Ockham on the other hand counted realism absurd and destructive of the whole Aristotelian philosophy as well as of all science and truth and reason.[2] It was in direct opposition to Duns that Ockham developed his nominalism and the difference between the two men is nowhere more evident than here. Since the time of Roscellin nominalism had been generally taboo, but in the thirteenth century it began to make its appearance again here and there in more or less inconsistent forms. The two Franciscans, Roger Bacon in the thirteenth and Aureoli in the early fourteenth century, were nominalists and their influence was undoubtedly felt by Ockham. With them he insisted that the individual alone exists and that the problem of individuation with which philosophers had struggled for centuries was no problem at all. Ockham, it would seem, completed and systematized the nominalism of his predecessors and gave it the standing of a recognized philosophical theory which for centuries disputed the ground with realism and in many quarters drove it completely from the field.

[1] Cf. Duns Scotus: *Rep. Par.* II. 1 : 7 (§§ 10–12). See Longpré: *Études Franciscaines*, vol. 35, p. 589.
[2] See Kugler: *Der Begriff der Erkenntniss bei Wilhelm von Ockham*, p. 10.

The nominalism of Ockham and his school had large practical as well as theoretical significance. For one thing, it promoted interest in the individual as alone real and turned attention away from universals which had been the chief object of thought and study ever since ancient times. It thus undermined the dominance of metaphysics and prepared the way for the scientific development of the modern age. Where nominalism prevailed the credit of philosophy in the traditional sense was bound to be lowered. Nominalism had large practical significance also in that it involved a divorce between philosophy and the traditional theology of the church. The latter, as has been already remarked, presupposed at least in certain essential features a realistic ontology of a more or less thoroughgoing kind. A consistent and clear-sighted nominalist like Ockham was therefore faced with one of two alternatives : either he must abandon certain doctrines of the Christian faith, or he must recognize the independence of philosophy and theology and give up altogether the effort to show the rational character of the Christian system. Though a nominalist in his philosophy Ockham was a devout and orthodox believer and he chose the latter alternative.[1] The Christian system is to be accepted in its entirety on the basis of divine revelation, but the claim that it is rational is to be abandoned once and for all.

Ockham went still further than this and denied that the divine unit, or infinity, or even the divine existence, could

---

[1] Cf. his words: "This is my faith because it is the Catholic faith. For whatever the Roman church believes that alone and nothing else I believe either explicitly or implicitly " (Quoted by Hoffmann, *Die Lehre von der fides implicita innerhalb der katholischen Kirche*, p. 161. Cf. also pp. 163 f.). In Ockham's words appears clearly the notion, emphasized by Tertullian and common in the church since his day, that faith is an act of obedience. The notion was shared by the schoolmen but only when the divorce between faith and reason was proclaimed, as it was by the nominalists, did its full significance become apparent.

be proved. This meant, of course, the rejection of the category of natural theology. Duns, with his more drastic criticism, had reduced somewhat the content of natural theology as accepted by Thomas; but he had not thought of denying the thing itself. He was as convinced as Thomas was that the existence of God, and of a God of a certain kind and character, could be proved quite independently of revelation. Moreover he saw in the divine existence the indispensable basis for a belief in revelation. But Ockham's attitude was radically different. It was not simply, as often said, that he went a step beyond Duns and reduced still further the number of demonstrable doctrines; the truth is he abandoned the whole conception of natural theology common to both Duns and Thomas and he did it on the basis of a changed philosophy which made their synthesis of reason and religion seem impossible to him.

Working in the same direction to bring about a severance of the traditional bond between philosophy and theology was Ockham's doctrine of the primacy of the will. This he took over from Duns — as a matter of fact it was in line with Franciscan tradition and congenial to the spirit generally prevalent within the Order — but he carried it further and drew from it conclusions which the older theologian would have repudiated.[1] The primacy of the will meant to Ockham that right and wrong are grounded not in the nature of things but in the will of God alone, his will being the only moral determinant. God might have commanded hate instead of love, selfishness instead of generosity, lying instead of truthfulness, and his command would have made them right. The primacy of the will meant also that God is not bound by his character or by principles of right and

[1] On Ockham's doctrine of the primacy of the will and the conclusions he drew from it see Seeberg's article " Ockham " in Herzog's *Realencyklopädie*[3], and Harris, *op. cit.* vol. I, pp. 296 ff.

reason in his own actions. It is impossible to say that God being of such and such a character must do so and so. What God has done and what he will do we can know only from revelation. He might have been men's enemy instead of their friend and might have treated them with cruelty instead of kindness. He might have become incarnate in a stone or an ass instead of in a man. He might have instituted an entirely different economy of redemption, or he might not have redeemed men at all.

The complete divorce between philosophy and theology and between reason and religion accomplished by Ockham, or by his school,[1] led to the conclusion that a proposition may be at once true in philosophy and false in theology, or false in philosophy and true in theology. To be sure, Ockham himself, so far as is known, did not draw this conclusion, but it is found in the writings of certain of his disciples and was widely accepted among the nominalists of later generations. This principle of the double truth, as it is called, which had been already condemned in the Paris decree of 1277 against the Averroists,[2] has an unpleasant sound, but it did not mean, as it seems at first sight to mean, dishonesty or double dealing on the part of those who held it. It meant only that they understood the Christian system as supernatural in such a sense that it transcends all the limitations that bind other systems. What is true of man is not true of God, and human reason is not one with the divine. Christianity is miraculous through and through. Hence it cannot be interpreted by ordinary categories or judged by the canons that are applied to the natural. It is not only superior to the natural, it is opposed to it in many ways. It teaches a supernatural ethic that runs counter to ordinary

[1] Just how far Ockham went in this matter and how far the opinions of his followers have been ascribed to him I do not feel sure.

[2] See Gilson: *Études de philosophie mediévale*, p. 60.

principles of morals, and similarly it teaches a theology that violates the conclusions of philosophy. The more unnatural it is the truer. Were it in accord with nature it might well be suspected to have come from man and not from God. It was not duplicity nor was it mere light-mindedness that was speaking here, but a genuine faith in the divine origin and miraculous character of Christianity which set it apart from and above all that is human.

Of course where Christianity is viewed in this way it must be accepted solely on the basis of divine authority; and this meant to Ockham the authority of the Catholic church. He insisted, to be sure, on the supreme authority of the Scriptures. But there was nothing new in this; Augustine, Anselm and many others had done the same. And though the principle was given practical application in Ockham's conflict with the pope, when he claimed that the latter was a heretic because he did not follow Scripture, he was throwing no discredit on the church. His appeal to the Bible was not from the church but from the pope, and it left the authority of the church untouched. The authority of the latter indeed was never more firmly entrenched than among the followers of Ockham who looked upon it as absolute and irrefragable and counted it an all-sufficient reason for the acceptance of the Christian system as true — an attitude very welcome to the ecclesiastical authorities especially in the troubled days of the fifteenth and sixteenth centuries.

Ockham's followers constituted a third party which for some time divided the theological field with the Thomists and the Scotists.[1] Their position was known as the via moderna in contrast with the via antiqua of both the latter, and for a couple of centuries they had wide influence within the church. Among them was no less a man than Peter

---

[1] On these three schools see Ueberweg's *Geschichte der Philosophie*, 11th edition, vol. II, pp. 583 ff.

d'Ailly, whose fame rests chiefly on his championship of the conciliar theory at the Council of Constance. The last of any note was Gabriel Biel, Professor at Tübingen in the late fifteenth century. He contributed nothing of his own, but his summary of Ockham's teaching [1] was widely used and gave him no little reputation. He has been called the last of the schoolmen but the title is misplaced. The last of the schoolmen is not yet, for scholastic theology still flourishes both in Catholicism and Protestantism. And quite apart from this the passing of the Ockhamist school did not mean the passing of the Thomists and the Scotists. They continued influential, the former indeed increasingly so, for a long time to come. Ockhamism and with it nominalism was but an episode within the Catholic church. But though too uncongenial to Catholic theology to remain permanently allied with it, nominalism at least has had a large place in the modern world of thought and the influence of Ockham, its greatest mediæval exponent, is still widely felt.

[1] *Epitome et collectorium ex Occamo super IV libros sententiarum* (1499).

CHAPTER XIV

THE SACRAMENTS

DURING the Middle Ages a large amount of thought was expended upon the sacraments by the theologians of the western church. The result was a doctrine which still remains substantially intact. The doctrine is so important a part of the Roman Catholic system and illustrates so admirably certain aspects of the religious thinking of the Middle Ages that it seems worth while to reproduce it here at least in its main features. For a long time there was great uncertainty both as to the nature and the number of the sacraments. The word sacrament indeed was widely used in a general sense for any holy act or rite which was thought to symbolize divine things or transmit divine grace. At first the tendency was to multiply the number of the sacraments and to include among them not only baptism and the eucharist, but also a large variety of sacred ceremonies and all sorts of religious practices, as for instance the dedication of churches, the consecration of bishops and abbots, the anointing of kings, monastic vows, prayer, fasting, and the like. Gradually theologians began to feel the need of distinguishing among the many and disparate ceremonies and practices indiscriminately spoken of as sacraments. It was quite evident that they were not all on the same plane. Some were necessary to salvation, others not ; some had immense importance for the spiritual life, others little or none ; some had to do only with individual Christians, others with the church as an institution or with

313

the Christian community as a whole. To call them all sacraments was to derogate from the worth and dignity of some and to give undue honour and importance to others. In the twelfth century, particularly, efforts were multiplying to bring order out of chaos and to determine just what a sacrament really was and which of the many and various sacred rites and practices were entitled to the name. Abelard, followed by many others, recognized five sacraments: baptism, confirmation, the eucharist, extreme unction, and marriage. Some of his disciples added penance and orders which had been widely regarded as sacraments since an early day. These seven were adopted by Peter Lombard and were dealt with at length in the fourth book of his Sentences. Through the influence of his famous work they soon came to be universally recognized and were officially sanctioned at the Council of Florence in 1439.[1] It is easy to understand why all of these should have been counted as sacraments but not why certain other rites and practices should have been excluded. Doubtless the traditional sanctity of the number seven had something to do with the result.

The seven sacraments, it was believed, were all of divine appointment, and according to Thomas they were instituted by Christ himself. The latter position was questioned by many, but in response to the denial of it by the Protestant reformers it was made official by the Council of Trent in its decree on the sacraments. In distinction from other sacred rites both of the old and the new dispensation the sacraments were generally supposed to impart divine grace. There was for some time, to be sure, considerable discussion over this point. Augustine's definition of a sacrament as a "sacred

---

[1] See the Bull *Exultate Deo* published by Eugene IV, Nov. 22, 1439. At this council the representatives of the eastern church also agreed, and the number seven has been official there too ever since.

sign" or "the sign of a sacred thing" [1] was universally
accepted, but there was a wide difference of opinion as to
how much was involved in it. Some insisted that the sacraments were only signs and nothing more; some that they
were efficacious signs, as had been believed from an early
day, and actually conveyed the grace which they signified.
Between these two extremes there were many shades of
opinion. Hugo declared that the sacraments contain grace.[2]
Bonaventura (with whom Duns Scotus agreed) denied this
and asserted that God confers grace when the sacraments
are administered but that the latter have no efficacy of their
own.[3] Thomas remarked that this made the sacraments no
more than mere signs and he himself maintained that they
not only signify but also cause grace.[4]

Peter Lombard has a careful and discriminating section
on the subject. He speaks of the sacrament as a "sign of a
sacred thing" and as the "visible form of invisible grace."
He then goes on: "Some signs are natural, as smoke signifies fire; others are artificial. And of the latter some are
sacraments, others are not. For every sacrament is a sign
but not every sign is a sacrament. A sacrament bears the
similitude of that whose sign it is; for if sacraments did not
resemble the things of which they are signs they could not
rightly be called sacraments. For a sacrament is properly
so called because it is a sign of the grace of God, and the
form of invisible grace, in the sense that it bears its image
and exists as its cause. Sacraments therefore are instituted
not only for the sake of signifying but also for the sake of

[1] "Signum sacrum," or "signum rei sacrae." The definition "a visible
sign of invisible grace" which is usually attributed to Augustine is not found
in his writings but was ascribed to him in the twelfth century and frequently
quoted as his. See Pourrat: *La théologie sacramentaire*, p. 34.

[2] *De sacramentis*, I. 9 : 2.

[3] See Loofs: *Dogmengeschichte*[4], p. 573.

[4] *Summa theologiæ*, III. 62 : 1. God himself, he explained, is the principal
cause of grace, the sacraments the instrumental cause. Cf. also III. 62 : 3, 4.

sanctifying. For those things that are instituted only for the purpose of signifying are merely signs not sacraments; as was true of the carnal sacrifices and ceremonial observances of the old law." [1] In the Bull Exultate Deo of 1439 and in the decrees of the Council of Trent it is said that the sacraments contain and confer grace and this remains the official doctrine. Moreover they confer grace ex opere operato (a phrase which became common in the thirteenth century), that is of themselves, or by virtue of what they are, and not because of the character of the one administering or the faith of the one receiving them.

Three things go to make a sacrament: the sensible sign, or matter; the words of institution, or form; the minister, or agent. If any of these be lacking or defective, there is no sacrament. The minister must be an ordained clergyman (except for baptism which may be performed in an emergency by a layman or a woman), and confirmation and ordination require a bishop. The ministrant need not be holy — he may even be immoral in his life and heretical in his beliefs — but he must be in regular standing and must have the intention of doing what the church does, as is said in the Bull Exultate Deo and in the Tridentine decree. There was much discussion as to how it might be known whether the minister had the proper intention. It was Thomas' opinion that if he used the correct form the intention might be assumed "unless the contrary were openly expressed both by him and by the recipient of the sacrament" [2] (as for instance in a mock marriage). This opinion, however, was not shared by everyone and an official decision upon the matter has never been reached, the church contenting itself with the general statement of the Bull and the Council of Trent. [3]

[1] *Libri quattuor sententiarum*, IV. 1.
[2] *Summa theologiæ*, III. 64 : 8.
[3] On the subject of intention see Hahn: *Die Lehre von den Sakramenten*, pp. 217 ff.

Augustine insisted that the sacraments benefit only those who receive them in faith, and recalling what Paul had said in relation to the Lord's Supper he maintained that if faith be wanting they do the recipient harm rather than good. The latter notion was early abandoned; the sacraments, it came to be generally agreed, never work injury to anyone. But that something was required of the recipient if they were to have their proper effect continued to be believed. Just what this was, however, has always been widely disputed.[1] Many mediæval theologians held that faith and penitence were needed; some that the absence of a bad disposition was enough, the bad disposition (motus malus interior) being commonly interpreted as contempt for the sacrament or positive disbelief in it, or as the presence of an unforgiven mortal sin. The Bull Exultate Deo says that the sacraments confer grace on those receiving them worthily; the Tridentine decree, on those that do not oppose an obstacle. Though the phrasing is different there is no reason to suppose a difference of meaning. To receive a sacrament worthily and to oppose no obstacle to it were substantially synonymous in the late Middle Ages. At the same time it may well be that the change from the positive to the negative expression in the Tridentine decree was due to the Reformers' insistence that where there is not faith the sacraments are without efficacy.

In addition to the grace received through the sacraments ex opere operato it was widely believed that the good disposition of the recipient (his faith and penitence) was meritorious and was rewarded by additional grace conferred, as the phrase has it, ex opere operantis.[2] Even where the condition required of the recipient was interpreted in negative terms, as the absence of a bad rather than the presence of a good disposition, the notion of merit continued and the belief

---

[1] See Hahn, *op. cit.* pp. 392 ff.   [2] *Ibid.* pp. 409 ff.

that the Christian partaking of the sacrament not unworthily receives a double grace. Thus the two ideas of divine grace and human merit which lay side by side throughout Catholic history were given a place in the doctrine of the sacraments. They convey grace because of what they are and they convey more grace as a reward to those that receive them not unworthily.

So far as concerns the individual sacraments, little need be said about baptism, for its nature and effects were settled long before the Middle Ages. The matter of the sacrament is water; the form the words, "I baptize thee in the name of the Father and of the Son and of the Holy Ghost." Only where the triune formula is used is the sacrament valid. The minister is ordinarily an ordained priest, but in case of necessity a deacon or even a layman or woman may baptize. Like lay baptism heretical baptism continued to be recognized as valid provided the correct formula was used. The sacrament is necessary to salvation and has a double effect: the birth of a new nature, or regeneration, and the forgiveness of all prebaptismal sin both original and actual. The term regeneration was commonly used to cover both effects, the birth of the new nature being thought of as removing all sin and hence the guilt attaching to it.[1] Baptism imparts an indelible character and is therefore not to be repeated. As Thomas expressed it, baptism is a kind of spiritual regeneration and one can be begotten only once.[2] It is worthy of remark that baptism was represented by Thomas and other mediæval theologians not as a social but as a wholly personal affair. Nothing was made of it as the incorporation of the child into the family of Christ with its mutual duties and responsibilities. It was treated solely as a means of individual regeneration and forgiveness.

[1] So, for instance, Thomas in *Summa contra gentiles*, IV. 59.
[2] *Summa theologiæ*, III. 66:9

The rite of confirmation — laying on of hands and anointing with oil — was originally a part of the baptismal ceremony, but as the practice of baptizing infants became increasingly common it was gradually separated from baptism and became an independent sacrament. Throughout the Middle Ages it retained and still retains its original character and purpose substantially unchanged. It is supposed to confer grace for the strengthening of the Christian already baptized that he may be the better fitted to meet the assaults of sin and to bear his part in the world as a soldier of Christ. Like baptism it imprints an indelible character and is not to be repeated. The matter of the sacrament is oil consecrated by the bishop; the form the words "I sign thee with the sign of the cross and confirm thee with the chrism of salvation in the name of the Father and of the Son and of the Holy Ghost." The minister must ordinarily be a bishop,[1] though in special circumstances a presbyter may be allowed by papal dispensation to take his place, as for instance in missionary lands. Whereas the sacrament of baptism was strictly individualistic the sacrament of confirmation bore also a social character. At least Thomas spoke of it as conferring spiritual strength which fits the recipient to be a soldier of Christ, to carry his banner, and to fight under his standard, and he recognized the psychological value of daring to confess publicly one's faith in Christ, for fortitude, as he remarked, casts out undue fear.[2] What was lacking in baptism was thus made good by confirmation in more ways than one.

The third of the seven sacraments is the eucharist which is counted the chief and greatest of all. Throughout the Middle Ages it was interpreted in traditional fashion as at

[1] In the eastern church confirmation like baptism was left to the priests, but in the west, in accordance with the general tendency to exalt the authority of the bishop, it was regarded as his prerogative. See above, p. 35.
[2] *Summa contra gentiles*, IV. 60.

once a means of grace, providing spiritual nourishment for those partaking of it, and a sacrifice for sin which could be offered for the benefit of those present or absent, living or dead. Thomas says of it: "This sacrament is not only a sacrament but also a sacrifice. For inasmuch as in it is represented the passion of Christ whereby he offered himself a victim to God, as is said in the fifth chapter of Ephesians, it has the nature of a sacrifice. Inasmuch as in it grace is truly conferred invisibly under a visible form it has the nature of a sacrament. Thus it benefits those who receive it both as a sacrament and as a sacrifice. . . . But others that do not receive it derive benefit from it as a sacrifice inasmuch as it is offered for their salvation." [1]

More and more as time passed the sacrificial aspect of the eucharist was emphasized.[2] The Council of Trent, in addition to a decree on the Most Holy Sacrament of the Eucharist, published another on the Sacrifice of the Mass,[3] in which it is said that in the divine sacrifice celebrated in the mass "the same Christ is contained and is immolated without blood who on the altar of the cross once offered himself in blood," that "the sacrifice is truly propitiatory," and that it is rightly offered "not only for the sins, punishments, satisfactions, and other necessities of living believers, but also for the dead in Christ that are not yet fully purified." The social character that attached to the Lord's Supper in the primitive church was altogether wanting in the Middle Ages. The eucharist was no longer a love feast in which the fellowship of Christian disciples with one another in devotion to their common Lord found chief expression. As a matter of fact it had lost this character long before and had become and remained, except for the use of it as a sac-

---

[1] *Summa theologiæ*, III. 79 : 7.
[2] Curiously enough it is not referred to in the Bull of 1439.
[3] The former in Session XIII; the latter in Session XXII.

rifice for the sins of others, as individualistic as baptism itself.

Augustine held a spiritual view of the presence of Christ in the eucharist : the bread and wine are not physically his body and blood, they only symbolize them. He frequently used realistic language, to be sure, after the example of John 6; but he interpreted the language spiritually as is evident from many passages in his writings. For instance he says : "It is a miserable slavery of the soul to take signs for things and to be unable to raise the eye of the mind above the bodily creature to the eternal light." [1] Though not shared by Augustine the realistic view which was already common was adopted by Gregory the Great and after his time spread rapidly. The first work upon the subject was by Paschasius Radbertus, a French Benedictine of the ninth century, and was entitled On the Body and Blood of the Lord. [2] Paschasius maintained that the bread and wine are really changed into the body and blood of Christ, the body being the one which he had on earth and which suffered on the cross. Yet in spite of this Paschasius held inconsistently that participation in the eucharist is spiritual, not carnal, and that only believers receive Christ's body and blood. The work marked no advance upon earlier views, but presenting the realistic doctrine as it did in systematic form it had large influence.

Paschasius was answered by Ratramnus and others but his opinion was the popular one and steadily grew in favour. In the eleventh century it was attacked by Berengar of Tours, one of the leading dialecticians of the day, who argued

---

[1] *De doctrina christiana*, III. 5. Cf. also his *De civitate Dei*, XXI. 25 and his work on the Gospel of John, particularly Tractatus XXVI–XXVII. It is irrelevant to call attention, as is often done, to the fact that symbol and reality were not necessarily mutually exclusive terms in ancient times.

[2] *De corpore et sanguine Domini.* On Paschasius' work see Seeberg: *Dogmengeschichte*[3], vol. III, pp. 70 ff.

against it chiefly on rational grounds, maintaining that the bread and wine are mere symbols of the body and blood of Christ who is present in the eucharist only spiritually not corporeally, and only for those receiving the sacrament in faith.[1] Berengar was replied to by Lanfranc,[2] Abbot of Bec, and others, Lanfranc going even further than Paschasius and asserting that unbelievers as well as believers receive Christ's real body and blood. Berengar was condemned as a heretic and forced to recant and sign a confession which asserted the doctrine of the real presence in the following extreme form: "The bread and wine which are placed on the altar after the consecration are not only a sacrament, but also the true body and blood of our Lord Jesus Christ, and sensibly not merely sacramentally but in verity are handled and broken by the hands of the priests and bruised by the teeth of believers."[3]

Serious opposition to the realistic view ceased with Berengar and the doctrine of the corporeal presence of Christ in the eucharist was officially stated at the fourth Lateran Council of 1215 which issued a dogmatic decree on the Trinity, the incarnation, the eucharist, baptism, and penance.[4] Concerning the eucharist it is said that Christ's "body and blood are truly contained in the sacrament of the altar under the form of bread and wine, the bread being changed into body and the wine into blood by divine power."[5]

[1] Berengar's original work on the subject is lost, but his views are given in his *Liber de sacra coena adversus Lanfrancum* (ed. by Vischer, 1834), an answer to the work of Lanfranc mentioned in the next note.

[2] In his *De corpore et sanguine Domini* (Migne, *Patrologia Latina*, vol. 150).

[3] Mirbt: *Quellen zur Geschichte des Papstthums und des römischen Katholizismus*, 4th ed. p. 144. On Berengar and his opponents see Seeberg, *op. cit.* pp. 196 ff.

[4] See Mirbt, *op. cit.* p. 179. For the entire decree see Hefele's *Conciliengeschichte*, vol. V. pp. 878 ff.

[5] Transubstantiatis pane in corpus et vino in sanguinem. The belief that the eucharistic bread and wine are changed into the actual body and blood of Christ was shared by John of Damascus and was common in the eastern church before his day. See vol. I. p. 323.

The word transubstantiation, which appears in this decree in the verbal form, was in common use already in the twelfth century and became the technical term for the change of the bread and wine into body and blood. The change which is effected instantaneously when the words of institution are repeated by the priest was supposed to be complete, the entire substance of the bread being transformed into body and the entire substance of the wine into blood, so that there is nothing left of the bread and wine except the form or appearance. Why the form should not also be changed when the substance is was explained by Thomas in the following way: "First, because it is not customary but horrible for men to eat the flesh of a man and drink his blood the flesh and blood of Christ are offered to us under the form of things which are more frequently used, namely bread and wine. Secondly, lest this sacrament might be ridiculed by unbelievers if we ate our Lord in his own form. Thirdly, that while we receive the body and blood of our Lord invisibly this may contribute to the merit of our faith." [1]

That the substance of the bread and wine is changed but not the form or appearance means that substance and accidents may be divorced from one another, that substance may exist without its properties and properties without their substance. As to the possibility of this there was much discussion among mediæval theologians and a great deal of ingenuity was expended in the effort to make it seem rational. It came finally to be generally agreed that the ordinary laws governing substance and accidents are suspended in the eucharist by the same divine power that brings about the transformation of the bread and wine. Thomas has the following to say upon the subject: "Thus it comes to pass

---

[1] *Summa theologiæ*, III. 75 : 5. There is a long and careful discussion of this and other objections brought against transubstantiation in the *Summa contra gentiles*, IV. 62 ff.

that in this sacrament the accidents remain without a subject. This indeed can be wrought by divine power. For since an effect depends more on the first cause than on the second, God, who is the first cause of both substance and accident, is able by his infinite power to preserve an accident in being when the substance by which it was preserved in being as by its own cause is withdrawn; as he is also able to produce other effects of natural causes without such causes, as when for instance he formed a human body in the Virgin's womb without the seed of man." [1]

Anselm, following Hilary and other early Fathers, had taught that the whole Christ was in every particle of the bread and wine. This doctrine of concomitance, as it was called by Thomas, was made official by the Council of Constance in 1415 and was there used to justify the withholding of the cup from the laity, a practice which had become general on prudential grounds, but had been attacked by various radical sects. If the whole Christ is present both in the bread and in the wine the Christian who partakes only of the former receives Christ as truly and as fully as if he took the communion in both kinds.

The sacrament of the eucharist which had at once, as Thomas put it, the nature of a sacrament and of a sacrifice, was the very heart of mediæval Christianity. In it the participant came into union with Christ and partook of his divine nature; in it too Christ's sacrifice was offered over and over again not merely as on the cross for the sins of men in general but particularly for one's own sins. No other ceremony or sacrament could equal it in its appeal to religious faith and sentiment. The very miraculous character of it enhanced its impressiveness in an age not inhospitable to miracle. Nothing more stupendous than the transformation of simple bread and wine into the very body and blood

[1] *Summa theologiæ*, III. 77 : 1.

of the divine Christ could well be conceived. Transubstantiation was not offensive to the piety of the age but congenial to it. It was but the formulation in theological terms of a belief that had long existed and had been confirmed over and over again in the religious experience both of common people and of theologians.

In spite of the new nature bestowed in baptism and nourished by the eucharist, and in spite of the grace given in confirmation, Christians continue to sin and hence require the sacrament of penance which may be repeated like the eucharist as often as there is need. Whereas in baptism nothing is demanded of the candidate but faith and repentance (if he has reached years of discretion), in penance there are required contrition, confession and satisfaction, all of which are essential parts of the sacrament and together constitute the matter of it. The form consists of the words of the priest "I absolve thee in the name of the Father and of the Son and of the Holy Ghost." Penance benefits no one unless his repentance is sincere and he truly desires to avoid sin. As Thomas says, spiritual health must come both from within and from without, from the man's own will and the assistance of divine grace.[1] At least once a year confession must be made to an ordained priest who alone has the power to perform the sacrament and pronounce absolution. The confession must cover all mortal sins, that is, all conscious, wilful and grave offenses, and as far as possible the attendant circumstances that the priest may be able to pass just judgment upon the penitent, a function which he is not called upon to perform in connection with baptism. The absolution pronounced by the priest conveys grace, removes guilt, and remits the eternal punishment, but satisfaction still remains to be rendered either here or in purgatory. Until this has been completed the penitent cannot

[1] *Summa contra gentiles*, IV. 72.

enter heaven. The satisfaction required was commonly summed up under the three heads of prayer, fasting, and almsgiving. As Thomas expressed it, a man humbles his spirit before God in prayer (an interesting interpretation of the value of prayer) ; he trains his flesh by fasting ; and he employs his worldly possessions to give alms to his neighbor.[1] Satisfaction was thought of as intended for the benefit not of another person but of the penitent himself who in rendering it did something that involved humiliation or labor or sacrifice, and thus atoned for his wrong-doing. In the Middle Ages to go on a pilgrimage to some sacred shrine, or even to the holy land, or to contribute to the building of churches or other memorials was a common form of penance.

The practice of granting indulgences, which meant originally the substitution of a less for a more onerous form of satisfaction, became common in the Middle Ages. The Franciscan theologian Alexander of Hales, an older contemporary of Thomas Aquinas, first worked out a consistent theory of indulgences, basing it on the treasury of merits laid up by Christ and the saints and put at the disposal of the church to be dispensed by the pope on such conditions as he might fix.[2] Indulgences do not affect eternal punishment — they release nobody from hell — but only the temporal penalties, including the purgatorial.

The practice of praying over the sick and anointing them with oil in the hope either of promoting their recovery or preparing them for death is very ancient. In the Middle Ages it came to be reckoned, under the name of Extreme Unction, as one of the seven sacraments, the authority for it being found in James 5 : 14-15. It was regarded as marking the end of the Christian's career as baptism marked its beginning, and was supposed to prepare him for death as

---

[1] *Summa contra gentiles*, IV. 72.
[2] Cf. his *Summa universæ theologiæ*, Bk. IV. Qu. 83.

baptism prepares him for life. According to Thomas the sacrament "removes the remains of sin and makes a man ready for final glory." [1] According to the Council of Trent it "wipes away offenses, if there are any still to be expiated, as also the remains of sin ; and raises up and strengthens the soul of the sick person by arousing in him great faith in the divine mercy, supported by which he bears more lightly the inconveniences and labors of illness and more easily resists the temptations of the devil who lies in wait for his heel ; and sometimes attains health when expedient for the welfare of his soul." [2] All agreed that whatever other benefits extreme unction might bring at any rate it secured forgiveness of sins, if there remained any still unforgiven. It thus had the same effect as the sacrament of penance and constituted an assurance to the recipient dying in the communion of the Catholic church, of escape from the pains of hell.

Unlike the first five sacraments which have to do only with the individual the sacrament of order is intended for the good of the church as an institution. Without it, indeed, the church could not continue to exist. By it grace is conferred which enables a man validly to perform the duties of the clergy and above all to administer the other sacraments. The administration of the sacraments, particularly the eucharist, is the highest function of the clergy, and for this the power conferred by ordination is especially requisite. Like baptism and confirmation the sacrament imparts an indelible character and is therefore not to be repeated.

The seventh sacrament, that of matrimony, seems at first blush something of an anomaly, for marriage is considered among Catholics a lower state than celibacy as it was

---

[1] *Summa theologiæ*, III. 65 : 1.
[2] Session XIV.

officially declared to be by the Council of Trent.[1] The chief reason for counting it a sacrament — and it was generally regarded as such already in the early Middle Ages — was the desire of the church to keep this most important human institution under its own supervision and control. Doubtless also there was the wish to prevent the general estimate of it as less worthy than celibacy from degrading and corrupting the relationship. Justification was found in Ephesians 5 : 25, 32 where marriage is used as a figure of the relationship between Christ and the church. Justification was found also in the fact that marriage is necessary as a means of raising up members for the church of Christ. This, indeed, was widely recognized as the only adequate ground for the institution. Accordingly, like Orders, the sacrament was regarded as existing primarily for the good of the church rather than of the individuals immediately concerned. To be sure, it was commonly assumed that grace is conferred in the sacrament, which purifies the conjugal relationship and keeps it free from the stain of sin and which sanctifies the mutual affection of the married pair. Nevertheless the primary purpose of the sacrament was not to benefit them but to insure future disciples of Christ and members of his church. Emphasis therefore was laid on the grace that enables parents to train up their children in Christian faith and virtue.

Marriage may not be dissolved, for it signifies the indissoluble union of Christ and his church, as the Bull of Eugene IV puts it. Like some of the other sacraments it imparts a character and may not be repeated by either the husband or the wife so long as the other is alive. That there should have been considerable divergence of opinion as to the

[1] "If anyone says that the married state is to be placed before the state of virginity or celibacy, and that it is not better and more blessed to remain in virginity or celibacy than to be joined in marriage let him be anathema" (Session XXIV : canon 10).

exact nature and effects of this particular sacrament was inevitable. To frame a consistent theory of it, indeed, proved very difficult if not impossible. But there was general agreement at least upon the points mentioned.

In his Summa theologiæ Thomas Aquinas gives an admirable and characteristic summary of the significance of the seven sacraments and their place in the Christian life which in spite of its length is well worth quoting. "The sacraments of the church are appointed for two purposes : namely, to perfect man in those matters that pertain to the worship of God according to the Christian religion, and to serve as a remedy against sin. On both accounts it is fitting that there should be seven sacraments. For the spiritual life has a certain correspondence with the bodily life, just as other corporeal things have a certain similitude to spiritual things. In his bodily life a man is perfected in two ways : first in his own person ; secondly in respect to the whole society in which he lives, for man is naturally a social animal. So far as he himself is concerned he is perfected in his bodily life in a double manner : first, directly, by acquiring a certain perfection of life ; secondly, indirectly, by removing the hindrances to living such as sickness and things of that sort. The bodily life is directly perfected in three ways, first, by generation, whereby a man begins to be and to live. To this, in the spiritual life, corresponds baptism which is spiritual regeneration, as is said in the Epistle to Titus : 'By the laver of regeneration, etc.' Secondly, the bodily life is perfected by growth, whereby one attains to full size and strength. To this in the spiritual life corresponds confirmation, in which the Holy Spirit is given for the sake of vigor, whence, according to Luke, it was said to the disciples who had already been baptized : 'Remain in the city until ye are endued with power from on high.' Thirdly, the bodily life is perfected by nourishment, whereby life and strength are preserved in a man. To this corresponds in the spiritual life the eucharist, whence it is said in John 6 : 'Unless ye shall eat the flesh of the Son of man and drink his blood ye shall not have life in you.' This, indeed, would suffice for man if he had an impassible life both corporeal and spiritual. But since he falls at times into bodily and spiritual infirmity, that is into sin, it is necessary that there should be a cure for his infirmity. The cure is twofold. First, there is the healing which restores health. To this corresponds in the spiritual life penance, according to the word of the Psalm : 'Heal my soul for I have sinned against thee.' In the second place there is the restoration of one's former health by proper diet and exercise. To this in the spiritual life corresponds extreme unction, which removes the vestiges of sin and renders a man ready for final glory. Whence it is said in James : 'If he be in sins, he shall be forgiven.' So far as concerns the whole community man is perfected in a twofold way. First, by receiving the power to rule over a multitude and to exercise public acts. To this in the spiritual life corresponds the sacrament of order, as it is said in Hebrews 7 : 1 that the priests offer sacrifices not for themselves alone but also for the people. Secondly, as regards natural propagation. This takes place through marriage whether in the corporeal or in the spiritual life. For marriage is not only a sacrament but an ordinance of nature." [1]

The significance of the sacraments for the life of the Christians of the Middle Ages it is impossible to exaggerate. They were not mere isolated rites ; they were bound together by their common quality as signs and vehicles of divine grace. They constituted the very heart of Christianity. By means of them the channel of communication between God and man and man and God was kept constantly open.

[1] *Summa theologiæ*, III. 65 : 1 ; cf. also *Summa contra gentiles*, IV. 56 ff.

Where the sacraments were there was life and salvation; where they were wanting man was left helpless and alone. They accompanied the Christian from the cradle to the grave, sanctifying all life for him, equipping him for its duties and responsibilities, giving him grace to live as God would have him live, and when he failed bringing divine forgiveness and renewed assistance. They prepared him not only for life but also for death. Receiving the last rites of the church he could depart in peace assured of a blessed resurrection and the life eternal. What all this must have meant to the Christians of the Middle Ages anyone may imagine but only a Catholic can fully know.

CHAPTER XV

THE CHURCH AND THE PAPACY

AUGUSTINE's twofold idea of the church as the community of saints, or the totality of believers, and as an external institution which dispenses sacramental grace and is the supreme authority on earth, persisted throughout the Middle Ages. But more and more as time passed the latter overshadowed the former. The spiritual notion of the church was not forgotten but it played relatively little part in mediæval thinking. Now and then it was appealed to by good Catholics who felt that the spiritual aims of the church were in danger of being lost sight of; frequently heretics and schismatics made use of it to justify their separation from the parent body; in general it served to keep the church from becoming completely mechanized and externalized. During the Middle Ages the Catholic church of the western world was the papal church. This gave it a distinctive character and marked it off sharply from the church of the east as also from the church of earlier days in west as well as east. According to Cyprian, who was followed by Augustine, the Catholic church was the institution ruled over by bishops that had received their appointment in regular succession from the Apostles and were thus qualified to dispense the saving grace to be had nowhere else. In other words the Catholic church of their day was an episcopal church. During the Middle Ages, on the other hand, the Catholic church was the church which acknowledged the pope as its head and was ruled over by him.

Church and pope were so closely bound together that the former cannot be adequately understood without the latter and unless we understand it the full significance of the Christian thinking of the Middle Ages will inevitably escape us. We shall do well therefore to acquaint ourselves with the nature and meaning of the mediæval papacy. This we can best do by tracing its rise and development, particularly the rise and development of the ideas that underlay it and found embodiment in it.

From an early day the church of Rome, the ancient capital of the Empire, was widely recognized as the most important church in Christendom. It was fully conscious of its own dignity and felt a special sense of responsibility for other churches, which showed itself in large generosity when they were in need and in copious advice and admonition when they were in difficulties. While the eastern church was torn by controversy and the patriarchs of Constantinople and Alexandria were doing all they could to weaken each other and advance their own power, Rome by following a conservative policy and avoiding all extremes of doctrine (as it could the more easily do because it was the home of no great theologians and its interest in theology was secondary only not primary) was building up for itself a reputation for orthodoxy which stood it in good stead in later centuries. Arianism never got a hold there and it was largely through the mediating influence of the Roman bishop Leo that the orthodox formula touching the person of Christ was adopted at Chalcedon in 451.[1]

This same Leo, who went beyond all his predecessors in his insistence upon the supremacy of the Bishop of Rome over the whole church of Christ both east and west, based his claim to supremacy on the theory that Peter was the

[1] See vol. I. pp. 284 ff.

founder of the church of Rome and that from him had descended to his successors, the Roman bishops, his prerogatives as prince of the Apostles to whom Christ had said: "Thou art Peter and upon this rock will I build my church." Leo's claim was sustained by the Emperor Valentinian III in an edict of the year 445 issued in his own name and that of his eastern colleague Theodosius.[1] The legitimacy of the claim did not go unquestioned. No one doubted that Peter was the founder of the Roman church but some held that all the Apostles were equal and that Peter enjoyed no prerogatives not shared by the rest; others while recognizing his primacy maintained that his prerogatives lapsed at his death; still others that they were inherited by all bishops not the bishop of Rome alone. Gradually, however, the soundness of the claim came to be generally recognized in the west, if not in the east, and a divine basis was thus given the primacy of Rome which has ever since been its principal support.

After Leo's time the authority of the Roman see grew apace and from the eighth or at any rate from the ninth century on there was no serious question that the Roman bishop was the primate of the west. How much this primacy involved, however, was widely disputed. Some held that it had to do only with religious and ecclesiastical affairs; others that it included also the sovereignty of the pope over civil states and rulers. Augustine's theory of the supremacy of the church has been already referred to. Bishop Leo, his younger contemporary, had nothing to say on the subject, but a generation later, whether under the influence of Augustine's City of God we do not know, Pope Gelasius I, in a letter to the Emperor Anastasius, explicitly

---

[1] Text of the edict in Mirbt: *Quellen zur Geschichte des Papstthums und des römischen Katholizismus*, 4th ed. p. 76; translated in part in Robinson's *Readings in European History*, vol. I. p. 72.

asserted the superiority of the spiritual power. "There are two, august Emperor, by which this world is principally ruled : the sacred authority of priests and the royal power. Of these two that of the priests is the more weighty since they are to give an account at the divine judgment even for the kings of men. For you know, most merciful son, that though you preside with dignity over the human race you submit yourself humbly to the rulers of divine things and look to them for the means of salvation, and you recognize that in receiving and rightly using the heavenly sacraments you ought to be subject to the clergy rather than superior to them, and depend in these matters upon their judgment rather than try to bend them to your will. For if in so far as pertains to public order the ministers of religion, recognizing the sovereignty which you have received from heaven, obey your laws that they may not seem to obstruct your will in worldly matters, how gladly, I ask you, should you not obey those who have the responsibility of administering the venerable mysteries? . . . And if to all priests who rightly handle divine things it is fitting that the hearts of the faithful should submit, how much more should obedience be rendered to the incumbent of that see which the supreme Divinity willed to rule over all priests and which the piety of the church universal has justly continued to honour." [1]

It is to be noticed that though the superiority of the spiritual to the temporal power is here asserted, and though the duty of the sovereign to submit in religious matters to the priest and particularly to the pope is emphasized, there is no hint that the latter has any authority in political affairs. His spiritual jurisdiction includes the persons of all Christians, rulers as well as subjects, but in his own province, that is where matters of state are concerned, the emperor

[1] Mirbt, *op. cit.* p. 85.

335

has complete control. This recognition of the mutual independence of the two spheres — the spiritual and the temporal — was very significant and long remained normative, biblical support for it being found in Jesus' words "Render unto Cæsar the things that are Cæsar's and unto God the things that are God's."

Some three centuries later, however, as a result of the prevailing political anarchy there arose a party in Italy which felt that only in the control by the pope of the civil as well as the religious affairs of the western world could peace be had and order reëstablished. To this party was due the production sometime in the eighth century and probably at Rome itself of one of the most remarkable forgeries history has seen, the so-called Donation of Constantine.[1] Purporting to be an official decree addressed by the Emperor Constantine to Bishop Sylvester of Rome, it declares that the most holy see of Peter should be exalted and glorified above all earthly power, even Constantine's own; that the Bishop of Rome should have supremacy over the sees of Antioch, Alexandria, Constantinople, and Jerusalem, and over all the churches of the earth; that he should be the chief of all priests throughout the world; and that in every matter pertaining to Christian faith or worship his judgment should be final. It also conveyed to Sylvester and his successors not only Constantine's own Lateran palace in Rome but the city itself together with "all the provinces and cities of Italy or of the western regions." [2] In order to give effect to this transfer of the sovereignty of the west from the emperor to the pope, Constantine declares his purpose to remove his own government to the east, "for where the dominion of priests and the

[1] Original text in Mirbt, *op. cit.* pp. 107–112; Eng. trans. in Henderson: *Select Historical Documents of the Middle Ages*, pp. 319–329.
[2] This is a sufficiently vague designation, but doubtless it was intended to be.

head of the Christian religion have been established by a celestial emperor it is not right that an earthly emperor should have jurisdiction." The decree closes with the threat of eternal damnation for anyone opposing it.

The purpose of the document was apparently not to enhance the actual authority of the pope, or to give him powers which he did not already possess in fact, but simply to supply a legal basis for an existing situation. For some time the pope had been the real sovereign of Rome and of a considerable part of Italy, but nominally he was only the representative and subordinate of the emperor at Constantinople. This situation had grown increasingly irksome and he finally determined to renounce allegiance to the east and rule in his own right. For this step the Donation of Constantine was intended to supply the legal sanction. Though meant primarily to meet a particular emergency, through its incorporation a century later in the famous collection commonly known as the Pseudo-Isidorian Decretals it acquired canonical authority and until the fifteenth century, when its spurious character was exposed, it constituted one of the strongest supports of the papal claim to political authority. If Christ's words to Peter formed the charter of the pope's spiritual power, Constantine's supposed gift to Sylvester was widely appealed to as the charter of his temporal power.

Soon after the middle of the eighth century, pressed anew by the Lombards who had been a thorn in the side of the Roman government for generations, and finding himself unable successfully to resist their encroachments, the pope turned for assistance and protection to the growing power of the Franks. An alliance was concluded with Pippin and afterwards with his son Charlemagne which proved to the advantage of both sides. The pope secured the support of the Frankish sovereign and the latter the support of the pope. The situation was not unlike that in the early fourth century when Constantine befriended the church and the church gave him in return its loyal devotion. Under Charlemagne anything like the supremacy of the church over the state was of course unthinkable, as unthinkable as it would have been under Constantine. He asserted his authority over church and pope as over all other institutions and persons within his realm. Supremacy in spiritual matters he was willing to concede, but the pope was his subject as was everyone else, and the thought of according him any measure of control in civil matters would have seemed absurd to him.

In the generations that followed, generations of religious and ecclesiastical chaos, the papacy passed through many vicissitudes and sank finally to the lowest level it has ever reached. Then came the Cluniac reformation. Beginning in the effort to purify monasticism and restore the earlier enthusiasm and devotion which had widely lapsed, it went on to awaken and vivify the religious life of the church at large. As the movement progressed it came to be recognized (as it had already been recognized by Pope Nicholas I in the middle of the ninth century) that one of the principal reasons for the low state of religion was the subjection of the ecclesiastical to the civil power, which prevented the church from fully carrying out its spiritual aims. This once realized it was soon seen by some of the more clear-sighted ecclesiastics that the church could free itself from the domination of the state only by becoming itself supreme and controlling the state for its own higher purposes. In the existing circumstances church and state could not stand side by side and on an equality one with the other; either the state must be master or the church.

It was this conviction that controlled the ecclesiastical policy of Hildebrand who became pope in 1073 as Gregory

VII. It is not necessary to trace the steps which he took in the effort to carry out that policy, or to recount his dramatic struggle with the Emperor Henry IV, but it is worth while to quote certain sentences from a remarkable document found among his papers. It is known as the Dictatus papæ and in it his principles find clear expression. "The Roman pontiff alone may rightly be called universal." "He alone may depose and reinstate bishops." "He alone may use the imperial insignia." "The feet of the pope alone shall be kissed by all princes." "He has the right to depose emperors." "No synod without his command may be called œcumenical." "He is to be judged by no one." "The Roman church has never erred and will not err to all eternity according to the witness of scripture." "He is not to be counted a Catholic who is not in harmony with the Roman church." "The Roman pontiff may absolve subjects from their oath of allegiance to wicked rulers." [1]

The supremacy over the nations of the earth claimed for the church by Gregory VII reached its fullest realization under Innocent III (1198–1216), perhaps the greatest of all the popes, certainly the most successful in achieving his aims. According to Innocent the pope is lord of earthly states as well as of the church. Princes, like bishops, are his agents, charged with the duty of carrying out his will. In one of his sermons Innocent said of him: "He has been placed in the middle between God and man, below God but above man, less than God but greater than man, and he judges concerning all and is judged by no one." [2] And in a decretal of the year 1202 dealing with the election of the emperor he declared: "The princes ought also to recognize, as they assuredly do recognize, that the right and authority to examine a person who has been chosen as ruler and is to

[1] Original in Mirbt, *op. cit.* p. 146.
[2] Migne: *Patrologia Latina*, vol. 217, col. 658.

be advanced to the sovereignty, belongs to us who anoint, consecrate and crown him. For it is a regular and general rule that to examine a person is the business of him to whom the laying on of hands belongs. For if the princes should choose, either by a divided vote or unanimously, a sacrilegious person, or one who had been excommunicated, or a tyrant, or a simpleton, or a heretic, or a pagan, are we under obligation to anoint, consecrate and crown such a man? God forbid!" [1] Nor were Innocent's words mere words as was the case with some of the popes, they were deeds as well. He succeeded in fact in making his claims good in an extraordinary degree.

At the end of the thirteenth century, during which the church enjoyed the very heyday of prosperity and the pope was at the zenith of his power, Boniface VIII in his famous Bull Unam sanctam gave the completest official expression to the high papal theory. The following abridged translation will give an adequate idea of the document. "By the prompting of faith we are compelled to believe and to hold — and this we do firmly believe and sincerely confess — that there is one holy catholic church outside of which there is neither salvation nor remission of sins. . . . This one and only church has one body and one head (not two heads like a monster), namely Christ and Peter the vicar of Christ, and the successor of Peter to whom the Lord said 'Feed my sheep.' 'My sheep' he said in general terms and not these or those sheep, thus showing that he committed them all to him. If therefore the Greeks or any others say that they were not committed to Peter and his successors, they confess that they are not of Christ's sheep, for the Lord says in John, 'There is one fold and one shepherd.' In this power of his there are two swords, the spiritual and the temporal, as we are taught in the gospels. . . . Both the spiritual

[1] Mirbt, *op. cit.* p. 175.

and material swords are in the power of the church, but the latter is wielded for the church, the former by the church; the one by priests, the other by kings and soldiers but at the command or with the approval of the priest.[1] Moreover one sword ought to be under the other and the temporal power ought to be subject to the spiritual. For when the Apostle says, 'There is no power but of God and the powers which be are ordered by God,' they would not be ordered unless sword were under sword and so the lower were led back by the other to the highest things. For according to the blessed Dionysius it is the divine law that the lowest be led back through the intermediate to the highest. . . . But that the spiritual excels every earthly power in dignity and nobility we ought as clearly to confess as that spiritual things are superior to temporal. . . . For the truth testifies that it belongs to the spiritual power to appoint the earthly and to judge if it be not good. . . . Therefore if the earthly power go astray it shall be judged by the spiritual power; if a lesser spiritual power, by its superior; if the supreme power, by God alone not by man, in accordance with the testimony of the Apostle: 'The spiritual man judges all things, but he himself is judged by no one.' . . . Furthermore we declare, we affirm, we define and pronounce that to be subject to the Roman pontiff is altogether necessary to salvation for every human creature." [2]

The principal architects of the papal theory of the Middle Ages were not theologians but canon lawyers. Peter Lombard, the "Master of Sentences," did not even mention the pope in his great work. For theology one went to Paris; for law to Italy, particularly to Bologna, the seat of the earliest university and of the most famous law faculty in Europe. Italy's interest, like Rome's, was not so much in

---

[1] Cf. Bernard of Clairvaux, *De consideratione*, IV. 3: 7.
[2] Mirbt, *op. cit.* pp. 210 f.

theology and philosophy as in government, not so much in doctrinal questions as in questions of organization and administration. Singularly enough there is no section on the church either in Lombard's Sentences or in any of the great mediæval Summæ. This is the more remarkable since the Holy Catholic Church is one of the articles of the Apostles' Creed and might well seem as appropriate a theme for discussion in a system of theology as the doctrine of God or of Christ. That Lombard did not include the subject may have been because it was omitted by John of Damascus,[1] and Lombard's example perhaps determined the course of the theologians that followed. But this hardly explains the situation. The omission seems rather to have been due to the general feeling that the ecclesiastical institution, including the papacy, demanded legal rather than theological treatment and could be dealt with better by canonists than by theologians.

Though there is no section on the church in the great systems of theology Thomas Aquinas had something to say about both the church and the papacy in more than one of his writings. It might be suggested that his interest in the subject, as also in many questions of civil law and government, was due to the fact that he was an Italian born and bred. However that may be, in the fourth book of his Summa contra gentiles, where he deals at length with the sacraments, he is led in discussing ordination to speak of the episcopal office and then of the pope, the supreme bishop.[2] The aim of all civil government, he says, is peace and unity, which can be most successfully maintained by a single ruler.[3] Similarly the best form of ecclesiastical government is the monarchical, and this Christ has provided for in appointing

[1] See vol. I. p. 325.
[2] *Summa contra gentiles*, IV. 76.
[3] See also his *De regimine principum*, Bk. I. chaps. 2–7 where he argues this at great length.

the pope as the successor of Peter and the ruler of the entire church. Other arguments urged in support of the primacy of the pope it is not necessary to refer to here.

In the late thirteenth century an effort was on foot to bring about a reunion of the Greek and Roman churches. The effort culminated at the Council of Lyons in 1274 where there were delegates present from the east and where an agreement was reached only to be rejected after all by the eastern church. At this council, the westerners made use of a brief work Against the Errors of the Greeks written by Thomas a few years before at the request of Pope Urban IV.[1] In it he discussed the principal points of difference in the hope of bringing the easterners to accept the positions of the Roman church. The points in question were the filioque (or the doctrine that the Spirit proceeds from both Father and Son), the primacy of the pope, the use of unleavened bread in the eucharist, and purgatory. The greater part of the work is devoted to the filioque, the acceptance of which, Thomas declares, is necessary to salvation; then the other three matters are dealt with briefly at the close. Speaking of the papacy he says that to deny the universal primacy of the pope is as serious an error as to deny that the Spirit proceeds from both Father and Son; that the Roman pontiff as the successor of Peter and vicar of Christ possesses the fullness of power (plenitudo potestatis) in the church; that it belongs to him to determine the faith; and that to be subject to him is necessary to salvation.[2] Though Thomas spoke so sweepingly of the power of the pope he recognized that it was not unlimited. Elsewhere he declared that the pope could not change either the faith of the church or its means of grace, that is, either its beliefs or its sacraments,

[1] *Contra errores Græcorum ad Urbanum IV Pontificem Maximum.*
[2] This last statement was repeated a few years later in the Bull *Unam sanctam* quoted above.

both of which Christ gave the church at its founding.[1] Within these limits, however, the power of the pope, according to Thomas, was absolute and universal.

Thomas' assertion that it belongs to the pope to determine the faith means that he regarded him as infallible. This appears also from the following passage in his Summa theologiæ. Speaking to the question whether the pope has the right to draw up a creed he says: "He has authority to issue a symbol to whom it belongs to determine finally what things are to be believed, that they may be held by all with unshaken faith. But this belongs to the authority of the supreme pontiff to whom the church's greater and more difficult questions are referred. . . . Whence also the Lord said to Peter in Luke 22: 'I have prayed for thee, Peter, that thy faith fail not.' And the reason for this is that there ought to be one faith in all the church according to 1 Cor. 1: 'That ye all say the same thing and that there be no schisms among you.' This cannot be assured unless when a question of faith arises it is determined by him who presides over the whole church, so that his opinion may be firmly held by all the church." [2]

Papal infallibility was but a natural conclusion from the belief that the church is infallible — a belief shared from an early day by all good Catholics — and that the pope is its head. The theory of papal infallibility was foreshadowed in the Dictatus papæ of Gregory VII, where the infallibility of the church of Rome was explicitly asserted. Whether it was widely held in Thomas' time is uncertain. His contemporary, the great Franciscan theologian and mystic Bonaventura, like him an Italian by birth, shared the belief,[3] and the more or less casual way in which Thomas

[1] See Leitner: *Der hl. Thomas von Aquin über das unfehlbare Lehramt des Papstes*, pp. 22 ff.
[2] *Summa theologiæ*, IIb. 1:10. Cf. IIb. 2:6.
[3] See Leitner, *op. cit.* pp. 156 ff.

refers to it suggests that it was not uncommon in his day, though it is clear from what followed that it was by no means universally accepted. In any event in the difficult days of the fourteenth and fifteenth centuries, when hostility to the papacy was growing on every side, there was no chance for the belief to make its way and the reforming councils of the fifteenth century put a quietus upon it for generations to come.

Of the power of the pope in temporal affairs Thomas had little to say. He recognized that the secular authorities are subordinate to the spiritual in all things pertaining to salvation, but that in worldly matters the rulers of the state are independent and may not be interfered with by the rulers of the church unless they pursue a course inimical to the spiritual welfare of their people. Should a prince apostatize from the faith and try to induce his subjects to do the same the pope might even go so far as to release them from their oath of allegiance but this only as a last resort.[1] Thomas' position was a moderate one. That he approved the sweeping claims of a Gregory VII and an Innocent III is hardly likely — certainly he says nothing to give that impression — but his general principle touching the relation of church and state was so elastic that it might be made to cover, if desired, even the extravagances of a Boniface VIII.

The political claims of the papacy that have been sketched in this chapter did not go uncontradicted. Emperors and kings battled for the independence of the civil power and strove sometimes successfully, sometimes not, to humble the pope and bring him into subjection to themselves. The counter claim was set up that civil rulers receive their sovereignty, not from the pope as the latter insisted, but directly from God himself. The Emperor Frederick Barbarossa, for instance, in a manifesto of 1157, declared em-

---

[1] See Leitner, *op. cit.* pp. 27 ff.

phatically : "Since by the election of the princes the royal and imperial power is ours from God alone who by the passion of his Son subjected the earth to the rule of two necessary swords, and since Peter the apostle made this doctrine clear to the world when he said 'Fear God, honour the king,' whosoever says that we have received the imperial crown as a benefice from the lord pope contradicts the divine appointment and the teaching of Peter and is guilty of falsehood." [1]

A similar position was taken in the early fourteenth century by Dante, Marsiglio of Padua, William of Ockham and many others. In his De monarchia, written not long after 1311, Dante spiritualized the secular order, insisting that the state is from God as truly as the church and that profane history is as completely under his control as sacred history.[2] Man was created by God to enjoy happiness both on earth and in heaven. The former he may attain by virtue and wisdom under the guidance of the emperor; the latter by faith and love under the guidance of the pope.[3] The power of the emperor is derived directly from God, not from the church or the pope; it is as truly divine in origin as is the power of the latter.[4] In the course of his discussion Dante took occasion to expose the fallacy of the proofs for the supremacy of the pope over the emperor drawn from the Donation of Constantine and from the analogy of the sun and moon and of the two swords. He also used Thomas' argument for the unique authority of the pope to support the unique authority of the emperor.[5] Though he thus undertook to vindicate the independence of the imperial power and to check the encroachments of the papacy which seemed to him — Ghibelline as he was — a major cause of

[1] Mirbt, op. cit. p. 169.
[2] De monarchia, Bk II.
[3] Ibid. III. 16.
[4] Ibid. III. 4 ff.
[5] Ibid. I. 14.

the ills of the time, he did not attack or question in any way the pope's authority over the church. He even spoke of him in passing as the "successor of Peter to whom belong the keys of the Kingdom of heaven."[1]

Ockham agreed in general with Dante in his theory of church and state though he differed with him at certain points. In his so-called Dialogue and in several other works written between 1330 and 1350 he had a good deal to say upon the subject. Church and state which are in reality only the whole body of citizens viewed now under one aspect, now under another, exist side by side and independently of each other. Of the two the dignity of the former is the greater, as the sun exceeds the moon in glory, but each has its own separate and peculiar sphere. The emperor is supreme in temporal affairs, the pope in spiritual, and neither must interfere with the other except in extraordinary circumstances, as for instance if the pope be a heretic he may be deposed by the emperor and if the emperor be a tyrant he may be deposed by the pope.

Marsiglio was more radical than either Dante or Ockham. Like them he considered the political power of the papacy a serious evil and he attacked it vigorously. In his famous Defensor pacis which appeared at Paris in 1324, some years before Ockham's anti-papal writings, he maintained that the state exists for the good of the people and the ultimate authority resides in them, not in any individual or group — a principle which he took from Aristotle's Politics and which he regarded as fundamental in any sound theory of the state. The state has two functions, temporal and spiritual, its aim being to promote the welfare of the people both in this world and in the next. The people as a whole choose a prince or other ruler (Marsiglio's ideal form of government was an elective monarchy) and he as their representative

[1] *Ibid.* III. 1.

appoints civil officials to look after their temporal well-being
and clergymen of higher and lower degree to look after their
religious interests.   The people are bound by the divine law
to support the clergy but are not required to pay tithes or
other taxes beyond what may be needed to supply them with
the necessaries of life.   The head of the state is supreme over
all officials, both civil and ecclesiastical, from the highest to
the lowest.   The emperor and the pope therefore are not
two independent and equal powers, but the latter is subject
to the former.   The clergy have no rights over the prince
and no voice in his selection.   If he be tyrannical he may
be deposed by the people as a whole but not by the pope.
From decisions rendered by a bishop or a priest appeal may
always be taken to the people.   To them, or to the prince
who rules by their authority, belongs the right to call an
ecclesiastical council, either general or local, and no one
may be compelled to obey the decrees of a council convoked
in any other fashion.   The prince alone, acting for the
people, is empowered to condemn heretics and to inflict
punishment upon them, and he should do it only if the welfare of the state is threatened.[1]

The question as to the relative authority of pope and civil
ruler was ultimately settled not by theoretical but by practical considerations.   Almost immediately after the death
of Boniface VIII who was defeated in his struggle with
Philip the Fair of France the papal court was removed to
Avignon, where it remained for nearly seventy years, much
of the time under the control of the French king.   The
so-called Babylonish captivity was succeeded by the papal
schism.   This still further reduced the respect in which the
papacy was held and led many thoughtful men to raise the

[1] For all this see the third book of Marsiglio's *Defensor pacis* which contains
his conclusions to the number of forty-one.   These are given in part by Mirbt,
op. cit. pp. 217 ff. ; Eng. trans. in Thatcher and McNeal, *A Source Book for
Mediæval History*, pp. 318 ff.

question whether any pope was needed. Popes still continued to claim authority, political as well as spiritual, over all the peoples and princes of the earth, but the claim after the days of Innocent III and his immediate successors was seldom made good and as time passed was taken less and less seriously by civil rulers and their subjects. Nationalism was more and more the watchword of the fifteenth and following centuries and nationalism had little place for the political claims of an international ecclesiastical power like the Roman church. It is not necessary to trace the development further. To do so would carry us beyond the horizon of the present volume; nor could the development be understood without taking account of the Protestant Reformation whose influence was particularly marked in the political field.

Meanwhile attacks on the pope were not confined to his secular power, though this was the head and front of his offending in the opinion of most; his spiritual authority was also assailed. Dante, as remarked above, did not question it, but Marsiglio did, claiming that all bishops derive their authority directly from Christ and that none of them is superior to any other, the bishop of Rome having no more right to excommunicate or control other bishops than they have to excommunicate or control him. He claimed, moreover, that to define the faith belongs not to the pope but to a general council. Ockham too attacked the spiritual prerogatives of the pope, basing his attack on the democratic idea of the church referred to at the beginning of this chapter. The church is the company of believers, not the pope or the bishops or the clergy; and the seat of authority is the Christian people as a whole. The pope is their representative, not their ruler, and derives his power from them. They are not dependent on him for salvation. The sacraments may be administered without his authorization or permission. He is not infallible and it does not belong to him but to the people to determine what is of faith. The pope, the cardinals, the bishops and even a general council may err; only the entire community of believers, whose head is Christ, cannot. The Scriptures are the final court of appeal in all disputed questions and the Scriptures interpreted not by the pope or the clergy but by the Christian people as a whole under the inspiration of the Holy Spirit.

Half a century later the Englishman John Wyclif followed Marsiglio and Ockham and even outdid them in attacking both the political and the spiritual supremacy of the pope.[1] It is not necessary to reproduce his positions in detail. They were in the main identical with those of his predecessors. But it is interesting to notice that while he agreed with them in denying that the true church is the external Catholic institution ruled by the pope he identified it, not with the company of Christian believers, as they did, but with the totality of the predestinated whether on earth, in purgatory, or in heaven, thus substituting an abstract concept for the concrete social entity envisaged by them. Though he did more than either of them for practical reform his idea of the church was less fitted than theirs to bear fruit in such an ecclesiastical revolution as occurred over a century later under the leadership of Martin Luther.

It was the growing desire to check the pretensions of the papacy that came to official expression in the reforming councils of the fifteenth century which were called primarily to heal the papal schism. At the Council of Constance where the Cardinals D'Ailly and Gerson were leading figures a decree was passed which ran in part as follows: "This holy synod of Constance . . . declares in the first place

---

[1] His attacks began with his *De civili dominio*, written between 1370 and 1377, and were continued in his *De ecclesia*, *De officio regis*, and other writings.

that being legitimately assembled in the Holy Spirit, constituting a general council and representing the Catholic church, it has its authority immediately from Christ and everyone of whatever status or dignity, even if it be the papal, is bound to obey it in those things that pertain to the faith and to the extirpation of the existing schism and to the reformation of the church in head and members." [1]

The effort at Constance was to turn the papacy into a constitutional monarchy. Instead of the absolute ruler of the church the pope was to be merely its chief executive, and general councils meeting at stated intervals and representing the church at large were to have supreme legislative authority. The effort, however, proved nugatory. In the protracted conflict between pope and council the former came off victorious and in the Bull Execrabilis of 1460 Pius II forbade anyone to appeal from the pope to a general council on pain of excommunication.[2] In spite of this prohibition, which was repeated more than once, Constance and Basle were not forgotten and appeals to a general council continued to be made. At the opening of the Protestant Reformation, indeed, the question of the relative authority of pope and council was still unsettled as was the whole question of the nature and extent of papal jurisdiction. For that matter the doctrine of the church itself still awaited official determination.

The democratic idea of the church as the totality of believers, which was shared by many of the critics of the papacy and was influential at the reforming councils, was the chief bulwark of most of the sects of the later Middle Ages. Monasticism with its many and diverse orders provided a safety valve for multitudes of adventurous and

---

[1] Mirbt, *op. cit.* p. 228. The action was confirmed by the Council of Basle in 1439 (see Mirbt, p. 233).

[2] See Mirbt, *op. cit.* p. 242.

impatient spirits and made the multiplication of sects such as marks our modern Protestantism unnecessary. Nevertheless sects were not wanting, though they were by no means so numerous as is often supposed. We have several contemporary lists of them, drawn up by their opponents, one containing the names of more than a hundred. Many of these, however, refer to the same heresy, or the same sect, which often bore different names in different localities. Still, though their number has been grossly exaggerated, there were enough of them to cause the Catholic church considerable anxiety.

From the theological point of view there were no important heresies in the Middle Ages, or at any rate none that had not been dealt with and disposed of long before. The great theological and christological heresies which had distracted the eastern church for centuries, though echoes of them were heard now and then in the west, made no serious trouble there. On the other hand dissent from the established order on other grounds, sometimes moral and religious, sometimes social and economic, was very common and caused the authorities both civil and ecclesiastical no little concern. The Catholic church, the great bulwark of the existing order, was the chief object of attack on the part of these dissenters and it seemed to the ecclesiastical rulers a matter of life and death to repel and overthrow them. In this effort they were as a rule abetted by the civil authorities who saw the entire fabric of society threatened by the assaults on the church. The question thus came to be in connection with any suspicious persons or groups, what was their attitude toward the church, rather than what were the particular errors taught by them. The latter were commonly appealed to as the ostensible grounds of condemnation, but the real ground was rebellion, not false teaching.

Among the most troublesome of mediæval sectaries were the Cathari, or Albigenses as they were also called from the town of Albi in southern France which was one of their important centres. As a matter of fact they bore many names which varied with the locality. Although recognized from an early day as heretical and repeatedly condemned, Gnostic dualism had never altogether died out, and reinforced by other forms of oriental dualism, including the Manichæan, it had considerable vogue in the west during the Middle Ages. Of the various dualistic sects of the time the Cathari were the largest and most important. Like the Manichæans, whom they most closely resembled and whose spiritual descendants they really were, they recognized two eternal powers, the good and the bad, which were in constant conflict with one another. The world, they maintained, is wholly evil and to escape from its bondage should be the aim of all right-minded men. They were ascetics on principle, insisting on celibacy and on complete abstinence from flesh and wine for the perfect, though they were more lenient with the rank and file. They rejected the Old Testament as the work of the bad god but they regarded the New as authoritative. In their Christology they were docetic as all dualists were.

They multiplied rapidly during the twelfth century especially in Lombardy and southern France. Little was done to check their spread until the end of the century, by which time they had become so numerous that in some regions they embraced a majority of the population and in certain places were actually threatening the existence of the Catholic church as the Donatists had done in North Africa in the time of Augustine. Finally it became evident to the ecclesiastical authorities that something radical must be done and Innocent III a few years after his accession launched a regular crusade against them, promising to those

who engaged in it the same spiritual rewards as awaited
the crusaders against the infidels and holding out to their
leaders the hope of financial gain and territorial aggrandize-
ment. The papal inquisition which had been recently
established to deal with heresy was also set in motion against
them. The repressive measures proved highly successful
and before long the sect was virtually extinct — one of the
instances in which persecution actually achieved its end.

Like the Manichæans the Cathari had their origin outside the Catholic church and remained always independent
of it and hostile to it, though drawing largely upon its
membership for their converts. But there were other less
radical groups that took their rise within the church and
whose quarrel was not so much with its theoretical principles
as with its lack of religious devotion and moral purity, or in
general with its failure to live up to the teachings of Christ.
Among these were the Waldenses who, unlike the Albigenses,
were fully in agreement with the Catholic church in their
theology so far as they can be said to have had a theology.
Their interests were exclusively practical. It was their
desire to improve existing moral and religious conditions
and to recall their fellows to the simplicity of primitive days.
The movement was begun about 1170 by Peter Waldo, a
wealthy merchant of Lyons, who gave away his property
and went about preaching the renunciation of all worldly
possessions and ambitions and the single-hearted devotion
of oneself to Christ in a life of purity, humility and service.
He was joined by others of like mind and the movement
spread rapidly as such movements always do. In Waldo's
day particularly the soil was well prepared for his message,
for impatience with the worldliness, rapacity and indifferent
morals of the clergy, higher and lower, was becoming more
and more common and was eliciting even from devout
Catholics criticism of the most drastic sort. Like the

Donatists whom they resembled in many ways the Waldenses insisted that sacraments administered by unworthy priests were invalid, and they even went so far as to maintain that in the absence of worthy priests their functions might be performed by laymen. This was the only theoretical point at which they differed with the Catholic church but it was a point of large practical significance, for it imperilled the validity of the sacraments performed by the Catholic clergy and thus undermined the authority of the hierarchy. The movement early aroused the hostility of the ecclesiastical rulers and Waldo and his associates were ordered to stop their preaching and when they refused to do so on the ground that they must obey God rather than men they were condemned for contumacy and the forces of the inquisition were turned against them. Though not exterminated, as the Albigenses were, they were driven into seclusion and their numbers greatly reduced, so that they ceased to be a menace to the church.

Surprise has been expressed that Waldo and his followers should have been persecuted when Francis of Assisi whose movement was similar in many ways was encouraged and supported by the authorities. But the reasons are not far to seek. For one thing the Waldensian view that the validity of the sacraments depends on the moral character of the person administering them could not be tolerated. For another the Waldenses appealed to the New Testament as the warrant for their message and drew from it ammunition for their attacks upon many current practices of the church. Finally, whereas Francis put himself at the service of the pope and wished to do nothing that he did not approve, Waldo and his followers showed themselves recalcitrant; in other words from the ecclesiastical point of view they were rebels while Francis was a loyal son of the church. Not heresy but resistance to the constituted authorities was the real ground of offense in their case as in that of most of the sects.

I have referred to the prevalence in the west during the Middle Ages of various forms of oriental dualism. Pantheism too was not without its exponents, as for instance Amalric of Bena, who felt the influence of Eriugena, and David of Dinant, who owed his ideas apparently in part to Amalric, in part to Averroes, the famous Arabic commentator on Aristotle. Their pantheism bore practical fruit in hostility to the Catholic church, in social radicalism, and often, if their opponents are to be believed, in moral indifferentism and antinomianism, it being maintained that the believer in whom God dwells cannot sin and is superior to all law, both civil and moral. Though their followers, of whom there were not a few in the late twelfth and early thirteenth centuries, were soon crushed by the authorities their ideas lived on here and there for a long time. Similar ideas appeared also in certain mystical sects of the fourteenth and fifteenth centuries, as for instance the so-called Brothers and Sisters of the Free Spirit. Speaking generally, however, the influence of these and other similar sects was not great and it is not important to dwell upon them here.

Because many of the sectaries appealed to the Scriptures in support of their positions and delighted in showing how far the church had departed from the teachings of the New Testament in various matters, the ecclesiastical authorities undertook to stop or at any rate to bring under strict supervision the reading of the Bible by the people. Thus Innocent III, while recognizing that the desire to know the Scriptures was to be commended not condemned, insisted that since they contained many things difficult to understand and liable to lead the ignorant and simple-minded astray, they should not be read except under the guidance of those competent to interpret them correctly. He also frowned upon unauthorized translations and after his day they were frequently proscribed and the faithful were forbidden to have copies of them in their possession.[1] All this was a marked departure from earlier custom. Jerome translated the Bible into Latin that it might be accessible to all and Gregory the Great explicitly urged the more diligent study of it on the part of everybody.[2] For centuries it was commonly taken for granted that its teachings and those of the church were in full agreement. But when this began to be seriously questioned and the authority of the Bible was appealed to over against the authority of the church, there seemed no other course left to the ecclesiastical rulers than to keep the Bible out of the hands of those who might employ it for heretical or seditious purposes.

As has been seen no doctrine of the church was officially formulated and promulgated in the Middle Ages and in the fourteenth and fifteenth centuries there was a wide difference of opinion even among good Catholics as to the constitution of the church and the relative authority of pope and council. But upon one thing there was general agreement. If a person is to be saved he must have the divine grace which is imparted through the sacraments alone. As the authorized dispenser of these sacraments the Catholic church seemed to most men indispensable. This it was above all else that gave it its hold upon them and kept them loyal to it even when they might, as was often the case, chafe under its restrictions, or feel impatience with its failures, or deplore the frequent worldliness of its rulers and unworthiness of its priests. Not only devout believers but even the most

---

[1] See Mirbt, pp. 173 ff.; 194; 227. G. G. Coulton, in his *Life in the Middle Ages*, vol. II. pp. 142 ff., quotes an interesting passage on this subject from Sir Thomas More.

[2] Mirbt, p. 98. During the greater part of the Middle Ages vernacular translations, particularly of the Psalms and the Gospels, of which there were several current, circulated without let or hindrance.

indifferent and least religious-minded men might well hesitate to cut themselves off from its ministrations, or die outside its pale, when to do so meant possibly if not certainly to forfeit the hope of eternal life and incur the risk of everlasting punishment.

But to leave the matter thus would be both misleading and unjust. Multitudes there were, clergy as well as laity, educated as well as uneducated, persons of high degree as well as of low, to whom the church, as it had always been, was an object of love and devotion and veneration, under whose guidance and in whose communion they found all they craved of spiritual nourishment and inspiration. Despite widespread discontent and multiplying complaints in many quarters the Catholic establishment was still strong and vigorous. The fourteenth and fifteenth centuries, indeed, though a time of change in many ways, was a time of life not death, of progress not decay, for church as well as people.

CHAPTER XVI

ECKHART AND THE MYSTICS

MYSTICISM of one or another type has existed in every period of Christian history and in every part of Christendom. In the Middle Ages there were notable mystics in Germany and the Netherlands, in Spain, Italy, France and England. No one country had a monopoly of them, though in Germany and the Netherlands they seem to have been more numerous than elsewhere; at any rate we know more about them there, particularly in the thirteenth and fourteenth centuries when their numbers were increasing rapidly. Of all of them there is none more interesting or better worth studying than Meister Eckhart, as he was called. He was born in central Germany (at Hochheim near Gotha) about 1260 and early joined the Dominican Order in which he later held important administrative posts and wielded considerable influence. True to the traditions of the order he received a careful training in theology and became a theological teacher of wide repute. He wrote many Latin works intended primarily for theologians. Some of these are still extant but most of them are lost. They set forth his theological views in the systematic and logical fashion common in that age. He was a follower of Thomas Aquinas and belonged ostensibly to his school, but he felt other influences as well and departed widely in some respects from the teaching of the great Dominican doctor.

The chief difference between them lay in the fact that Eckhart was a mystic of the most thoroughgoing kind.

while Thomas, though he read the future life of the saved in mystical terms, was far from being a mystic in his interpretation of the present life. Compared with this fundamental contrast all theological divergences were of relatively minor importance. Nevertheless, to understand Eckhart we must acquaint ourselves with certain aspects of his theology, for his significance was due not only to the extreme and uncompromising character of his mysticism but also to his grounding of it in a speculative theology of a very daring type. It meant much for his influence that he was a great preacher, that he preached and wrote extensively in German, and that he did not hesitate to express his most profound and abstruse ideas in the vernacular for all to read and hear. He made extraordinary demands upon his public. Much of what he said must have been quite beyond their comprehension; but he was enormously popular and had an immense following, lay as well as clerical.

Eckhart's great aim as a preacher and religious teacher was to promote the Christian's union with God. This he counted the end of all religion and the essence of salvation as brought to the world by Jesus Christ. In his own person Christ united God and man and thus made it possible for man in his turn to become one with God. Union with God Eckhart interpreted in the most intimate possible sense. It is not simply communion with God, or oneness of will and affection with him, but a complete fusion of man's nature with the nature of God. "God must become I," Eckhart declares, "and I must become God."[1] "The fire," he says elsewhere, "changes into itself whatever is brought to it, and gives it its own nature. The wood does not change the fire into wood; rather the fire changes the

---

[1] In a sermon on "Renewal in the Spirit" in Pfeiffer's *Meister Eckhart,* Sermon 99, p. 320.

wood into fire. Thus we are transformed into God and know him as he is, as Saint Paul says." [1] This union with God, this transformation into God, Eckhart speaks of frequently as deification : the man united to God " is deified" ; "he is a deified person." [2] "Blessedness is always God ; and everyone who is blessed is in his experience of blessedness God, both God's nature and God's substance itself." [3] This does not mean that man loses his individual consciousness. However closely united with God and however completely transformed into God he still retains something of himself ; his personal identity is not destroyed but rather conserved and enriched.[4]

Union with God was possible, so Eckhart believed, because man and God are at bottom really one. Man came from God and is himself in some sense truly divine. It is not simply that he was made in the image of God and still retains vestiges of the divine likeness, but that he shares the being of God. Upon this essential oneness of God and man Eckhart laid great emphasis. One of the chief difficulties, he was convinced, in arousing men's desire for God and in bringing them to him was their mean idea of their own nature and capacities. Thinking of themselves as fallen creatures, altogether alien to the divine, to imagine that they might really become one with God and live their lives in him was quite beyond them. To meet their doubts and hesitations Eckhart proclaimed in ringing terms their divine origin and their genuine kinship with God. Not only might they become one with God if they would, they were already one with him if they but knew it. All they had to do was to open their eyes and live in the light of the

---

[1] *Ibid.*, Sermon 65, p. 206.
[2] 'So wird er vergottet' (Pfeiffer, Sermon 76, p. 240) ; 'Er ist ein vergotteter Mensch' (p. 643).
[3] Büttner: *Meister Eckehart's Schriften und Predigten*, vol. I. p. 202.
[4] Cf. Lasson: *Meister Eckhart der Mystiker*, pp. 212 f.

vision that would then be theirs. God, Eckhart insisted, is within man and is to be found not by traveling to some distant sphere but by turning one's gaze upon one's inner self, where the soul of man and the Spirit of God are inseparably joined.

The union with God which Eckhart preached he was fond of calling the birth of Christ in the soul. There is a twofold begetting of the Son: his eternal generation as the second person of the Trinity, and his generation in the soul of man. "In eternity the Father begets his Son like himself. 'The Word was with God and the Word was God,' the same in the same nature. I say still more: he has begotten him in my soul. Not only is my soul with him and he equally with my soul, but he is in my soul, and the Father begets his Son in the soul in the same way as he begets him in eternity and not otherwise. He must do it whether he likes it or not. The Father begets his Son without ceasing; and I say furthermore he begets me as his Son and the same Son. I say more: he begets me not alone as his Son, he begets me as himself and himself as me — me his essence and his nature." [1]

There is a faculty in the soul by which a man may know God directly. "I have a power in my soul which is always sensible of God. I am as certain as I live that nothing is so near as God. God is nearer to me than I to myself. My existence depends on God's being near me and present with me. He is also present with a stone and a stick of wood but they know it not. If the wood knew about God and were conscious how near he is, as the highest angel is conscious of it, the wood would have the same blessedness as the angel. Therefore man is more blessed than a stick of wood, because he recognizes God and knows how near God is. The more conscious of it the more blessed, the less

[1] Pfeiffer, Sermon 65, p. 205.

conscious of it the less blessed he is. He is not blessed
because God is in him and is so near to him, or because he
has God, but only because he is aware of God and knows
how near he is and that he is dear to him and present with
him." [1] The faculty by which one knows God is not merely
human like the senses, or the reasoning power, but divine.
"The eye wherewith I see God," Eckhart says, "is the
same eye wherewith God sees me. My eye and God's
eye are one eye — one seeing, one knowing, one loving." [2]
Eckhart had many names for this faculty: divine spark,
power, eye of the soul, ground of the soul, uncreated light,
and so on. The important thing is that because of it man
may know God directly instead of being obliged to content
himself with learning about God from others or with drawing
conclusions concerning him from the data supplied by the
senses.

There are three kinds of knowledge: sensible, rational,
and super-rational. In his lower consciousness man depends
wholly on the senses and knows only finite things. He must
renounce and rise above both the sensible and the rational,
that is all ordinary human knowledge, in order to know God.
This he can do because of the divine faculty just referred to,
the faculty that makes him truly one with God and opens
to him the vision of the divine. The vision of God which
Thomas put into the future life, when man shall have laid
off the flesh with its limitations, Eckhart put into the present
(not the perfection of it to be sure, but its real beginning),
for even here we are one with God, if we but know it. Few,
to be sure, are aware of it, and hence few now enjoy the vision,
but all might if they only would, for God is not apart from
us but in us. God's kingdom is himself, and hence when
it is said the kingdom of God is within us it means that
God is within us. If we would know God we must first

[1] *Ibid.*, Sermon 69, p. 221.   [2] *Ibid.*, Sermon 96, p. 312.

know ourselves, since it is in ourselves not in the world outside or in the heavens above that we shall find him.[1]

Eckhart, as I have said, was a philosopher as well as a mystic and he did not content himself with asserting the essential oneness of God and man. He made it part of a general system of philosophy and read it in the light of a larger whole. God he represented as the fountain from which all things flow and to which all things return. God is being and the source of all being. The universe is not simply his creation; it is God unfolded and revealed. It is not of another nature but of the nature of God himself, for God alone truly is. All things are in God and outside of him there is nothing. God and the whole world together are no more than God alone. Everything is in God and is identical with him. All creatures are God so far as they are in him; all creatures are nothing so far as they are in themselves. God works and creates and knows and loves nothing outside himself. The smallest thing seen in God is nobler than the whole world seen apart from him. Not only are all things in God, God is in all things as their being, for he alone is being.[2]

The whole universe, spiritual as well as material, is part of an eternal process, the process of the divine unfolding and refolding.[3] In begetting the eternal Word God begets the eternal ideas in which every thing, from angels down to the lowest creatures, has its eternal existence. The visible world is but the temporal manifestation of this eternal world of ideas. Out of the fullness of God all things came and to him all things return. The process is circular not rectilinear — God is not simply the source, but the goal of all things, not simply the beginning but the end of the

[1] Pfeiffer, Sermon 69, p. 221; also p. 617 and often.
[2] For all this see the quotations in Karrer: *Meister Eckhart*, pp. 76, 80 ff, 85, 87.
[3] For this and what follows see the quotations in Karrer, pp. 84 ff.

process. To bring all things back to himself is the purpose of all that God does. Not man alone but nature as well seeks God. All creatures long for unity and desire to return to the source whence they came. There there is complete rest. Movement belongs only to the imperfect. Through the imperfect and the finite the process goes on until it reaches the perfect quiescence of Deity in which all things are eternally at peace. All this reminds us of Eriugena. Whether Eckhart drew directly upon that great thinker, or only felt the influence, as Eriugena did, of Plotinus and the Neoplatonists, at any rate his thought moved along similar lines. Not altogether inappropriately he might be called a mystical Eriugena or Eriugena become mystic.[1]

To God in himself — the undifferentiated unity lying back of the process of evolution — Eckhart gave the name deitas or Gottheit (Deity or Godhead), distinguishing him from the personal God, the creator of the world.[2] Of God in himself, or Deity, we can speak truly only in negative terms. He is not this or that or anything that we can say or think. He is pure being without qualities or attributes of any kind. To define him is to limit him. If he were comprehensible, Eckhart says, he were no God. It is a fault of nature that we cannot avoid sensible images in referring to him. These, however, do not express the truth about him; they are only symbols and as such quite inadequate to give us real knowledge. That God is incomprehensible and beyond all human understanding was no new idea. From the beginning it had been recognized by

[1] Denifle (*Meister Eckeharts lateinische Schriften und die Grundanschauung seiner Lehre*) attempts to show that practically all Eckhart's teaching is to be found in Thomas and was the common property of the schoolmen. But though Eckhart quoted largely from Thomas and though parallels to many of his utterances can be found in him the emphasis lies elsewhere and the general impression is very different. We are moving indeed in another realm of thought, the Neoplatonic not the Aristotelian, and that despite the fact that there is no little Aristotelianism in details.

[2] See the quotations in Büttner, *op. cit.* I. 198 f.

Christian theologians, but some made more of it and others less. Like Dionysius the Areopagite, who influenced him largely, Eckhart went further than most in his emphasis upon this aspect of the divine. Even in his German sermons he had much to say on the subject and employed the strongest possible language in trying to express his thought. "God," he says, "is nameless; no one can know or say anything of him. . . . If I say God is good, it is not true: I am good, God is not good. I say more: I am better than God is, for what is good can be better and what is better can be best. But God is not good, therefore he cannot be better, and since he cannot be better, therefore he cannot be best. These three: good, better, best are remote from God who is above all. And if, again, I say that God is wise, it is not true: I am wiser than he. Or if I say God is a being, it is not true: he is a transcendental essence, a superessential nothing. Saint Augustine says, 'The finest thing a man can say of God is that he is silent from consciousness of interior fullness.' Wherefore hold thy peace and prate not about God, for prating of him thou dost lie, committing sin. If thou wouldst be perfect and free from sin babble not of God. Neither know anything of God, for God is beyond knowledge." [1]

This Being who is above all being and utterly beyond human comprehension Eckhart distinguished, as I have said, from the personal God, the creator and ruler of the world. The latter, the triune God of the Christians, has been revealed; the former remains hidden. The latter is Deity manifest, Deity in relations; the former is Deity apart and alone, the Absolute, out of touch with anything else that is.[2] It was not the Absolute but the personal

[1] From Evans' translation of Pfeiffer's *Eckhart*, p. 246 (in the original, p. 318).
[2] The difference between the two is similar to that marked by Clement's use of the terms God and Logos: his God is Eckhart's Deity, his Logos Eckhart's God.

God of the Christians that Eckhart ordinarily meant when he used the term God.[1] He could therefore say with perfect consistency, as he did frequently, that without the creature God were not God, that God depends on the creature as well as the creature on God. "Before there were creatures God was not God: he was what he was. And when creatures came into being and their created existence began he was not God in himself but in the creatures."[2] "Before there were creatures God was not God, but he was Godhead."[3] "God alone works and has created all things; the Godhead works not and knows no creative activity."[4] It was the same thing he had in mind when he said in still more striking terms, "If I were not God were not";[5] and, "It is due to me that God is God."[6]

The practical significance of all this lies in the fact that Eckhart taught that union with the personal God revealed by Christ was not enough and that Christians should not be content with it. They should press on until united with the ultimate fountain of being, the oneness that lies back of all differences, the unknown and unknowable Deity. God in himself, in his apartness and stillness, should be the supreme object of the soul's desire. "Now if with this faculty the soul sees form, whether she see the form of an angel or her own form, it is an imperfection in her. But when all forms are detached from the soul and she sees nothing but the one alone, then the naked essence of the soul finds the naked, formless essence of the divine unity, the superessential being, passive, reposing in itself. O surpassing wonder, what lofty suffering is that when the soul suffers nothing but the absolute unity of God."[7]

---

[1] He was not always consistent, to be sure, in his use of terms and often employed the word God indifferently both for the Absolute and for the personal God.

[2] Büttner, I. 172. [4] *Ibid.* 199. [5] *Ibid.* 176.

[3] *Ibid.* 198. [6] *Ibid.* 198.

[7] From Evans' translation of Pfeiffer, p. 245 (in the original, p. 318).

God, Eckhart says later in the same sermon, is to be loved not because he is lovable but because he is one. "If you love God as God, or spirit, or person, or image — this must all be abandoned. How then shall I love God? You must love him as he is: not God, not spirit, not person, not image, but rather a mere pure, clear One, alien from all duality. And in this one let us sink down eternally from nothingness to nothingness. Thereto God help us. Amen."[1] Knowledge in the ordinary sense is impossible at this level. The relationship between the soul and the absolute is superrational and indefinable but it means the closest possible union and the highest conceivable beatitude. Like Plotinus and Dionysius Eckhart speaks of the soul thus one with God as in an ecstasy. What the soul enjoys, however, is not less than knowledge but more, and it is along the path of an ever ascending and increasing knowledge that the soul ultimately attains to it.

Psychologically Eckhart's desire for unity meant revolt against the distractions of the world of every day. This desire lies back of all mysticism and dominates it to a greater or less degree. Though Eckhart carried it further and interpreted it in more extreme terms than many others it was in itself nothing new or singular. In the form given it by him it was not distinctively Christian, indeed hardly Christian at all. Rather it was genuinely Neoplatonic. Not Christ himself and not the Christian God, the God revealed by Christ and in him, was the supreme object of Eckhart's desire, but a mysterious Being unknown and unknowable lying back of God, a Being who though called Deity is really nothing but a metaphysical abstraction, the conception of unity in which the philosopher finds satisfaction in the midst of all the disunities and diversities and inconsistencies of the phenomenal universe. It has been

[1] Pfeiffer, Sermon 99, p. 320.

said that Eckhart's mysticism was more philosophical than religious. The statement is not without truth, but it implies a distinction between philosophy and religion which is hardly justified.[1] As a matter of fact the genuinely religious value to Eckhart himself of the metaphysical conception of unity is unquestioned. The very essence of mysticism resides in the realization of one's unity with what is higher and larger than oneself. That by Eckhart this higher and larger was interpreted in philosophical terms did not mean that he was less religious than those to whom the supreme object of desire was the personal God revealed by Jesus Christ.

That in his sermons, where the distinction might seem wholly out of place, Eckhart emphasized Deity unrevealed as distinguished from the revealed God was due perhaps to the desire to impress vividly upon his hearers the importance of complete detachment from all earthly and finite things. The very paradox of God's immediate presence and yet his remoteness and unknowability tended to make the supernatural character of union with him more evident. It was no mere everyday human exercise to which Eckhart was exhorting his hearers but something of an altogether different sort : miraculous, wonderful, incomprehensible, and yet profoundly real. He would have them think of it as extraordinary not commonplace. He would challenge their attention and fire their imagination by emphasizing the seeming impossibility of the very thing he was urging upon them. Something marvelous — yes, but something all the more appealing ; and impossible as it seemed, not really impossible if they pursued the right path and fulfilled the required conditions.

Eckhart had much to say about these conditions, the

[1] Eriugena, it should be remembered, identified philosophy and religion. See above, page 169.

conditions prerequisite to union with God. And first of all, surprisingly enough, he put the imitation of Christ in his life of active Christian service rather than solitude and separation from the world. In a discourse on the contemplative life he says: "Too few there are who give themselves wholly to gazing in God's magic mirror; few there are, indeed, who possess the contemplative life at all here on earth. Many begin it and complete it not. That is because they have not practised enough the active life, the life of Martha. He that would build high must lay a strong foundation. The right foundation is the pattern of our Lord Jesus Christ's conduct and way of living. He himself said: 'I am the way, the truth and the life.'" [1] Whether Eckhart felt the influence of Saint Francis at this point, as he may well have done (though he was a Dominican not a Franciscan), at any rate his attitude showed his practical Christian interest and marks him off from many of the great mystics of history. Upon the indispensable necessity of active Christian service he insisted over and over again. "As I have often said, even were one in a rapture like Saint Paul, if he saw a sick man who needed his help it were much better that out of love he should abandon the rapture and serve the needy one in greater love. Nor should he fear that he would thus be robbed of grace. For what one leaves willingly and deliberately that will be much more richly his, as Christ said 'Whoever forsakes anything on my account will receive it again a hundredfold.'" [2]

In disagreement with common opinion Eckhart ranked Martha higher than Mary. Mary was still at school, he declared; Martha had already learned her lesson.[3] Sustaining and vitalizing all her activity was a life of oneness

---

[1] Büttner, I. 24.   [2] Pfeiffer, p. 553.
[3] See the sermon on Martha and Mary in Pfeiffer, pp. 47 ff.

with God out of which she drew strength for her daily tasks. Active Christian service, as Eckhart viewed it, was at once the condition and the fruit of union with God. Love for one's fellows draws upon the vision of God for its sustenance ; and yet at the same time love is itself a condition of that vision — only he who follows Christ in his life of active service may enjoy the rapture of knowing God and being one with him. To bring these two under a common formula may be impossible, but Eckhart was speaking evidently out of his own experience which has been duplicated over and over again in Christian history.

In calling attention to Eckhart's emphasis on active Christian service both as the condition and the fruit of oneness with God, I have been presenting only one aspect of his teaching, and an aspect of it which bulks less largely in his extant writings than another and very different one. Notwithstanding his recognition of the importance of love for others expressing itself in deeds of charity and helpfulness he commonly spoke of the contemplation of God as the noblest of all exercises. The smallest inner work, he insisted, is greater than the largest outer one. To become one with God is the highest of all things, and this is possible only to him who eschews all works both outer and inner, both bodily and spiritual.[1] Speaking in one of his tracts of detachment (Abgeschiedenheit) he explicitly ranks it above love and humility and mercy and then goes on : "Peradventure thou wilt say, what then is detachment that it should be so noble in itself? True detachment means a mind as little moved by what befalls, by joy and sorrow, honour and disgrace, as a broad mountain by a gentle breeze. Such motionless detachment makes a man superlatively Godlike. For that God is God is due to his motionless detachment, and it is from this that he gets his purity and his simplicity

[1] Büttner, I. 27.

and his immutability. If then a man is going to be like God, so far as any creature can resemble God, it will be by detachment. This leads to purity and from purity to simplicity and from simplicity to immovability; and it is these three which constitute the likeness between man and God, which likeness is in grace, for it is grace which draws a man away from mortal things and purges him from things corruptible. I would have you know that to be empty of creatures is to be full of God and to be full of creatures is to be empty of God." [1]

This detachment from the world and from all finite things was interpreted by Eckhart as self-abnegation of the most thoroughgoing sort. One must be poor in spirit, which means that one must give up one's own will completely and know no will but God's. Indeed one must go further and cut off all desire whatever, even the desire to fulfill God's will. In an extraordinary sermon on the poor in spirit Eckhart says: "Supposing someone asked me, What then is a poor man who wills nothing? I should answer this. As long as it can be said of a man that it is in his will, that it is his will, to do the will of God, that man has not the poverty that I am speaking of, because he has a will to satisfy the will of God, which is not as it should be! If he is genuinely poor a man is as free from his created will as he was when he was not. I tell you by the eternal truth, as long as ye possess the will to do the will of God, and have the least desire for eternity and God, ye are not really poor: the poor man wills nothing, knows nothing, wants nothing." [2] No one could well go further than this. If one is tempted at times to say that Eckhart's mysticism was ethical through and through — dynamic rather than static, active rather than passive — one is driven to recognize that it was also

[1] From Evans' translation of Pfeiffer, p. 343 (in the original, p. 486).
[2] *Ibid.*, p. 218 (in the original, p. 281).

quietistic to the last degree. To attempt to make him consistent with himself in this matter is wholly vain. Though he was a theologian and a philosopher of a profound type he was even more of a religious genius, and quite unconcerned about consistency he gave his religious emotions free play in sermons whose eloquence and splendor and moving power have seldom been approached.

Eckhart's mysticism led him to value somewhat lightly the sacraments and other external means of grace, as also the priesthood, the appointed ministers of salvation. In this he differed with Dionysius who in his work on the Ecclesiastical Hierarchy gave them a prominent place. To Eckhart the Christian's oneness with God made all intermediate agencies seem superfluous, and he was inclined to think that they were often obstacles rather than aids to devotion.[1] To be sure he did not go so far in this matter as many another. He recognized that external means of grace might be of value at any rate to the young and immature and he did not suggest their abolition. He was a loyal son of the church. To attack its institutions or its clergy was the last thing he would have thought of doing; he preferred rather to let all externals remain as they were. To cultivate an attitude of spiritual independence toward them while continuing to make use of them as others did was better, he felt, than to abandon them altogether. But it may well be that his teaching on the subject tended to undermine dependence on both hierarchy and sacraments and made the break with the old church which came with the Protestant Reformation easier in Germany than it might otherwise have been.

Much the same is true of his attitude toward good works. Man is not saved by them but by love for God alone. "God cares little about our works but much about the spirit in

[1] Cf. Pfeiffer, Sermon 76, p. 239.

which we do them, that we love him alone in all things." [1]
Love alone, he says elsewhere, makes work worthy.[2] "A
man should not think he is advancing in the good life because
he fasts often or does many good works. A sure sign of
advancement is when his love for the eternal increases and
his love for the temporal decreases." [3] But again Eckhart
did not go to extremes. In the spirit of Paul he denounced
the antinomians of the day who maintained that the Christian in defiance of all the rules of morality might do what
he pleased quite without regard to the will of God. "Some
people say, If I have God and the love of God then I am at
liberty to follow my own will. They labor under a mistake.
So long as thou art capable of anything against his law thou
hast no love of God though thou cozen the world that thou
hast it. One who is in God's will and in God's love is fain
to do the things God likes and leave undone the things God
hates, and he can no more leave undone a thing that God
wants done than he can do a thing that God abhors." [4]
Still further, Eckhart insisted that one should not quarrel
with another's way of living, whether more or less punctili-
ous than one's own. "What is one man's life," he declared,
"is often another man's death." [5] There was thus a refresh-
ing and wholesome freedom about his attitude which may
well have leavened the soil of Germany and prepared it for the
seed later sown by the Protestant reformers. But to speak
of him as a reformer before the Reformation or as a Protestant before Luther is wholly to misunderstand him. For
all his freedom and independence he was a genuine Catholic
and his piety like that of many another mystic of the Middle
Ages was at bottom Neoplatonic not evangelical.

[1] Pfeiffer, p. 560.
[2] Karrer, p. 151.
[3] *Ibid.*, p. 169.
[4] From Evans' translation of Pfeiffer, p. 180 (in the original, p. 232).
[5] Pfeiffer, p. 565.

Toward the close of his life he fell under the suspicion of heresy and after his death several propositions drawn from his writings were condemned by Pope John XXII who denounced him for "wishing to know more than he should." It is not surprising that teaching such as his should have been condemned. Both in substance and in form of expression large parts of it were out of harmony with the common faith of the church. Eckhart himself, to be sure, had no thought of heresy. He was a loyal son of the church, as already said, and when the storm began to gather he declared himself ready to make full submission if that should be desired. His death, however, spared him the humiliation of a recantation. In spite of his condemnation his name continued to be revered and his memory cherished by multitudes. Among those who felt his influence were the German Dominicans, Henry Suso (Seuse) and John Tauler, the latter one of the most famous preachers of the age, and the Flemish mystic John Ruysbroeck. They were interesting figures, especially Ruysbroeck, but after what has been said of Eckhart it is unnecessary to dwell upon them here. While they reproduced many of his ideas they were not so profound and philosophical as he; and Tauler and Suso, at any rate, were much more careful not to offend the weaker brethren. Their writings which are thoroughly devotional in spirit are less extreme and paradoxical than Eckhart's and better calculated to promote a type of mystical piety in harmony with Catholic tradition, though the independent and venturesome spirit of the great master shines through now and then.

The most famous religious documents of the period, both of them mystical in tendency though only moderately so, are the fourteenth-century tract known as Theologia Germanica, or Deutsche Theologie, which Luther prized so highly, and the fifteenth-century Imitation of Christ, a beautiful example of the finest monastic piety in which humility and poverty and the other monastic virtues receive chief emphasis while almost nothing is said of Jesus' active life of service or of the Christian's duty toward his fellows. Both of these writings, indeed, devotional as they are in temper and lofty and moving in their delineation of the reality and beauty of the spiritual life, fall below the ideal not only of a Saint Bernard and a Saint Francis but of a Meister Eckhart as well.

The mystics that have been referred to and their associates among the "Friends of God," the "Brethren of the Common Life," and other similar circles, were as a rule orthodox Catholics and sound if not zealous churchmen.[1] But there were other more radical groups which denounced the church and attacked it bitterly. The freedom of the Spirit was their watchword and they often carried to extreme lengths their hostility to outward forms and means of grace, to social and ecclesiastical institutions, and to all the laws and conventions by which men are bound. To say without reserve, as is often said, that mediæval mysticism was a revolt of individual against corporate religion, and that it undermined the authority of the church and the respect in which it was held by western Christians, is seriously to distort the facts. That many of the mystics did rebel against the church and condemn sacerdotalism and sacramentarianism is true. But far more of them then as now felt themselves quite at home within the Catholic establishment and found in its cultus a fitting expression for their mystical piety and in its sacraments a potent means of union with the divine. To imagine that mysticism is necessarily opposed to the spirit of Catholicism is to mistake both Catholicism and mysticism. History has abundantly

[1] On these various mystical brotherhoods, see Rufus M. Jones: *Studies of Mystical Religion*, chaps. X ff.

shown that there is nothing incompatible between the two. Mysticism indeed has been called, with some exaggeration to be sure but not altogether inaccurately, the classical form of Catholic piety. It might better be said one of its classical forms, for from the beginning, as has been seen, it was paralleled by another and different type. But even so it has been no alien in Catholic Christianity. While, as was said above in connection with Eckhart, his teaching and that of others like him may have weakened the hold of the church upon many a Christian of the later Middle Ages, it must be recognized that there were others whose mystical beliefs and experiences only made the church dearer to them and heightened and enriched their devotion to it. Not simply religion but the ecclesiastical institution as well was given a new vigor by the great revival of which the mysticism of the period was the most notable expression. By it the ground was prepared for both the Catholic and Protestant reformations of the sixteenth century.

CHAPTER XVII

ERASMUS AND THE HUMANISTS

THE propriety of including in this volume a chapter on Erasmus and the humanists may perhaps be questioned. Do they not belong to the modern age? And should they not be dealt with, if dealt with at all, in another volume rather than in this? I have no disposition to argue the question. It is at best an artificial one. The phrases Middle Ages and Modern Age represent not so much the realities of history as the convenience of historians. I conclude the present volume with a chapter on the humanists not because I count them mediæval rather than modern but for other reasons. For one thing I wish to avoid the impression that they were separated from those that went before them by any sharp line of division; for another to make it clear that their significance was not exhausted in their influence on the Protestant reformers, as is suggested when humanism is treated, as it too often is, merely as an introduction to the Reformation. Humanism had its rise within Catholicism and was as much at home there as in Protestantism. The Reformation was not a humanist movement. Men did not become Protestants because they were humanists but on altogether different grounds. It is of humanism within the Catholic church that I propose to speak in this chapter and I wish to speak of it not as a preparation for Protestantism but as a stage in the development of Catholic thought.

Humanism was only one phase, but for our purpose

the most important phase, of a larger movement which commonly goes by the much-abused name Renaissance. It was not the first movement of the kind in Christian Europe,[1] but it was far and away the most pervasive and enduring. The revival of interest in Greek and Roman antiquity denoted by the name meant first and foremost a new enthusiasm for the classics — the literæ humaniores as they were called — and it is this particular enthusiasm with all that it involved which is known as humanism. Despite continued opposition on the part of many theologians the reading at any rate of the Latin classics had never been altogether abandoned. No century was without those who studied and enjoyed and often made theological use of Cicero, Seneca, Ovid, Virgil, Horace and other ancient Latin authors. But in the fourteenth and fifteenth centuries these more or less rare individuals grew into a host, first in Italy, later in northern Europe as well. Classical literature became the staple of education, and the man of literary ambitions strove above all to bring both his style and his thought into conformity with classical models. At first it was the Latin classics, the glory of ancient Rome, as Petrarch and the Italian humanists were fond of calling them, that received attention, but before long the new enthusiasm extended to ancient Greek literature as well. The study of Greek, almost wholly neglected in the west for nearly a thousand years, was taken up again and pursued with diligence, and it was not long before a knowledge of it was generally regarded as indispensable to the educated man. Under Pope Nicholas V, in the middle of the fifteenth century, humanism invaded the papal court itself and found in him and in Leo X, early in the sixteenth

---

[1] Cf. Taylor's account of the Carolingian renaissance (though he refuses to use the word " renaissance ") in his *The Mediæval Mind*, Chapter x ; also Haskins' *The Renaissance of the Twelfth Century.*

century, devoted supporters and patrons. In their time humanistic tastes and attainments became a favored road to high ecclesiastical preferment.

The influence of humanism was not confined to language and literature; it extended over wide areas of life and thought. The humanists were interested in the ideas of the ancient Greeks and Romans on all sorts of subjects — social, political, moral and religious — as also in their general way of looking at things and their prevailing attitude toward life. Many were so carried away by their devotion to the past that they looked with contempt upon everything modern — especially everything Christian — and undertook to substitute pagan beliefs and ways of living for the traditional faith and morals of the Catholic church. Often this meant a complete loss of interest in religion, and in Italy especially a spirit of secularism grew increasingly common.

On the other hand there were large numbers of humanists, like Petrarch himself, who notwithstanding their zeal for the classics remained devout and loyal Christians. Some of them were entirely satisfied with the existing situation; others felt that religious conditions were not what they should be and undertook so to reinterpret Christianity as to make it a more powerful factor in the life of the times and a greater influence for good. These latter humanists were the modernists of the age, as certain Aristotelians were in the thirteenth century. Many thinkers of that day, as was seen in an earlier chapter, were led by Aristotle into scepticism and atheism, but others remained believers and devoted themselves to the reconciliation of Christianity and Aristotelianism that the Christian faith might not lose the confidence of modern men. The situation in the fifteenth century was similar. Not a few humanists did what they could, as Albert and Thomas had done in the thirteenth century, to bring Christianity into line with the new way of looking at things, that it might be possible for men of modern sympathies to retain their interest in it. The new way of looking at things, however, varied widely. There was no one attitude and no one set of principles common to all humanists. As a consequence to adjust Christianity to the new situation meant now one thing, now another.

An interesting example of what it might mean is seen in the effort of the Italian philosopher Pico della Mirandola of the late fifteenth century to Platonize Christianity. A leading figure in the Florentine Academy, one of the great humanistic centres of the day which made the revival of Platonism its great concern, he attempted, like his older contemporary Marsiglio Ficino, to combine Christianity and Platonism, or rather Neoplatonism, in a vast philoso-phico-religious system of universal reach. The result was a mystical form of religion of a highly symbolic char-acter which owed much to Pseudo-Dionysius and even to the Jewish cabbala and which had considerable vogue in the early sixteenth century in Italy and elsewhere.

More significant and of wider influence was the work of Erasmus, the greatest humanist of northern Europe. As one of his biographers remarks, he is the only humanist whose name is still a household word in all parts of the world. He was born in Rotterdam in 1469 or thereabouts, the natural son of a priest (the Gerard of Charles Reade's historical novel, The Cloister and the Hearth). He got most of his early training under the instruction of the Brethren of the Common Life, a religious society founded a century before by the famous scholar and mystic, Gerard de Groot. The society regarded the education of the young as one of its principal responsibilities and its schools, notably the one at Deventer which Erasmus attended for a number of years, were famous throughout the country.

Already before Erasmus' day humanism had found its way to the Netherlands, as to other parts of northern Europe, and had worked a great change in educational ideals and methods. The Brethren of the Common Life were awake to the situation and made a place for the new learning in their schools, and while the instruction, according to Erasmus, left much to be desired it was here that he gained the love for the classics which lasted him all his life. Though the new learning was given a place in the schools conducted by the brotherhood the religious and moral training of the boys committed to their care was still the chief concern of the instructors and nothing was allowed to interfere with it. Many of their pupils found their way into the priesthood or the monastery. Among them were such well-known figures as Thomas à Kempis, author of The Imitation of Christ, and Cardinal Nicholas of Cusa, author among other works of the famous philosophico-mystical treatise De docta ignorantia. The religion fostered by the brotherhood was of a mystical type, simple and practical, with little regard for theology or for external rites and ceremonies compared with holiness of life and devotion to Christ. But though they emphasized life rather than doctrine and the inner spirit rather than the outer form they were orthodox in their beliefs and genuinely loyal to the church. A change in the traditional faith or a revolt against the existing ecclesiastical organization was the last thing they desired. To understand Erasmus' attitude in mature life it is necessary to take account of this religious environment in which he grew up. Though he later revolted against it he never ceased to feel its influence.

While still in his teens he was persuaded by his guardian (his parents having died some years before) to enter a monastery, a not unnatural step for a youth with scholarly ambitions such as he already cherished and with a religious training such as he had had. An essay written about this time on the familiar theme De contemptu mundi shows the common monastic spirit and attitude. After some years, however, chafing under the restrictions of the monastic life and convinced that he had no vocation for it, he secured a papal dispensation which permitted him to lay off the habit of his order and live where he would. Thenceforth he pursued the career of a scholar and littérateur, untrammeled by ties of any kind. He was offered more than one scholastic appointment, but save for brief periods when he taught at the University of Cambridge and again at Louvain he declined all such calls, preferring to keep his independence and not be fettered by academic routine. Freedom was always very dear to him and he found the academic bondage no less irksome than the monastic. He was also too restless and impatient to remain long in any one place. He was almost constantly on the move, settling down for a little where conditions seemed propitious and then breaking away again and seeking other surroundings. He liked to think of himself as a citizen of the world. Patriotism he regarded rather as a vice (or a natural weakness) than a virtue. For some time he lived at Venice, where the printing house of Aldus offered him special facilities for publication, but the later years of his life were passed chiefly at Basle in intimate relations with the famous publisher Froben. It was here he died in 1536.

Erasmus was at once a great scholar and a literary artist of the highest distinction. He was widely read and thoroughly at home in the classics, both Greek and Latin. Unlike some of his contemporaries he eschewed the vernacular altogether and wrote his letters as well as his books and pamphlets exclusively in Latin. During much of his life, indeed, Latin was more familiar to him than his native Dutch, which he seldom had occasion to use, and he did not take the trouble to learn any other modern tongue. Latin had been the language of scholars and literary men throughout the Middle Ages, but by the humanists it was reformed after classical models, and the possession of a good Latin style was counted an essential mark of an educated man. Upon this Erasmus particularly prided himself, and was generally recognized as the most accomplished stylist of his time. Always whatever else he might be he remained a genuine humanist.

But he was not simply a humanist. He was also a religious man with a deep concern for religious conditions in his day. His preoccupation with religion revealed itself in his famous satire, The Praise of Folly, as also in many of his Familiar Colloquies, a favorite subject of which was one or another religious institution or practice. That there was much mockery in these writings, particularly when he was speaking of pilgrimages, rites and ceremonies, and similar matters, proves nothing to the contrary. He wrote not as a sceptic or an outsider but as one who was concerned to bring about improvement by attacking abuses.

He was especially severe in his criticism of monasticism. The theme was one he never tired of and he returned to it over and over again and in all sorts of connections. He denounced the common notion that the monastic life is meritorious and that by ascetic practices one may gain favor with God. Not explicitly but by implication he repudiated altogether the double standard of morality when he declared that he who does not strive to be perfect is not really good.[1] He did not, like Jovinian in the fourth century and Luther in the sixteenth, pronounce monasticism itself wrong and the monastic life unchristian, but only the common estimate of it both within and without the monastery. If one wished to live the life of a solitary or

[1] *Enchiridion militis christiani*, chap. xv.

to immure oneself in a convent with others of like mind no harm was done, though an active life of Christian service in the midst of the world was much more Christlike and socially valuable. His polemic against monasticism, however, had to do not merely with monastic principles and ideals, but even more largely with the personal character of the monks. Their conduct he pictured in the darkest colors and satirized unmercifully. In this he was simply following a common custom, for monks and friars had been a favorite subject of ridicule for generations.

Erasmus also turned his criticism upon the schoolmen. They were very unpopular with the humanists because of their literary style, so unlike that of the classics, their prolixity and repetitiousness, their endless distinctions, and their tiresome disputes over questions that seemed both futile and uninteresting. Erasmus criticized them for all these shortcomings, but also and especially because they lost sight of the simple gospel of Christ and magnified unimportant at the expense of really important matters. In his Praise of Folly, after ridiculing them at great length for devoting so much attention to dialectical subtleties quite without practical significance, he continues: "These most subtle subtleties are made even more subtle by the countless tribes of schoolmen, so that you might sooner find your way out of a labyrinth than out of the complications of the Realists, Nominalists, Thomists, Albertists, Occamists, Scotists — not to mention all the sects but only the principal ones. In all of which there is so much erudition and so much difficulty that I fancy the Apostles themselves, if they had been compelled to join hands with this new crowd of theologians in dealing with such things, would have had need of another spirit. Paul was able to show what faith is, but when he said, 'Faith is the substance of things to be hoped for, the evidence of things not seen,' he did not define it in the manner of a pedagogue. And while he exhibited charity most excellently in the thirteenth chapter of First Corinthians, he did not divide or bound it dialectically."[1] And then Erasmus goes on with an enumeration of the practical matters in which the Apostles, as he claims, were really interested in contrast with the abstruse and religiously indifferent questions which the schoolmen spent their time over.

Erasmus is often thought of as a mere satirist who was interested simply to castigate the follies and vices of the age. But he was much more than that. He had ideals and principles of his own which he was eager to see realized, and when he criticized existing conditions it was always with the purpose of promoting what seemed to him the better way. This appears most clearly in his charming little Handbook of a Christian Soldier.[2] He wrote it, so he says, at the request of a pious woman whose husband was a man of dissolute life. It was her hope that as he was a friend and admirer of Erasmus, the latter might be able to recall him to a sense of religion and lead him to amend his way of living. The result was not simply a warning against vice and an exhortation to virtue, but a treatise on Christian living which reveals with delightful clarity Erasmus' general attitude and point of view. In a letter to Dean Colet of St. Paul's, one of the friends to whom he owed most, he declared that he wrote the Enchiridion not to display his genius or eloquence but to correct the error of those who made religion consist of external observances while neglecting true piety. This was a favorite theme with him in his Colloquies and elsewhere, and in his Enchiridion he laid special stress upon it, returning to it again and again in the course of the work. "Whether it be through negligence or ignorance, most Christians," he says,

---

[1] *Stultitiæ laus*, chap. LIII.   [2] *Enchiridion militis christiani.*

"are superstitious instead of pious and except for the name of Christ are not far from the superstition of the heathen."[1] Not that Erasmus condemned religious observances. He admitted they might be useful, if not put in the place of inner piety which is alone essential. "To observe these things is salutary, but to lean upon them is pernicious. Paul does not forbid you to use rites and ceremonies, but it is not his wish that he who is free in Christ should be bound by them. He does not condemn the law of works if only one use it lawfully. Without these things perhaps you will not be pious but they do not make you pious."[2]

Erasmus did not content himself with attacking the common subordination of the inner to the outer, he also undertook to show what piety really is and how it may be attained. True piety consists in following Christ. At baptism we promise to fight under his standard and we are Christians only if we make him our master, do all for his sake, obey his precepts, and follow him in all things. He is "the only archetype, from which if anyone swerve even by a nail's breadth he goes astray and runs outside the way."[3] "Think not that Christ is an empty voice. On the contrary count him nothing else than charity, simplicity, patience, purity, in short whatever he himself taught."[4]

The piety inculcated by Jesus Erasmus was fond of calling in good humanistic fashion, the philosophy of Christ, and he was careful to point out its kinship with the teaching of the ancient philosophers. The essence of it he found in charity or love for one's neighbor. "For this cause chiefly," he says, "Christ was born and died that he might teach us not to do as the Jews do but to love." And he goes on : "Paul, when writing to the Corinthians, put charity before miracles and prophecy and the tongues of angels.

---

[1] *Enchiridion*, XIII. I.
[2] *Ibid*. XIII. 49.
[3] *Ibid*. XIV. I.
[4] *Ibid*. XII. I.

And do not tell me that charity consists in going often to church, in bowing before the images of the saints, in lighting candles, in repeating the prescribed prayers. God has no need of these things. Paul means by charity to edify your neighbor, to count all men members of the same body, to think of them all as one in Christ, to rejoice in the Lord over your brother's good fortune as over your own, to relieve his misfortunes as if they were yours, to correct the erring with gentleness, to instruct the ignorant, to lift up the fallen, to console the dejected, to aid the toiling, to help the needy; in short to employ all your wealth, all your effort, all your care, for this end, that in Christ you may be as useful as possible." [1]

It is interesting to notice in this connection that Erasmus committed himself explicitly to Jesus' principle of non-resistance, with all that it implied. He even carried the principle over into the international sphere and wrote against war in strong terms as for instance in his Complaint of Peace (Querela pacis) and in a still more radical treatise on the subject in the 1515 edition of his Adages. [2] He condemned war as inexpedient and bound to harm victors as well as vanquished, as unchristian, and as wrong in any and all circumstances — a position in striking contrast with that of most of his contemporaries.

Erasmus not only set forth clearly and in great detail the nature of true piety, he also showed how it is to be attained. No man, he insisted, can live the Christian life in his own strength. He must exert himself to the utmost, must have courage and confidence, must be ever watchful

---

[1] *Enchiridion*, XIII. 46 f.

[2] This treatise had as its text the proverb " Dulce bellum inexpertis " and was published separately, under the title *Bellum*, in 1517. An English translation of it (entitled *Antipolemus: or the Plea of Reason, Religion and Humanity against War*) appeared in 1794 and was reprinted in America, together with a translation of the *Querela pacis*, in 1813.

and persistent in resisting the devil, but even so he cannot overcome evil and live as he ought without divine help. In view of what is commonly said about human worth and ability and independence, as cardinal principles of the humanists, Erasmus' attitude is instructive. In one passage in his Enchiridion he emphasized the dignity of man, but this was only for the purpose of bringing out more clearly the unworthiness of vice and uncleanness, and he based man's dignity not on what he was in himself but on what he owed to God who created him and bought him with a great price, who framed the world for his sake, who made him a son of God, an heir of immortality, a member of Christ and of the church, his body a temple of the Holy Spirit and his mind the image and the secret habitation of Deity.[1] Pride Erasmus attacked in good Catholic fashion as the worst of all vices, most hated both by God and men. He concludes a long disquisition on the meanness and littleness of man with the words: "Two things chiefly will keep you from pride, if you consider first what you are in yourself, filthy at birth, a bubble throughout life, the food of worms at death, and secondly what Christ was made for you." [2]

Two special weapons Erasmus says a man needs in the conflict with sin: prayer and knowledge. "Paul who commands us to pray without ceasing wishes we should always be armed. Pure prayer raises the affections to heaven, a fortress inaccessible to one's enemies. Knowledge strengthens the mind with wholesome opinions, so that neither the one nor the other ought to be wanting. The one requires the aid of the other and the two are bound together in unity. That one prays, but this one suggests what is to be prayed for." [3] It is significant that prayer appears here not as itself a part of piety but as a means to

[1] *Enchiridion*, XXVII. 2.   [2] *Ibid.* XXXVI. 5.   [3] *Ibid.* II. 3.

piety, the latter, as already said, being thought of as life rather than religious practices or observances. Similarly it is not mystical knowledge that is spoken of — there was nothing of the mystic about Erasmus — but only a knowledge of what the Christian life is, how one may attain it, and why one should strive to do so. Upon all of these Erasmus dwells at length. Among the motives to Christian living, while he appeals to self-respect, he gives prominence to the consequences that follow upon virtue and vice not only in this world but also in the world to come, for there God rewards the good and punishes the wicked everlastingly. "For what are more unequal than eternal death and life everlasting? Than to enjoy without end the highest good in fellowship with the citizens of heaven, and to suffer without end the worst evils in the most unhappy community of the damned? He who doubts about this is not even a man, much less a Christian. He who does not think upon it is more insane than insanity itself."[1] One who wrote thus can hardly be counted an unbeliever or a sceptic. The words testify anew — if testimony were needed — to the fundamental place in mediæval as well as ancient Christianity of the belief in a future life of rewards and punishments.

The Enchiridion was published while Erasmus was still in his thirties, and at first attracted little attention. But later it became very popular and passed through several editions. Though many, especially among monks and scholastic theologians, were outraged by it as by others of his writings, the work was warmly approved by multitudes including even high ecclesiastics. It is evident that in its eloquent presentation of a simple, ethical, undogmatic Christianity it met a widely felt need. There was nothing heretical in it, but it was unlike what people were accus-

[1] *Enchiridion*, XXIX. I.

tomed to, and both in its emphases and in its omissions it was a very significant book.

Erasmus also showed his religious interest by editing, either alone, or in coöperation with others, the works of various church Fathers, both Greek and Latin : among them Athanasius, Basil, Chrysostom, Cyprian, Jerome, and Augustine. Among all the Fathers Jerome was his favorite, and that in spite of his extreme asceticism so unlike Erasmus' own attitude. The younger humanist could not say enough in praise of the older : of his scholarship, his literary gifts and his services to theology.[1] On the other hand with Augustine he had little sympathy. The great African's predestinarianism and denial of all moral power to man represented a tendency wholly uncongenial to him.

More important and memorable than his editions of the Fathers was his epoch-making publication in 1516 of the New Testament in Greek. It was issued, as were his Latin paraphrases which appeared later and proved very popular, with the purpose of calling Christians back to the true sources of Christianity. These he believed had been overlaid and obscured by later theologians, so that few knew what Christianity really was, or what it was meant to be by its founder Jesus Christ. In the introduction to his first edition Erasmus complained bitterly of the wide-spread ignorance of Christ's teaching. He would have the New Testament read by everybody, laymen as well as theologians, and with that in view, he would have it translated into all modern languages, that it might be accessible to the people of every land, even if they could read neither Latin nor Greek. Though he did not himself make a vernacular translation, as Luther did, the attitude of the

[1] See for instance his letter to Greverade (in Allen: *Erasmi Epistolæ*, vol. I. p. 331 ; and Nichols: *The Epistles of Erasmus*, vol. I. p. 288).

two men was similar. Back to the primitive church was their common watchword. Unlike Luther, however, Erasmus returned to Christ rather than to Paul, finding in Christ's teaching not the doctrine of justification by faith alone, which Luther found in Paul, but the simple, ethical Christianity which appears in the Enchiridion. Not that he disregarded Paul any more than Luther disregarded Christ, but that he based his interpretation of Christianity on Jesus, while Luther based his on Paul.

As has been said, Erasmus was troubled by the prevailing religious conditions of his day, and was profoundly convinced of the need of a reformation. But he was no revolutionist, and he wanted only such a reformation as could be brought about within the existing establishment and by the slow and peaceful process of education. He was a loyal and orthodox Catholic to the end of his life, and to break with the Catholic church, or to undermine its influence, was the last thing he wished. Because he remained within it and refused to go with Luther and his followers, among whom were many of his own disciples, he was denounced as a coward and a time-server. But the accusation was misplaced. Not simply because he deplored the violence of the evangelical movement and saw that it meant the destruction of much he held most dear, but also because his principles were utterly opposed to Luther's he remained within the old church. There was much about it he did not like, but the simple, ethical, undogmatic Christianity which he championed was more at home within Catholicism than it could have been within Protestantism, at any rate the Protestantism of those days. The fundamental difference between Erasmus and Luther comes out clearly in the former's work on Free Will (published in 1524), in which he maintained the traditional Catholic belief that salvation is the product of divine grace and human effort, in opposition to the high Augustinianism of Luther and his rejection of all human merit. This did not mean that Erasmus belittled or minimized divine grace. On the contrary, he says explicitly toward the close of the work just mentioned: "To me the opinion of those is pleasing who ascribe something to free will but most to grace." [1] To Erasmus, Luther's doctrine seemed to threaten the very foundations of morality and true piety. To expect him to go with the Protestant reformer was to expect the impossible. Had he been a coward or a time-server, he might have done so; for he passed much of his later life in the reformed city of Basle and counted many Swiss evangelicals among his friends. As it was, he remained true to his convictions in spite of criticism and calumny from both parties.

Erasmus was a representative man. Though there may have been few that fully agreed with him — many were more conservative, many more radical than he — there was abroad in all parts of Europe, even in Spain where he had a host of devoted admirers, a type of piety akin to his, a piety that with all loyalty to the church laid the emphasis on life rather than dogma, and wished to substitute the simple teaching of Christ for the dialectic subtleties of scholastic theologians. It was an attitude congenial to the humanists and common, though by no means universal, among them. Many, particularly in Italy, were out of sympathy with religion altogether; for them Erasmus had no attraction. Many went over into Protestantism; to them he seemed a backslider and a traitor. But many others stood substantially where he stood, and he became their spokesman. Like them, he recognized the authority of the church and accepted its teachings loyally. Though he minimized the importance of theological dogmas in

[1] *De libero arbitrio*, IV. 16.

comparison with the gospel of Christ, he neither attacked them nor threw suspicion on them. Ockham had maintained that all religious truths are unprovable and are to be accepted solely on the authority of the church, thus weakening their appeal to many thinking men. Eckhart and others like him had put the emphasis on mystical oneness with God, and though they might accept the dogmatic teaching of the church, their influence tended to make it seem of relatively minor importance, compared with the great central experience of union with the divine. Similarly the humanists, while they might not reject Catholic dogma, as Erasmus did not, were primarily interested in other things. The golden age of theology had passed and neither the intellectual leaders of the day nor the rulers of the church wished to call it back.

Had it not been for Luther and the Protestant revolt such a simple, ethical Christianity as that of Erasmus might well have prevailed within the Catholic church alongside of such a mystical Christianity as that of Eckhart and his associates.[1] In that event while Catholic dogma might have remained untouched and sacrosanct it would have ceased to dominate the religious situation and to restrain the free working of the human mind. But the Protestant revolt made all this impossible. It brought dogma to the front again and gave it a place of prominence it had not enjoyed for generations. In opposition to Protestantism the Catholic church was driven to define its own dogmatic position with a completeness and definiteness never before approached, and to anathematize all that departed from it. Like other liberals, Erasmus now came to be regarded as a dangerous heretic, even by many of those who had

[1] The two were very different, but differences equally great abound in Catholic history. Erasmus and Eckhart, indeed, represented each in his own way the two disparate types of Christianity that have always been present within the church and to which I have repeatedly called attention.

hitherto thought most highly of him. He was condemned by the Sorbonne, his books were burned in several countries and were put on the Index by Pope Paul IV in 1559. There was, it seemed, no longer a place for his form of Christianity and that of others like him within the Catholic church. The Protestant Reformation was a double tragedy for the old church. It meant not only the loss of vast territory and multitudes of adherents but also such a hardening of temper and narrowing of platform as unfitted it to meet the needs of the dawning modern age. The forces of reaction, hitherto more or less balanced by the forces of progress, now took complete control and the church lost the leadership that had belonged to it for a thousand years.

BIBLIOGRAPHY

GENERAL

In addition to the books listed under this heading in the Bibliography of Volume I (most of which cover also the period dealt with in this volume) may be mentioned the following:

H. M. Gwatkin: *The Knowledge of God and Its Historical Development*, 2 vols., 1906; 2nd ed., 1907.

F. W. Bussell: *Religious Thought and Heresy in the Middle Ages*, 1918.
> Deals more largely with oriental religious thought outside Christendom than with Christian thought but contains much that is suggestive in connection with the latter.

E. Troeltsch: *Die Soziallehren der christlichen Kirchen und Gruppen*, 1912. Eng. trans., 1932.
> Fruitful in ideas; many fresh points of view.

F. J. Foakes Jackson: *An Introduction to the History of Christianity* (A.D. 590–1314), 1921.

F. Ueberweg: *Geschichte der Philosophie:* Theil II. *Die patristische und scholastische Philosophie;* 11th ed., by B. Geyer, 1928.
> Contains very elaborate bibliographies.

R. McKeon: *Selections from Medieval Philosophers:* vol. I. *Augustine to Albert the Great*, 1929; vol. II. *Roger Bacon to William of Ockham*, 1930.
> English translation of selected works or parts of works not hitherto translated.

Shailer Mathews: *The Atonement and the Social Process*, 1930; *The Growth of the Idea of God*, 1931.

> In these two books the author emphasizes the social origin of Christian doctrines and the influence upon them of political and economic ideas and institutions.

BOOK THREE

P. Monceaux: *Histoire littéraire de l'Afrique chrétienne depuis les origines jusqu'à l'invasion Arabe*, 1901 ff.
> A large and important work, not yet completed. Vol. VII on Saint Augustine and the Donatist controversy appeared in 1923.

H. O. Taylor: *The Classical Heritage of the Middle Ages*, 1901; 3rd ed., 1912.
> A capital little book, forming an excellent introduction to the author's larger and more important work mentioned on p. 403.

BIBLIOGRAPHY

H. Leclercq: *L'Afrique chrétienne*, 2 vols., 1904.

S. A. Donaldson: *Church Life and Thought in North Africa*, 1909.
Small and popular.

G. Krüger: *Die christliche lateinische Litteratur von Augustinus bis Gregor der Grosse* (in M. Schanz: *Geschichte der römischen Litteratur*, IV. 2), 1920.
Important.

P. de Labriolle: *Histoire de la littérature latine chrétienne*, 1920. English translation, 1924.
Excellent. Ends with Isidore of Seville.

E. K. Rand: *Founders of the Middle Ages*, 1928.
Interesting and informing. Written from the literary rather than the theological point of view.

CHAPTER I

Complete edition of Tertullian's works by F. Oehler; 3 vols., 1853. Some of his works have already appeared in the Vienna edition of the Latin Fathers (*Corpus scriptorum ecclesiasticorum latinorum*). Eng. trans. in the *Ante-Nicene Fathers*, vols. 3–4. There is an admirable English translation of his Apology by J. E. B. Mayor: *Tertullian Apologeticus*, 1917.

E. Noeldechen: *Die Abfassungszeit der Schriften Tertullians*, 1888 (in *Texte und Untersuchungen*, V. 2).
Important for the chronology of Tertullian's writings.

E. Noeldechen: *Tertullian dargestellt*, 1890.

K. H. Wirth: *Der Verdienstbegriff in der christlichen Kirche:* vol. I. *bei Tertullian*, 1892; vol. II. *bei Cyprian*, 1901.

G. Esser: *Die Seelenlehre Tertullians*, 1893.
Careful and thorough.

C. Guignebert: *Tertullien: Étude sur ses sentiments à l'égard de l'empire et la société civile*, 1901.

A. d'Alès: *La théologie de Tertullien*, 1905.
Excellent.

R. E. Roberts: *The Theology of Tertullian*, 1924.

J. Lortz: *Tertullian als Apologet*, 2 vols., 1927 f.
An extended discussion of the apologist Tertullian and his Greek predecessors.

J. Morgan: *The Importance of Tertullian in the Development of Christian Dogma*, 1928.

CHAPTER II

The best edition of Cyprian's works is that of Hartel, in the Vienna edition of the Latin Fathers; 3 vols., 1868–1871. Eng. trans. in the *Ante-Nicene Fathers*, vol. V.

BIBLIOGRAPHY

O. Ritschl: *Cyprian von Karthago und die Verfassung der Kirche*, 1885.
Important.

K. G. Götz; *Das Christenthum Cyprians*, 1896.
Careful and thorough.

J. A. Faulkner: *Cyprian the Churchman*, 1906.
Brief and popular.

A. d'Alès: *La théologie de Saint Cyprien*, 1922.
Excellent.

H. Koch: *Cyprianische Untersuchungen*, 1926.
Has to do chiefly with literary problems but also deals instructively with the question of penance.
An adequate biography of Cyprian is a desideratum.

CHAPTER III

Arnobius' *Adversus nationes* is in the Vienna edition of the Latin Fathers, vol. IV. Eng. trans. in the *Ante-Nicene Fathers*, vol. VI.

A. Röhricht: *Die Seelenlehre des Arnobius nach ihren Quellen und ihrer Entstehung untersucht*, 1893.

F. Gabarrou: *Arnobe: son œuvre*, 1921.
Excellent.

Lactantius' works are in the Vienna edition of the Latin Fathers, 3 vols., 1893 ff. Eng. trans. in the *Ante-Nicene Fathers*, vol. VII.

R. Pichon: *Lactance: Étude sur le mouvement philosophique et religieux sous le règne de Constantin*, 1901.
The best biography.

The best complete edition of Ambrose is that of Ballerini, 6 vols., 1875–83. Several of his works have already appeared in the Vienna edition of the Latin Fathers. Eng. trans. of some of his writings, including *The Duties of the Clergy*, in the *Nicene and Post-Nicene Fathers*, Series II, vol. X.

T. Förster: *Ambrosius, Bischof von Mailand: Eine Darstellung seines Lebens und Wirkens*, 1884.
The principal biography; still valuable.

R. Thamin: *Saint Ambroise et la morale chrétienne au IVᵉ siècle*, 1895.
Important.

P. de Labriolle: *Saint Ambroise* (in the series *La pensée chrétienne*), 1908. Eng. trans., 1928.
Excellent.

W. Haller: *Jovinianus, die Fragmente seiner Schriften, die Quellen zu seiner Geschichte, sein Leben und seine Lehre*, 1897 (in *Texte und Untersuchungen*, Bd. XVII, Heft 2).

BIBLIOGRAPHY

A. Harnack: *Geschichte der Lehre von der Seligkeit allein durch den Glauben in der alten Kirche* (in *Zeitschrift für Theologie und Kirche*, 1891).

The works of Jerome are in Migne's *Patrologia Latina*, vols. 22–30. Eng. trans. of some of his writings in the *Nicene and Post-Nicene Fathers*, Series II, vol. VI.

G. Grützmacher: *Hieronymus, eine biographische Studie zur alten Kirchengeschichte*, 3 vols., 1901 ff.
   Important.

F. Cavallera: *Saint Jérôme: sa vie et son œuvre.* Pt. I in 2 vols., 1922.
   The most comprehensive biography, not yet completed.

CHAPTER IV

Augustine's writings are in Migne, vols. 32–47. Many of them have already appeared in the Vienna edition of the Latin Fathers. I have used this edition so far as available. Eng. trans. of a number of his most important writings in the *Nicene and Post-Nicene Fathers*, Series I, vols. I–VII. Several of his works have been published separately both in the original and in translation.

Books about Augustine are legion. Only a few representative ones can be mentioned here.

H. Reuter: *Augustinische Studien*, 1887.
   Still valuable.

L. Grandgeorge: *Saint Augustin et le Néoplatonisme*, 1896.

T. Hahn: *Tyconius Studien: Ein Beitrag zur Kirchen- und Dogmengeschichte des vierten Jahrhunderts*, 1900.
   Shows that in his lost commentary on the Apocalypse, Tyconius (a former Donatist) anticipated by some years Augustine's contrast between the civitas Dei and the civitas terrena.

J. Martin: *St. Augustin*, 1900; 2nd ed., 1923.

O. Scheel: *Die Anschauung Augustins über Christi Person und Werk*, 1901.

W. Thimme: *Augustins geistige Entwickelung in den ersten Jahren nach seiner Bekehrung*, 1908.
   Important.

J. Mausbach: *Die Ethik des heiligen Augustinus*, 1909.
   The most complete work on Augustine's ethics.

H. Scholz: *Glaube und Unglaube in der Weltgeschichte: ein Kommentar zu Augustins De civitate Dei*, 1911.
   An important work. Scholz remarks that Tyconius was the creator of the idea of the City of God and Augustine only its first prophet.

W. Montgomery: *St. Augustine, Aspects of His Life and Thought*, 1914.

E. Troeltsch: *Augustin, die christliche Antike und das Mittelalter*, 1915.
   Fresh and suggestive. Troeltsch maintains that Augustine was the end

of an old not the beginning of a new era. And he denies all connection between civitas Dei and church as well as between civitas terrena and state.

P. Alfaric: *L'évolution intellectuelle de Saint Augustin:* vol. I. *Du Manichéisme au Néoplatonisme,* 1918.
   Very important.

C. Boyer: *Christianisme et Néoplatonisme dans la formation de Saint Augustin,* 1920.
   An excellent summary. Contains a good outline of the early dialogues.

J. N. Figgis: *The Political Aspects of St. Augustine's City of God,* 1921.
   A brief but valuable series of lectures.

K. Holl: *Augustins innere Entwickelung* (in *Abhandlungen der preussischen Akademie der Wissenschaften,* 1922).
   An admirable sketch.

P. von Sokolowski: *Der heilige Augustin und die christliche Zivilisation,* 1927.
   Brief but suggestive. Represents Augustine as the real creator of Christian civilization.

E. Gilson: *Introduction à l'étude de Saint Augustin,* 1929.
   Excellent. Contains an annotated bibliography.

W. J. Sparrow Simpson: *Saint Augustine's Conversion: An Outline of His Development until the Time of His Ordination,* 1930.

W. P. Tolley: *The Idea of God in the Philosophy of St. Augustine,* 1930.
   A careful treatment. Contains a useful annotated bibliography.

A. Harnack's *Dogmengeschichte,* vol. III, contains an admirable account of Augustine, and there is a long and important article by E. Portalié in the *Dictionnaire de théologie catholique.*

CHAPTER V

Pelagius' letter to Demetrias and his (interpolated) commentary on the Pauline epistles are printed in Migne, vol. 30 (the eleventh volume of Jerome's works). We have also his *Libellus fidei ad Innocentium* in Hahn: *Bibliothek der Symbole und Glaubensregeln der alten Kirche* 3, p. 288 ff.; and the editio princeps of his original and unexpurgated commentary in A. Souter's *Pelagius's Expositions of Thirteen Epistles of St. Paul,* No. 1: Introduction, 1922; No. 2: Text, 1926 (in *Cambridge Texts and Studies,* IX. 1 and 2). An important publication. Vincent of Lerins' *Commonitorium* is in Migne, vol. 50. There is a handy edition of the Latin text, with introduction and notes, by R. S. Moxon (*The Commonitorium of Vincentius of Lerins*) in *Cambridge Patristic Texts,* 1915. Eng. trans. in the *Nicene and Post-Nicene Fathers,* vol. XI.

F. Wörter: *Der Pelagianismus,* 1866; 2nd ed., 1874.
   Old but still valuable.

F. Klasen: *Die Innere Entwickelung des Pelagianismus,* 1882.

BIBLIOGRAPHY

A. Bruckner: *Julian von Eclanum: sein Leben und seine Lehre*, 1897.

F. Wörter: *Beiträge zur Dogmengeschichte des Semipelagianismus*, 1898.

H. von Schubert: *Der sogenannte Praedestinatus*, 1903.

A. Bruckner: *Quellen zur Geschichte des pelagianischen Streites*, 1906.
A brief but convenient collection of sources.

H. Zimmer: *Pelagius in Irland: Texte und Untersuchungen zur patristischen Litteratur*, 1901.

E. Jauncey: *The Doctrine of Grace up to the End of the Pelagian Controversy*, 1925.
Contains a careful account of the controversy.

F. Loofs: *Pelagius und der pelagianische Streit;* in Herzog's *Realencyklopädie für protestantische Theologie und Kirche*, 3rd ed.

G. Krüger in Schanz: *Geschichte der römischen Literatur*, vol. IV, 2.

CHAPTER VI

Gregory's works are in Migne, vols. 75-79. There is a critical edition of his epistles, edited by P. Ewald and L. Hartmann, in the *Monumenta Germaniae, Epistolae*, vols. 1 and 2 (1891, 1899). Many of his letters and the *Pastoral Rule* (*Liber regulae pastoralis*) are translated in the *Nicene and Post-Nicene Fathers*, Series II, vols. XII and XIII; and the *Moralia* in *A Library of Fathers of the Holy Catholic Church*, 4 vols., 1844 ff. (a free translation, often hardly more than a paraphrase). An English translation of the *Dialogues* was published in the seventeenth century (reprint, edited by E. G. Gardner, 1911).

G. J. Lau: *Gregor I. der Grosse*, 1845.
Still valuable.

F. H. Dudden: *Gregory the Great: His Place in History and Thought*, 2 vols., 1905.
Important. The best work on Gregory's theology.

H. H. Howorth: *Gregory the Great*, 1912.

W. Stuhlfath: *Gregor I. der Grosse: sein Leben bis zu seiner Wahl zum Papste nebst einer Untersuchung der ältesten Viten*, 1913.
Chiefly a critical study of the sources.

P. Batiffol: *Saint Gregoire le Grand*, 1928.
Best brief biography of Gregory, but devoted to his work rather than his thought.

BOOK FOUR

B. Hauréau: *Histoire de la philosophie scolastique*, 1872.

Reuter: *Geschichte der religiösen Aufklärung im Mittelalter*, 1875.
Both of these books are still valuable but are to be used with caution.

BIBLIOGRAPHY

J. Schwane: *Dogmengeschichte der mittleren Zeit* (787–1517), 1882.
By a Roman Catholic.

R. L. Poole: *Illustrations of the History of Mediæval Thought and Learning*,
1884; 2nd ed., 1920.
Contains much interesting material.

H. Rashdall: *The Universities of Europe in the Middle Ages*, 2 vols., 1895.
An important work.

M. De Wulf: *Histoire de la philosophie médiévale*, 1905; Eng. trans., 1909.

F. Picavet: *Esquisse d'une histoire générale et comparée des philosophies médié-
vales*, 1907.

T. Heitz: *Essai historique sur les rapports entre la philosophie et la foi de Béren-
ger de Tours à S. Thomas d'Aquin*, 1909.

M. Grabmann: *Die Geschichte der scholastischen Methode*, 2 vols., 1909, 1911.
An important work. Vol. II contains an account of several theological
Summæ of the thirteenth century which have not yet been printed.

H. O. Taylor: *The Mediæval Mind: A History of the Development of Thought
and Emotion in the Middle Ages*, 2 vols., 1911; 4th ed., 1925.
A comprehensive work broadly conceived and admirably carried out.

C. Baeumker: *Der Platonismus des Mittelalters*, 1916.
Excellent.

E. Gilson: *La philosophie au moyen âge de Scot Érigène à Guillaume d'Occam*,
1925.
Brief but good.

C. H. Haskins: *The Renaissance of the Twelfth Century*, 1927.
Excellent.

W. Betzendörfer: *Glaube und Wissen bei den grossen Denkern des Mittelalters*, 1931.
Excellent.

CHAPTER VII

Eriugena's works are in Migne, vol. 122.

J. Huber: *Johannes Scotus Erigena: Ein Beitrag zur Geschichte der Philosophie
und Theologie im Mittelalter*, 1861.
Still valuable.

Alice Gardner: *Studies in John the Scot*, 1900.
A good, brief treatment.

J. Draeseke: *Johannes Scotus Erigena und dessen Gewährsmänner in seinem
Werk De Divisione Naturae Libri V*, 1902.

E. K. Rand: *Johannes Scottus:* I. *Der Kommentar des Joh. Scottus zu den
Opuscula Sacra des Boethius;* II. *Der Kommentar des Remigius von Aux-
erre zu den Opuscula Sacra des Boethius*, 1906.
The first part contains a brief commentary which Rand ascribes to
Eriugena. The commentary, as is not surprising, is more conventional
and orthodox than the *De divisione naturae*.

BIBLIOGRAPHY

A. Schneider: *Die Erkenntnisslehre des Johannes Eriugena im Rahmen ihrer metaphysischen und anthropologischen Voraussetzungen nach den Quellen dargestellt*, 2 Theile, 1921, 1923.
Important.

H. Bett: *Johannes Scotus Erigena*, 1925.

H. Dörries: *Zur Geschichte der Mystik: Erigena und der Neuplatonismus*, 1925.

S. M. Deutsch: article "Scotus, Johannes Eri(u)gena" in Herzog's *Realencyklopädie für protestantische Theologie und Kirche*, 3rd ed.
Excellent.

CHAPTER VIII

Anselm's works, including more than four hundred letters, are in Migne, vols. 158 and 159. Eng. trans. of his *Devotions* by C. C. J. Webb, 1903; of his *Monologium, Proslogium* and *Apology in Reply to Gaunilon* by S. N. Deane, 1903; of his *Cur deus homo* by J. G. Vose in the same volume; and of his *De veritate* in McKeon's *Selections from Medieval Philosophers*, vol. I.

F. R. Hasse. *Anselm von Canterbury*, 2 vols., 1843, 1852. Abridged translation, 1850.
An admirable biography, still valuable.

M. Rule: *The Life and Times of St. Anselm*, 2 vols., 1883.
Voluminous and unduly eulogistic.

J. M. Rigg: *St. Anselm of Canterbury: A Chapter in the History of Religion*, 1896.
Good.

D. de Vorges: *Saint Anselme*, 1901 (in the series *Les grands philosophes*).
Excellent.

J. Fischer: *Die Erkenntnisslehre Anselms von Canterbury*, 1911.
Excellent.

C. Filliatre: *La philosophie de Saint Anselme*, 1920.
Contains a good account of the philosophy of Anselm's day.

C. Bayer: *La vérité dans S. Anselme*, 1921.

CHAPTER IX

Abelard's works are in Migne, vol. 178. Since the appearance of Migne other writings have been discovered of which the most important have been published in *Peter Abaelards philosophische Schriften: I. Die Logica 'Ingredientibus'* (1. *Die Glossen zu Porphyrius*, 1919; 2. *Die Glossen zu den Kategorien*, 1921; 3. *Die Glossen zu Περὶ Ἑρμηνείας*, 1927) *zum ersten male herausgegeben von B. Geyer* (in *Beiträge zur Geschichte der Philosophie des Mittelalters*, vol. XXI). The *Glosses on Porphyry* are translated in McKeon's *Selections from Medieval Philosophers*, vol. I. The letters of Abelard and Heloise have been translated more than once, for instance by Scott Moncrief, 1926.

BIBLIOGRAPHY

E. Vacandard: *Abélard, sa lutte avec St. Bernard, sa doctrine, sa méthode,* 1881.

S. M. Deutsch: *Die Synode zu Sens, 1141, und die Verurtheilung Abälards,* 1881.

S. M. Deutsch: *Peter Abälard, ein kritischer Theologe des 12ten Jahrhunderts,* 1883; 2nd ed., 1895.
> An admirable biography, with a good account of Abelard's thought.

Denifle: *Die Sentenzen Abälards und die Bearbeitungen seiner Theologie* (in *Archiv für Literatur- und Kirchengeschichte des Mittelalters,* 1885).

A. Hausrath: *Peter Abälard,* 1893.

J. McCabe: *Peter Abelard,* 1901.

E. Kaiser: *Pierre Abélard critique,* 1901.

J. G. Sikes: *Peter Abailard,* 1932.
> An excellent account of Abelard's thought which came into my hands after this volume was in press.

CHAPTER X

Bernard's works are in Migne, vols. 182 and 183. His letters and many of his sermons, including those on the Song of Songs, have been translated into English by S. J. Eales in *The Life and Works of St. Bernard,* 4 vols. (a free translation, in parts a paraphrase); also a few of his treatises as, e.g., *De consideratione* (by George Lewis, 1908), *De diligendo Deo* (by M. C. and C. Patmore, 1881), and *De gratia et libero arbitrio* (by W. W. Williams, 1920).

J. C. Morison: *The Life and Times of St. Bernard,* 1863; 3rd ed., 1884.
> Fair and sound.

A. Neander: *Der heilige Bernhard;* revised edition with Introduction and Notes, by S. M. Deutsch, 1889.

E. Vacandard: *Vie de St. Bernard,* 2 vols., 1895; 2nd ed., 1897.
> Excellent.

J. Ries: *Das geistliche Leben in seinen Entwicklungsstufen nach der Lehre des hl. Bernhard,* 1906.

R. Linhart: *Die Mystik des hl. Bernhard von Clairvaux,* 1923.

W. Williams: *The Mysticism of St. Bernard of Clairvaux,* 1931.

The writings of St. Francis edited by H. Boehmer: *Opuscula S. Francisci Assissiensis,* 1904. Eng. trans. by P. Robinson: *The Writings of St. Francis of Assisi,* 1906 (an annotated translation).

P. Sabatier: *Vie de S. François d'Assise,* 1894 and many later editions. Eng. trans., 1894.
> The best biography.

W. Goetz: *Die Quellen zur Geschichte des hl. Franz von Assisi: Eine kritische Untersuchung,* 1904.
> Important.

BIBLIOGRAPHY

Father Cuthbert: *Life of St. Francis of Assisi*, 1912.

J. Jörgensen: *Saint Francis of Assisi: A Biography.* Eng. trans. from the Danish, 1912.
 Interesting but over-romantic.

H. Felder: *Die Ideale des hl. Franziskus*, 1923; Eng. trans., 1925.

L. Salvatorelli: *Vita di Francesco d'Assisi*, 1926. Eng. trans., 1928.

CHAPTER XI

Hugo's works are in Migne, vols. 175–177; Peter Lombard's in Migne, vols. 191 and 192.

A. Liebner: *Hugo von St. Viktor und die theologischen Richtungen seiner Zeit*, 1832.
 Still valuable.

F. Protois: *Pierre Lombard, son époque, sa vie, ses écrits et son influence*, 1881.

A. Mignon: *Les origines de la scolastique et Hugues de Saint Victor*, 2 vols., 1895.

J. Kilgenstein: *Die Gotteslehre des Hugo von St. Viktor, nebst einer Untersuchung über Hugos Leben und hervorragendsten Werke*, 1897.

O. Baltzer: *Die Sentenzen des Petrus Lombardus, ihre Quellen und ihre dogmengeschichtliche Bedeutung*, 1902.
 Important.

J. Sauer: *Symbolik des Kirchengebäudes und seine Ausstattung in der Auffassung des Mittelalters*, 1902.
 Very interesting.

H. Ostler: *Die Psychologie des Hugo von St. Viktor: ein Beitrag zur Geschichte der Psychologie in der Frühscholastik*, 1906.

CHAPTER XII

Thomas' complete works have been printed many times. A new and sumptuous edition, sponsored by Pope Leo XIII and commonly known as the Leonine edition, has been in course of publication since 1882. Fifteen volumes, containing with some other writings the *Summa theologiæ* and the *Summa contra gentiles*, have already appeared. I have used this edition so far as available, otherwise the Venice edition of 1777. There is an English translation of the *Summa theologiæ* (1911 ff.) and of the *Summa contra gentiles* (1924 ff.) by Fathers of the English Dominican Province. P. Mandonnet and J. Destrez: *Bibliographie thomiste* (1921) contains an exhaustive bibliography of the very extensive Thomistic literature down to 1920, which is continued in the *Bulletin thomiste* carried on by J. Destrez, 1924 ff.

P. Rousselot: *L'intellectualisme de St. Thomas*, 1908; 2nd ed., 1924.

BIBLIOGRAPHY

M. Grabmann: *Thomas von Aquin: Eine Einführung in seine Persönlichkeit und Gedankenwelt,* 1912; 5th ed., 1926. Eng. trans., 1928.
Brief but important; an excellent account of Thomas' philosophy.

A. Sertillanges: *St. Thomas d'Aquin* (in the series *Les grands philosophes*), 2 vols., 1912.

P. Wicksteed: *Dante and Aquinas,* 1913.
Interesting and suggestive.

A. Sertillanges: *La philosophie morale de St. Thomas d'Aquin,* 1916.

E. Gilson: *Le Thomisme: Introduction au système de S. Thomas d'Aquin,* 1919: 3rd ed., 1927. Eng. trans. (*The Philosophy of St. Thomas Aquinas*), 1925; 2nd ed., 1929.
Excellent.

M. Grabmann: *Einführung in die Summa theologiæ des hl. Thomas von Aquin,* 1919; 2nd ed., 1928. Eng. trans., 1930.
An excellent introduction to the *Summa.*

M. Grabmann: *Die Werke des heiligen Thomas von Aquin. Eine literarhistorische Untersuchung und Einführung,* 1920; 2nd ed., 1931.
Important for the authenticity of Thomas' works.

M. Grabmann: *Die Kulturphilosophie des heiligen Thomas von Aquin,* 1925.
Excellent.

J. Mausbach: *Thomas von Aquin als Meister christlicher Sittenlehre,* 1925.

St. Thomas Aquinas: Papers read at the celebration of the Sixth Centenary of his Canonization at Manchester, 1925.

M. C. D'Arcy: *Thomas Aquinas,* 1930.
An interesting and convenient summary of his philosophy.

CHAPTER XIII

Duns Scotus' works, both genuine and spurious, have been published by Vivés, 26 vols., Paris, 1891 ff. This edition is in the main simply a reprint of the uncritical edition of Wadding, Lyons, 1639, in 13 volumes. There is no collected edition of Ockham's works and one is much needed. Several of his most important writings exist only in copies printed in the late fifteenth century which are not always easily accessible. Certain of his anti-papal writings were published in 1614 by M. Goldast: *Monarchia* II; and R. Scholz's *Unbekannte kirchenpolitische Streitschriften aus der Zeit Ludwig des Bayern,* Theil II, 1914, contains some others hitherto unprinted. See A. G. Little: *The Grey Friars in Oxford* (1892), pp. 225 ff., and Ueberweg's *Geschichte der Philosophie,* Theil II; 11th ed., p. 572.

K. Werner: *Die Scholastik des späteren Mittelalters:* vol. I, *Johannes Duns Scotus,* 1881; vol. II, *Die nachscotistische Scholastik,* 1883; vol. III, *Der Augustinismus in der Scholastik des späteren Mittelalters,* 1883; vol. IV, pt. 1, *Der Endausgang der mittelalterlichen Scholastik,* 1887; pt. 2, *Der Übergang der Scholastik in ihr nachtridentinisches Entwickelungsstadium,* 1887.

BIBLIOGRAPHY

R. Seeberg: *Die Theologie des Johannes Duns Scotus*, 1900.
> The best book on Duns' theology; but it represents in certain matters the old point of view and is based in part on doubtful sources.

G. Hoffmann: *Die Lehre von der fides implicita innerhalb der katholischen Kirche;* 3 vols., 1903 ff.
> Excellent.

P. Minges: *Der Gottesbegriff des Duns Scotus*, 1907.

P. Minges: *Das Verhältnis zwischen Glauben und Wissen, Theologie und Philosophie nach Duns Scotus*, 1908.
> To these and other writings by Minges is due in no small part the revolution in the interpretation of Duns.

S. Belmond: *Études sur la philosophie de Duns Scot: I. Dieu: existence et cognoscibilité*, 1913.

J. Klein: *Der Gottesbegriff des Johannes Duns Scotus*, 1913.

B. Landry: *Duns Scot*, 1922.
> Interesting but uncritical and based in part on doubtful sources.

E. Longpré: *La philosophie du B. Duns Scot* (in *Études Franciscaines*, vols. 34–36; 1922–1924).
> Contains a severe criticism of Landry's book and a careful discussion of the authenticity of Duns' alleged writings. Follows the revised interpretation of Minges and others.

C. R. S. Harris: *Duns Scotus*, 1927: vol. I. *The Place of Duns Scotus in Medieval Thought;* vol. II. *The Philosophical Doctrines of Duns Scotus*.
> A careful piece of work and in the main sound though based in part on doubtful sources. The best book in English on Duns.

J. Kranz: *Die Lehre des Johannes Duns Scotus von der natura communis*, 1927.
> An excellent discussion of realism.

J. Hofer: *Biographische Studien über Wilhelm von Ockham*, 1913.

L. Kugler: *Der Begriff der Erkenntniss bei Wilhelm von Ockham: Ein Beitrag zur Geschichte mittelalterlicher Noetik*, 1913.

E. Hochstetter: *Studien zur Metaphysik und Erkenntnislehre Wilhelms von Ockham*, 1927.
> Important.

R. Seeberg: article "Ockam" in Herzog's *Realencyklopädie für protestantische Theologie und Kirche*, 3rd ed.
> For further literature on Ockham (mostly in periodicals) see Ueberweg, *Geschichte der Philosophie*, Theil II; 11th ed., p. 781.

CHAPTER XIV

G. L. Hahn: *Die Lehre von den Sakramenten*, 1864.
> Still valuable.

K. Müller: *Der Umschwung in der Lehre der Busse während des 12ten Jahrhunderts*, 1892.

BIBLIOGRAPHY

H. C. Lea: *A History of Auricular Confession and Indulgences in the Latin Church*, 3 vols., 1896.

F. Renz: *Die Geschichte des Messopferbegriffs:* vol. I. *Alterthum und Mittelalter*, 1901.

P. Pourrat: *La théologie sacramentaire: Étude de théologie positive*, 1906; 2nd ed., 1907.

D. Stone: *A History of the Doctrine of the Holy Eucharist*, 2 vols., 1900.
Written from the high Anglican point of view.

J. Hilgers: *Die katholische Lehre von den Ablässen und deren geschichtliche Entwicklung*, 1914.

O. D. Watkins: *A History of Penance*, 2 vols., 1920.

N. Paulus: *Geschichte des Ablasses im Mittelalter vom Ursprunge bis zur Mitte des 14ten Jahrhunderts*, 3 vols., 1922 f.
Contains elaborate bibliographies.

A. J. MacDonald: *Berengar and the Reform of Sacramental Doctrine*, 1930.
A careful and thorough piece of work.

CHAPTER XV

F. X. Leitner: *Thomas von Aquin über die unfehlbare Lehramt des Papstes*, 1872.

J. Langen: *Geschichte der römischen Kirche*, 4 vols., 1881 ff.
Carries the history down to the close of the pontificate of Innocent III.

C. Mirbt: *Quellen zur Geschichte des Papstthums und der römischen Kirche*, 1895; 4th ed., much enlarged, 1924.
A very useful collection of extracts from the sources. In connection with Mirbt may be mentioned the following source books in English translation:

E. F. Henderson: *Select Historical Documents of the Middle Ages*, 1896.

J. H. Robinson: *Readings in European History*, vol. I, 1904.

Thatcher and McNeal: *A Source Book for Mediæval History*, 1907.

T. F. Tout: *The Empire and the Papacy* (918–1273), 1899; 9th printing, 1921.

K. Hirsch: *Die Ausbildung der Konziliarentheorie im XIV. Jahrhundert*, 1903.

R. Scholz: *Die Publizistik zur Zeit Philipps des Schönen und Bonifatius VIII. Ein Beitrag zur Geschichte der politischen Anschauungen des Mittelalters*, 1903.

J. Haller: *Papstthum und Kirchenreform: Vier Kapitel zur Geschichte des ausgehenden Mittelalters;* Erster Band, 1903.
An important work.

G. Krüger: *Das Papstthum: seine Idee und ihre Träger*, 1907; 2nd ed., 1932.
Eng. trans., 1909.
An admirable summary.

BIBLIOGRAPHY

E. Emerton: *The Defensor Pacis of Marsiglio of Padua*, 1920.
An admirable introduction to Marsiglio's work.

The Cambridge Mediæval History: vol. V. *Contest of Empire and Papacy*, 1926.

C. W. Previté-Orton: *The Defensor Pacis of Marsilius of Padua*, 1928.
A critical edition of the text.

E. Caspar: *Geschichte des Papstthums von den Anfängen bis zur Höhe der Welt-herrschaft.* Erster Band: *Römische Kirche und Imperium Romanum*, 1930.
An important work of which only the first volume has appeared, carry-ing the history through the reign of Leo I.

CHAPTER XVI

Many of Eckhart's sermons and other writings in German are still extant and until a few years ago, when some of his Latin works were dis-covered, constituted practically our only source for a knowledge of his teaching. The principal edition of his German writings is Pfeiffer's *Meister Eckhart*, 1857 (frequently reprinted). Eng. trans., with some omissions and additions, by C. de B. Evans, 1924. See also Büttner: *Meister Eckeharts Schriften und Predigten aus dem Mittelhochdeutschen übersetzt*, 2 vols., 1903; and F. Schulze-Maizier: *Meister Eckharts deutsche Predigten und Traktate*, 1927 (in modern German). For a list of other editions of Eckhart's writings see Karrer: *Meister Eckehart*, 1926, p. 10. Karrer's book contains a useful collection of quotations from Eckhart, arranged topically. On Eckhart's Latin works and the views contained in them see Denifle: *Meister Eckeharts lateinische Schriften und die Grund-anschauung seiner Lehre*, 1886 (in *Archiv für Litteratur- und Kirchen-geschichte des Mittelalters*, vol. II).

A. Lasson: *Meister Eckhart der Mystiker*, 1868.
Still valuable.

W. Preger: *Geschichte der deutschen Mystik im Mittelalter*, 3 vols., 1874–1893.

W. R. Inge: *Christian Mysticism*, 1899.

H. Delacroix: *Essai sur le mysticisme spéculatif en Allemagne au XIVe siècle*, 1900.

R. M. Jones: *Studies in Mystical Religion*, 1909.

J. Bernhart: *Meister Eckhart* (in *Deutsche Mystiker*, vol. III), 1914.

E. L. Schellenberg: *Die deutsche Mystik*, 1920; 2nd ed., 1927.

J. Bernhart: *Die philosophische Mystik des Mittelalters von ihren Ursprüngen bis zur Renaissance*, 1922.

X. de Hornstein: *Les grands mystiques allemands du XIVe siècle*, 1922.

O. Karrer and H. Piesch: *Meister Eckeharts Rechtfertigungsschrift vom Jahre 1926: Einleitungen, Uebersetzung und Anmerkungen*, 1927.

BIBLIOGRAPHY

R. Otto: *Mysticism East and West: A Comparative Analysis of the Nature of Mysticism*, 1932.
> An illuminating comparison of Eckhart's mysticism with that of the Indian Sankara.

CHAPTER XVII

Collected edition of Erasmus' works, edited by J. Clericus in ten vols., 1703 ff. A critical edition of his letters by P. S. Allen, 1906 ff., is in course of publication. Six volumes have already appeared. Eng. trans. of the earlier letters by F. M. Nichols; 3 vols. 1901 ff. Many of his works have been published separately, and several of them have been translated into English, some of them repeatedly.

R. B. Drummond: *Erasmus, His Life and Character*, 2 vols., 1873.
> An old standard life; still valuable.

J. A. Froude: *The Life and Letters of Erasmus*, 1894.
> The most vivid portrait of Erasmus but marred by serious inaccuracies.

E. Emerton: *Desiderius Erasmus of Rotterdam*, 1899.
> Excellent.

The Cambridge Modern History: vol. I. *The Renaissance*, 1902.

J. A. Faulkner: *Erasmus the Scholar*, 1907.
> Brief and popular.

A. Humbert: *Les origines de la théologie moderne.* I. *La renaissance de l'antiquité chrétienne* (1450–1521), 1911.

A. Renaudet: *Préréforme et humanisme à Paris pendant les premières guerres d'Italie* (1494–1517), 1916.
> Important.

P. Mestwerdt: *Die Anfänge des Erasmus: Humanismus und "Devotio moderna,"* 1917.
> An admirable account of Erasmus' intellectual and religious background.

P. Smith: *Erasmus: A Study of His Life, Ideals and Place in History*, 1923.
> Sound and good, with an elaborate bibliography.

J. Huizinga: *Erasmus*, 1924.
> An admirable brief biography.

A. Hyma: *The Christian Renaissance: A History of the "Devotio moderna,"* 1924.

J. J. Mangan: *Life, Character and Influence of Desiderius Erasmus of Rotterdam*, 2 vols., 1927.

E. Cassirer: *Individuum und Kosmos in der Philosophie der Renaissance*, 1927.

R. Stadelmann: *Vom Geist des ausgehenden Mittelalters*, 1929.

INDEX

413

INDEX

INDEX

INDEX

Latin: authors, 379; literature, 73; in Middle Ages, 384.

Law: Christian and Jewish, 281; divine, 15; human, 281, 286; kinds of, 281 f.; natural, 272, 281, 286; revealed, 281.

Legalism, 127, 161.

Leo, Bishop of Rome, 333–336.

Leo X, Pope, 379.

Logic, 202. *See also* Dialectics, Reason.

Logos, 52, 178–179, 366 n.

Louis of Bavaria, 306.

Love: Abelard, 215; Anselm, 192; Augustine, 101; Bernard of Clairvaux, 231–233; Eckhart, 361, 371, 374; Erasmus, 387–388; Francis of Assisi, 235 f.; for God, 272, 281–282, 285, 286, 302, 368; Gregory, 150; for neighbors, 272, 285, 387–388; for oneself, 285–286; Thomas Aquinas, 272, 281–282, 285–286.

Luther, Martin, 283, 374, 376, 384, 391–392.

Lyons, Council of, 140, 343.

Majorinus, Bishop, 108.

Man, 255; Anselm, 142; Arnobius, 40; Augustine, 89–90; chief end of, 46, 86, 124, 192, 280; Dante, 346; divine origin of, 361; Duns Scotus, 300; Eckhart, 361; Erasmus, 389; Gregory the Great, 151, 154; Hugo of St. Victor, 247; John Scotus Eriugena, 179; Lactantius, 46; Pelagius, 126–128; Thomas Aquinas, 267–268, 271.

Manichæism, 114, 353; asceticism, 74; the Bible, 74; Catholicism, 74; dualism, 74; evil, 92; Jesus Christ, 74; rationalism, 74, 75; spread, 74.

Mariolatry, 62–63.

Marriage, 272.

Marsiglio Ficino, 347–348, 381.

Martyrs, 28, 163.

Mass, Sacrifice of, 320. *See also* Eucharist.

Massilianism, 136 f., 139. *See also* Semi-Pelagianism.

Materiality, 10–11.

Matrimony, Sacrament of, 327–329.

Maximus the Confessor, 171.

Melito, Apologist, 255.

Merits, 65, 67, 151, 326.

Metaphysics: Duns Scotus, 303; Ockham, 308.

Middle Ages: education, 166, 379, 381; freedom, 167; Latin, 166; piety of, 157; science, 123–124; symbolism, 254; theology, 161, 166 f.; unity of, 166.

Millennium, 118–119.

Minucius Felix, 52.

Miracles, 120, 271–272.

Monasticism, 144, 338, 351; Ambrose, 59; Erasmus, 384–385; Jovinian, 64; Lactantius, 49; spread, 62.

Montanism, 22.

Morality: Duns Scotus, 300–301; Erasmus, 384; Lactantius, 46, 50–51; Ockham, 310, 311; pagan, 101; Thomas Aquinas, 282. *See also* Ethics, Virtue.

Motion, 262.

Mystery, 43, 161.

Mysticism: Augustine, 99, 143; **Bernard of** Clairvaux, 227–228; books, 376; **and** Catholicism, 376–377; ethics, 369 f.; Hugo of St. Victor, 245 f.; in **Middle** Ages, 143, 359 f., 375 f.; motivation of, 368–369; Neoplatonism, 99; **Thomas** Aquinas, 268–269.

Nationalism, 349.

Naturalism, 127.

Nature: Augustine, 121; John Scotus Eriugena, 176; mediæval symbolism, 254–255; Ockham, 309; of things, 309; Thomas Aquinas, 272, 283; Vincent of Beauvais, 254.

Necessity and contingency, 297.

Neoplatonism, 76–77, 80–81, 84–87, 89, 93, 99, 124, 149, 171 f.; 182, 190, 245, 260–261, 295, 365, 368.

Nestorius, 133.

New Testament, 391.

Nicene doctrine, 54.

Nicholas I, Pope, 338.

Nicholas V, Pope, 379.

Nicholas of Cusa, Cardinal, 382.

Nominalism, 178, 308 f.

Novatian, 30.

Numidia, 4.

Obedience, 20, 99, 238.

Ockham, William of, 394; Aristotelian, 307; authority, 311; Christianity, 310; church and state, 347 f.; Duns Scotus, 306 f.; heresy, 305–306, 311; life, 305–306, 311; nominalism, 306 f.; work, 308, 310, 312.

Ockhamism, 310 f.

Odo of St. Victor, 248.

Old Roman Symbol, 37.

Old Testament, 55, 77, 353. *See also* Bible.

Ontological argument, The, 192 f., 262.

Opinion, 246.

Optatus, Bishop of Milevis, 109, 110.

Orange, Second Council of, 140 f., 151.

Order of Lesser Brothers, 238.

Orders, 327. *See also* Bishops.

Origen, 46, 55, 154, 181, 267.

Orphism, 153.

Otherworldliness, 22–23, 61, 102, 122.

Othloh, 222.

Oxford, University of, 296.

Pantheism, 88, 278, 356, 362–363.

Papacy: attacks on, 345 f.; Babylonish captivity of, 348; and church, 342–343; Gregory VII, 338–339; growth of, 333 f.; Innocent III, 339–340; Ockham, 349–350; Peter and, 333–334, 340; reform of, 350–351; rise of temporal power, 336; Thomas Aquinas, 342–343.

Paris, University of, 257, 296.

Paschasius Radbertus, 321.

Paul, The Apostle, 66–67, 97, 124, 161, 271, 317, 374, 392.

Paul IV, Pope, 395.

Pelagians, 83, 103, 133 f.

Pelagius: Augustine, 125 f., 131–132; freewill, 125, 127; God, 127; grace, 129, 135;

INDEX

heresy trials, 132–133; Jesus Christ, 127; legalism, 127; life, 125 f., 131–132; man, 126 f.; naturalism, 127; original sin, 126; perfectionism, 128; reasons for condemnation, 134–135; Stoicism, 126; writings, 126.

Pelagius II, Pope, 45.

Penance, 36, 325; Anselm, 198; Cyprian, 37; Gregory the Great, 152, 156; Pelagius, 128; Tertullian, 21.

Perfectionism, 128, 134.

Perseverance, 96, 137.

Personality, 361.

Peter Damiani, 222.

Peter Lombard, 248, 252, 288, 342; authorities, 250–251; dialectics, 250; the Fathers, 250–251; life, 249; sacraments, 314; *Sententiarum libri quattuor*, 248 f.; significance, 251–252; things and signs, 249–250; traditionalist, 251; work, 251, 252.

Petrarch, 380.

Philo, 55.

Philosophy: Duns Scotus, 298; Eckhart, 369; John Scotus Eriugena, 170–171; Lactantius, 48; Ockham, 308 f.; Thomas Aquinas, 273.

Pico della Mirandola, 381.

Piety: Ambrose, 60; Bernard of Clairvaux, 227 f.; Catholic, 377; Erasmus, 387, 388 f., 393; Francis of Assisi, 237; in Middle Ages, 157; monastic, 376; Thomas Aquinas, 302.

Pilgrimage, 326.

Pippin, 337.

Pius II, Pope, 351.

Plato, 10, 12, 179, 260, 267.

Platonism, 77, 79, 122, 187–188, 364.

Plotinus, 76, 365, 368.

Pope, The, 338 f. *See also* Papacy.

Poverty, 376; Francis of Assisi, 237; and the papacy, 305; Thomas Aquinas, 272.

Prayer, 271, 326, 389.

Praxeas, 12.

Predestination, 140, 183, 300; Augustine, 95–97, 113, 137; Gregory the Great, 151; Thomas Aquinas, 278; unconditional, 96–97, 136, 141.

Premillenarianism, 22.

Presbyters, 29.

Pride, 389.

Progress, 138–139.

Property, 286.

Prophecy, 269–270, 272.

Prosper of Aquitaine, 136–137.

Providence, 46 f., 271.

Psalms, 124.

Pseudo-Dionysius, *see* Dionysius the Areopagite.

Pseudo-Isidorian Decretals, 337.

Psychology, 8 f., 72.

Punishment, 99, 152, 325, 326. *See also* Rewards and Punishments.

Purgatory, 102, 153, 156, 325–326.

Radbertus, *see* Paschasius Radbertus.

Radicalism, Social, 356.

Rationalism, 247.

Ratramnus, 321.

Realism, 177 f.; Anselm, 187–188; moderate, 306; and nominalism, 178, 202–203.

Reality, 87.

Reason: Abelard, 205–206; 210; Anselm, 186 f.; Arnobius, 40–41; Augustine, 81; Bernard of Clairvaux, 227; Hugo of St. Victor, 243 f.; John Scotus Eriugena, 169; Thomas Aquinas, 261, 272–273, 293. *See also* Faith.

Reconciliation, 291.

Redemption, 242 f., 245.

Reformation: Catholic, 394–395; Protestant, 96, 165, 317, 349, 351, 373–374, 377–378, 394–395.

Regeneration, 65–66, 100, 129, 318.

Religion: Francis of Assisi, 239; Hugo of St. Victor, 242 f.; John Scotus Eriugena, 171; Lactantius, 52; Thomas Aquinas, 272, 287.

Renaissance, 379.

Repentance, 19–20, 152, 216.

Reprobation, 278, 279 n.

Responsibility, 96. *See also* Will.

Resurrection, 118–119, 273, 291.

Revelation, 254, 256; Abelard, 206; Anselm, 186–187; Hugo of St. Victor, 244–245; of John, 118–119; Lactantius, 52; Ockham, 308–310; special, 96; Tertullian, 17; Thomas Aquinas, 269, 272–274, 277.

Rewards and Punishments, 46–47; Augustine, 103; Erasmus, 390; Gregory the Great, 9 f., 151; Jovinian, 65; Lactantius, 53; Pelagius, 129–130; Tertullian, 19, 21; Thomas Aquinas, 272.

Roland of Bologna, 249.

Rome, 108; Church of, 27, 111, 333. *See also* Papacy.

Roscellin, 187–188, 201 f., 206, 210, 212, 221, 307.

Ruysbroeck, John, 375.

Sabellianism, 212.

Sacraments: Abelard, 214–215; Augustine, 110, 112–113, 314–315, 317; Bonaventura, 315; of the church, 376–377; conditions of receiving, 317–318; Cyprian, 35; definition, 313–315, 329–330; Donatism, 108–109; Eckhart, 373; efficacy of, 316–317; and faith, 317; grace, 314 f., 317, 330–331; history, 313–314; Hugo of St. Victor, 315; mediaeval significance, 330–331; ministry of, 316; nature of, 314 f.; number, 313–314; Pelagius, 135; Peter Lombard, 314–315; Thomas Aquinas, 282, 314 f., 329–330; Waldenses, 255. *See also* Eucharist.

Saints, 63, 158, 184, 326.

Salvation: Abelard, 214 f.; Arnobius, 42–43; Augustine, 100 f.; Boniface VIII, 340 f.; Cyprian, 31–32; Eckhart, 360; means of, 100 f., 214 f.; Tertullian, 19; Thomas Aquinas, 283, 343.

Satan, 18, 66–67, 154, 197, 255, 289.

Satisfaction, 20, 290–291, 326.

Scepticism, 40–41, 43, 44, 76.

Schismatics, 30–32, 109–110.

Scholasticism, 248, 312.

418

INDEX

Science: mediæval, 121–123, 256; modern, 308.

Scotists, 294, 304–305.

Scriptures, 114, 169 f., 311. *See also* Bible.

Sects, 351 f., 356, 376.

Secularism, 380.

Self-denial, 372.

Self-interest, 49.

Semi-Augustinianism, 140 f.

Semi-Pelagianism, 136–138, 141, 151, 279.

Seneca, 48.

Sens, Council of, 204.

Serenity, 371.

Service, 370–371, 385.

Siger of Brabant, 257–258.

Sin: Ambrose, 55–56; Augustine, 90–91, 105; forgiveness of, 37; John Scotus Eriugena, 182–183; original sin, 18–19, 56, 125–126, 136; Pelagius, 125–126; post-baptismal, 36; remission of, 105; seven deadly, 21; Tertullian, 18–19, 21; Thomas Aquinas, 284.

Soissons, Council of, 204, 209.

Son of God, 52, 128. *See also* Jesus Christ.

Song of Songs, 225.

Soteriology, 243 f.

Soul: Arnobius, 41; Augustine, 81, 86; Pelagius, 126; Plato, 10; Tertullian, 18–19, 88.

Space and time, 179, 190, 191.

Spinoza, 175.

Spirit: Ambrose, 55; Augustine, 93; Bernard of Clairvaux, 226; Eckhart, 362; indwelling, 93; and matter, 10; Tertullian, 10; Thomas Aquinas, 282.

Stephen, Bishop of Rome, 32–33, 37.

Stoicism, 8 f., 18, 89, 126.

Subjective and objective, 86.

Substance, 188, 191–192, 228, 323.

Summum bonum: Abelard, 219; Duns Scotus, 302–303; Eckhart, 368; Thomas Aquinas, 264, 268.

Supernatural, 120, 310, 369.

Suso, Henry, 325.

Symbolism: church, 253–254; man, 255; nature, 254–255; Peter Lombard, 249, 250; religious significance, 256; Scriptures, 252 f.; Thomas Aquinas, 254.

Synods, 33–34, 132–134.

Tauler, John, 375.

Teleological argument, The, 263.

Tertullian, 25, 26, 51, 52, 56, 90, 91, 94, 99, 124, 125, 151, 153, 200, 301; *Apology*, 8; authority, 9, 16–17; baptism, 19–20, 36; Clement, 16; confession, 20; *De anima*, 8; demons, 8; dualism, 10; eschatology, 22; forgiveness, 20; God, 12–14; heresy, 16–17; Irenæus, 19; legalism, 7, 11, 15; Montanism, 6, 17; obedience, 20; originality, 7; otherworldliness, 22–23; penance, 21; revelation, 17; satisfaction, 20; sin, 18–19, 20; soul, 8 f., 18–19; summary, 24; Trinity, the, 12; work, 6, 7.

Theft, 286–287.

Theodosius, Emperor, 55, 334.

Theologia Germanica, 370.

Theology: Augustine, 83; Catholic, 251; Duns Scotus, 303; mediæval, 166 f., 394; natural and revealed, 244–245, 247, 260 f., 272 f., 291 f., 298–299, 309; negative, 172, 190; western, 261–262.

Thomas a Kempis, 382.

Thomas Aquinas, 124, 304–305, 380; *Against the errors of the Greeks*, 343–345; angels, 279–280; Aristotle, 259 f.; authority, 269, 275, 293; baptism, 318; canonized, 294; Catholic theology, 292 f.; Duns Scotus, 298 f.; Eckhart, 359; ethics, 280 f.; faith, 277, 284–285; God, 262 f., 271–272; grace, 282; incarnation, 288 f.; intellectualism, 301–302; law of nature, 272; life, 259; modernist, 259–260, 294; mysticism, 268–269; opposition to, 295 f.; papacy, 343–344; purpose, 259 f.; revelation, 272 f.; sacraments, 329–330; *Summa contra gentiles*, 261 f.; *Summa theologiæ*, 270, 274 f., 292; summum bonum, 268; symbolism, 254; synthesis, 292, 294; theology, 260 f., 272 f.; vision of God, 363; work, 292; work of Christ, 288 f.

Thomists, 294.

Tradition, 160, 251.

Traducianism, 10.

Trajan, Emperor, 36.

Transubstantiation, 321 f. *See also* Eucharist.

Trent, Council of, 316, 317, 320, 327, 328.

Trinity, The: Abelard, 210 f.; Anselm, 188; 191–192; Augustine, 87, 106; Bernard of Clairvaux, 228; Eckhart, 362; of properties, 212; Roscellin, 188; Tertullian, 12; Thomas Aquinas, 273, 274.

Truth, 112, 244; doctrine of double, 293–294, 310.

Unam Sanctam, Bull, 340–341.

Unbelievers, 284.

Understanding, 269.

Union with God, 246–247, 360 f., 367, 370, 376–377.

Union with Christ, 228–229, 237, 324.

Universe, 89, 119 f., 364. *See also* Creation.

Universities, 166.

Unworldliness, 239.

Urban IV, Pope, 343.

Valentinian III, Emperor, 334.

Vandal invasion, 137.

Via antiqua, 311; via moderna, 311; via negativa, 172.

Victor, Bishop of Rome, 33.

Vigilantius, 63.

Vincent of Beauvais, 254.

Vincent of Lerins, 160; Augustine, 139; authority, 138–139; Bible, 138; tradition, 138.

Virgin Mary, 62 f.

Virtue, Virtues: Abelard, 216–217; Ambrose, 57 f., 61; Augustine, 101; Erasmus, 389–390; Francis of Assisi, 234 f.; Lactantius, 46–47; monastic, 376; natural, 286–288;

419